# Zonal
# Marking

ALSO BY MICHAEL COX

*The Mixer*

# Zonal Marking

## From AJAX to ZIDANE, the MAKING of MODERN SOCCER

## MICHAEL COX

BOLD TYPE BOOKS
*New York*

Bold Type Books
116 East 16th Street, 8th Floor New York, NY 10003
www.boldtypebooks.org
@BoldTypeBooks

Printed in the United States of America

Originally published in 2019 by HarperCollins*Publishers* in Great Britain

First US Edition: August 2019

Published by Bold Type Books, an imprint of Perseus Books, LLC, a subsidiary of Hachette Book Group, Inc. Bold Type Books is a co-publishing venture of the Type Media Center and Perseus Books.

The Hachette Speakers Bureau provides a wide range of authors for speaking events. To find out more, go to www.hachettespeakersbureau.com or call (866) 376-6591.

The publisher is not responsible for websites (or their content) that are not owned by the publisher.

Library of Congress Cataloging-in-Publication Data has been applied for.

ISBNs: 978-1-56858-933-6 (paperback), 978-1-56858-932-9 (e-book)

LSC-C

10  9  8  7  6  5  4  3  2

# Contents

# Introduction

Despite this book's chronological nature, it was not originally intended to be a history of modern European football. The primary intention was to analyse the various playing styles that dominate Europe's seven most influential footballing countries – the Netherlands, Italy, France, Portugal, Spain, Germany and England – a fairly unarguable septet, based on a combination of recent international performance and the current strength of their domestic leagues.

A nation's footballing style is reflected in various ways. It's not simply about the national side's characteristics, but about the approach of its dominant clubs, the nature of its star players and the philosophy of its coaches. It's about the experiences of a country's players when moving abroad, and about the success of its imports. It's about how referees officiate and what the supporters cheer. That's what this book was always going to be about.

But then came the issue of structure – in which order should the countries be covered? Geographically? Thematically? By drawing balls out of bowls at UEFA's headquarters? It immediately became clear that the story wasn't simply about the different style of each country. It was also about how Europe's dominant football country, and dominant style, had changed so regularly.

# Introduction

1992 was the obvious start date, heralding the back-pass law, the rebranding of the European Cup to Champions League and the formation of the Premier League. From that point, each country could be covered in turn, by focusing on a four-year period of success.

In the early 1990s the Dutch footballing philosophy was worshipped across the continent, but its influence declined after the Bosman ruling. The baton passed to Italy, which clearly boasted Europe's strongest league. But then France started winning everything at international level and its national academy became the template for others, before suddenly, almost out of nowhere, Europe's most revered player and manager both hailed from Portugal. Next, Barcelona and Spain won across the board during a very obvious four-year period of dominance, before tiki-taka's decline meant Bayern and Germany took control. Finally, Europe's most successful coaches found themselves competing in England, introducing various styles to the Premier League.

Naturally, each section strays outside these four-year boundaries. You can't analyse Dutch football in the mid-1990s without relating it back to the Total Football of the 1970s, and you can't analyse Didier Deschamps' performances for France at the turn of the century without noting that he won the World Cup as manager in 2018. None of the chapters are named after specific individuals or teams from each period; they're based around more general concepts that have been reflected in each nation's football over a longer period.

The seven sections are different in style. The Netherlands section is about how the Dutch dictated the nature of modern European football, the Italy section focuses on specific tactical debates and the France section is about its production of certain types of player. The Portugal section is about its evolution into a serious footballing force, the Spain section about its commitment to a specific philosophy, the

Germany section about its reinvention and the England section about how it borrows concepts from elsewhere.

By virtue of the book's structure, some noteworthy teams aren't covered extensively here: there are only passing mentions of Greece's shock Euro 2004 triumph, Italy's World Cup success two years later and Real Madrid's Champions League-winning sides of recent years. But the most influential players, coaches and teams since 1992 feature heavily, and therefore, while it wasn't the original intention, this book hopefully serves as a history of modern European football by outlining its crucial innovations, including gegenpressing, playing out from the back, tactical periodisation, tiki-taka and, of course, zonal marking.

Part One

# Voetbal, 1992–96

# 1

# Individual versus Collective

At the start of football's modern era in the summer of 1992, Europe's dominant nation was the Netherlands. The European Cup had just been lifted by a Barcelona side led by Johan Cruyff, the epitome of the Dutch school of Total Football, while Ajax had won the European Cup Winners' Cup. And there was strength in depth domestically – PSV had won the league, Feyenoord won the cup.

Holland failed to retain the European Championship, having won it in 1988, but played exciting, free-flowing fotball at an otherwise disappointingly defensive Euro 92, the last tournament before the back-pass change. Europe's most dominant player was also a Dutchman – that year's Ballon d'Or was won by Marco van Basten, while his strike partner at international level, Dennis Bergkamp, finished third.

But the Dutch dominance wasn't about specific teams or individuals; it was about a particular philosophy, and Dutch sides – or those coached by Dutch managers like Cruyff – promoted this approach so successfully that football's modern era would be considered in relation to the classic Dutch interpretation of the game.

When Total Football revolutionised the sport during the 1970s, the nature of the approach was widely associated with the nature of

Amsterdam. The Dutch capital was the centre of European liberalism, a mecca for hippies from all across the continent, and that was reflected in Dutch football. Ajax and Holland players supposedly had no positional responsibilities, and were seemingly allowed to wander wherever they pleased to create vibrant, free-flowing, beautiful football.

But in reality the Dutch approach was heavily systematised – players interchanged positions exclusively in vertical lines up and down the pitch, and if a defender charged into attack, a midfielder and forward were compelled to drop back and cover. In that respect, while players were theoretically granted freedom to roam, in practice they were constantly thinking about their duties in response to the actions of others. In an era when attackers from other European nations were often granted free roles, Ajax and Holland's forwards were constrained by managerial guidelines. Arrigo Sacchi, the great AC Milan manager of the late 1980s, explained it concisely: 'There has only been one real tactical revolution, and it happened when football shifted from an individual to a collective game,' he declared. 'It happened with Ajax.' Since that time, Dutch football has held an ongoing philosophical debate – should football be individualistic like the stereotypical depiction of Dutch culture, or be systematised like the classic Total Football sides?

During the mid-1990s, this debate was epitomised by the rivalry between Johan Cruyff, the golden boy of Total Football now coaching Barcelona, and Ajax manager Louis van Gaal, who enjoyed a more prosaic route to the top. Both promoted the classic Ajax model in terms of ball possession and formation, but whereas Cruyff wholeheartedly believed in indulging superstars, Van Gaal relentlessly emphasised the importance of the collective. 'Van Gaal works even more structurally than Cruyff did,' observed their shared mentor Rinus Michels, who had taken charge of those legendary Ajax and

Holland sides in the 1970s. 'There is less room in Van Gaal's approach for opportunism and changes in positions. On the other hand, build-up play is perfected to the smallest detail.'

The Dutch interpretation of leadership is somewhat complex. The Dutch take pride in their openness and capacity for discussion, which in a footballing context means players sometimes enjoy influence over issues that, elsewhere, would be the responsibility of the coach. For example, Cruyff sensationally left Ajax for Barcelona in 1973 because Ajax employed a system in which the players elected the club captain, and was so offended when voted out that he decamped to the Camp Nou. When you consider Cruyff's subsequent impact at Barcelona, it was a seismic decision, and one that owed everything to classic Dutch principles.

Dutch players are accustomed to exerting an influence on their manager, and helping to formulate tactical plans. As Van Gaal explained of the Ajax system, 'We teach players to read the game, we teach them to be like coaches ... coaches and players alike, we argue and discuss and above all, communicate. If the opposition's coach comes up with a good tactic, the players look and find a solution.' While in many other countries, players instinctively follow the manager's instructions, a team of Dutch players may offer eleven different opinions on the optimum tactical approach, which partly explains why the national side are renowned for constantly squabbling at tournaments – they've always been encouraged to articulate tactical ideas. This inevitably leads to disagreements, and players in the national side only ever seem to agree when they decide to overthrow the coach.

Michels, the father of Total Football, actively encouraged dissent with his so-called 'conflict model', which involved him luring players into dressing-room arguments. 'I sometimes deliberately used a strategy of confrontation,' he admitted after his retirement. 'My objective was to create a field of tension, and improve the team spirit.' Crucially, Michels acknowledges he always picked on 'key players', and when a nation's most celebrated manager admits to provoking his best players into arguments, it's hardly surprising that those in future generations saw nothing wrong with squabbling.

This emphasis on voicing opinions means Dutch players are often considered arrogant by outsiders, and this is another concept linked to the nature of Amsterdam. The original Total Footballers of the 1970s Ajax team were described by Cruyff as being 'Amsterdammers by nature', the type of thing best understood by his compatriots. Ruud Krol, that side's outstanding defender, outlined it further: 'We had a way of playing that was very Amsterdam – arrogant, but not really arrogant, the whole way of showing off and putting down the other team, showing we were better than them.' Dennis Bergkamp, on the other hand, claims it is simply 'not allowed to be big-headed in the Netherlands', and describes the notoriously self-confident Cruyff as 'not arrogant – it's just a Dutch thing, an Amsterdam thing.'

Van Gaal was arguably even more arrogant than Cruyff, and was so frequently described as 'pig-headed' that critics sometimes appeared to be making a physical comparison. Upon Van Gaal's appointment as Ajax boss he told the board: 'Congratulations for appointing the best manager in the world,' while at his first press conference, chairman Ton Harmsen introduced him with the words, 'Louis is damned arrogant, and we like arrogant people here.' Van Gaal was another who linked Ajax's approach to the city. 'The Ajax model has something to do with our mentality, the arrogance of the capital city, and the discipline of the small Netherlands,' he said. Everyone in Amsterdam acknowledges their collective arrogance, but no one seems to admit to individual arrogance, which rather underlines the confusion.

His long-time rival, Cruyff, was arrogant for a reason: he was the greatest footballer of the 1970s and the greatest Dutch footballer ever. His career was littered with successes: most notably three Ballons d'Or and three straight European Cups. He also won six league titles with Ajax, then moved to Barcelona and won La Liga, spent some time in the United States before returning to Ajax to win another two league titles. In 1983, when not offered a new contract at Ajax, he took revenge by moving to arch-enemies Feyenoord for one final year, won the league title, was voted Dutch Footballer of the Year, and then announced his retirement. Cruyff did what he pleased and got what he wanted, enjoying all this incredible success while simultaneously claiming that success was less important than style. He personified Total Football, which made his status – as the only true individual in an otherwise very collective team – somewhat curious. He was a popular choice as Ajax manager in 1985, just a year after his playing retirement. He won the Cup Winners' Cup in 1987 and inevitably headed to another hero's welcome in Barcelona, where he won the Cup Winners' Cup again in 1989, then Barca's first-ever European Cup in 1992 and their first-ever run of four straight league titles. A legendary player had become a legendary coach.

In stark contrast, when Van Gaal was appointed Ajax manager in 1991 after several disappointing post-Cruyff managerial reigns, supporters were unhappy. Cruyff had been heavily linked with a return and Ajax fans chanted his name at Van Gaal's early matches, while *De Telegraaf*, the Netherlands' biggest-selling newspaper, led a campaign calling for Cruyff's return. Some believed Van Gaal was merely a temporary solution until Cruyff's homecoming was secured, so it would be understandable if Van Gaal harboured resentment towards him based on those rumours. In fact, the tensions had their origins two decades earlier.

Van Gaal was a relatively talented footballer, a tall and immobile player who started up front, more playmaker than goalscorer, and later dropped back into midfield. He enjoyed a decent career, primarily with Sparta Rotterdam, but considered his playing career something of a disappointment, mainly because he had expected to become an Ajax regular. He'd joined his hometown club in 1972 at the age of 20 and regularly appeared for the reserve side, but he failed to make a single first-team appearance before being sold. The player in his position, of course, was Cruyff, and therefore Van Gaal's entire Ajax career was spent in Cruyff's shadow: first as his understudy when a player, then unpopular second-choice as coach.

By the early 1990s Cruyff was Barcelona manager and Van Gaal was Ajax manager, and the two were not friends. 'We have bad chemistry,' Cruyff confirmed. Initially, as coaches, they'd been on good terms. In 1989, when Van Gaal was Ajax's assistant coach, he studied at a coaching course in Barcelona over Christmas and spent many evenings at the Cruyff family home, getting along particularly well with Cruyff's son Jordi, then a Barca youth player. This, however, is supposedly where things turned sour. Van Gaal received a phone call from the Netherlands, bringing the news that his sister was gravely ill, and he rushed back to Amsterdam to see her before she died. Much later, Van Gaal suggested Cruyff was angry with him for leaving without thanking the Cruyffs for their hospitality, something Cruyff strongly denies, claiming they had a friendly encounter shortly afterwards in Amsterdam. It seems implausible that Cruyff would use Van Gaal's tragic news to start a feud, and more likely that there was a misunderstanding at a moment when Van Gaal was emotional. But the truth is probably much simpler: this was a clash of footballing philosophies, and a clash of egos.

Cruyff devoted a considerable amount of time to winding up Van Gaal, while increasingly becoming wound up himself. By 1992 journalists were inevitably comparing Cruyff's Barcelona to Van Gaal's Ajax, the European Cup winners and the European Cup Winners' Cup winners respectively, which prompted a furious response from Cruyff. 'If he thinks Ajax are much better than Barcelona, then he's riding for a fall, he's making a big mistake,' he blasted. 'When you look at Ajax at the moment, you can see the quality is declining.' He became increasingly petty. In 1993 he said he wanted Feyenoord to win the league ahead of Van Gaal's Ajax. In 1994, when asked which teams across Europe he admired, Cruyff replied with Auxerre and Parma – the two sides that had eliminated Ajax from European competition in the previous two seasons. In February 1995, when a journalist suggested that Ajax might be stronger than Barcelona, his response was blunt: 'Why don't you stop talking shit?' But Van Gaal's Ajax demonstrated their superiority by winning the Champions League that year.

Van Gaal eternally stressed the importance of collectivism: 'Football is a team sport, and the members of the team are therefore dependent upon each other,' he explained. 'If certain players do not carry out their tasks properly on the pitch, then their colleagues will suffer. This means that each player has to carry out his basic tasks to the best of his ability.' Simple stuff, but you wouldn't find Cruyff speaking about football in such functional, joyless language. Cruyff wanted his players to express themselves, to enjoy themselves, but for Van Gaal it was about 'carrying out basic tasks'. When Ajax failed to win, Van Gaal would typically complain that his players 'did not keep to the arrangement', effectively accusing them of breaking their teammates' trust by doing their own thing. However, Van Gaal's sides were not about grinding out results – they would play in an extremely attack-minded, if mechanical, way. 'I suspect I'm fonder of playing the game well, rather than winning,' he once said.

A fine example of Van Gaal's dislike for individualism came in 1992, when he controversially sold the exciting winger Bryan Roy, which prompted criticism from Cruyff, who complained that his rival didn't appreciate individual brilliance. Van Gaal's reason was intriguing; he ditched Roy because 'he did not mind running for the team, but he could not think for the team'. He was hardly the first autocratic manager to become frustrated with an inconsistent winger, but whereas others eschewed them entirely in favour of narrow systems, Ajax's approach depended heavily on width, and Van Gaal needed two outright wingers.

Left-sided Marc Overmars and right-sided Finidi George were given strict instructions not to attempt dribbles past multiple opponents: in one-against-one situations they could beat their man, but if faced with two defenders they were told to turn inside and switch the play. Ajax supporters, accustomed to wingers providing unpredictability and excitement, were frustrated by their lack of freedom, as were the players themselves. Finidi eventually left for Real Betis, where he spoke of his delight at finally being able to express himself. Van Gaal, though, hated dribbling; not only did he consider it inefficient, he thought it was the ultimate example of a footballer playing for himself. 'We live in a laissez-faire society,' said Van Gaal. 'But in a team, you need discipline.'

Van Gaal's schoolmasterly approach was entirely natural considering he'd juggled his playing career with teaching for 12 years, following in the footsteps of his hero Michels, who was also a schoolteacher. Van Gaal was by all accounts a hard taskmaster who worked in a tough school with difficult pupils, often from poor backgrounds, and this shaped his managerial philosophy. 'Players are really just like big children, so there really is a resemblance between being a teacher and being a coach,' he said. 'You approach students in a certain way, based on a particular philosophy, and you do so with football players in exactly the same manner. Both at school and in a football team you encounter a pecking order and different cultures.'

Before becoming Ajax's first-team coach, Van Gaal took charge of the club's youth system, where he coached an outstanding group featuring the likes of Edgar Davids, Clarence Seedorf and Patrick Kluivert. This, rather than managing a smaller Eredivisie club, served as his bridge between being a teacher and becoming a first-team coach. He enjoyed working with youngsters precisely because they were malleable; once a footballer was 25, Van Gaal believed, he could no longer change their identity. The only veterans in Ajax's 1995 Champions League-winning side were defenders Danny Blind, in his ninth year at the club, and the returning Frank Rijkaard, who had initially risen through the club's academy in the 1980s. Van Gaal wouldn't have countenanced signing a fully formed, non-Ajax-schooled superstar, even if they were individually superior to an existing option. 'I don't need the eleven best,' Van Gaal said. 'I need the best eleven.'

Whereas Van Gaal was a teacher, Cruyff wasn't even a student. He'd been appointed Ajax manager in 1985 despite lacking the requisite coaching badges: Cruyff was Cruyff, and so, as always, an exception was made. And whereas Van Gaal was highly suspicious of individuals, Cruyff was delighted to indulge superstars, and his Barcelona side featured far more individual brilliance in the final third because he could, at various stages, count on four of the most revered superstars of this era: Michael Laudrup, Hristo Stoichkov, Romario and Gheorghe Hagi. The rise and fall of Cruyff's Barcelona depended largely on his treatment of these players.

The most fascinating individual was Laudrup, effectively the Cruyff figure in Cruyff's Dream Team. Cruyff had been his childhood hero, and at World Cup 1986, a tournament for which Holland failed to qualify, Laudrup was the outstanding player in the fabulous 'Danish Dynamite' side that drew comparisons to the Dutch Total Footballers of the 1970s. Laudrup signed for Barca in 1989 and immediately became the side's technical leader, dropping deep from a centre-forward role to encourage midfield runners into attack. He could play killer through-balls with either foot, and possessed an uncanny ability to poke no-look passes with the outside of his right foot while moving to his left, leaving defenders bamboozled. He would finish his career, incidentally, with a one-year stint at Ajax in 1997/98.

On one hand, Cruyff adored Laudrup's natural talent. When Laudrup scored a stupendous last-minute equaliser at Real Burgos in 1991/92, flicking the ball up with his left foot and smashing it into the top-right corner with his right, Laudrup rushed over to celebrate with a delighted Cruyff, among the warmest embraces between player and manager you'll witness. But Cruyff also labelled him 'one of the most difficult players I've worked with', believing that Laudrup didn't push his talents hard enough, and he constantly complained about his lack of leadership skills. Cruyff used Michels's 'conflict' approach, but it only served to annoy the Dane, who was a nervous, reserved footballer requiring more delicate treatment.

The beneficiary of Laudrup's measured through-balls was another supremely talented superstar, Bulgarian legend Stoichkov. 'From more than 100 goals I scored, I'm sure that over 50 were assisted by Michael,' Stoichkov said of his period at Barca. 'To play with him was extremely easy – we found each other by intuition.' That was a telling description; in a Van Gaal side attacking was about pre-determined moves, in a Cruyff side it was about organic relationships.

Like Laudrup, Stoichkov idolised Cruyff and still owned videos of the Dutchman when he agreed to join him at Barcelona, but he was completely different from Laudrup in terms of personality: aggressive, fiery and unpredictable. He'd been handed a lifelong ban from football in his homeland, later reduced to a year, for fighting at the 1985 Bulgarian Cup Final. After impressing Cruyff by scoring a wonderful chip over the head of Barcelona goalkeeper Andoni

Zubizarreta for CSKA Sofia in the Cup Winners' Cup, he arrived at the Camp Nou in 1989. 'He had speed, finishing and character,' Cruyff remembered. 'We had too many nice guys, we needed someone like him.' But in Stoichkov's first *Clásico* he was shown a red card, stamped on the referee's foot on his way off and was handed a ten-week ban. At another club Stoichkov might have been sacked, but Cruyff kept faith and he scored the winner on his return, then the following week scored four in a 6–0 victory at Athletic Bilbao. Stoichkov was worth indulging, even if he received ten red cards while at Barca, an incredible tally for a forward.

Unlike Laudrup, Stoichkov was well suited to Cruyff's 'conflict model', perfectly understanding the purpose of his manager's attacks. 'In front of the group he told me that I was a disaster, that I wasn't going to play the next game and that he was going to sell me,' Stoichkov explained. 'But at the end of training we would go and eat together.' He repeatedly professed his hatred for Real Madrid, and supporters loved his attitude – Stoichkov would refuse to sign autographs, yet fans would just laugh at his anarchic nature. 'He shook things up,' said Zubizarreta. 'Although he sometimes went too far, I am grateful for people like him who are capable of breaking the monotony of everyday life.'

Yet by 1993/94, when Cruyff won his final league title, Stoichkov wasn't even the most arrogant forward at Barcelona, because Cruyff had raided Ajax's rivals PSV to sign Brazilian striker Romario, an extraordinary talent who also had a reputation for skipping training sessions. 'People say he's a very difficult individual,' suggested a journalist upon Romario's arrival. 'You could say the same thing about me,' Cruyff fired back, delighted to sign a footballer who possessed his individualistic nature. Romario declared himself the world's best-ever striker, announced he would score 30 league goals (he did, winning the Pichichi Trophy as La Liga's top goalscorer), then spent the season promising that the 1994 World Cup would be 'Romario's tournament' (it was, and he was then voted World Player of the Year). Whereas at PSV Romario was regularly involved in build-up play, at Barcelona he would vanish for long periods before providing a ruthless, decisive finish. His acceleration was incredible, he had a knack of surprising goalkeepers with toe-poked finishes and he unashamedly celebrated goals solo, even when he'd simply converted into a gaping net after a teammate had done the hard work.

Stoichkov and Romario had a love–hate relationship throughout their 18 months together. Cruyff said they had 'the same problem', thinking the side was built around them, and they sometimes appeared to be competing to score the most goals rather than combining as a traditional strike partnership. Yet it spurred both on to new heights, and they struck up a surprising friendship. 'It seems bizarre and even now I ask myself how it was possible,' Stoichkov said later. 'But we became good friends right from the start; we were inseparable.' Their wives became best friends, their children went to school together, Stoichkov became godfather to one of Romario's sons and acted as a minder when Romario visited the hospital to visit his newborn, getting a photographer out of the way by punching him.

On the European stage their most memorable display was a 4–0 thrashing of Manchester United at Camp Nou in November 1994. Stoichkov scored the first, Romario grabbed the second, then Stoichkov dribbled forward, slipped in Romario, who backheeled a return pass for Stoichkov to smash in the third. Full-back Albert Ferrer rounded off the scoring. 'We just couldn't handle the speed of Stoichkov and Romario,' admitted United manager Alex Ferguson. 'The suddenness with which they attacked was a new experience.' But for Barcelona fans the 5–0 thrashing of Real Madrid earlier that year meant more. Romario hit a hat-trick, including an opener featuring him outwitting Real centre-back Rafael Alkorta with an incredible move that became known as 'the cow's tail': receiving the ball with his back to goal, then turning on the spot by touching the ball twice in one movement, dragging it around into his path and finishing. 'It will go down in history,' said Stoichkov, referring to Romario's move when he could have been speaking about the scoreline. But Barca were hugely inconsistent at this point, and only an excellent late run meant they pinched the title from Deportivo on goal difference, the second straight season they'd triumphed courtesy of a rival slipping up on the final day. That wasn't, in itself, disastrous – but a 4–0 loss to Milan in the 1994 European Cup Final was.

Things started to fall apart. Cruyff and Laudrup's relationship had broken down, the Dane was omitted from the squad for that Milan final and his contract wasn't renewed. He promptly imitated Cruyff's controversial switch to Feyenoord in 1983, joining Real Madrid and inspiring them to the league title while Cruyff, intriguingly, claimed Laudrup had become too individualistic. 'He lacked discipline,' Cruyff protested. 'If you have a lot of stars in a team, there has to be a limit as to what each does as an individual.' This was something of a curious explanation, though, considering that Laudrup was evidently a selfless player who loved assisting others. The reality was that Barcelona simply now had brighter stars, and with the three-foreigner rule still in place, Laudrup had become fourth in the pecking order behind Romario, Stoichkov and centre-back Ronald Koeman.

Romario, meanwhile, was proving equally problematic, and his friendship with Stoichkov had broken down because of his complaints about the Brazilian's increasingly hedonistic lifestyle. Other Barca players became equally exasperated. Having won the 1994 World Cup, Romario inevitably spent a month partying in Rio and returned to Barcelona late. Cruyff wasn't too bothered by his tardiness, but

Barcelona's committee of senior players, including Koeman, Zubizarreta, José Bakero and Txiki Begiristain, demanded a meeting to address the situation. Cruyff reluctantly agreed, and sat down with the players, asking them to spell out their grievances. Romario listened attentively, before launching into an angry tirade. 'You, you and you got knocked out early,' he fired at the Spanish trio, before turning to Koeman and reminding him, 'You got eliminated by me. You guys lost! I am the winner here! I thought this meeting would be to welcome me, to congratulate me, that you would give me a trophy. What am I doing answering to you guys? Go shove it up your arse!' Cruyff's response was typical: 'Right, back to training.'

Meanwhile, in response to Laudrup's departure, Cruyff recruited another absurdly talented attacker, Hagi, a magnificent player sometimes regarded almost interchangeably with Stoichkov, as two glorious number 10s who inspired their country to their peak in the mid-1990s. Only Cruyff would be crazy enough to pair them, and he welcomed the Romanian's arrival by directly comparing him with Laudrup: 'If you exchange Laudrup for Hagi, you have to assume you're not trading down ... I bet that Hagi scores at least double the number of goals Laudrup managed, and provides at least as many assists.' Cruyff was wrong, and it was unusual to witness a manager so directly comparing the output of two footballers, especially considering he was denigrating a player so fundamental to his Dream Team.

Hagi was signed on the strength of his World Cup performances, which meant Cruyff had assembled three of that tournament's All-Star Team XI: Romario, Stoichkov and Hagi. The Romanian was a tempestuous character: individualistic, aggressive, inconsistent, arrogant and lazy, but capable of producing genuine moments of magic. His injury-hit Barcelona spell was disappointing, but Hagi considered it successful because of the freedom he was granted.

'There were several rumours and discussions about me, but Johan Cruyff had faith in me and gave me the opportunity to show what I could do. I repaid his confidence,' he declared. Hagi produced a moment of genius in a 4–2 victory at Celta Vigo, taking the ball straight from kick-off in thick fog and shooting directly from the halfway line into the net, surely the ultimate example of individualism.

But Cruyff's obsession with individualistic players was spiralling out of control. Romario's attitude upon returning from the World Cup was a sign of things to come, and he spent most of his time in Barcelona partying, permanently renting two hotel suites to entertain guests. 'Have sex every day, but three times at the most,' was his self-declared motto. Throughout that second season, various Barcelona players suggested that Romario turned up for training barely able to move, having been up all night. Cruyff was forced to send him home, and Romario was frequently late for team meetings having overslept. 'Romario never came back after the World Cup. His body was there but his mind was still in Rio', sighed Stoichkov, while Cruyff simply complained that 'he lacked discipline', the exact words he'd used to describe Laudrup. The beginning of the end came exactly a year after Barcelona had defeated Real Madrid 5–0. Now, they lost to Real Madrid 5–0, with Laudrup sensational. Stoichkov was dismissed in the first half, while a desperately useless Romario was hauled off at the interval, never to play for Barca again. Cruyff had kept faith in the wrong individuals.

The following week Romario was voted World Player of the Year, while Stoichkov came second, the Bulgarian also winning the Ballon d'Or, which was then only open to Europeans. This was the starkest demonstration of Cruyff's problem: Barcelona officially had the world's two greatest players, but they were barely speaking to one another, or their manager, and their most recent performance saw neither making it into the second half of a 5–0 defeat. Cruyff was angry that Stoichkov even wanted to attend the presentation and made him train on the day of the ceremony, meaning he arrived late. 'Something has gone wrong between me and the coach,' bemoaned Stoichkov when he finally arrived, before referencing the individual versus collective dilemma again. 'When we lose I am always the one singled out for blame. When we win, the whole team get the praise.' Later he said something similar, but hardened his attack on his manager. 'When we win it's down to Cruyff, when we lose it's the players' fault.' Cruyff's conflict model had finally worn him down.

By the summer Stoichkov was gone, Romario had already returned to Brazil, Laudrup was celebrating a title victory in Madrid and only the underwhelming Hagi remained. Cruyff's management had been undermined by his feuds with superstars and he responded, perhaps having enviously noted Van Gaal's model at Ajax, by promoting from within, extending his trust to a host of youth products – Iván de la Peña, brothers Roger and Óscar García and his son Jordi – none of whom fulfilled their promise. New signing Luís Figo wasn't yet ready to lead the side, while up front was the unspectacular and very un-Barca Bosnian Meho Kodro, who managed just nine goals. Cruyff was dismissed at the end of 1995/96 amidst a fall-out with club president José Luis Núñez, but arguments with star players had been equally decisive.

The Cruyff versus Van Gaal debate continued when Van Gaal took charge of Barcelona only a year after Cruyff's departure. He proudly declared 'Louis van Gaal is the star now' at his presentation, and attempted to import his Ajax model, including several of his old players. This initially proved successful, as Van Gaal won the Double in his first season and retained the league title in his second. But, predictably, he couldn't cope with Barcelona's big names, and in particular Rivaldo, the bandy-legged Brazilian genius who was briefly the world's greatest player. Compared with Stoichkov and Romario, Rivaldo was a true professional, and whereas Cruyff's rows with star players were largely about off-field discipline, Van Gaal's problems with Rivaldo were about tactical discipline.

In their third season together at Barca, Van Gaal became infuriated by Rivaldo's determination to dribble past opponents, a quality that would have been worshipped in the Dream Team, not least by Cruyff. In an incident that recalled Stoichkov's row with Cruyff, Rivaldo openly criticised his manager on the day he was confirmed as European Footballer of the Year, explaining he would no longer play wide-left. 'It's different in Brazil – there, people don't talk about tactics, and that means freedom,' he said. 'Here's it's a bit complicated, it's more tactical … for years I have been doing things for the team, and I've done nothing for myself. I want to enjoy it more. I have played on the wing for a while, and now I want to play in the centre, not just with the shirt number 10, but as a number 10.'

Van Gaal couldn't tolerate this level of self-importance, and so for the trip to Rayo Vallecano two days later he omitted Europe's best footballer from his 18-man squad. Barca could only draw. Rivaldo was also omitted for a 3–1 win over Real Sociedad, before Van Gaal relented, with the Brazilian coming off the bench to score the second in a 2–0 win over Celta Vigo. He didn't miss a minute for the next seven games. Rivaldo had won the power struggle, which was the beginning of the end for Van Gaal. 'I've given him too many chances,' he later rued. 'The equilibrium in the dressing room is gone – that was my biggest mistake this season. This culture needs stars. Now, I have two players who rank among the ten best in the world [Figo was the other]. At Ajax in 1995, when I did not lose a single game, I had nobody on that list.' A dressing room lacking stars suited him much better. Van Gaal also rowed with Sonny Anderson and Geovanni, two of Rivaldo's teammates and, significantly, compatriots. Brazilian footballing culture places emphasis on individual attacking inspiration, which simply didn't register with Van Gaal, and he was dismissed at the end of the campaign.

For two legendary coaches both obsessed with promoting the classic Ajax style, Cruyff and Van Gaal were remarkably different in almost every respect. Consider, for example, their approach towards match preparation. Cruyff backed his players to outplay anyone, and didn't even think about the tactical approach of the opposition. In stark contrast, Van Gaal would study videotapes of upcoming opponents and explain, in extensive detail, their build-up play and how to disrupt it, while his assistant Bruins Slot constantly surprised the players with his level of knowledge about specific opponents.

It was Cruyff's art versus Van Gaal's science. The latter sat in the dugout with a tactics notepad on his lap, depended on data to measure his players' performance and employed a man named Max Reckers, who was generally described as a 'computer boffin' in an era before statistical analysts were common. When Van Gaal moved between clubs, his 'archives', including endless piles of dossiers and videotapes, needed to be physically moved across the continent at great expense. This was anathema to Cruyff, who once said that his great footballing qualities 'were not detectable by a computer', said his football understanding was a 'sixth sense', and repeatedly admitted he had a dreadful memory and wasn't big on detail. He was all about instinct, and embodied a philosophy in the truest sense of the word. Van Gaal believed in a studious approach, and developed robotic footballers discouraged from demonstrating flair.

The Van Gaal versus Cruyff saga continued over the next 15 years. Van Gaal was appointed Holland coach in 2000 and immediately ripped up Cruyff's plans for developing Dutch youth talent. The Netherlands' failure to qualify for the 2002 World Cup, however, meant that his tenure proved disastrous and he returned to Ajax as technical director in 2004, where he infuriated a young striker who boasted the requisite arrogance for Amsterdam. 'Van Gaal wanted to be a dictator,' Zlatan Ibrahimović wrote in his autobiography. 'He liked to talk about playing systems. He was one of those in the club who referred to the players as numbers. There was a lot of "5 goes here" and "6 goes there" ... the same old stuff about how number 9 defends to the right, while number 10 goes to the left. We knew all that, and we knew he was the one who came up with it.' By this point, Cruyff had been retired from coaching for eight years but continued to repeat a familiar message in interviews. 'What I notice particularly is that policy-makers in football are never really concerned about individuals, all they're concerned about is the team as a whole,' he said. 'Yet a team consists of 11 individuals, who each need attention.'

In 2009 Van Gaal took the Bayern Munich job, leading them to the Double and the Champions League Final. 'My team has a bond and a trust in me that I have never experienced before,' he raved, and he attracted rare praise from Cruyff. But his old rival pointedly suggested that 'Bayern Munich and Van Gaal is a particularly good match – the management and players at the club were prepared to accept his way of thinking and operating.' Which, coming from Cruyff, was barely disguised criticism, an accusation that Van Gaal was more Bayern than Ajax, more German than Dutch.

Van Gaal later even linked himself with the German national team job. 'I dream of winning the World Cup with a team that can do it, and Germany is one of them,' he admitted. This fitted with constant complaints in the Dutch media that Van Gaal was simply not very Dutch, and was more typical of the joylessly efficient Germans, traditionally Holland's biggest rivals. Van Gaal was repeatedly considered 'a dictator', and in an intriguing biography of the coach, Dutch journalist Hugo Borst entitled one of the chapters 'Hitler' and examined the similarity between the two men. It's a slightly unsettling part of the book, featuring Geovanni, the former Barcelona playmaker, referring to Van Gaal as 'sick', 'crazy' and 'a Hitler', and containing the story that a Romanian newspaper once ran a headline simply reading 'Van Hitler', stating that this was a common nickname for Van Gaal in the Netherlands. It was completely false, yet the fact it seemed plausible speaks volumes about his reputation.

The last squabbling between the two old foes came in 2011, after Van Gaal was announced as Ajax's general director. Cruyff, by this stage, was on Ajax's board of directors but Van Gaal's appointment was made when he was on holiday in Barcelona. He objected so strongly that the issue ended up in court, which ruled against him. Yet in a sense Cruyff won, because Van Gaal never started his job, instead taking charge of the Dutch national side for a second time, an appointment that led to another round of mudslinging between the two old foes.

'Van Gaal has a good vision on football,' accepted Cruyff. 'But it's not mine. He wants to gel winning teams and has a militaristic way of working with his tactics. I don't. I want individuals to think for themselves, and take the best decision on the pitch that is best for the situation. He wants to control all these situations as a coach. We need to make the club successful, including the youth academy, and that means individual coaching and not straitjacket tactics. If Louis comes to Ajax, I won't be around for long. We think differently about everything in life.'

Van Gaal was more pragmatic, although he couldn't resist one final wind-up. 'There is no more a "Cruyff line" than there is a "Van Gaal line,"' he insisted. 'There is only an Ajax line, and it has been in place for at least 25 years. I have contributed to that, just as Cruyff has – with the difference that I was there longer.'

# 2
# Space

The Netherlands, by its very nature, is based around the concept of space. A country whose name literally means 'lower countries' is a remarkable construct, gradually reclaimed from the sea through the revolutionary use of dikes. Seventeen per cent of the Netherlands' landmass should be underwater, and only around 50 per cent of the country is more than one metre above sea level.

The Netherlands is also Europe's most densely populated major country (excluding small countries such as Malta, San Marino and Monaco) and worldwide of countries with similar-sized or larger populations only South Korea, Bangladesh and Taiwan boast higher population densities. The history of the Netherlands has therefore been about increasing the perimeters of the nation, and then desperately trying to find space within those perimeters.

This is, of course, reflected in Dutch football. It's through the prism of the country's geography that David Winner explains Total Football in his seminal book *Brilliant Orange*. 'Total Football was built on a new theory of flexible space,' he begins. 'Just as Cornelis Lely in the nineteenth century conceived and exercised the idea of creating new polders, so Rinus Michels and Johan Cruyff exploited the capacities of a new breed of players to change the dimensions of the football pitch.'

It was Michels who introduced the ideas, and Cruyff who both epitomised them and explained them most poetically. He outlined the importance of space in two separate situations: with possession and without possession. 'Michels left an indelible mark on how I understood the game,' Cruyff said. 'When you've got possession of the ball, you have to ensure that you have as much space as possible, and when you lose the ball you must minimise the space your opponent has. In fact, everything in football is a function of distance.' This became the default Dutch footballing mentality, ensuring everything was considered in terms of positioning and shape. Some nations considered the characteristics of footballers most important ('strong and fast'), some focused on specific type of events ('win fifty–fifty balls'), others only considered what to do with the ball ('get it forward quickly'). But, from the Total Football era onwards, Dutch football was about space, and gradually other European nations copied the Dutch approach.

Michels considered Total Football to be about two separate things: position-switching and pressing. At Ajax, the latter was inspired by Johan Neeskens' aggressive man-marking of the opposition playmaker, combined with Velibor Vasović, the defensive leader, ordering the backline higher to catch the opposition offside. It became the defining feature of the Dutch side at the 1974 World Cup.

'The main aim of pressure football, "the hunt", was regaining possession as soon as possible after the ball was lost in the opponents' half,' Michels explained. 'The "trapping" of the opponents is only possible when all the lines are pushed up and play close together.' Holland's offside trap under Michels was astounding, with the entire side charging at the opposition in one movement, catching five or six opponents offside simultaneously, before interpretations around who exactly was 'interfering with play' made such an extreme approach more dangerous in later years.

This tinkering with the offside law notwithstanding, pressing remained particularly important for Cruyff and Louis van Gaal during the era of Dutch dominance, with both managers encouraging their players to maintain an extremely aggressive defensive line and to close down from the front. Cruyff's Barcelona and Van Gaal's Ajax dictated the active playing area, boxing the opposition into their own half and using converted midfielders in defence because they spent the game close to the halfway line.

'I like to turn traditional thinking on its head, by telling the striker that he's the first defender,' Cruyff outlined. 'And by explaining to the defenders that they determine the length of the playing area, based on the understanding that the distances between the banks of players can never be more than 10–15 metres. And everyone had to be aware that space had to be created when they got possession, and that without the ball they had to play tighter.'

Van Gaal's approach was similar, with speedy defenders playing a high defensive line, and intense pressing in the opposition half. 'The Ajax number 10 is Jari Litmanen, and he has to set the example by pressuring his opponent. Just compare that with the playmaker of ten years ago!'

The best representation of the Dutch emphasis on space, however, was in terms of the formations used by Cruyff's Barcelona, Van Gaal's Ajax and the Dutch national team. The classic Dutch shape was 4–3–3, although in practice this took two very separate forms.

The modern interpretation of 4–3–3, epitomised by Pep Guardiola's Barcelona, prescribes one holding midfielder behind two others, effectively a 4–1–2–3; the Dutch would often flip the triangle, creating a 4–2–1–3, but would still consider this a 4–3–3. Nowadays it seems curious that the two can be conflated, especially considering this is essentially the difference between 4–3–3 and 4–2–3–1 formations, the two dominant shapes of the 2010s. But during this earlier period, 4–3–3 was a philosophy as much as a system, and with other major European countries generally preferring boxy 4–4–2 systems or sometimes a defensive-minded 5–3–2, the concept of a three-man attack spread across the field was in itself audacious. The precise positioning of the midfielders was a minor detail.

But both Cruyff and Van Gaal became even bolder. Upon his appointment at Ajax, Cruyff reduced the four-man defence to a three-man defence, explaining that the majority of Eredivisie sides played two up front, and therefore a trio of defenders could cope. He effectively replaced a defender with a number 10, forming a diamond midfield between the three forwards and three defenders. This was the Dutch 3–4–3, which was very different from the Italian-style 3–4–3 with wing-backs that would later be popularised, for example, by Antonio Conte at Chelsea. Cruyff's holding player would move between defence and midfield, and the number 10 would move between midfield and attack, with two box-to-box players either side. 'Cruyff put up with the risks connected to this decision,' Michels outlined. 'The success of the 3–4–3 is dependent upon the individual excellence that serves this spectacular but risky style of play … it places high demands on the tactical cohesion of the central players, and it demands that they have a high level of football intelligence.'

Van Gaal disagreed with Cruyff on many topics, but he largely followed Cruyff's basic formation, using 3–4–3 throughout his tenure at Ajax. Michels, Cruyff's old mentor, was himself a convert and utilised the system when taking charge of the Dutch national side at Euro 92, although he considered 3–4–3 a mere variation on his old 4–3–3. At this tournament, the uniqueness and fluidity of the Dutch shape confused foreign observers, and the same system was described as, variously, 4–3–3, 3–4–3 and even 3–3–4, a notation that looks absolutely ludicrous on paper compared with the dominant 4–4–2 and 5–3–2 systems of the time, but shows how the Dutch were thinking about the game in an entirely different manner to German, Italian and Scandinavian sides.

The crucial, non-negotiable element of these systems was width. Regardless of the number of defenders, the tilt of the midfield or whether or not the centre-forward was supported by a number 10, Dutch coaches insisted on two touchline-hugging, chalk-on-the-boots wingers. Again, this was unfashionable at the time, with the 4–4–2 system requiring midfielders who tucked inside, and the 5–3–2 relying on overlapping runs from wing-backs to provide width. The Dutch, though, intrinsically believed in the importance of stretching play and prising the opposition defence apart to create gaps for others. Michels spoke about the importance of using 'true flank players who have great speed and good skills … they must be selected and trained at a very young age,' he said. 'The Netherlands is one of few countries that actually develop this kind of player in the 4–3–3 system.'

Van Gaal's 1992 UEFA Cup-winning side depended on right-winger John van 't Schip, a classic old-school winger who boasted the three classic qualities: a turn of speed, a drop of the shoulder and a good cross. Van 't Schip would never receive the ball between the lines, nor would he cut inside; he was a winger and stayed on the touchline. Left-sided Bryan Roy was similar, albeit quicker and less of a crosser. He was supposed to perform an identical task to Van 't Schip, although he infuriated Van Gaal by drifting inside too frequently. The contrast in systems in their 1992 UEFA Cup Final victory against Torino was particularly stark: the Italian side played 5–3–2, the Dutch played 3–4–3.

Roy also played wide-left for Michels' Netherlands side at Euro 92, although the right-winger was Ruud Gullit, an atypical player for this system, essentially a central player that had to be accommodated somewhere because he was too important to omit. By the 1994 World Cup the Dutch were coached by Dick Advocaat, who continued with Roy but also discovered the exciting Gaston Taument – and, more significantly, Ajax's Marc Overmars.

Overmars was the most typical, and most accomplished, Dutch winger of this period. He offered searing acceleration, was happy on either flank because of his two-footedness, loved riding a tackle, and could cross and shoot excellently. He was exciting yet efficient, a winger based around end product rather than trickery, which made him perfect for Van Gaal.

'I was a coach who wanted to attack with wingers – there aren't a lot of good wingers around, and Overmars was one of the best,' remembered Van Gaal. 'He was a good dribbler who could beat people one-on-one and that was important for a winger in our system, but he also had a very good assist record and he could score goals. Every season he got 10–15 goals and they were nearly always important goals. We need his kind of player to maintain the game as an attractive spectacle.' If Van Gaal could have fielded two Overmarses, one on either flank, he would have. Instead, he fielded him wide-left, and the speedy Nigerian Finidi George on the opposite flank.

The curious thing about Van Gaal's use of wingers, however, was that they were almost decoys, part of the overall framework rather than star performers. Something similar can be observed of the centre-forwards: the likes of Stefan Pettersson and Ronald de Boer (who was also used as a midfielder) were tasked with leading the line rather than dominating the goalscoring, instructed to stretch play and occupy opposition centre-backs. Van Gaal's reasoning was simple: if the wingers dragged the opposition full-backs wider, and the centre-forward forced the opposition centre-backs backwards, it would create more space for the star – the number 10.

For both Ajax and Holland during this period, that meant one man: Dennis Bergkamp. While not necessarily the best Dutch footballer of this period – Marco van Basten won the Ballon d'Or in 1992, while Bergkamp came third and then second in 1993 – he was certainly the most typically Dutch footballer of the 1990s, because his entire mentality was based around that familiar concept. 'On the field, my greatest quality was seeing where the space was, and knowing where you can create space,' he explained. Throughout his autobiography, Bergkamp explains everything about his game, and everything about his career path, with the same word: space. Why was he so obsessed with scoring chips? 'It's the best way – there's a lot of space above the goalkeeper.' Why did he struggle to connect with his Inter Milan teammates during his spell in Serie A? 'There was a huge space between us, and it was dead space.' Why did he transfer to the Premier League? 'I knew you could get space in England.' What was the key to his legendary 1998 World Cup winner against Argentina? 'It was a question of creating that little space.' And, even, what did he dislike so much about aeroplanes? 'There was hardly any space – it was so cramped it made me claustrophobic.'

Bergkamp was an Amsterdammer who had risen through Ajax's academy, although his journey to becoming the club's number 10 was curious. As a teenager he was considered a pure centre-forward, and initially appeared under Cruyff in 1986/87 as a right-winger. 'Wingers played a simpler game back then,' Bergkamp recalled, confirming the accepted manner of wing play at the time. 'You weren't expected to get into the box and shoot – you had to stay wide, feel the chalk of the touchline under your boots. Your job was to stretch their defence, get past your man at speed and cross the ball.'

After Cruyff's departure, Bergkamp was demoted to the B-team by Kurt Linder, a German coach who didn't understand the Dutch mentality and preferred a rigid 4–4–2. In Ajax's reserves, however,

Bergkamp played under Van Gaal, who recognised his talent and fielded him as the number 10. When Linder was dismissed, Antoine Kohn became caretaker manager, but it was Van Gaal, now his assistant, who was in charge of tactics. Van Gaal insisted on fielding Bergkamp in the number 10 role, which prompted Bergkamp to set a new Eredivisie record by scoring in ten consecutive matches. When Leo Beenhakker was appointed first-team manager, however, he misused Bergkamp, deploying him up front or out wide again. It took the appointment of Van Gaal as manager, in 1991, for Bergkamp to regain his rightful position. The Dutch press were so captivated by Bergkamp's performances in the number 10 role that they felt compelled to invent a new term for it: *schaduwspits*, the 'shadow striker'.

In that role Bergkamp was sensational. At Ajax he developed an excellent partnership with Swedish centre-forward Pettersson, a more conventional forward who also made intelligent runs to create space for him. During this period Bergkamp won three consecutive Eredivisie top goalscorer awards, jointly with Romario in 1990/91, then outright in the following two seasons, despite not being a number 9 – or, in Dutch terms, precisely because he wasn't a number 9. Cruyff is the obvious example of a prolific forward who dropped deep rather than remaining in the box, but the Eredivisie's all-time top goalscorer – Willy van der Kuijlen – was also a second striker, not a number 9. Van der Kuijlen, who spent nearly his entire career with PSV, had the misfortunate to be playing in the same era as Cruyff, and squabbles between Ajax and PSV players meant he was underused at international level. But in the Eredivisie he was prolific, and formed a partnership with Swedish number 9 Ralf Edström that was identical in terms of nationalities and style to Bergkamp and Pettersson's relationship two decades later: the Swede as the target man, the Dutchman as the deeper-lying but prolific second striker.

That was the Dutch way: the number 9 sacrificing himself for the number 10, and this arrangement continued at international level, despite the fact that Holland's striker was the wonderful Van Basten. At Euro 92, when Holland sparkled before losing to Denmark in the semi-final, their best performance was a famous 3–1 thrashing of fierce rivals Germany. Their third goal was significant: midfielder Aron Winter attacked down the right and assessed his crossing options. Van Basten was charging into the penalty box, seemingly ready to convert a near-post cross. But when Winter looked up, Van Basten had just glanced over his shoulder, checking Bergkamp was in support. He was. So, while occupying both German centre-backs and sprinting frantically to get across the near post, Van Basten threw out his right arm and pointed behind him, towards his strike partner. Winter saw Van Basten's signal and chipped a pull-back behind him, towards Bergkamp, who neatly headed into the far corner. It was the most fantastic example of the Dutch number 9 creating space for the Dutch number 10.

Bergkamp was the tournament's joint-top goalscorer, while Van Basten finished goalless but was widely praised for his selflessness, and both were selected in UEFA's XI of the tournament. Their partnership worked brilliantly. 'Marco was a killer, a real goalscorer, always at the front of the attack – whereas I was more of an "incoming" striker,' Bergkamp said. 'If records had been kept they'd show how often Marco scored from ten yards or less. For me, it was from about 15 yards.'

Bergkamp had a curious relationship with Van Gaal, who had initially shown tremendous faith in him, 'inventing' his shadow striker role. When Bergkamp missed the second leg of Ajax's victorious UEFA Cup Final against Torino because of flu, Ajax's celebratory bus parade detoured to take the trophy past his apartment, and at the reception Van Gaal took the microphone and bellowed

Bergkamp's name from the balcony of the Stadsschouwburg Theatre to the assembled masses below, who responded with their biggest cheer of the day. But the two constantly quarrelled in Bergkamp's final season at Ajax in 1992/93, before his move to Italy. Having already announced his intention to leave, Bergkamp's performances were criticised by Van Gaal, who substituted him at crucial moments when Ajax needed goals to keep their title bid alive. In Van Gaal's opinion, Bergkamp had become too big for his boots. By treating him harshly, he sent a message to Ajax's emerging generation that superstars would not be tolerated – the team, and the overall system, were far more important.

Bergkamp endured two unhappy seasons at Inter, before becoming the catalyst for Arsenal's evolution into the Premier League's great entertainers. The reason for his failure in Italy, and his unquestionable success in England, was inevitably about the amount of space he was afforded. 'English defences always played a back four, with one line, which meant they had to defend the space behind,' he said. 'In Italy they had the *libero*, but the English had two central defenders against two strikers, so they couldn't really cover each other. As an attacker I liked that because it meant you could play between the lines.' From that zone, Bergkamp became the Premier League's most revered deep-lying forward, although he became more prolific in terms of assists than goals.

Ajax, however, didn't desperately miss him. In Bergkamp's three seasons as Eredivise top goalscorer, Ajax didn't win the title – PSV triumphed twice and Feyenoord once – but in the three seasons after his departure, Ajax won three in a row, while winning the Champions League in 1995 and reaching the final the following year. This wasn't solely down to Bergkamp's departure, of course, and more about Ajax's emerging generation of players. It helped, however, that Bergkamp was replaced by an equally wonderful talent, the Finnish number 10 Jari Litmanen. 'Dennis Bergkamp was brilliant for Ajax, but the best number 10 we have ever had was Jari,' said Frank Rijkaard. Litmanen was Finnish rather than Dutch, and therefore his qualities are less salient here, but he perfectly encapsulated the Ajax idea of a number 10. He was excellent at finding space, had a wonderful first touch and could play the ball expertly with either foot. Van Gaal said that whereas Bergkamp was a second striker, Litmanen was the fourth midfielder.

After his retirement, when asked to name his 'perfect XI' of past teammates by *FourFourTwo* magazine, Litmanen spent two days mulling over his options – Ballon d'Or winners like Luís Figo, Michael Owen and Rivaldo, and other world-class options like Michael Laudrup, Steven Gerrard, Zlatan Ibrahimović and Pep Guardiola – before simply naming the entire 1995 Ajax side. That underlined the harmony of Van Gaal's Champions League winners; Litmanen didn't want to upgrade in terms of individuals, because the collective might suffer.

1994/95 was an extraordinary campaign for Ajax; not only did they lift Europe's most prestigious club trophy, they also won the Eredivisie undefeated. Van Gaal counted on a sensational generation of talent, but also created the most structured, organised side of this era.

Tactical organisation, at this point, was often only considered an important concept without the ball; teams defended as a unit, while attackers were allowed freedom to roam. But Van Gaal was obsessed with structure within possession, almost robbing his attacking weapons of any spontaneity. The crucial difference between Van Gaal's system and the approach of his predecessors Michels and Cruyff was that Van Gaal effectively prohibited the classic position-switching up and down the flanks, the hallmark of Total Football. Previously, Ajax's right-back, right-midfielder and right-winger, for example, would often appear in each other's roles, but Van Gaal ordered his midfielders to stay behind the wingers; not because he didn't subscribe to the concept of universality, but because it harmed the side's structure. Ajax were supposed to occupy space evenly, efficiently and according to Van Gaal's pre-determined directions. 'Lots of coaches devote their time to wondering how their players can do a lot of running during a match,' he guffawed. 'Ajax trains its players to run as little as possible on the field, and that is why positional games are always central to Ajax's training sessions.'

The classic starting XI featured Edwin van der Sar in goal, behind a three-man defence of Michael Reiziger, Danny Blind and Frank de Boer, three technical, ball-playing defenders. Ahead of them was Frank Rijkaard, an exceptional all-rounder who played partly in defence and partly in midfield, allowing Ajax to shift between a back three and a back four. The midfielders on either side of the diamond were the dreadlocked, Suriname-born duo of Clarence Seedorf and Edgar Davids. They were both technically excellent but also energetic enough to battle in midfield before pushing forward to support the central attackers rather than the wingers, Finidi George and Marc Overmars, who were left alone to isolate opposition full-backs. Then Litmanen would play between the lines, dropping deep to overload midfield before motoring into the box to support Ajax's forward, generally Ronald de Boer, although he could play in midfield with Patrick Kluivert or Nwankwo Kanu up front.

Ajax's 1995 side is certainly comparable to Pep Guardiola's Barcelona side a decade and a half later – possession-based, tactically flexible, adept at pressing – but whereas Barca attempted to score following intricate passing combinations through the centre, many of Ajax's goals were much simpler. The midfielders would service the wingers, who would dribble past the opposition full-backs and cross for the forwards. When Ajax were faced with a deep defence, the most fundamental part of their possession play involved building an attack on one flank, realising they were unable to get the nearest winger in a one-against-one situation, so quickly switching play to the opposite flank, where there would be more space, to try the other winger. This was generally achieved with two or three quick passes flowing through Davids, Rijkaard and Seedorf, rather than with a long crossfield ball. This way, opponents were momentarily drawn towards those central midfielders, which allowed the opposite winger a little extra space.

Ajax's crowning moment was the 1995 Champions League Final victory over Fabio Capello's AC Milan. While Capello almost always selected a 4–4–2 formation, for the final he narrowed his midfield quartet to help compete with Ajax's diamond. Capello tasked his creative number 10, Zvonimir Boban, with nullifying Rijkaard before dropping back towards the left, while defensive midfielder Marcel Desailly performed a man-marking job on Litmanen. With hard-working forwards Marco Simone and Daniele Massaro cleverly positioning themselves to prevent Blind and De Boer enjoying time on the ball, and therefore directing passes to the less talented Reiziger, Ajax struggled before half-time.

After the break Van Gaal made three crucial changes that stretched the usually ultra-compact Milan, allowing Ajax extra space. First, Rijkaard was instructed to drop back into defence, in the knowledge that Milan's midfielders wouldn't advance high enough to close him down. Rijkaard started dictating play. Second, Van Gaal withdrew Seedorf, shifted centre-forward Ronald de Boer into a midfield role, and introduced Kanu, whose speed frightened Milan's defence and forced them to drop deeper. Third, he added yet more speed up front by sacrificing Litmanen, widely considered Ajax's best player, and introducing the extremely quick 18-year-old Patrick Kluivert.

In typical Dutch fashion, Ajax had increased the active playing area by tempting Milan's attack higher and forcing their defence deeper, thereby giving themselves more space in midfield. The winner came five minutes from full-time, with substitute Kluivert exploiting Milan's uncoordinated defensive line and poking home after Rijkaard had assisted him from the edge of the box. That might sound peculiar: Ajax's holding midfielder, who had been told to drop into defence, playing the decisive pass from inside the final third. Defenders showcasing their technical skill, however, was another key feature of Dutch football during this period.

## 3
# Playing Out from the Back

European football's epochal moment in 1992 wasn't about the formation of the Premier League nor the European Cup being rebranded as the Champions League, but about the back-pass law. Forced into action by the disastrously negative 1990 World Cup, and the increasing popularity of time wasting by knocking the ball around in defence before returning it to the goalkeeper, FIFA ruled that a goalkeeper could no longer handle the ball if deliberately kicked to him by a teammate. The final major tournament under the old rules was Euro 92, with Denmark triumphing courtesy of a defensive strategy that relied heavily on Peter Schmeichel picking up back passes.

The impact of the law change was overwhelmingly positive – goalkeepers and defenders, now forced to play their way out of danger, became more comfortable in possession and the speed of matches increased dramatically. The first major tournament under the new rules, incidentally, was the football tournament at the 1992 Olympics, a largely entertaining competition with the gold medal won at the Camp Nou by a Spain side featuring Pep Guardiola.

Initially, reaction to the law change was universally negative. *World Soccer* magazine launched a 'Save Our Backpass' campaign, while more surprising criticism came from Johan Cruyff, a man usually determined to promote technical, fast-paced football. 'The law changes don't make sense to me,' he blasted. 'All they're doing is complicating life for officials, coaches and players. What's been done is a typical product of people who play their football sitting behind desks in an office and have never been out on the pitch in their lives.' But the biggest beneficiary would be the Dutch, and those who represented Cruyffian football. In most other European nations, goalkeepers suddenly needed to adjust and develop their kicking, while rudimentary old-school defenders quickly became extinct. The Dutch, however, were already producing technically gifted goalkeepers and defenders.

Cruyff, possibly more than anyone in the history of football, had very particular and influential ideas about goalkeepers, which is somewhat curious considering Cruyff was not a goalkeeper himself. Except for one thing – he was. Such was Cruyff's all-round football-ing ability, he kept goal for Ajax's third team even after his first-team debut in 1964. Saving, catching and throwing were no problem for Cruyff, who had previously excelled at baseball as a youngster, show-ing potential as both pitcher and catcher. But for Cruyff, goalkeeping wasn't about using your hands; it was 'a question of vision', and few could rival him in that respect. He believed the goalkeeper should act as an 11th outfielder, starting attacking moves and sweeping behind an advanced defensive line, and as a thoughtful and outspoken Dutch superstar Cruyff exerted a considerable influence on his managers' tactical approach, acting as a catalyst for the development of the goalkeeper.

When Total Football changed the game at the 1974 World Cup, there was a perfect example of the Dutch goalkeeping approach. The incumbent number 1, PSV's Jan van Beveren, was a fine shot-stopper revered across Europe, but he wasn't a footballing goalkeeper. 'I could not play football! I was a born goalkeeper: reflexes, jumping, strength,' he admitted. But Cruyff was more concerned with speed, intelligence and passing, so he convinced manager Rinus Michels to drop Van Beveren and also overlook the highly rated Pieter Schrijvers of FC Twente. Holland instead fielded Jan Jongbloed, who played for the relatively obscure FC Amsterdam and had made a single appearance for the national team 12 years previously. Jongbloed was quick, comfortable sweeping behind his defence, good with his feet and therefore perfect for Total Football. The model for Dutch goalkeepers was thereby established, and upon the start of football's modern era in 1992, the Dutch adjusted better than anyone. Dutch goalkeepers had always been, quite literally, several steps ahead of their European rivals.

In 1992 Ajax's goalkeeper was Stanley Menzo, who was typical of many Ajax players during this period; he hailed from the former Dutch colony of Suriname, was a product of the club's youth academy and was an all-round footballer rather than a specialist blessed with the traditional skillset for his position. Menzo was a footballing goalkeeper in Europe's best footballing side, and was successful at Ajax because he was excellent with his feet. His spell as first-choice Ajax goalkeeper started under Johan Cruyff in 1985 and ended under Louis van Gaal in 1994 – he won the Eredivisie and European trophies under both, and unsurprisingly names them as the two greatest coaches he worked under. Both loved his footballing ability. Significantly, but not entirely unsurprisingly, Menzo offered plenty of experience in a different position. 'I started as a sweeper, a central defender, but after less than a year I started to become a goalkeeper,' he said. 'Honestly, I could play goalkeeper but I could also play football. I was both, I could do both. And in the end … not I *chose*, but I *became*, a goalkeeper.'

This was in keeping with Ajax's long-standing, forward-thinking goalkeeping approach introduced by Cruyff during his playing days, and when Cruyff was appointed Ajax manager in 1985, the athletic, speedy Menzo was promoted from back-up to succeed Hans Galjé as Ajax's number 1. Menzo became renowned for his aggressive starting position and his excellent long throws, and was consistently showered with praise by Cruyff, who said he was Ajax's most important player in the 1987 Cup Winners' Cup because of his distribution. Menzo could play as an outfielder, Cruyff believed.

While Cruyff was stereotypically opinionated regarding the role of the goalkeeper, he also appreciated the requirement for a genuine specialist, and appointed the Netherlands' first-ever goalkeeping coach, Frans Hoek, the most influential of the modern era. While also running a shop in the outskirts of Amsterdam that solely stocked goalkeeping paraphernalia, Hoek's first pupil was Menzo, and the pair continued working together throughout the late 1980s and into Van Gaal's reign as Ajax manager. The problem, however, was that Menzo was somewhat erratic in a traditional goalkeeping sense. The stubborn ideologist Cruyff was entirely forgiving of mistakes, declaring that Menzo's footballing ability compensated for sporadic errors, but Van Gaal was more pragmatic. The final straw came when Ajax's UEFA Cup defence was surprisingly ended by Auxerre in March 1993, with Menzo making a dreadful mistake, palming Pascal Vahirua's inswinging corner into his own net. Van Gaal dropped Menzo and turned to Ajax's back-up, the previously little-known Edwin van der Sar.

Van der Sar shared Menzo's initial footballing experience – he originally played in defence, but when his youth team's regular goalkeeper failed to turn up for a game, Van der Sar was handed the gloves purely because he was the tallest player in the side; he eventually grew to be 1.97 metres tall, enormous even by the standards of the Netherlands, the loftiest nation in the world. His early outfield experience ensured he became a significant goalkeeping revolutionary, as he adapted instinctively to the 1992 law changes. 'The back-pass law changed my life, because I was already good with my feet,' he recalled after his retirement.

'We looked at what qualities an Ajax keeper should have, and Edwin already had most of them,' said goalkeeping coach Hoek. 'He had a good understanding of space around his goal and could play out to the defenders. That was difficult for many keepers, because most of them were "line-keepers" who stayed on their line and were primarily ball-stoppers. Also, he was tall and therefore had enormous range. He was calm, stable and a great foundation to build plays from. And importantly, he was ambitious and very coachable.' As Jonathan Wilson outlines in his history of the goalkeeper, *The Outsider*, Van der Sar was 'the first goalkeeper to operate as a genuine sweeper'.

That might surprise those who only witnessed the end of Van der Sar's career, which continued into his 40s – by which point he'd split eight league titles and two Champions League successes between Ajax and Manchester United, and won a then-record 130 caps. Towards the end of his career, Van der Sar was less mobile and more of a classic goalkeeper; his brief, unhappy spell with Juventus saw him being encouraged to remain on his goal line, and at Manchester United he was also more conservative. But the early Ajax-era Van der Sar was renowned for his bravery and confidence in terms of positioning and distribution, and he became the obvious and outstanding role model for the following generation of goalkeepers. Indeed, Van der Sar was so influential that what was considered remarkable in his Ajax days became entirely commonplace by the time of his retirement.

'One of the first to bring a new perspective was Edwin van der Sar, who played a lot with his feet and allowed the position to enter a new phase,' Germany's World Cup-winning goalkeeper Manuel Neuer later declared. 'I was inspired by his style of play and enjoyed the philosophy of Ajax.' Thibaut Courtois, David de Gea and Vincent Enyeama also cite him as a major inspiration. Of course, others attempted to play as a sweeper; at the 1990 World Cup, Colombia's extravagant René Higuita was famously dispossessed well outside his area by Roger Milla, who converted into an empty net. But such goalkeepers were considered crazy, with Higuita, most notorious for his scorpion kick, famously nicknamed 'El Loco'.

But Van der Sar wasn't in any way *loco*. Van der Sar was boring, efficient and business-like. When he retired from playing, he didn't choose coaching or punditry, but instead became Ajax's CEO. When approached about writing an autobiography, he was worried he wouldn't have enough material to fill the pages. 'I'm sorry, I'm just not very rock and roll,' he insisted. But his understated calmness was perfect for promoting the role of the 'footballing goalkeeper', demonstrating it was a logical, valuable undertaking rather than a self-indulgent experiment. When constructing passing moves, Ajax used their goalkeeper considerably more than other top-level European sides, because few teams were so committed to building from the back. A back pass to the goalkeeper was widely considered a last resort, especially as the goalkeeper would simply thump the ball downfield. But Ajax's outfielders treated Van der Sar as one of their own, safe in the knowledge he would recycle possession.

Van der Sar was certainly better than his predecessor Menzo in a traditional goalkeeping sense, but he didn't make many spectacular saves when compared with, for example, Peter Schmeichel or David de Gea, Manchester United's other two most celebrated goalkeepers of the Premier League era. Van der Sar once explained his duty very simply as 'stopping the balls that people expect you to save'. His only indulgence was taking a couple of penalties when Ajax were thrashing Eredivisie minnows – he had one saved against Sparta Rotterdam, then converted another against De Graafschap, although he was annoyed to subsequently lose his clean sheet in the final minute, making the score 8–1.

Van der Sar's most impressive piece of 'footballing' skill came at the start of a famous goal Ajax scored away at MVV Maastricht in May 1995, shortly before their Champions League triumph. Defender Michael Reiziger found himself under pressure in the right-back zone, and his underhit back pass meant Van der Sar had to sprint laterally out of his goal, almost on the byline, to reach the ball. The accepted practice for goalkeepers in this situation is simple: smash the ball into the stands, shout obscenities at the appropriate defender and sprint back furiously towards goal. But not Van der Sar. Instead, he nipped in ahead of the opposition striker, sidestepping the challenge and playing a calm return pass to Reiziger, now beside the corner flag. What happened next demonstrated the importance of the goalkeeper's coolness.

Reiziger dribbled past an opponent and passed forward to Litmanen, who fed Ronald de Boer. He evaded a tackle and passed left to Edgar Davids, who also slalomed past an opponent before knocking a through-ball into the path of the onrushing defender Danny Blind, who charged through on goal in the inside-right position, then knocked a square pass for left-winger Marc Overmars to convert at the far post. It was a remarkable team goal, the single greatest summary of Ajax's footballing style under Van Gaal, and it all started with the composure of Van der Sar. Ajax's attackers rushed to celebrate – but not with the goalscorer Overmars, who looked confused by the lack of teammates around him and awkwardly turned to hail the supporters on his own, but instead with the defensive section of the side, because they'd built the move from deep. A delighted Van Gaal emerged from his dugout with enthusiastic applause for a wonderful team goal. This was Ajax all over: forwards dropping deep, defenders running through on goal, rapid passing and, more than anything else, a footballing goalkeeper.

When Ajax won the Champions League, a watching Cruyff suggested that their key player was Van der Sar. Cruyff had been determined to introduce the Dutch goalkeeping model at Barcelona, but was frustrated with the performances of Andoni Zubizarreta. In terms of character, 'Zubi' could be likened to Van der Sar; he was hugely professional and statesmanlike, won a then-record 126 caps for Spain and later became Barca's director of football. But in a goal-keeping sense Zubizarreta was distinctly old-school, happily remaining on his line, and Cruyff frequently criticised his lack of technical skills, which became a more obvious issue after the back-pass change. 'Cruyff hasn't changed me as a goalkeeper, but he's changed my position,' said Zubizarreta, which rather summed it up. Cruyff told him to act as a sweeper, yet at heart he was a pure shot-stopper, a 'serious, reliable type of keeper', in the Basque's own words. Cruyff deployed him in midfield during training matches, desperate to improve his confidence in possession.

Zubizarreta lasted until 1994, before Cruyff turned to long-serving back-up Carles Busquets, father of future Barcelona midfielder Sergio. He was considerably more receptive to Cruyff's tactics, playing miles off his line with typically mixed results. His first major appearance for Barcelona came when Zubizarreta was suspended for the 1991 European Cup Winners' Cup Final, a 2–1 defeat to Manchester United, and was characterised by three major errors. First, Busquets raced outside his box towards a high ball, got nowhere near it and United's Lee Sharpe volleyed narrowly wide of an empty net. Next, he was caught in no-man's land for United's opener, half-coming to claim a long free-kick before belatedly changing his mind. Steve Bruce headed over him, and former Barca striker Mark Hughes smashed in. Hughes doubled United's lead seven minutes later, when he received a through-ball and immediately encountered Busquets 25 yards out of his goal, making a desperate sliding tackle. Hughes rounded him and again fired into an empty net.

Cruyff invested huge faith in Busquets. He was relatively short for a goalkeeper, at 1.81 metres, but was incredibly confident in possession and loved playing chipped passes over opposition attackers to his teammates. For most observers' tastes, however, he was still incredibly haphazard. Shortly after replacing Zubizarreta as number 1, he made a characteristic error for the decisive goal in a shock 2–1 defeat at Gothenburg, charging off his line to intercept a long ball. Approaching the edge of his box, and unsure whether to head or punch, he did neither and Jesper Blomqvist, a winger hardly renowned for his aerial prowess, headed into the empty goal. This was typical of Busquets' style, and the type of mistake the great Zubizarreta would never have made. More significantly, Busquets' footballing skills were far from flawless and he was caught in possession rather too often. Even his attire prompted nerves, as he insisted on wearing long tracksuit bottoms, and when combined with the muddy goalmouths of this era, meant he looked too scruffy to inspire much confidence.

Journalists constantly linked Cruyff with a move for Van der Sar, to which Cruyff would diplomatically respond by pointing out that he didn't have any slots left for foreign players. Besides, he forgave errors from footballing goalkeepers, believing that subtler positive contributions from sweeping and distributing compensated for the odd cheap concession. This became the mantra at Barcelona, and Busquets' approach was considered so important that he later became the club's goalkeeping coach, mentoring the likes of Pepe Reina and Víctor Valdés, and ensuring that Cruyff's vision of a footballing goalkeeper remained integral to the Barcelona way.

There's one final, forgotten Barcelona goalkeeper from this period who deserves belated recognition: Jesús Angoy. Another sweeper-keeper from Barcelona's academy, he played just nine La Liga games between 1991 and 1996, largely without distinction, serving as back-up to Zubizarreta and then Busquets. But for two non-footballing reasons he is significant: first, he was married to Cruyff's daughter Chantal, suggesting that the Cruyffian affection for footballing goalkeepers was somehow genetic. When Chantal gave birth, the beaming new grandfather Johan told the media that the newborn 'has got big feet and big hands – the feet are for playing football and the hands are for picking up his wages', with not even a passing thought that the hands might be useful for following his father into goalkeeping. Second, Angoy departed Barca in 1996 at the same time as Cruyff, but stayed in the city to continue his playing days over at the Olympic Stadium. Busquets didn't move to Barca's city rivals Espanyol, however; he switched sports and signed for NFL Europe side Barcelona Dragons. You might think this would be a natural transition for a goalkeeper, as American football is all about catching and throwing, but Angoy was actually the Dragons' placekicker – and a very good one. He ended his second career as the second-highest points scorer in the history of NFL Europe, and turned down a transfer to the Denver Broncos because he wanted to remain in Barcelona with Chantal. Even in a sport that overwhelmingly involves using your hands, the former Barca goalkeeper specialised in the role that involves using your feet. His father-in-law presumably approved.

Playing out from the back was not, of course, solely about goal-keepers being comfortable in possession, and Dutch football placed great emphasis on defenders who offered, in Van Gaal's words, 'more than just defensive skills'. English football supporters were stunned when former Ballon d'Or winner Ruud Gullit, a world-class attacking midfielder, signed for Glenn Hoddle's Chelsea in 1995 and promptly declared his intention to play as a sweeper, the position he'd played in his teenage years. 'As a central defender I could move into midfield and would dash from there into an attacking position,' he said. But the experiment lasted only a couple of months at Chelsea, because Gullit's teammates simply weren't on the same wavelength. 'I would take a difficult ball, control it, make space and play a good ball in front of the right-back,' Gullit recalled. 'Except, he didn't want that pass. Eventually, Glenn said to me, "Ruud, it would be better if you do these things in midfield."' The Dutch were well ahead of the game.

This had been a crucial feature of Total Football in the 1970s: defenders bursting forward when opportunities arose, with midfielders and attackers providing cover by dropping back. To make this worthwhile, however, the Ajax and Holland sides of the 1970s required defenders to be genuinely good footballers, capable of using their freedom to provide decisive contributions in the final third. Because of the importance of pressing, meanwhile, they also needed to offer speed, to play in a high defensive line and cover the space in behind.

When the Dutch adopted this policy during the 1970s it was genuinely revolutionary. Their defensive leader was Ajax's Ruud Krol, a gloriously complete footballer who possessed the three qualities Dutch defenders would come to be renowned for – intelligence, speed and ball-playing ability. He read the game beautifully, swept up behind his fellow defenders and knocked long, diagonal balls to the wingers, sometimes doing all three in the same move. He was the only defender aside from the legendary Bobby Moore and Franz Beckenbauer to be voted into the top three of the Ballon d'Or in the 1970s, such was his impact on club and country, and he also provided the most concise summary of the Dutch approach to defending. 'We looked to keep our opponent on the halfway line,' he said. 'Our standpoint was that we were not protecting our own goal – we were attacking the halfway line.'

Krol played left-back during Holland's run to the 1974 World Cup Final, and his three defensive colleagues were also particularly attack-minded. Right-back Wim Suurbier, also of Ajax, was renowned more for his speed and stamina than his defensive ability, and constantly charged up the wing. In the middle, Holland converted Feyenoord's Wim Rijsbergen from a right-back into a centre-back, and most significantly redeployed Ajax's Arie Haan, a reliable midfielder, as the side's fourth defender, although he had never previously played in defence. It's also telling that the only two significant foreigners who turned out for Ajax during this period, Yugoslavian Velibor Vasović and German Horst Blankenburg, both played the physical, old-school hardman role, because Ajax simply didn't produce that kind of defender themselves. 'The foreign players brought something different,' Cruyff acknowledged of the 1970s Ajax side. That kind of statement in England or Italy would be about foreigners bringing flair, but in the Netherlands it was about foreigners bringing fight.

By the time Cruyff's and Van Gaal's sides were dominating Europe in the 1990s, both were determined to promote the concept of the ball-playing defender, helped by the back-pass reform. Cruyff continued to talk about the importance of attacking the halfway line rather than defending the goal even after his retirement, complaining about 'defenders running back towards their own goal when they lose the ball, rather than moving forward to put pressure on the players in possession'. His Barcelona side, more than any other team of the 1990s, attempted to play in the opposition half.

Such was the emphasis on ball-playing defenders, Van Gaal referred to them using a word previously reserved for attacking midfielders. 'In modern soccer the players in the middle of the back four – the numbers 3 and 4 – have really become the playmakers,' he said. 'That's why Danny Blind and Frank Rijkaard were so important to Ajax. The number 10 certainly can't be called a playmaker because the space in which he operates is too restricted ... today's playmakers are to be found in the centre of the back four. This means, of course, you can no longer deploy the old-fashioned, solid type of player in these positions. You have to use technically and tactically gifted players like Blind and Rijkaard.' Blind, Ajax's captain, had played alongside Van Gaal for seven years at Sparta Rotterdam and was a calm, technically gifted footballer. But his defensive partner Rijkaard was the real star, hailed by Cruyff in his autobiography as 'one of the best all-round footballers I've ever seen – he could defend with the best of them, he organised the midfield and he still had scoring potential. All of that in one person, who also had the right mentality and a good set of brains.'

Rijkaard was a curious, reserved figure constantly suffering some form of identity crisis. He was considered a thug by many for his quite literal 1990 World Cup spat with Rudi Völler, but was actually among the most amiable footballers around. He appeared a natural leader, but when Ajax manager Cruyff wanted him to become more involved in off-field duties, Rijkaard stormed out and refused to play under him again. He became a celebrity by virtue of his footballing ability, yet he found fame suffocating. He later became a successful coach, winning the Champions League with Barcelona in 2006, but walked away from management at 50, saying, 'I don't see myself as an authentic coach. I've done something for about 16 years which isn't a match for me.' But, most crucially in this context, Rijkaard was an outstanding defender who didn't just want to defend.

This was nothing new for Dutch defenders, of course, but Rijkaard's case was particularly extreme. He emerged from Ajax's academy and became an outstanding, forward-thinking defender, partnering Ronald Koeman at Euro 88 and finishing third in that year's Ballon d'Or voting. While Dutchmen were accustomed to Rijkaard's attacking quality, other managers appeared surprised. 'This is the best central defender I've seen in the last few years,' raved Argentina manager Carlos Bilardo. 'He wins everything in the air, he marks perfectly, reads the game well, has a great long pass and a great shot. He is the perfect defender, born for today's game.' Ireland boss Jack Charlton repeated the praise. 'He can do everything! In England he would be worth gold. We hardly have any like him, a player who can defend and attack brilliantly.'

Rijkaard moved to AC Milan in 1988, and because Arrigo Sacchi had created the most formidable defensive quartet of that era – Mauro Tassotti, Franco Baresi, Alessandro Costacurta and Paolo Maldini – Rijkaard was deployed in midfield alongside another future Champions League-winning manager, Carlo Ancelotti. This came to be Rijkaard's established position; he won the 1989 European Cup from midfield and was again voted third in the Ballon d'Or, and then helped Milan retain the European Cup by scoring the only goal in the final, breaking forward from midfield, receiving a through-ball from Marco van Basten and finishing coolly. Rijkaard was now a box-to-box midfielder. But for Holland he was fielded as a central defender at the 1990 World Cup, with the midfield based around the underperforming Ruud Gullit, his Milan teammate and childhood friend. Being deployed at centre-back frustrated Rijkaard and contributed to his decision to quit the national side. He wanted to be the playmaker, not a man-marker, and only returned to international duty when promised a midfield role.

Upon his return to Ajax in 1993, Rijkaard was less mobile, more mature and happier playing defensively – so the position Van Gaal had earmarked for him was perfect. In Ajax's 3–4–3, he played as the number 4, essentially anchoring the midfield ahead of captain Blind but dropping back to become a defender when necessary. But crucially, for a player who always wanted to be a playmaker, that's precisely what Van Gaal demanded from him, and although asked to track opposition forwards, Rijkaard was also free to join the attack.

Rijkaard played a crucial role in Ajax's 1995 European Cup Final win against Milan with his assist for Patrick Kluivert, but arguably more significant was the fact that he had taken control in the Ajax dressing room at half-time, laying into Clarence Seedorf and rallying his teammates, a moment Van Gaal would repeatedly cite as an example of a teammate stepping up and assuming responsibility. Rijkaard retired from football immediately after the triumphant final – which meant that his first departure from Ajax, in 1987, came after his manager Cruyff complained about his lack of leadership skills, and his second departure, in 1995, came after his manager Van Gaal was delighted with them.

Alongside Blind and Rijkaard was Frank de Boer, capable of playing left-back or left-sided centre-back, and therefore ideal for the flexible nature of Ajax's defence. He was a wonderful distributor, particularly when spraying long, diagonal passes to a centre-forward who had drifted into the opposite channel. The classic example was the most famous Dutch pass of the 1990s, the pinpoint 60-yard diagonal to Dennis Bergkamp in the dying seconds of the 1998 World Cup quarter-final against Argentina. It was a good ball, made into a great one by Bergkamp's extraordinary feat of bringing the ball down, beating Roberto Ayala and lifting the ball into the net with three quick touches. But Bergkamp's favourite goal owed everything to his existing relationship with De Boer, as he explained when outlining how he received the pass. 'You've had the eye contact … Frank knows exactly what he's going to do. There's contact, you're watching him.

He's looking at you, you know his body language: he's going to give the ball.'

Bergkamp knew, because De Boer had played that pass to him so often at club level, the best instance coming on Valentine's Day 1993 at PSV. De Boer moved forward on the left of the Ajax defence and thumped a perfect curling ball into the right-hand channel for Bergkamp, who responded with a typical three-card trick: controlling the ball with his right thigh, then knocking the ball past the defender with his left foot, before chipping the ball over the goalkeeper with his right. Stripping away the context and looking purely at the technical skill involved, it was arguably more impressive than the Argentina strike. 'It wasn't a simple thing to do, but I'd done it so often with Dennis when we'd played together at Ajax,' De Boer recalled when speaking of the Argentina goal. 'When you watch the footage of Dennis at Ajax, I must have given him assists like that three or four times. We felt good together – when he went forward, I knew he wanted to go deep, and vice-versa … everything went right, and the pass was beautiful. But that was one of my strengths, and the chances of the pass getting there are higher for me than for other players.' That's because De Boer was simply an excellent passer, and that specific diagonal ball, from De Boer to the centre-forward, became a familiar part of Ajax's attacking under Van Gaal.

Ajax's final defender, right-sided Michael Reiziger, was a different type of footballer entirely: less creative but extremely quick, which meant he was the most effective defender at covering the space in behind, and lithe and tricky when bursting forward. Reiziger was another academy product, and when loaned out to Groningen was deployed as a right-winger, such were his attacking skills. 'He's quick, has good anticipation and sufficient ability to participate in build-up play,' said Van Gaal, with 'sufficient' a telling choice of word. 'Initially his defensive play was not so good, but this is an aspect which can be taught quickly – I give a player like him more time to play himself into the team. It's not such a big gamble, we play near the halfway line, so Reiziger has time to use his basic speed to correct any mistakes.'

It's crucial that Van Gaal suggested defending could be 'taught quickly', whereas Ajax's passing patterns took longer to master. It was therefore much easier to convert an attacker into a defender than the other way round. In truth, Reiziger sometimes appeared to be Ajax's weak link, but the importance of his speed shouldn't be underestimated in combination with the guile of his defensive colleagues, and athleticism and adaptability meant that Van Gaal once declared him 'the symbol of this Ajax side'. In all, this was the most technically gifted four-man defence football had witnessed. Significantly, three would later head to Barcelona: Reiziger in 1997, De Boer in 1999 and Rijkaard, as coach, in 2003.

But the Dutch defensive style had already been imposed at the Camp Nou by Cruyff in the early 1990s, and was naturally best epitomised by a Dutchman, the magnificent Ronald Koeman, who demonstrated a determination to attack like few other centre-backs in history. The most notable feature of his career – among eight league titles, two European Cups, the European Championship and 78 Dutch caps – is his extraordinary goalscoring tally at club level, 239 in all. He even finished joint-top goalscorer in the 1993/94 Champions League, with eight goals. Three were penalties, and Koeman also scored a number of free-kicks throughout his career – the 1992 European Cup Final winner against Sampdoria the most significant – but 239 remains a staggering figure for a player in his position. It's 39 more than Kluivert and only 25 behind Bergkamp. Koeman is regarded as the most prolific central defender of all time.

'I was a defender who wasn't really a defender,' Koeman explained. 'I scored so many goals because I used to step forward out of defence a lot, and my coaches asked and expected me to do that. My set-pieces were a big strength too, but even in general play, I would be in those kind of positions, able to take long-range shots.' His greatest mentor was clearly Cruyff, whom he'd played under at Ajax in 1985/86 and then, after a controversial switch to PSV, rejoined at Barcelona in 1989. His booming diagonal balls became a regular feature of Barca's play, particularly when switching the ball out to left-winger Hristo Stoichkov, and Cruyff had a very special trust in Koeman, perhaps only rivalled by his affection for Pep Guardiola. 'Koeman likes the football that I preach about,' said Cruyff. 'He's the ideal man at the back, a defender who is good for 15 goals a season. He can live in that position because I want players like him, who can make decisive moves in tiny spaces.'

'Koeman was one of the first central defenders with the quality not just to defend,' said Guardiola, who Koeman took under his wing at Barca. 'I think Johan Cruyff bought Ronald Koeman to show us, to teach us, why we need a central defender like Ronald … most of the quality was his build-up, amazing long balls, forty metres, quick balls. He is one of the best central defenders I've ever seen in my life.' Koeman's regular forward charges rarely exposed Barcelona in a defensive sense because they could rely on Guardiola's selfless, intelligent play in the holding midfield position. This was particularly crucial when Cruyff played the 3–4–3, with Koeman the centre-back and Guardiola the holding midfielder. Guardiola, often wearing number 3 at this stage, would effectively become Barcelona's main defender, covering for his attack-minded teammate in the original manner of Total Football.

While Guardiola is widely considered a deep midfielder, Cruyff often referred to him as a defender. 'As a player he was tactically perfect but he said he couldn't defend,' said Cruyff. 'I said: "I agree – in a limited way. You're a bad defender if you have to cover this whole area. But if you have to defend this one small area, then you're the best. Make sure that there are people to cover the other areas. As long as you do that, you can be a very good defender." And he did become very good.' Cruyff sometimes deployed Guardiola as a conventional centre-back; in late 1991 Cruyff even handed him the job of man-marking Real Madrid's outstanding striker Emilio Butragueño, the reigning Pichichi. Perhaps the most significant example came in a 2–2 UEFA Cup draw away at Bayern Munich in April 1996; the idea of Guardiola, a midfielder, being deployed in defence would prove particularly prescient considering his own use of Javier Mascherano and Javi Martínez when later coaching these two clubs.

Cruyff insisted that Koeman and Guardiola, two players he praised primarily for their passing, were a perfectly functional pairing because of their positional strength and intelligence. 'As the central defensive duo, they weren't fast and they weren't defenders,' Cruyff admitted. But he believed there were only three passes that Barca needed to worry about: balls over the top would be intercepted by his goalkeeper, the aggressive Busquets; crossfield balls would be dealt with by his speedy full-backs Albert Ferrer and Sergi Barjuán, academy products and converted wingers; balls down the centre, meanwhile, wouldn't be a problem because Cruyff was confident Koeman and Guardiola communicated well, and were flawless in a positional sense. Sometimes he referred to the duo as both 'midfielder-defenders', which summarised the Dutch interpretation of defenders – they aren't really defenders at all.

# Transition: Netherlands–Italy

Juventus required a penalty shoot-out to confirm their triumph over Ajax in the 1996 Champions League Final, but this nevertheless felt like a turning point in European football, the moment when Dutch dominance gave way to Italian ascendency. Ajax, the previous season's Champions League winners, found themselves unable to cope with the speed and power of Juve's forwards, and the Italian side should have killed the game before half-time.

For Ajax, the problem wasn't simply defeat and the failure to retain their trophy, but the knowledge it was the end of an era. Midway through 1995/96 European football had been shaken by the Bosman ruling, which had two major impacts. First, players could run down their contracts and transfer elsewhere for free. Second, the three-foreigner rule was now illegal, and European clubs could field as many EU nationals as they liked.

No club suffered as much as Ajax. At the end of 1995/96 Edgar Davids, arguably Europe's most coveted midfielder, left for AC Milan on a free transfer – previously, Ajax would have received a fee and reinvested the proceeds. Meanwhile, the liberalisation of the rules regarding the number of foreign players permitted meant there was now extra overseas demand for Ajax's other stars, and within three years they found almost their entire Champions League-winning side had departed. Davids, Winston Bogarde, Edwin van der Sar, Michael Reiziger, Nwankwo Kanu and Patrick Kluivert all headed to Serie A, mirroring the shift in power. Bosman had made players, and Europe's major leagues, considerably more powerful, and Ajax were no longer among Europe's elite.

1996 also saw Ajax depart their much-loved De Meer Stadion, moving to the Amsterdam Arena – later renamed the Johan Cruyff Arena – in the south of the city. They encountered serious problems with the new stadium, which wasn't simply a football ground, but a multipurpose arena also used for concerts. Grass didn't grow properly, which hampered Ajax's passing football, and to many supporters it just didn't feel like home. Louis van Gaal initially intended to leave in 1996, but stuck around one more year for personal reasons. Cruyff, meanwhile, left Barcelona in 1996 and would never coach again, while Holland were hugely disappointing at Euro 96, thrashed 4–1 in the group stage by England, and exiting after a quarter-final penalty shoot-out defeat to France. Holland's customary tournament arguments seemed particularly serious, too, with various suggestions of a divide between black and white players.

With Dutch football's reputation taking a battering, then, Italy became the centre of European football. Serie A had been Europe's strongest league throughout the 1990s, evidenced by their clubs' dominance of the European competitions, but only now, with the sexier, more forward-thinking Ajax out of the picture, was its superiority unquestionable.

Whereas Ajax focused on youth development, Italian clubs depended on financial clout. The country's major clubs were owned by absurdly wealthy businessmen – at least in theory, as many later found themselves financially ruined – who competed to sign the world's greatest talents. The so-called 'seven sisters' of Italian football had emerged: Juventus, Milan, Inter, Roma, Lazio, Parma and Fiorentina all boasted world-class players, and all seven started each season with a genuine chance of glory. In terms of overall strength and competitiveness, there has probably never been a better league than Serie A during the mid- to late-1990s.

Stylistically, Serie A was in a peculiar place. Italian football had always been considered defensive, with its infamous *catenaccio* of the 1960s still influencing tactical thought. While the attack-minded Milan boss Arrigo Sacchi had revolutionised football in the late 1980s by overhauling *catenaccio* and introducing the pressing game, he'd been inspired by Ajax's Total Football, and his approach was atypical for an Italian coach.

During this period Italian football's major tactical themes were essentially debates between coaches who were pro-Sacchi and those who were Italian traditionalists. Sacchi promoted a proactive style of football in an inflexible 4–4–2 system, which featured no *trequartista* (the number 10) or *libero* (the sweeper). But, by nature, Italian coaches adapted their system to the opposition's approach, most loved their *trequartisti* and many still insisted on a *libero*. Italian football during this era was not about following Sacchi's Dutch-centric ideals, but about returning Serie A to the old Italian way.

Part Two

# Calcio, 1996–2000

# 4
# Flexibility

In the closing stages of Juventus's 1996 Champions League Final victory over Ajax, there was an unusual incident that summed up so much about Juventus, and so much about Italian football.

Ajax, in keeping with their customary approach, constantly switched play in the first half between right-winger Finidi George and left-winger Kiki Musampa. Juve's aggressive 4–3–3 system, featuring three outright forwards in Alessandro Del Piero, Gianluca Vialli and Fabrizio Ravanelli, meant that neither of Juventus's most impressive performers on the night, the unheralded full-back pairing of Gianluca Pessotto and Moreno Torricelli, were afforded protection against Ajax's wingers, but both defenders were magnificent, sticking tight and refusing to let the Ajax wingers turn. Pessotto completely nullified Finidi, while Torricelli intercepted passes and launched quick counter-attacks. Louis van Gaal evidently decided that Ajax weren't likely to get the better of Torricelli, and at half-time he removed Musampa. Ronald de Boer, who had started in central midfield, moved to the left.

Late in the game, however, Torricelli started to struggle with cramp, so for extra-time Van Gaal introduced Nordin Wooter, another speedy winger, to attack Torricelli, testing the right-back's mobility. Juventus boss Marcello Lippi had already used his three substitutes, and therefore devised a novel solution: he switched his full-backs. Pessotto had played 90 minutes at left-back, but played extra-time at right-back, and stopped Wooter. Torricelli made the reverse switch, and was less troubled by the fatigued Finidi.

It was, on paper, a simple solution, but it's difficult to imagine other full-back pairings of this era doing likewise. You wouldn't have witnessed Brazil switching Cafu and Roberto Carlos, or Barcelona moving Albert Ferrer to the left and Sergi Barjuán to the right; it would have been unthinkable and fundamentally compromised their natural game. Italian sides, though, weren't about playing their natural game; they were about stopping opponents from playing theirs. They were – and still are – defensive-minded, reactive and tactically intelligent. Torricelli and Pessotto weren't playing out of position, they were in another position they could play.

For all Juventus's superstars during the mid- to late-1990s, it's those underrated, jack-of-all-trades, versatile squad players who best exemplify the nature of Italian football. Lippi could depend on four players who would struggle to identify their best position, something that would be considered a sign of weakness elsewhere but was very much a virtue in Serie A. Torricelli, Pessotto, Angelo Di Livio and Alessandro Birindelli could play as full-back, wing-back or wide midfielder, they could play on the left or the right and sometimes through the centre. These were the club's leaders. 'Every year we sold our best players, but the backbone of the squad stayed,' remembered Lippi. 'And when new players would arrive and wouldn't work as hard, players like Di Livio or Torricelli would put an arm around them and say, "Here, we never stop, come on!," and the message would come from these players who had won the league and the Champions League, and on the pitch they worked their arses off. They were exceptional examples.'

This quartet of players were workers rather than geniuses, with a single year of Serie A experience between them upon their arrival at Juventus. Torricelli was plucked straight from amateur football at a cost of just £20,000; Pessotto had played five of his six full campaigns in the lower leagues; Di Livio had played eight seasons without any Serie A experience; and Birindelli had played more in Serie C than Serie B, never mind in Serie A. 'It's not just the real quality players like Zinedine Zidane or Del Piero that captured everyone's attention,' observed Roy Keane, whose Manchester United side regularly faced Juventus in the Champions League during this era. 'But tough, wily defenders, guys nobody's ever heard of, who closed space down, timed their tackles to perfection, were instinctively in the right cover positions and read the game superbly.'

That described Torricelli, Pessotto and Birindelli perfectly; they were probably defenders who could play in midfield, while Di Livio was the reverse. He was nicknamed *Il soldatino* by Roberto Baggio, who observed that he continually sprinted up and down the touchline like a little solider. It didn't matter which touchline, and while Di Livio was right-footed, he occasionally took corners with his left. Usually the mark of a technically outstanding player, the workman-like Di Livio hardly falls into that category. In his case, it was a sign of a flexible player who had worked hard to improve his weaknesses and could adapt to any situation.

The rest of Juventus's backbone were similarly versatile. Ciro Ferrara and Mark Iuliano were centre-backs, but when Juventus defeated Ajax again the following season, this time in the semi-finals, both were deployed in the full-back positions and performed excellently, while Alessio Tacchinardi, usually a holding midfielder, filled in at centre-back. Meanwhile, Antonio Conte was the epitome of the Italian midfielder: a dependable general capable of performing equally well in the centre or out wide. These players could seemingly be deployed anywhere within the defensive section of the side, which allowed their manager, Lippi, to become Europe's most revered tactician, changing formations regularly, between games and within games. 'If you have smart players who understand tactics and are comfortable in big systems, then making frequent changes can be a big plus,' Lippi believed. So did his compatriots.

Lippi was the most celebrated graduate from Coverciano, the Italian Football Federation's technical headquarters. Based in Florence, just over a mile east of Fiorentina's Stadio Artemio Franchi, Coverciano was different from Clairefontaine in France, for example, which was famous for its development of players. Instead, Coverciano focused primarily on the development of coaches, and was effectively football's version of Oxford – Europe's greatest university of football coaching.

Coverciano's highest coaching certificate was necessary to coach in Serie A, but entry requirements were strict, with only 20 places per year. You needed to be an Italian citizen or to have resided in the country for two years, you needed to have qualified from the second level of coaching course, and then you had to complete an assessment based upon your playing career (35 points), coaching career (40 points) and academic career (5 points), with 20 points on offer for your performance in an interview.

Playing and coaching careers were assessed according to an absurdly complicated points system that awarded 0.02, 0.04 and 0.06 points for club appearances in Serie C, B and A respectively, with bonus points available for winning Serie A, playing internationally or appearing in the World Cup. The famous quote from Arrigo Sacchi, who never played football professionally, about how 'a jockey doesn't need to have been a horse', becomes more significant when you realise the extent to which the Italian coaching school was predisposed to favour former players.

In all, graduating from Coverciano involved over 550 hours of study, and because it is mandatory for coaching in Serie A, Italian coaches were furious when Sampdoria circumvented the rules and appointed the underqualified David Platt, although technically he was only an assistant because he lacked the requisite certificates. 'It's like a student nurse conducting a heart operation,' blasted Bari manager Eugenio Fascetti. There was widespread glee when Platt departed after an unsuccessful two-month tenure. Luciano Spalletti unexpectedly found himself as a manager in Serie A without the necessary qualifications after back-to-back promotions with Empoli and, after publicly questioning whether he was good enough for the top flight, juggled coaching with studying, regularly making the trip across Tuscany to Coverciano. The academic approach has proved invaluable to numerous Italian coaches. With modules on 'Football technique', 'Training theory', 'Medicine', 'Communication', 'Psychology' and 'Data', they are thoroughly prepared for the rigours of Serie A. Before graduation, students are obliged to write a dissertation. Carlo Ancelotti wrote about 'Attacking Movements in the 4–4–2 Formation', Alberto Zaccheroni's was concisely titled 'The Zone' and Alberto Malesani offered 'General Considerations from Euro 96'. These documents are stored in Coverciano's library, which boasts 5,000 such papers.

Lippi is among the greatest advocates of Coverciano. 'I started to understand why, as players, you were asked to do certain things,' he explained in Vialli's book *The Italian Job*. 'It was an eye-opener because it encouraged me to question and evaluate everything we take for granted in football. That's what I truly found important about Coverciano, the exchange of ideas between myself and my colleagues. The more I think about it, what I hold dear is not just the course in itself, it's the atmosphere around it, that challenging, thought-provoking environment ... Coverciano does not give you truths, it gives you possibilities.'

That sense of openness was echoed by Gianni Leali, head of Coverciano during the mid-1990s. 'We don't teach one system,' he said. 'We teach them all, and then show the advantages and disadvantages of each one. There's a variety here, and that makes Serie A a lot more interesting.' Whereas Dutch football was fixated on 4–3–3 or 3–4–3, Italian football featured almost every possible formation, and just as Juventus's versatile defensive players had no defined position, Lippi and other Italian coaches had no defined system. They reacted to the opposition's tactics to a greater extent than coaches elsewhere, and they routinely substituted star forwards to introduce defensive reinforcements.

Lippi's Juventus defined Italian football during this period. They became European and World champions in 1996, won Lo Scudetto in the next two campaigns, while reaching the Champions League Final in both years too, being beaten by Borussia Dortmund and Real Madrid in turn. Juve had long maintained a reputation for losing superstars yet continuing to prosper, sacrificing World Cup winners like Paolo Rossi and Marco Tardelli in the 1980s without suffering, while the players themselves declined after departing Turin. After the 1996 final it wasn't just their defeated opponents Ajax who suffered because of the Bosman ruling; Juve lost Ravanelli and Vialli to newly monied Premier League clubs. Ravanelli had finished as Juventus's top goalscorer that season, while Vialli had been named Player of the Year by *World Soccer* magazine, who commended him for being 'equally at home on the right, the left or the centre of the attack – he defends like a tiger and attacks like a lion'. In other words, in keeping with the Juventus ethos, he could do whatever job Lippi demanded.

Juve still had Alessandro Del Piero, their golden boy, and replaced the outgoing duo with three players: Alen Bokšić, who led the line effectively but rarely scored; Christian Vieri, a complete striker who changed clubs every summer; and youngster Nicola Amoruso, who didn't quite fulfil his potential, although his arrival was certainly appreciated by Del Piero, who married Amoruso's sister. Veteran Michele Padovano was still around too, and proved a useful supersub.

Lippi therefore had five good options up front, and the nature of Juventus's goalscoring throughout their 1996/97 title-winning campaign underlined how he used different strikers in different situations. Bizarrely, for champions, none of the five strikers recorded more than eight goals: half as many as Sandro Tovalieri, who played half the season for Reggiana and half for Cagliari, both of whom were relegated. Lippi had fully embraced rotation, and his five centre-forwards all played a similar amount: Bokšić scored just three goals from 51 per cent of Serie A minutes, an injury-affected Del Piero managed eight from 48 per cent, Vieri eight from 43 per cent, Padovano eight from 39 per cent and Amoruso four from 36 per cent. There was no grand hierarchy, no divide between untouchable first-teamers and frustrated back-ups, and everyone provided different qualities. Bokšić offered hold-up play, Del Piero provided invention, Vieri lent his aerial power, Padovano was a good poacher and Amoroso brought speed.

Significantly, Bokšić was the least prolific striker and yet also the most used, because he consistently worked hard and brought the best out of others. 'No prima donnas, no privileges,' declared Lippi. 'If a player doesn't agree with that, he can walk. You might like the antics and the eccentricities of a champion, but I believe people appreciate things like humility and intelligence.' Lippi's tendency to rotate forwards by using them tactically remained one of his trademarks throughout a long coaching career. When leading Italy to World Cup success in 2006, Lippi named six forwards in his 23-man squad: Francesco Totti, Pippo Inzaghi, Luca Toni, Alberto Gilardino,

Vincenzo Iaquinta and his old favourite Del Piero. All six found themselves on the scoresheet.

When Ronaldo, the world's most exciting striker, was destined to leave Barcelona and move to Serie A, Juventus declined to become involved in a bidding war, not because the sums of money were too vast, but because Umberto Agnelli, the club chairman, believed such an overt superstar would ruin the club's spirit. Even Zinedine Zidane, who joined in 1996 and soon became Europe's most celebrated player, was diligent, introverted and hard-working, a world away from the self-indulgent *galáctico* that he would later become at Real Madrid.

Zidane was shocked by the intensity of Juventus's fitness sessions, led by the notorious Giampiero Ventrone. 'Didier Deschamps told me about the training sessions but I didn't believe they could be as bad as all that,' he gasped. 'Often I would be at the point of vomiting by the end, because I was so tired.' Ventrone was nicknamed 'The Marine' by the Juventus players, and he had three terrifying mottos: 'Work today to run tomorrow'; 'Die but finish'; and 'Victory belongs to the strong'. The players had a love–hate relationship with him; Ravanelli said he couldn't cope without him, while Vialli once became so incensed by Ventrone's approach that he locked him in a cupboard and called the police, not the last time the Carabinieri would take an interest in Juve's methods of physical conditioning. It was Lippi, however, who remained Juventus's most important asset. 'He was like a light switch for me,' Zidane said. 'He switched me on and I understood what it meant to work for something that mattered. Before I arrived in Italy, football was a job, sure, but most of all it was about enjoying myself. After I arrived in Turin, the desire to win things took over.'

This is essentially what defines Italian football: the absolute primacy of winning. In other major footballing nations, to varying extents, emphasis is placed on the spectacle; attacking football is respected and sometimes considered an end in itself. But in Italy the result is paramount and the end justifies the means, which largely explains why Italian sides are content to win tactically rather than through finesse and panache. There's certainly a reverence towards certain types of stylish player, particularly classy *liberos* and gifted *trequartisti*, but teams are under little pressure to provide dazzling collective performances like Ajax or Barcelona. Italian football therefore places huge emphasis on workmanlike players performing functional roles.

'To Italian players, it's a job. It's not fun, not a game,' said Fabio Capello. 'When I was coaching Real Madrid, training would end and everyone would stay and eat, get a massage, go to the gym together … in Italy, they'll stay as long as they have to, then they'll go. We don't have this joy inside us. It's almost as if they don't like being footballers.' Capello was another celebrated Italian tactician, and his experience at Real Madrid during 1996/97 was particularly enlightening.

Capello had succeeded Arrigo Sacchi at Milan in 1992 and won four Serie A titles in five seasons, strung together an unprecedented 58-game unbeaten run and won the Champions League in 1994 with a memorable 4–0 thrashing of Barcelona. Capello was less ideologically attack-minded than the revolutionary Sacchi, but he provided creative players with more licence to express themselves, usually from wide roles in a 4–4–2. After Real Madrid slumped to sixth place in 1995/96, their worst season in nearly two decades, they turned to Capello. President Lorenzo Sanz declared him 'the greatest manager in the world' upon his appointment. Capello won the league in his first season. He then promptly returned to Italy.

While Capello brought success to the Bernabéu, that wasn't enough for Real's supporters and president, none of whom appreciated Real's style – or lack of it – under Capello. While Barcelona showcased speed and trickery courtesy of Ronaldo's legendary single season at the Camp Nou, Real were boring, functional and tactical; essentially, Capello had made them Italian. Raúl González, Spanish football's new superstar forward, was asked to play from the left, with new signings Davor Šuker and Predrag Mijatović preferred up front. Real's most common tactic involved centre-back Fernando Hierro launching long balls for overlapping left-back Roberto Carlos, a perfectly legitimate tactic that Real supporters nevertheless considered too direct, too brutal. Real insisted on inserting a clause in Capello's contract that prevented him from joining Barcelona for three years after leaving Madrid, but if Real were so determined to compete with Barcelona in terms of attractive football, Capello heading for Catalonia would have helped redress the balance. 'I believe the most important thing is to win,' Capello once said. 'Nothing else matters.'

'In Spain, everything that comes from Italy is seen in a negative light,' said defender José Amavisca, quoted in Gabriele Marcotti's biography of Capello. 'Because he's Italian, everything Capello did was seen as ugly, dirty, nasty or boring.' Capello's training sessions were typically Italian: long periods spent drilling the back four into the correct shape, and a strong emphasis on hardcore fitness work. He spent much of the season squabbling with Sanz, the Real president, partly because Capello consistently refused to select his son Fernando, a graduate of the club's academy. He also encountered problems with forwards Mijatović and Šuker, who were frequently substituted when Capello summoned defensive reinforcements. 'My matches only ever last 75 minutes,' complained Šuker. More than half of the Croatian's La Liga starts ended with his withdrawal, a stark contrast to the star treatment Real Madrid forwards are usually afforded. His replacement was always a defender or defensive midfielder.

Capello was justified in sacrificing big names, because his tactical acumen was outstanding. During 1996/97 Real Madrid regularly started poorly and found themselves a goal behind, before Capello's instructions enabled them to readjust and clinch victory. Real came from behind to win with incredible regularity: against Real Sociedad, Valencia, Atlético Madrid, Deportivo de La Coruña, Hércules, Racing Santander, Sevilla and Sporting Gijón.

The Sevilla comeback, in mid-April, was most significant. Capello started with his usual 4–4–2, with Raúl drifting inside from the left, but Real were absolutely battered by a rampant Sevilla, particularly down the flanks. Tarik Oulida, the Ajax-schooled left-winger, crossed for right-winger José Mari to head home in the first minute, then Oulida made it 2–0. Real could have easily been 4–0 down. Therefore, Capello made two tactical changes midway through the first half. Veteran defender Manuel Sanchís replaced beleaguered right-back Chendo. Next, Capello sacrificed Šuker and introduced defensive midfielder Zé Roberto. The home supporters were understandably bemused; at 2–0 down Real needed goals, and Capello had taken off a striker.

First, though, Capello knew Real required defensive solidity. Raúl pushed up front, Zé Roberto played on the left of a midfield diamond and screened Roberto Carlos. Real now coped down the flanks and could work their way into the game. On the stroke of half-time, Clarence Seedorf got a goal back, then Raúl scored the equaliser in the second half. Hierro headed home seven minutes from time, and then Seedorf teed up Mijatović. Real had been 2–0 down, Capello had made two first-half substitutions purely for tactical reasons, including substituting his top scorer, and they ended up winning 4–2.

Winning in this fashion would have been celebrated in Capello's home country, but Real demanded more spectacular performances, and despite the title success, this was a loveless marriage that lasted just a year. Curiously, a decade later Capello returned for a second spell at the Bernabéu, with somewhat familiar consequences; he won the league, then he was sacked. 'We have to find a coach who gives us a bit more,' said Real's sporting director, after Capello's second departure. 'We need a coach who, as well as getting results – which are very important – can help us enjoy our football again.' The identity of the sporting director? Mijatović, the frequently substituted forward from Capello's first stint. Two seasons, two titles, two acrimonious departures. Italian methods were not popular outside Italy.

But they were clearly conducive to success, because the three most respected Italian coaches of this era completed an extraordinary treble in 1996/97. Lippi triumphed in Serie A with Juventus, Capello was victorious in La Liga with Real Madrid, while Giovanni Trapattoni won the Bundesliga with Bayern Munich.

This was Trapattoni's second spell with Bayern, after a disappointing 1994/95 campaign that he blamed on not mastering German properly, although upon his return his communication skills had only improved slightly. Trapattoni initially attempted to use a four-man defence, before reverting to the sweeper system that was more typically German, and indeed more typically Trapattoni, after some disappointing early results, including a 3–1 aggregate UEFA Cup defeat to Valencia. 'Too many changes have upset their rhythm,' claimed Trapattoni's predecessor Otto Rehhagel after that European exit. 'Bayern are paying for the mistakes in signing the wrong players and not sticking to a definite tactical system.' Not sticking to a definite tactical system, though, was entirely Trapattoni's plan.

His tactical tinkering continued to frustrate and caused problems among his key players. In late November Bayern were 2–0 up at half-time against relegation strugglers Hansa Rostock, so Trapattoni ordered his players to concentrate on keeping a clean sheet. But centre-forward Jürgen Klinsmann encouraged his teammates to continue attacking. The players were caught in two minds, conceded 20 minutes into the second half and limped to a 2–1 victory. 'That's why we lost our shape,' complained left-wing-back Christian Ziege. 'One defensive player would make a forward run, and everyone else would stay back and watch him disappear into the distance. Very confusing.' But Trapattoni's focus on tactical discipline, and his refusal to indulge FC Hollywood's superstars, proved successful; compared with the previous campaign, Bayern only scored two more goals, but they conceded 12 fewer. 'Under him, I learned how to defend,' explained midfielder Mehmet Scholl. 'But I also learned that if I played a bad pass, I would be substituted.'

Just like Capello in Madrid, Trapattoni's substitutions proved particularly controversial in Munich, particularly with Klinsmann, who took a break from squabbling with long-time foe Lothar Matthäus to row with Trapattoni instead. Klinsmann knew exactly what to expect, having previously played under Trapattoni at Inter, but he frequently complained about the Italian's defensive tactics and about being hauled off midway through the second half, generally so Trapattoni could introduce a defensive player. The final straw came three games from the end of the campaign, in a 0–0 home draw with Freiburg. Trapattoni summoned youngster Carsten Lakies for his first – and last – Bundesliga appearance, in place of Klinsmann, who screamed at Trapattoni on his way off, made an 'It's over' hand gesture and then furiously booted a large, battery-shaped advertising hoarding, momentarily getting his foot stuck. 'I was just trying to open the game up a bit,' explained Trapattoni afterwards, gesturing as if he wanted more runs from wider positions.

The advertising hoarding later found its way into Bayern's museum, a monument to Klinsmann's rage and Trapattoni's ultra-Italian tendency to sacrifice stars when tactically necessary.

Bayern won the league and, after the celebratory parade, Trapattoni, in traditional Bavarian dress, treated Bayern's supporters to some Italian songs from the balcony of Munich's town hall. It was indeed over for Klinsmann after winning his only league title – he returned to Serie A, joining Sampdoria. 'I wanted a club where the philosophy of football was right for me,' he announced. 'Sampdoria is that club and César Menotti is that sort of coach.' It was a pointed dig at Trapattoni.

'As an Italian coach in Germany, I was trying to change their mindset,' remembered Trapattoni. 'I was met with resistance, because you don't change a mentality in two or three months. I wanted them to get accustomed to thinking tactically, developing the play and seeking options. I had to let them play their way and gradually blend in my tactics. After my first year, they began to change a little, but it was a cultural clash. In Germany, they follow a fixed plan. In Italy, we are more flexible.'

Trapattoni's second campaign was less successful, and was most notable for his infamous press-conference rant in broken German, during which he screamed into the microphone, justifying his decision to omit Scholl, a classy playmaker, and Mario Basler, an unpredictable winger, neither of whom had been pulling their weight defensively. Trapattoni was keen to stress that Bayern played positive football in his diatribe. 'No team in Germany plays attacking football like Bayern,' he declared. 'In the last game, on the pitch we had three strikers – Giovane Élber, Carsten Jancker and Alexander Zickler. We mustn't forget Zickler! Zickler is a striker, more than Scholl, more than Basler!' Even in this irritated state, Trapattoni felt compelled to underline that his selection wasn't too defensive, too Italian.

In Italy itself, of course, no one had a problem with defensive football, and Lippi's Juventus won the 1996/97 Serie A title in stereotypically unspectacular fashion. In their 34 matches they only scored the joint-fourth highest number of goals, but they conceded the fewest. They won fewer matches than second-placed Parma, but Parma lost four more. Juventus weren't about scoring goals and winning matches, they were about not conceding goals, and therefore not losing matches.

Juve's centre-back duo of Ciro Ferrara and Paolo Montero were hugely dominant, although both found themselves in trouble with referees. Montero was sent off away at Napoli and Cagliari, and both were suspended for the home contest with Milan in mid-November, a furiously contested game, delayed because of heavy downpour in Turin, with the touchlines needing to be repainted beforehand. Juventus, as ever, coped without key players, and the makeshift partnership of Sergio Porrini and Alessio Tacchinardi, a right-back and a central midfielder respectively, excelled against Roberto Baggio and George Weah. It finished goalless.

There were starring performances from Zidane, who recovered from a slow start to dominate Juve's attacking play, and Del Piero, who suffered from injuries but also netted some crucial goals, including the winner in the Intercontinental Cup victory over River Plate. Lippi evolved his default system from the previous season, shifting from 4–3–3 to 4–4–2, which became 4–3–1–2 with Zidane shifting forward into the number 10 position. As always, Lippi used his functional players excellently. The wider midfielders, often Di Livio and Vladimir Jugović, played busy roles, tucking inside to support Didier Deschamps, who became Juve's primary holding midfielder after Paulo Sousa's move to Dortmund. Genuine width came from the left-back, usually Pessotto, and Juve shifted towards a three-man defence in possession with the right-back – Porrini or Torricelli – tucking inside, a trademark move from Italy's old *catenaccio* system.

Lippi's policy of switching full-backs, as witnessed in the Champions League Final against Ajax, was again used after 20 minutes in a 2–1 victory over Perugia in February. Porrini, playing as a right-sided centre-back alongside Ferrara, departed through injury but was replaced by Iuliano, who was left-footed and therefore played to the other side of Ferrara. Lippi decided Iuliano needed more protection, so switched Torricelli from right-back to left-back, and Pessotto made the opposite move. Again, only an Italian side would switch their full-backs so readily.

Lippi was never afraid to make early defensive changes, sacrificing Pessotto after 30 minutes against a rampant Udinese because he needed extra pace. Di Livio, a right-midfielder in the previous game, came on at left-back. Converting energetic right-sided midfielders into rampaging left-backs became something of a Lippi speciality; in a second stint with Juventus he did something similar with Gianluca Zambrotta, who became the world's best in that position, and played both right-back and left-back under Lippi during the World Cup triumph in 2006.

Even when Lippi's Juventus thrashed the opposition, they often did so efficiently rather than joyfully. In the 6–1 battering of PSG in the European Supercup first leg at a snowy Parc des Princes, Juve's first four goals came from set-pieces. In fairness, they also defeated a shambolic Milan side by the same scoreline at San Siro in an incredibly dominant display, while the season's most impressive victory was the 4–1 Champions League semi-final victory over familiar foes Ajax.

In the previous year's final, Juventus were superior but only won after a shoot-out. This time they were rampant, underlining Italy's dominance over Holland. Lippi, typically, sprung a tactical surprise in his 4–3–1–2 by using Ferrara and Iuliano, two centre-backs, in the full-back positions either side of Montero and Tacchinardi, forming a formidable, physically dominant defensive quartet. Up front, Juve pressed energetically, with Zidane joining Bokšić and Vieri in shutting down Danny Blind, Mario Melchiot and Frank de Boer. Ajax's build-up play was disrupted and they uncharacteristically resorted to long balls, which played into the hands of Juve's four centre-backs. Juventus, meanwhile, played direct football excellently, constantly launching the ball for Vieri and Bokšić, their strongest forward partnership, to batter Ajax's defenders.

Zidane, meanwhile, ran the show. Supported by the positional discipline of Deschamps, and the energy of Di Livio and Attilio Lombardo – who switched flanks midway through the first half – the Frenchman was superb. In the first half he collected possession 40 yards from goal, advanced with the ball then slowed his dribble, before jinking past three challenges towards the left flank. He then crossed for Vieri, whose shot was deflected wide. Zidane swung in the corner, and Lombardo headed home. The Frenchman was involved in the build-up to the second, scored by Vieri. For the third, Zidane's speed allowed him to intercept the ball in midfield and he launched a counter-attack, wrongfooted Danny Blind with a stepover and allowed substitute Amoroso to tap into an empty goal. Zidane scored the fourth himself, receiving a pass from Didier Deschamps and faking a shot to leave Edwin van der Sar on the ground, before finishing into an open goal. 'He is, without a doubt, the greatest player I ever coached,' said Lippi. 'And I also think he's the greatest player of the next 20 years. The previous 20 it was Maradona, and the next twenty, Zidane. I am convinced of that.'

The Ajax victory was arguably Juventus's greatest under Lippi, and highlighted the three areas in which Italian football had an advantage over Dutch football: tactical flexibility, physical power and a standout individual performance from a world-class talent. 'Zidane was different class, even in such a remarkable team,' declared a defeated Louis van Gaal. 'They are a great team with great skills, a pleasure to watch. I'll repeat what I said after the first leg: I have never met opponents who beat us like Juventus did.'

Juve were surprisingly defeated 3–1 in the final by Dortmund, who were better prepared for Juventus's physicality and nullified Zidane through Paul Lambert's excellent marking. Yet the game could have been very different; Juventus created the better chances, twice hit the woodwork and Bokšić had a goal controversially disallowed. After Juve found themselves 2–0 down at half-time, they switched from 4–3–1–2 to 4–3–3, with Del Piero on for Di Livio. This forced Dortmund to retreat, and Del Piero's backheeled goal from Bokšić's cross seemed set to launch a comeback. Soon afterwards, however, 20-year-old Dortmund youth product Lars Ricken was summoned in place of Stéphane Chapuisat, and took all of 16 seconds to make it 3–1, scoring with his first touch after streaking away on a counter-attack and producing a remarkable long-range shot that curled around Angelo Peruzzi. It was a shock win. 'Having watched that final as a spectator, the only sentiment I have is anger,' said the injured Conte. 'Because the weaker side won, and because there's nothing you can do to set it straight – nothing except turn out again in next season's Champions League, and win it.'

1997/98 marked a shift in Lippi's approach up front. Vieri had departed for Atlético Madrid, and the arrival of Pippo Inzaghi, Italian football's brightest young goalscorer, meant Juventus now had a solid first-choice centre-forward. Lippi rotated less, and there was more combination play between the front three. 'Now, we have to keep the ball on the ground, rather than trying to knock it onto Vieri's head as we did last season,' explained Del Piero. Zidane, Del Piero and Inzaghi were largely allowed freedom from defensive responsibilities, and there was a clear split in Juventus's system: the back seven players were functional, the forward trio were allowed freedom to express themselves. 'This time, we have the best defence *and* the best attack,' bragged Lippi.

Juventus regularly played a 4–3–1–2, taking advantage of their attackers' natural qualities, but versatility in defensive positions meant plenty of switches to 3–4–1–2, particularly when playing against two strikers. On occasion, Lippi would ask Zidane and Del Piero to drift inside from the flanks in a 3–4–3. 'There's not a lot between 4–3–3 and 3–4–3,' Lippi explained. 'I want a foundation of seven players who make up a block between defence and midfield, and then in attack I need another three players who don't need to worry about chasing back. They should have freedom to create chances.' There was a major change from the previous season's goalscoring figures, when no one had managed more than eight league goals; now Del Piero managed 21 and Inzaghi 18.

Juventus, and Lippi, excelled during the run-in. In mid-March, Juventus were 2–0 down at half-time to Parma. Lippi made two changes at the break, introducing Di Livio and Tacchinardi for Deschamps and Birindelli, then sacrificed Zidane for a third striker, Marcelo Zalayeta. Juve went from 4–3–1–2 to 3–4–3, and brought the game back to 2–2. The next weekend, with Zidane on the bench, Juve demolished Milan 4–1. Del Piero scored a penalty and a free-kick, Inzaghi finished a couple of one-on-ones.

But the most famous win came over Inter – their major title rivals – in April, when Juventus triumphed courtesy of a classic Italian combination: tactical thinking from the coach, magic from the number 10 and a hugely controversial decision from the referee.

Juventus's tactics focused on hitting long balls into the space on the outside of Inter's three-man defence for Del Piero and Inzaghi, and when Inter defender Taribo West advanced dangerously upfield and lost possession, Juve immediately broke into the space behind him. Edgar Davids slipped in Del Piero, dribbling forward in his classic inside-left position against Salvatore Fresi, the sweeper who had been dragged across to cover for West. Juve's number 10 produced an extraordinary goal, pretending to change direction twice, courtesy of a stepover and then a feint, before attempting to cut the ball into the six-yard box and getting it stuck under his foot, then pivoting and somehow steering a shot into the far corner.

In response, Inter pushed forward in numbers. The intensity was increasing, with various skirmishes between players, and then came the infamous 69th minute. Inter played a long ball that bounced kindly for Iván Zamorano, who was held up by Birindelli's desperate lunge on the edge of the box. Zamorano's strike partner Ronaldo quickly raced on to the second ball, knocked it into a favourable shooting position, but was flattened by a body-check from Juve defender Iuliano. To the fury of Inter's players, referee Piero Ceccarini waved play on. Juve launched an immediate counter-attack through Davids and Zidane. The Frenchman played the ball on to Del Piero, who was clumsily fouled by West. Ceccarini pointed to the spot.

Even by the standards of 1990s Serie A, when players weren't afraid of confronting referees, the subsequent reaction was unprecedented. Within seconds Ceccarini was surrounded by ten furious Inter players, which eventually became 11 once Ronaldo had picked himself up from the opposition's penalty box. Inter's usually placid coach Gigi Simoni was sent to the stands, restrained on his way by a policeman, while shouting 'Shameful!' towards the officials. West's tackle on Del Piero was definitely a penalty, his challenge so wild that his boot made contact with Del Piero's shoulder. Iuliano's challenge on Ronaldo was arguably also a penalty, but it was the type of coming-together that, in real-time, could be wrongly called by a referee making an honest mistake, especially just two seconds after Birindelli's challenge on Zamorano.

But Italians don't believe in honest mistakes when it comes to favourable decisions towards Juventus, and this decision prompted years of conspiracy theories. The debate peaked three days after the game inside Italy's Chamber of Deputies. Parliament was suspended after an extraordinary row between far-right politician Domenico Gramazio, who pointedly declared that 'a lot of Italian referees drive Fiats' – Fiat being Juventus's parent company – and Massimo Mauro, a former Juventus player turned politician, who repeatedly chanted 'Clown' at him, with ushers being forced to physically restrain Gramazio, who was attempting to punch Mauro. Del Piero, for the record, had his penalty saved by Gianluca Pagliuca, but his earlier piece of brilliance meant Juventus still won 1–0.

Juve wrapped up the title with a 3–2 victory over Bologna, courtesy of an Inzaghi hat-trick, including two trademark goals from inside the six-yard box, and a fine finish after brilliant interplay between Zidane and Del Piero between the lines. The target, though, was recapturing the Champions League, and Juventus fell at the final hurdle for the second year running, losing 1–0 to Real Madrid, courtesy of a Predrag Mijatović goal.

Lippi appeared unable to explain the defeat. 'It was one of those evenings where a large part of the team played well below the level they are capable of,' he said. 'The reality is that over the whole 90 minutes, we were never dangerous.' That sole Champions League victory in 1996 doesn't adequately represent Juventus's dominance of European football during this period – it probably should have been three in a row.

5

# The Third Attacker

During the mid-1990s, Serie A boasted the most staggering collection of world-class attackers ever assembled in one country. With billionaire owners investing vast sums in various top clubs, moving to Serie A was an inevitability for the world's best footballers. Yet among so much individual talent, one particular forward represented Italian football perfectly.

Roberto Baggio was a legendary footballer, an all-round attacker who could do almost anything with the ball: weave past opponents, play delicate through-balls, score from impossible angles. His brilliance on home soil at the 1990 World Cup planted an Italian flag in the footballing landscape, signifying that Italy would be the home of football for the coming decade, with his mazy dribble against Czechoslovakia the goal of the tournament. His performances had prompted Juventus to pay a world-record fee to Fiorentina, their bitter rivals, to secure Baggio's services, a transfer that prompted full-scale riots in Florence, leaving dozens injured. Baggio supposedly objected to the transfer, and the following season famously refused to take a penalty against Fiorentina on his return to the Stadio Artemio Franchi. When substituted, a Fiorentina fan threw a purple scarf towards him. Baggio picked it up and took it into the dugout, a move that infuriated Juventus fans, who never entirely took to him. After leaving Fiorentina, he always felt more like an Italy player who happened to play club football, rather than a club footballer who occasionally played for his country; worshipped by the country overall rather than by supporters of his club.

Baggio was neither an attacking midfielder nor a conventional forward; he was the archetypal number 10 who thrived when deployed behind two strikers, orchestrating play and providing moments of magic. He was the type of player that demanded, and justified, the side being built around him, the type Italian football adores. However, the classic Italian *trequartista* role, which generally refers to a number 10 playing behind two strikers, was under threat. Arrigo Sacchi's emphasis on a heavy pressing 4-4-2 left no place for a languid *trequartista*, and therefore players like Baggio were having to prove their worth.

Baggio was a reclusive, amiable character who nevertheless constantly talked himself into trouble. 'I'm a ball-player, and I think it's better to have ten disorganised footballers than ten organised runners,' he declared, which couldn't have been a more obvious put-down of Sacchi's methods. Ahead of the 1994 World Cup, Sacchi couldn't ignore Baggio's talent, considering he was the reigning European Footballer of the Year, but Sacchi always deployed him as a forward in a 4-4-2, rather than in Baggio's preferred role behind two strikers. Their most famous dispute came in the group stage match against Norway, when goalkeeper Gianluca Pagliuca was sent off in the opening stages. Italy needed a replacement, and Sacchi elected to substitute Baggio, who trudged off while calling his manager 'crazy'. Supporters sided with the footballing genius rather than the totalitarian coach, but it was probably the right decision, and Italy won 1-0 with a goal from a Baggio – Dino, no relation. Sacchi's Italy eventually reached the final, losing to Brazil in a penalty shootout with Roberto Baggio the unfortunate fall guy, blasting the decisive penalty over the crossbar. Nevertheless, the general feeling amongst Italian supporters was that their country had reached the final because of Baggio's brilliance rather than Sacchi's tactics. He was omitted from Italy's disastrous Euro 96 campaign, with Sacchi citing fitness concerns. Nevertheless, his absence supported the growing public feeling that Italian managers were placing too much prominence on the system, and not enough on creative geniuses.

Baggio started 1996/97 at Óscar Tabárez's AC Milan, playing as a number 10 behind Marco Simone and George Weah. But after disappointing results, Milan made two decisions that hampered Baggio. First, they reverted to their tried-and-tested 4–4–2 and then, even worse, they re-appointed Sacchi after he was sacked by Italy. 'He's two-faced. He tells me that I'm playing well during the week, but come Sunday he leaves me on the bench,' blasted Baggio after a couple of months. 'I feel like a Ferrari being driven by a traffic warden. A coach must, above all, be a good psychologist. If he imposes his demands harshly, he suffocates the personalities and creativity of his players.' Baggio started searching for a new club ahead of 1997/98.

That club should have been Parma, who emerged as a serious title challenger thanks to the apparent wealth of Calisto Tanzi, founder and CEO of Parmalat, a locally based multinational dairy producer. As with various Serie A owners of the time, Tanzi's wealth later proved to have been acquired by fraud, and Parmalat later collapsed in Europe's biggest-ever bankruptcy; the club went bust too, and Tanzi was imprisoned. But during the mid-1990s, Tanzi's beneficiary attracted a variety of superstars.

Not every coach, however, wanted superstars, and in 1996 Tanzi appointed an up-and-coming manager by the name of Carlo Ancelotti. He only had one season of Serie B experience, coaching

Reggiana, but had previously been Sacchi's assistant for the national side. Ancelotti was considered the next great Italian manager, and from the outset he followed Sacchi's template perfectly, insisting on a compact side, aggressive pressing and, crucially, a 4–4–2.

This proved controversial at Parma, for two reasons. First, he'd inherited the wonderful Gianfranco Zola, a classic number 10 who had finished sixth in the previous year's Ballon d'Or voting. But Ancelotti refused to change his system to incorporate Zola in his best position, and didn't believe he could play as one of the two strikers, who were instructed to stretch the play and run in behind. Ancelotti instead deployed Zola awkwardly on the left of a 4–4–2. 'We are no longer wanted,' complained Zola, speaking about the plight of *trequartisti*. 'At the moment everything is about pressing, doubling up as a marker and work rate.' He fled to Chelsea, pointedly remarking that he would 'be able to play in my proper role in England', and made an instant impact in the Premier League, winning the 1996/97 Football Writers' Player of the Year award despite only joining in November. His form attracted the attention of new Italy boss Cesare Maldini, who briefly based his Italy side around him, and he also received praise from Baggio, a kindred spirit. 'I admire Zola, he's taking brilliant revenge on all his doubters,' he said. 'That's the beauty of football. When you have been written off, you can just as easily rise up again.'

In the summer of 1997, Tanzi was desperate to sign Baggio for Parma, and a contract had been agreed, but Ancelotti vetoed the deal at the last minute. 'He wanted a regular starting position, and wanted to play behind the strikers, a role that didn't exist in 4–4–2,' explained Ancelotti. 'I'd had just got the team into the Champions League and I had no intention of changing my system of play. I called him up and said, "I'd be delighted to have you on the team, but I have no plans for fielding you regularly. You'd be competing against Enrico Chiesa and Hernán Crespo.'" Baggio instead signed for Bologna. Ancelotti clearly wasn't against the idea of signing unpredictable geniuses; he sanctioned the return of Faustino Asprilla, explaining that the difference was because the fiery Colombian was happy to play up front, whereas Baggio and Zola would have demanded a withdrawn role. Ancelotti simply didn't want a *trequartista*. It wasn't merely a very public snub to the country's most popular footballer; it also cast Ancelotti as an inflexible coach who favoured the system over individuals. 'I was considered "Ancelotti, the anti-imagination", give me anything but another number 10!' he self-deprecatingly remembered. 'At Parma, I still thought that 4–4–2 was the ideal formation in every case, but that's not true, and if I had a time machine I'd go back. And I'd take Baggio.'

At this stage, Italian formation notation was slightly confusing. The determination to keep a compact team meant a number 10 was generally considered a third attacker, rather than deserving of his own 'band' in the system, and therefore what would be considered a 4–3–1–2 elsewhere was a 4–3–3 in Italy. 'There are several types of 4–3–3 formation,' outlined Marcello Lippi. 'There's the 4–3–3 formation with a centre-forward and two wingers, the 4–3–3 with two forwards and a player behind, and the 4–3–3 with three proper forwards.' Lippi considered his later Juventus side, with Zinedine Zidane in support of Alessando Del Piero and Pippo Inzaghi, a 4–3–3 rather than a 4–3–1–2. Therefore, the debate was not necessarily about whether managers would deploy a number 10, but whether they'd deploy any kind of third attacker. Luckily, a couple of managers remained committed to fielding a front three.

An extreme example was Zdeněk Zeman, Serie A's most eccentric coach. Zeman was born in Czechoslovakia but as a teenager moved to live with his uncle, Čestmír Vycpálek, who would coach Juventus to two Scudettos in the 1970s. Zeman therefore grew up surrounded by Italian football culture, but he never played professionally, drew inspiration from handball and remained a mysterious outsider. He was a contemporary of Sacchi at Coverciano and the two became kindred spirits, determined to demonstrate that other Italian coaches placed too much emphasis on results. Zeman said he preferred to lose 5–4 than draw 0–0, because that way the supporters had been entertained. It wasn't a philosophy shared by his contemporaries.

Zeman focused on short passing, zonal defending and developing youngsters. His idol was Ştefan Kovács, who had won two European Cups with Ajax in the early 1970s, and he remained committed to the classic Ajax 4–3–3. But whereas Dutch coaches prescribed touchline-hugging wingers, Zeman's three-man attack generally comprised three goalscorers, dragging the opposition narrow and opening up space for rampaging full-backs. It was all-out attack.

Zeman performed impressively at Foggia in the early 1990s, before moving to Lazio in 1994, taking the club to second in 1994/95 and third in 1995/96, when his forward trio featured three proper strikers: Alen Bokšić, Pierluigi Casiraghi and the wonderful Giuseppe Signori, who won the *Capocannoniere* – the title given to Serie A's top scorer – jointly in 1995/96 with Bari's Igor Protti. Bokšić then departed for Juventus, so Zeman signed a replacement: Protti, of course. His forward trio now included the two top goalscorers from the previous campaign, although he only lasted midway through 1996/97 before being dismissed. What happened next was somewhat unexpected; Zeman spent the rest of the campaign attending Lazio matches at the Stadio Olimpico, joking that, having frequently been criticised for overseeing a leaky defence, he was assessing how his successor Dino Zoff would fix things. The following season, he was again regularly at the Olimpico, for a very different reason. Now he was coaching Roma.

At Roma, Zeman's attacking trio offered greater balance. Rather than a trio of outright strikers, Zeman deployed just one, Abel Balbo, flanked by the speedy Paulo Sérgio and a young Francesco Totti, who drifted inside from the left into clever positions between the lines. Zeman's 4–3–3 became more of a 4–3–1–2, with Totti the number 10.

'Zemanlandia', as his style of football became known, exploded into life with Roma's 6–2 victory over Napoli in early October 1997, an extraordinarily dominant display in which Roma could have reached double figures. Balbo helped himself to a hat-trick, but Roma players were queueing up to provide finishes to their direct passing moves. They subsequently beat Empoli 4–3, Fiorentina 4–1, and both Milan and Brescia 5–0, although their defeats were often heavy too, and traditional Italian coaches particularly enjoyed putting Zeman in his place.

In December Roma lost 3–0 away at a Marco Branca-inspired Inter. 'Some managers like to play possession football,' Inter boss Gigi Simoni grinned afterwards. 'I like to counter-attack. Everyone's right, so long as they win.' Zeman, however, insisted he was right even when Roma lost. His team became increasingly attack-minded as the season unfolded, scoring 17 goals in their final five matches to finish fourth, as joint-top scorers alongside champions Juventus. Zeman's attacking trio provided balance in terms of style and goalscoring contribution: Balbo netted 14 times, Totti 13 and Sérgio 12. Totti also recorded ten assists; this proved to be his breakthrough campaign, and he would dominate Roma for the next two decades.

Roma slipped to sixth place in 1998/99, but again Zeman's front three sparkled. Balbo had left for Parma, so Zeman promoted the tall, slightly awkward Marco Delvecchio, who managed 18 league goals with Totti and Paulo Sérgio chipping in with 12 apiece from either side. But Zemanlandia became a parody of itself; Roma scored the most goals in Serie A, 65, but conceded 49, more than relegated Vicenza.

The match that summed everything up came four games from the end of the campaign, when Roma hosted an Inter side that hadn't scored away from home in open play for 700 minutes and had just appointed their fourth manager of the season, the returning, perennially cautious Roy Hodgson. Roma hit four goals, with Totti, Sérgio, Delvecchio and Eusebio Di Francesco all on the scoresheet. But they conceded five. Inter forwards Ronaldo and Iván Zamorano constantly breached Roma's high defensive line to score two apiece, and then Diego Simeone headed a late winner. Defensive horror shows like this, and the 3–2 loss to Milan, the 3–2 loss to Perugia and the 4–3 loss to Cagliari, meant that Zeman wasn't considered pragmatic enough to win a title.

Zeman also cemented his outsider status by dramatically accusing Juventus of taking performance-enhancing drugs. Juve doctor Riccardo Agricola was initially given a suspended prison sentence in 2004, then later acquitted. Zeman believes his determination to highlight Serie A's dark practices hampered him in terms of future employment, and he's probably right: he spent the next two decades managing the likes of Salernitana, Avellino, Lecce, Brescia, Foggia and Pescara, a succession of modest clubs for a coach who had significantly improved the fortunes of Lazio and Roma, regularly finished in the top five, and helped launch the careers of Alessandro Nesta and Francesco Totti. For all Zeman's popularity with neutrals, his influence on managerial colleagues was negligible. He remained a cult figure.

Instead, the manager most instrumental in promoting the third attacker was Alberto Zaccheroni. He'd toiled his way up through Italy's lower divisions, winning promotion from the fourth and third tiers, before working in Serie B and then landing his first Serie A job with newly promoted Udinese, finishing 11th in 1995/96. He was originally a disciple of Sacchi, a 4–4–2 man, so when he found himself with three quality centre-forwards throughout 1996/97, he played only two. He could pick from Oliver Bierhoff, the prolific old-school German target man whose two goals as a substitute had won the Euro 96 final; Paolo Poggi, a hard-working forward who made good runs into the channels; and Márcio Amoroso – a shaven-headed, explosive Brazilian who was inevitably compared to Ronaldo and who topped the goalscoring charts in Brazil, Italy and Germany. Bierhoff and Poggi started the season up front, with Amoroso playing when Bierhoff was injured. With a couple of months remaining in 1996/97, Udinese found themselves three places clear of the relegation zone in Serie A, with tricky trips to Juventus and Parma, first and second in the table, in their next two games.

These contests proved significant. Udinese's trip to Juventus, defending champions and on their way to another title, produced an unthinkable 3–0 away victory, despite Zaccheroni's side going down to ten men inside three minutes. Zaccheroni switched to a 3–4–2, and somehow his forwards ran riot: Amoroso scored a penalty, Bierhoff scored a header, then Bierhoff's flick-on found Amoroso running in behind to make it three. It was perhaps the most surprising Serie A victory of the decade. After Udinese recorded such an extraordinary win with three defenders and four midfielders, Zaccheroni retained that defensive structure for the trip to Parma, introducing Poggi as the third forward. Udinese again recorded a shock victory, 2–0, and the 3–4–3 was here to stay. The new formation helped Udinese surge up the table – having been battling relegation, they finished fifth and secured European qualification for the first time in the club's history.

Zaccheroni continued with 3–4–3 for 1997/98, taking Udinese to a historic third-placed finish. Bierhoff led the line, flanked by Poggi and Amoroso running into space. Udinese scored in every game that season, and Zaccheroni constantly pointed to his side's goalscoring figures to underline his belief in open, expansive football. Udinese beat Lecce 6–0, Brescia 4–0, Bologna 4–3 and Zeman's Roma 4–2. 'My system was not the 3–5–2, which you could observe elsewhere, but a system that included four midfielders,' Zaccheroni later recalled. 'And there's a big difference. I looked around, I studied and I observed things that I didn't like. Often there were five across the midfield, which I don't like at all because eventually it becomes a 5–3–2 and you lack an attacking threat. I observed Cruyff's Barcelona and Zeman's Foggia, but these weren't the solutions I was looking for; I didn't want three in midfield [in a 4–3–3], which inevitably forced you to defend in a 4–5–1. A midfield four, however, can effectively support the attack and defence simultaneously. My target was to keep three up front, so they didn't have to retreat all the time, so I started working on it, first with pen and paper, and then on the pitch.'

Zaccheroni became defined by 3–4–3, and beyond the simple numbers game, Udinese were demonstrating that underdogs could attack. 'Once, when coaches took their teams to, say, San Siro to play Milan or Inter, they had to pray for a result,' said Zaccheroni. 'Now the mentality is different. We can go there with our own ideas and our own style of play.'

Zaccheroni took his style to San Siro somewhat literally, by becoming the Milan coach in 1998. This was, theoretically at least, a dramatic step down. Zaccheroni's Udinese had finished fifth and third in the previous two campaigns, while Milan had endured two disastrous campaigns, finishing 11th and 10th. Zaccheroni was a highly promising coach, but the prospect of implementing a 3–4–3 at the club which had dominated Italian football with Sacchi's 4–4–2, and largely stuck to that system since, seemed daunting. 'Don't expect an Udinese photocopy,' he declared, despite the fact he'd brought both striker Bierhoff and right-wing-back Thomas Helveg with him from Udine. 'Milan will play with three defenders, four midfield players and three forwards, but that doesn't mean that it will be the same as Udinese's play. Anyway, 3–4–3 is not a magical formula. Perhaps it will be a new interpretation of 3–4–3.'

That proved prescient. Zaccheroni commenced the campaign with his usual system, although there was only one guaranteed starter up front. His old favourite Bierhoff began all 34 games and managed 19 goals: two penalties, three from open play with his feet, and 14 headers. Out wide, Zaccheroni struggled to find the right balance. George Weah wasn't suited to the left-sided role, and despite his unquestionable talent, the 1995 Ballon d'Or winner wasn't prolific, never finishing within ten goals of Serie A's top goalscorer. Meanwhile, Maurizio Ganz scored some crucial late goals, but was workmanlike rather than explosive. Zaccheroni tried deploying playmakers rather than forwards in his front three. The magical Brazilian Leonardo showed flashes of brilliance, but was more effective coming off the bench.

Milan, Lazio and Fiorentina emerged as the three title contenders that season. Fiorentina were briefly favourites, but slumped after Gabriel Batistuta injured his knee in a goalless draw with Milan, and then his strike partner Edmundo allowed himself a mid-season break because he fancied heading to the carnival in Rio. Milan's goalless draw at Lazio in early April, with eight games remaining, meant Lazio were nailed-on title favourites. But then came a major tactical shift.

Throughout the season Zaccheroni had only ever deployed Zvonimir Boban, the wonderfully gifted, tempestuous Croatian number 10, as one of his two central midfielders. Boban's two dismissals in the first half of the campaign, meanwhile, meant two suspensions, two dressing-downs from Zaccheroni and widespread speculation that he would leave in January. However, a week after that goalless draw with Lazio, Milan welcomed Parma to San Siro and, for the first time, Zaccheroni deployed Boban as a number 10, floating behind Bierhoff and Weah in a 3–4–1–2, in a tactical change supposedly suggested by Demetrio Albertini and Alessandro Costacurta, two dressing-room leaders. Milan started nervously, and went behind. But Boban took control, and after Paolo Maldini smashed a brilliant right-footed equaliser past Gianluigi Buffon from outside the box, Milan piled on the pressure.

Boban, a tall, swaggering figure and the only Milan player to wear his shirt untucked, provided the game's pivotal moment. Collecting the ball in the left-back position under pressure, he nonchalantly poked it past Parma's Diego Fuser with the outside of his boot, charging onto it before teammate Guly could get in his way. Then, from just inside his own half, Boban launched a long pass over the top of the Parma defence with such perfect weight that it tempted Buffon to advance, but also enabled Milan striker Ganz to prod it past the Parma goalkeeper on the volley, before he outpaced the recovering Fabio Cannavaro to slide it into an empty net. 2–1. Boban was magnificent, and received a standing ovation from the Milan supporters as he was substituted. Later that day Lazio lost the Rome derby 3–1 to a Francesco Totti-inspired Roma. Suddenly, the title race was on. More importantly, number 10s were now sexy again.

The following weekend Zaccheroni and Bierhoff returned to Udinese. Both received a rapturous reception upon emerging from the tunnel; Zaccheroni put on his sunglasses as if trying to hide the tears, while Bierhoff, strangely, was presented with Udinese's Player of the Year award ten months after he'd departed the Stadio Friuli. But neither were in the mood for niceties. Milan won 5–1, their most dominant performance of the campaign and a perfect demonstration of their new attacking trident's powers. Boban scored the first two, Bierhoff added the next two – both headers, of course – and then came the most telling goal of Milan's run-in. Boban received the ball in the number 10 position, casually sidestepped a dreadful two-footed lunge from Udinese defender Valerio Bertotto, and found himself with Weah running into the left-hand channel and Bierhoff running into the right-hand channel. Boban glanced towards Weah but slipped in Bierhoff, who chipped a cross over goalkeeper Luigi Turci, allowing Weah to nod into an empty net. Milan were rampant, and now top for the first time, having suddenly stumbled on this system. It was the perfect trio: Boban offered the invention, Weah the speed and Bierhoff the aerial power. 'The type of player I am means I'm best suited to being behind the main strike force,' Boban said. 'I can't be at my best in that role for all of the 34 games but I much prefer being in the centre of the field, where I'm more involved ... Zaccheroni has made it possible for me to give my best. A lot has changed.'

It wasn't plain sailing all the way to the title, and Milan had to rely on a last-minute own goal to defeat Sampdoria 3–2. Their most crucial victory came away at Juve. Milan were on the back foot throughout the first half, but after half-time a long, bouncing ball in behind gave Weah the chance to open the scoring by cleverly nodding over Angelo Peruzzi. Their second was another showcase of their front trio's varied skill sets; Bierhoff battled for a high ball, Boban picked up possession and delicately half-volleyed the ball over the defence for Weah, who raced through, steadied himself and drove the ball home. The next week Milan defeated Empoli 4–0, with a Bierhoff hat-trick, and then recorded a final-day 2–1 victory at Perugia, a match interrupted when rioting home fans invaded the pitch, supposedly to delay the game and allow their relegation-threatened side an advantage by knowing the results of rivals' matches. This delayed Milan's confirmation as champions, too, but Zaccheroni's side were eventually home and dry. It was one of the less convincing title victories of this era, but Milan captain Paolo Maldini declared it the most memorable of his seven Scudetti because it was so unexpected. Zaccheroni had overcome Milan's obsession with 4–4–2, implemented a front three, and taken the *Rossoneri* – who finished in the bottom half the previous season – to the title.

Questions persisted about precisely who had suggested the change in system, and one man inevitably insisted on taking all the credit. Milan owner Silvio Berlusconi claimed it was his idea to deploy Boban as the number 10, which deeply offended Zaccheroni.

Whatever the truth, the number 10 had returned to prominence, and while 1999/2000 was an ugly season in Italian football, dominated by refereeing conspiracies and settled in controversial fashion on the final day, it was nevertheless a wonderful campaign for *trequartisti*.

A good example came at Giovanni Trapattoni's Fiorentina, who finished as last of the seven sisters but offered arguably the most cohesive attacking trident. Gabriel Batistuta was the most complete striker of this era, and his closest support came from Enrico Chiesa, a speedy, two-footed forward capable of operating wide and shooting from acute angles. Behind them was Rui Costa, a classic number 10 adept at dribbling past challenges and slipping delicate passes in behind.

Fiorentina's equaliser in a 1–1 draw with fierce rivals Juventus shortly before Christmas was a perfect example of their attacking potential; Rui Costa brought the ball through midfield and prodded it into the path of Chiesa down the left, and he fired a near-post cross into Batistuta, who converted smartly. This was precisely how the attacking trident was supposed to operate: the number 10 initiating the break, the second striker running into the channel, the number 9 scoring. Fiorentina's opener in a 2–1 victory over Inter was another typical goal, coming when Rui Costa passed out to Chiesa on the left; his devilish cross tempted Angelo Peruzzi to advance, but the goalkeeper grasped at thin air, and Batistuta nodded into an empty net. However, Fiorentina didn't produce these moments consistently enough, and their underwhelming league finish meant Batistuta's nine-year love affair with Fiorentina was over – he moved to Roma.

Fabio Capello's Roma had only finished one place above Fiorentina, but they were an exciting prospect. Capello was previously a strict 4-4-2 man, and therefore his decision to build the side around Totti, Italian football's next great *trequartista*, was a significant moment in the revival of the number 10. Cafu and Vincent Candela were ready-made wing-backs, so Capello was another who turned to 3-4-1-2.

Fielded permanently behind two strikers, Totti was sensational. He dropped deep to create from midfield, and could arrive late in the penalty area to score. But Totti's natural home was between the lines, and his speciality was a specific pass – retreating slightly to receive a ball from midfield and then whipping the ball around the corner first-time for a runner down the right, usually either Vincenzo Montella breaking in behind or Cafu sprinting from deep.

Roma's best performance was their 4-1 derby victory over Lazio in November. All four goals came within the first half-hour and were scored in similar circumstances, with Delvecchio and Montella racing in behind, scoring two apiece, while Totti prowled between the lines. Roma briefly went top in autumn, although they collapsed dramatically in spring, winning just one of their last ten, failing to score in five of them. But that was a blessing in disguise, as it prompted Roma's signing of Batistuta, and his goals fired Roma to Totti's only Serie A title in 2000/01.

Fifth-placed Parma had a disjointed campaign. They were hindered by the inconsistency of their number 10 Ariel Ortega, who, having replaced Juan Verón successfully at Sampdoria, now replaced him less convincingly at Parma. A 3-0 victory over Verona in October showed their 3-4-1-2 had potential, with Ortega grabbing a goal, an assist and a pre-assist, and the two forwards, Hernán Crespo and Márcio Amoroso, all getting on the scoresheet.

Ortega linked particularly well with the wing-backs Fuser and Paolo Vanoli, but sadly struggled with alcoholism throughout his career, rarely justified his tag as the first of the many 'new Maradonas' and started fewer than half of the matches in 1999/2000. Without him, the manager Alberto Malesani varied between a more cautious 3–5–2, or a 3–4–3 with Amoroso and Di Vaio flanking Crespo, but in both systems Parma missed a *trequartista*.

Significantly, however, Parma finished level on points with Inter, who started 1999/2000 with unrivalled attacking options: Ronaldo, Christian Vieri, Iván Zamorano, Álvaro Recoba and – last and very much least in the eyes of coach Marcello Lippi – Roberto Baggio. His excellent season at Bologna had convinced Inter to sign him in the summer of 1998, although he endured a difficult first campaign, in a typically chaotic Inter season that featured three changes of coach.

Just as Baggio had been devastated at being reunited with Sacchi at Milan, now at Inter he suffered from the appointment of Lippi, with whom he'd rowed at Juventus. Lippi had little interest in Baggio, and even less interest in fielding a number 10; Vieri and Ronaldo were expected to cope by themselves, although injury problems meant they only once started together all season, in a 2–1 derby defeat to Milan, when Ronaldo was dismissed after half an hour for elbowing Roberto Ayala.

Like Parma, Inter struggled to create chances when playing 3–5–2, collecting only ten points from the nine matches before the opening of the January transfer window. They then completed a significant signing: Real Madrid's Clarence Seedorf. Although the Dutchman had spent the majority of his career in a deeper position, he was instantly deployed as a number 10, and transformed Inter. On his debut, Inter defeated Perugia 5–0. Seedorf assisted the first, then dribbled inside from the left flank, produced a stepover so mesmeric that it left Perugia defender Roberto Ripa on the ground, and lifted the ball into the corner. Three more Inter goals followed, and Seedorf was substituted to a standing ovation. His arrival, and the shift from 3–5–2 to 3–4–1–2, meant Inter collected 23 points from their next ten games.

Baggio, meanwhile, didn't start a single Serie A game until mid-January – Lippi was using anyone else he could find. For a January trip to Verona, Ronaldo, Vieri and Zamorano were all out, so Seedorf played behind Álvaro Recoba and unknown 21-year-old Adrian Mutu, making his first-ever Serie A start. Inter went 1–0 down, and Lippi spent the final stages of the first half speaking to a nonplussed Baggio on the edge of the technical area, giving him instructions with a succession of hand gestures in such a deliberate, overt way that he was surely asserting his authority as much as detailing specific plans. At half-time, Lippi introduced him as his number 10.

Baggio, never one for instructions, did his own thing. Two minutes into the second half, his through-ball to Vladimir Jugović bounced fortuitously to Recoba, who swept the ball home. Fifteen minutes from time, Recoba attacked down the left and stabbed a cross into the box that was met by Baggio, who slid in and diverted the ball into the far corner. Baggio celebrated passionately and, in typical fashion, used his post-match interview to slam Lippi for having questioned his level of fitness.

This didn't stop Baggio from being handed his first start the following week, at home to Roma. Once again he won the game for Inter. After eight minutes he collected a pass from Seedorf in the inside-left channel, dribbled menacingly towards goal before poking a through-ball into the path of Vieri, who finished. Vieri, Baggio and Seedorf embraced, a trident on the same wavelength. They again connected shortly afterwards, but Vieri's touch failed him. Roma equalised, but Inter responded; Vieri scuffed a shot into a defender, and the ball broke for onrushing wing-back Francesco Moriero, whose shot was saved by Francesco Antonioli and looped up into the air. Baggio took a couple of steps backwards to catch up with the ball, then produced a perfect over-the-shoulder volley, lobbing the ball over the recovering Cafu and delicately into the net. Baggio again celebrated wildly, and so did Lippi. Yet with others returning from injury, Baggio was dropped for the following weekend and used sparingly until the final weeks, once more omitted by an authoritarian coach.

Inter's city rivals Milan started the campaign as defending champions, although their campaign was handicapped by injuries to Boban, who missed the first and last couple of months, meaning Zaccheroni sometimes reverted to 3–4–3. Milan were clearly better with Boban; he ran the show in a 2–1 victory over Parma, scoring both goals from free-kicks, which inevitably meant Berlusconi approved the system. 'Boban was brilliant today, back to his best,' he declared. 'Today he had him playing behind a front two, which is one of the formations I like.'

Zaccheroni remained frustrated by Boban's languidness and petulance, but he kept on proving his worth. In January 2000, Milan trailed Lecce 2–0 at San Siro having started with three outright strikers, so Zaccheroni replaced José Mari with Boban and switched from 3–4–3 to 3–4–1–2. Milan got a goal back immediately, then Boban crossed to Bierhoff for the equaliser, with the German striker wheeling away and pointing to Boban in his celebration. Then, in the final stages, Boban stepped up to take a free-kick and bent the ball over the wall and onto the angle between crossbar and post. The match finished 2–2, and Boban was the star despite playing only half an hour.

He was also the game's outstanding player in a 2–1 victory over Lazio in February, receiving a standing ovation when he was substituted, before encountering yet more injury problems. These derailed Milan's campaign. 'We'd got very used to him playing behind us,' said Andrei Shevchenko, who won the *Capocannoniere* with 24 goals in his first Serie A campaign. 'He created the chances, he was the brains of the team, with amazingly creative ideas which he translated into balls for us to score. Now we have to take other routes to goal. That will take time.'

Second-placed Juventus were yet another side who used 3–4–1–2 throughout 1999/2000. That wasn't particularly surprising considering they'd previously played that way under Lippi, but it became more significant when you considered the identity of their manager: Ancelotti. He was previously a strict 4–4–2 man who refused to accommodate a number 10. He didn't want Zola, he didn't want Baggio. At Juve, though, he couldn't resist Zidane.

Upon his arrival at Juventus, Ancelotti discovered the squad were happy to make allowances for Zidane. One day, before an away trip, Zidane was late for the team coach and no one could get hold of him. A furious Ancelotti ordered the driver to leave without him, only for centre-back Paolo Montero to rush to the front of the coach and declare that they weren't leaving without their talisman. Ancelotti relented, Zidane arrived ten minutes later, played well, and Juventus won the game. Gradually, Ancelotti understood the need to indulge number 10s, and started to regret his treatment of Baggio.

'I should have worked with Baggio and found a way,' Ancelotti conceded many years later. 'I learned my lesson, and appreciated the quality of being more flexible with systems when I went to Juventus. I had to change my idea of football to accommodate Zidane, building the system around him rather than forcing him into my preferred 4–4–2. I didn't want to put Zidane on the left of a 4–4–2 where he wasn't comfortable. Instead we played 3–4–1–2, and he played between the lines.' Ancelotti's U-turn was the single greatest indication of the number 10's return.

Zidane showed flashes of brilliance, his starring performances often capped by free-kick goals, as against Roma, Perugia and Lecce. But Juventus's attacking performance in 1999/2000 was atrocious – in 34 games they managed only 46 goals, the lowest of the seven sisters. The contributions of Juve's attacking trio were questionable: Zidane managed just one goal from open play, and only one assist, from 32 starts. Creativity came from Del Piero, who provided 14 assists, the most in the league. But while he converted eight penalties, Del Piero didn't score from open play until the penultimate game of the campaign. Inzaghi managed a respectable 15 goals, but the three Juve attackers lacked cohesion, mainly because Del Piero and Inzaghi didn't get along.

Things came to a head in February's trip to Venezia – a 4–0 Juve win – with problems between the two strikers becoming evident in the closing stages. Del Piero opened the scoring with a penalty, but was still desperately searching for his first goal from open play, a huge topic of discussion in the media. With ten minutes remaining, Inzaghi pounced on a defensive mistake and rounded goalkeeper Fabrizio Casazza. Del Piero was coming on to the ball at a better angle, but Inzaghi took the shot himself, and scored. Not too much wrong with that in itself – Inzaghi had created the opportunity and deserved the chance to finish it.

But then, in stoppage time, Inzaghi streaked away again. Casazza advanced, and Inzaghi could have squared to Del Piero for an open goal. But Inzaghi being Inzaghi, he took on the shot. Casazza saved, and the ball rebounded back to Inzaghi. Others might have passed Del Piero at the second opportunity, almost out of guilt, but Inzaghi shot once more, this time successfully. He hailed the away supporters all by himself, with Del Piero standing motionless in the six-yard box.

Finally, Inzaghi completed his hat-trick by racing into a goalscoring position right in front of an exasperated Del Piero, to convert a pull-back into an open goal. There was still time for one final chance, when the ball fell perfectly between the two forwards. Inzaghi swung with his right boot, but Del Piero got there first with his left, and Casazza turned the ball onto the post. It finished with a clear Juve win, and they were top of the league, but it was obvious that this wasn't a proper strike partnership.

'Inzaghi and Del Piero made a good pair, but they got along only in theory,' Ancelotti later admitted. 'The problem was always the usual problem between players. One of them was the least selfless player in history – and I'm not talking about Alessandro.' Their souring relationship cost Juventus dearly in the final eight matches, when the team failed to score in four matches and Inzaghi failed to score at all. Having led the table for 13 weeks, Juventus lost the league on the final day.

The final day of 1999/2000 was a chaotic affair. Juventus started with a two-point lead over second-placed Lazio, and simply needed an away win at mid-table Perugia, who had nothing to play for, so there was no tactical rioting from the home supporters this time around. Juve started strongly and should have gone ahead when Zidane shot wastefully rather than passing to an unmarked Inzaghi, but shortly before half-time there was a sudden downpour, which left the Renato Curi pitch looking more suitable for Mark Spitz than Marco Materazzi. Half-time lasted an hour, as the players sheltered in the dressing room, watching TV footage of Pierluigi Collina wandering around the pitch beneath an umbrella and dropping the ball onto the pitch amid huge areas of standing water. The match surely would have been postponed at any other time in the season, but it needed to be finished on the final day. There was only one goal, a fine finish from journeyman Alessandro Calori, Perugia's centre-back. Juventus, and their selfish forwards, had blown it.

That opened the door for Sven-Göran Eriksson's Lazio, who lifted their first title since 1974 with a 3–0 victory over Reggina, including a penalty from the younger Inzaghi brother, Simone. Eriksson wasn't a particular admirer of *trequartisti*, and generally deployed a 4–4–2 formation, rotating Inzaghi, Marcelo Salas, Alen Bokšić, Fabrizio Ravanelli and Roberto Mancini up front.

That spring, however, he turned towards a 4–5–1, and while this essentially involved fielding Salas up front alone and introducing an extra midfielder, it allowed Juan Verón and Pavel Nedvěd extra freedom. Verón was Lazio's outstanding performer in two crucial games, scoring the winning goal in the Rome derby with an incredible long-range free-kick to make it 2–1, and the following weekend assisting Diego Simeone for the only goal against title rivals Juventus.

When Eriksson returned to 4–4–2, he found space for three natural number 10s in the final day victory over Reggina: Verón, Nedvěd and Mancini, playing his 541st and final Serie A match. Half-time in that contest lasted 35 minutes, as the governing bodies wanted Lazio and Juventus to start their second halves simultaneously, before eventually giving up and letting Lazio play their second half. 'It would be tough to write a better thriller than this,' Eriksson said afterwards, with typical calmness. It was an extraordinary ending to a remarkable campaign.

Except, however, it wasn't quite the ending. Each team had played their allotted 34 matches, and Lazio had been crowned champions. According to Serie A rules at the time, however, sides that finished level on points for a crucial position – the title, a European slot or relegation places – had their final position decided not according to goal difference or head-to-head results, but on the basis of a one-legged play-off. Therefore, because Inter and Parma finished on 58 points, a one-off contest would decide who accompanied Lazio, Juventus and Milan into the following season's Champions League.

If Inter failed to win the play-off, Lippi would lose his job. The problem was that Inter were suffering from a huge injury crisis, which had forced Lippi to re-summon Baggio. For the final four games of the Serie A campaign he'd played up front with Recoba, a partnership lacking the physical power that Lippi preferred. Nevertheless, Baggio scored a powerful shot on the run against Bari, then a penalty against Cagliari, and assisted Seedorf with a lovely long-range pass against Perugia. In the other game, Inter lost 4–0 to Fiorentina, their heaviest-ever home league defeat, and Baggio was fuming when substituted after 55 minutes. Lippi was bemused. 'If players don't want to be taken off, then they should go and sign for clubs who have only 13 players in their squad,' he blasted. 'That way they can always play.' Lippi, however, needed Baggio one last time.

Parma dominated the opening stages of the play-off, hitting the woodwork. Vieri, starting his first Inter match in three months and evidently unfit, pulled up after half an hour and was ruled out of Euro 2000. Inter were struggling. But then Baggio tempted Lilian Thuram into a foul on the edge of the box. It was in a difficult shooting position, to the right of the area rather than in front of it. Only a left-footed player could reasonably score from that position. Or Roberto Baggio. When everyone expected a cross, Baggio unleashed a magical free-kick that curled around the wall and dipped under the bar at the near post, past the world's best goalkeeper, Gianluigi Buffon.

Parma hit back when Mario Stanić headed in a corner. But with seven minutes remaining, Inter knocked a long ball into the box, and Iván Zamorano – on for Vieri – nodded the ball backwards into the D towards Baggio, who let the ball bounce, steadied himself, then unleashed a brilliant left-footed shot that swerved away from Buffon's dive and flew into the corner. Two Baggio goals from outside the box: the first was precision with his right foot, the second was power with his left.

In stoppage time Zamorano added a third. But it was Baggio's day, and, in a sense, Baggio's final day. He subsequently spent four happy years at Brescia, where he became friends with Pep Guardiola, and he was later honoured with a 'ceremonial' farewell appearance for Italy, five years after his previous cap. But this was Baggio's last appearance for a major club. He'd generously saved the job of Lippi, the coach who had so often overlooked him, and more importantly he'd reminded other coaches about the value of the *trequartista*.

# 6

# Catenaccio

No other football nation produces as many top-class defenders as Italy, and this era of Italian dominance witnessed one outstanding generation of defenders passing the baton on to their successors. The likes of Franco Baresi and Giuseppe Bergomi were winding down their careers, while Alessandro Nesta and Fabio Cannavaro were establishing themselves as Europe's next great centre-backs. The remarkable Paolo Maldini acted as the bridge between the two generations, midway through his record 647 Serie A appearances.

But during this period Italian football was subject to an incredibly bitter war over the fundamental issue of precisely what defending meant. Were defenders supposed to be concerned with nullifying a specific opponent or focusing on a particular zone? It wasn't merely about which approach was most effective, but also about which approach was most Italian.

Throughout the post-war period Italian football had been synonymous with the sport's most infamous tactic: *catenaccio*. Although frequently used as a simple synonym for 'negative football', *catenaccio* – which literally means 'door bolt' – actually referred to a very specific defensive tactic: the use of a *libero*, or sweeper, playing behind 'stopper' centre-backs who performed strict man-marking duties on opposition forwards. The notion of a spare defender was a relatively novel idea, and inevitably meant a shortfall in more advanced positions, which generally produced defensive football.

*Catenaccio* was popularised – if that's the right word – primarily by the two Milanese clubs in the 1960s, whose European Cup successes came immediately after Real Madrid and Benfica sides had dominated through free-scoring, attractive football. It was quite a contrast, and the Italian approach was widely reviled across the continent. Its most famous practitioner was Inter manager Helenio Herrera, who admitted that his brand of *catenaccio* was simply about removing a midfielder to introduce an extra defender, the sweeper. Herrera insisted that this liberated legendary left-back Giacinto Facchetti to perform an attack-minded role, and that other managers copied the sweeper without adjusting the positional responsibilities of the defenders, therefore ensuring *catenaccio* became more defensive than he'd intended. AC Milan's Nereo Rocco also won two European Cups with *catenaccio*, but unlike Herrera he never rejected the defensive tag. His motto was brilliantly telling: 'Let's hope it's a good game, but that the better team doesn't win.' He was content to be overrun in midfield to ensure security at the back.

Gradually, to solve the numerical inferiority in midfield, *liberos* became more gifted in possession, pushing into midfield and starting attacks, but the basic system remained. *Catenaccio* was effectively rebranded in Italy as '*il giocco all' Italiana*' (effectively 'the Italian game'), although elsewhere the '*catenaccio*' moniker stuck. Whatever it was called, this system continued to dominate Italian football. Its most famous modern practitioner was Giovanni Trapattoni, the most successful coach in Serie A history with seven Scudettos and the most obvious disciple of Rocco, having played as a defensive midfielder for his Milan side throughout the 1960s. 'Thanks to the achievements of Inter, Milan and the Italian national team between 1960 and 1980, Italy became one of the most heterogeneous countries in terms of tactics,' Trapattoni proudly explained in the introduction to his book about tactics. 'The Italian game necessitates a player placed behind the defensive line, the *libero*.' Trapattoni, more than most, stuck to that approach.

Trapattoni's Juventus, six-time Serie A champions between 1977 and 1986, played a hybrid of 3–5–2 and 4–4–2, with zonal marking in midfield but strict man-marking at the back. Trapattoni firmly believed that *liberos* and stoppers were very different types of players; *liberos* were about 'being able to read the play and anticipate the situation', while stoppers required 'physical strength, aerial power, determined tackling skills and intelligent aggression'. Italians admired both types – elegant sweepers like Gaetano Scirea and aggressive man-markers like Claudio Gentile, beauty and beast respectively.

Then, in the late 1980s, along came Arrigo Sacchi. In stark contrast to most Italian coaches, Sacchi had never been a professional footballer, spending his formative years as a shoe salesman, and he therefore developed ideas independently from ex-players accustomed to playing *catenaccio*. Rather than worshipping Rocco's Milan, Herrera's Inter or Trapattoni's Juve, Sacchi loathed *catenaccio* and adored the Dutch school of Total Football. He was determined to create teams that played positively, and re-educated his defenders according to the principles of zonal marking.

With Parma and then Milan, where he won two European Cups in 1989 and 1990, Sacchi overhauled the Italian obsession with sweepers and stoppers, and introduced a 'flat' back four. Whereas other Italian sides dropped deep, Sacchi's flat defence played an aggressive offside line that compressed play into the opposition half, enabling Milan to dominate. This was a genuine revolution in Italy, particularly in terms of playing positively away from home. 'Italian sides used to try to sneak by their opponents,' remembered Carlo Ancelotti, who worked under Sacchi as both player and assistant. 'They weren't trying to show that they were better; they were trying to show that they were shrewder. Sacchi changed that. His teams took the pitch to win, to dominate the other side.' Sacchi remains widely admired for his revolutionary thinking, a key influence on the next generation of Champions League-winning managers like Pep Guardiola, Rafael Benítez and, of course, Ancelotti.

But Italy is nothing if not conservative, and while Sacchi's approach received rave reviews across Europe, within his home country his methods were considered an affront to Italian traditions – he was, after all, overhauling a system his compatriots called 'the Italian game'. He'd turned Milan into a Dutch-style side, complete with three Dutchmen in Frank Rijkaard, Ruud Gullit and Marco van Basten, and when he transferred his methods onto the Italian national side upon his appointment in 1991, he was almost considered a traitor. Italy reached the 1994 World Cup Final, losing to Brazil on penalties, and yet Sacchi was loathed for his obsession with pressing, 4–4–2 and zonal defending. At the beginning of this *calcio* era in 1996, Sacchi remained in charge of Italy despite a disastrous European Championship in England, where the Azzurri exited at the group stage. He claimed Italy had played the best football at the tournament, but most fans wanted him sacked.

Sacchi's most vociferous and significant critic was, inevitably, Trapattoni. 'Sacchi's Italy has only looked like a good side in about five matches,' he complained. 'Sacchi's Milan only won one out of four championships, but their style of play was glorified by an effective propaganda machine. I'd like to have seen that Milan without the three Dutchmen and all those Italian internationals. You can try explaining the same tactical dispositions to 11 ordinary players and they'd still be ordinary players. The idea that zonal defence equals spectacle is a colossal mistake, yet the idea has been fed to TV-dependent fans and they've swallowed it: hook, line and sinker.'

But Trapattoni was evidently biased, because he'd been deeply affected by Sacchi's achievements. Having enjoyed sustained success with traditional Italian methods, Trapattoni was now considered an anachronism in some quarters for continuing to play the Italian way. He accused Sacchi of stealing zonal play from basketball, and said he preferred Sacchi's successor at Milan, Fabio Capello, who had played more defensively and won more trophies. Far from being an isolated critic, however, Trapattoni's views were echoed by many within Italian football. Indeed, for all his complaints about Sacchi's 'propaganda', the majority of the Italian press were pro-Trapattoni and anti-Sacchi.

The most obvious example was the esteemed *La Gazzetta dello Sport* editor Gianni Brera, who famously once opined that 'the perfect game of football would finish 0–0' and happily referred to himself as a believer in 'defensivist' football. Brera was close friends with Rocco, the godfather of *catenaccio*, and therefore heavily promoted Trapattoni, his modern-day equivalent. 'When you build a house, you start with the foundations and not the roof,' Brera explained. 'Rocco and then Trapattoni have always built their sides on the basis of the principle that it is easier to concede one less goal than your opponents, than to score one goal more than your opponents. It seems perfectly logical.' While a section of the Italian public appreciated Sacchi's revolution, Brera's beliefs dominated.

Sacchi was finally sacked by the Italian FA in late 1996, after half a decade attempting to overhaul Italy's obsession with deep defending. He left behind a country divided between his disciples, and those who remained loyal to Italy's past.

Sacchi's replacement was Cesare Maldini. While his son, Paolo, was a mainstay of Sacchi's zonal defence for both Milan and Italy, the elder Maldini was an Italian traditionalist. He'd been a classy *libero* in his playing days, had featured in Rocco's classic *catenaccio* Milan side and later became his assistant manager, before succeeding him and also serving as Enzo Bearzot's assistant for Italy's 1982 World Cup triumph, then coaching the U21 side for a decade. Maldini's appointment represented a U-turn, and while Maldini attempted to play down the significance of his appointment, insisting 'there is no new and no old in football', his return was widely considered a return to a typically Italian approach. After years spent learning the Sacchi methods, Italy's defenders now reverted to playing with a *libero*, and even Maldini's own son appeared bewildered by the prospect of *catenaccio*. 'If Dad tells me how it is done, then no problem,' he joked after his father's appointment. 'But before I line up as a *libero*, he'll need to explain a few things to me.'

Maldini, Italy's captain, was the most respected defender of his generation, and was typically versatile. Although he became the world's greatest left-back, he had initially broken through as a right-sided defender, only switching flanks because of the presence of established right-back Mauro Tassotti. He was admirably two-footed, so playing on the wrong side was never an issue. Maldini was also capable of shifting inside to play centre-back, including during Italy's run to the 1994 World Cup semi-final, and became renowned for defending in a calm, composed manner, never resorting to slide tackles – clean sheets, clean shorts. He would have made a fine *libero*.

Instead, Maldini was fielded in his customary left-back position, and his father's return to the Italian game benefited others. The outstanding Fabio Cannavaro became a regular, confirming his brilliance by marking England's Alan Shearer out of a World Cup qualifier in 1997, while Giuseppe Bergomi, a veteran of Italy's 1982 World Cup victory and the Azzurri's captain for the 1990 World Cup, was handed a surprise call-up after six years away from the national side

– he was a classic man-marker, but had been overlooked by Sacchi because he wasn't suited to playing in a flat back four. Milan's Alessandro Costacurta, like Maldini Jr, was flexible enough to adjust, and became Italy's *libero*.

The Italian public, and particularly the press, adored the new regime. 'After Sacchi, we wanted more simple football, a very Italian style of football that has so often demonstrated its worth, and that's what we got,' read *Corriere dello Sport* after Maldini's first game, a 2–0 win over Northern Ireland. Gianni Mura of *La Repubblica* declared that Maldini's regime 'gives me the impression of bread and salami after years of *nouvelle cuisine*'. This might sound like a downgrade to many, but Mura was welcoming the return of familiar Italian fare.

Not everyone, however, was thrilled by the Italian national side regressing to *catenaccio*, and plenty of Serie A managers preferred Sacchi's zonal system. Another zonal advocate was Roy Hodgson, enjoying the first of two spells at Inter, whom he took to the 1997 UEFA Cup Final. Hodgson had first emerged when 'doing a Sacchi' in Sweden during the 1970s, introducing zonal marking into a country previously fixated on man-marking, taking lowly Halmstad, who had survived relegation on goal difference the season before his appointment, to their first league title. Twenty-five years later, Hodgson was fighting the same war in a new country. 'All the best teams in Italy play a four-man defence,' he declared. 'Will it stay that way? No. The Italians are trying to change it. The new era that has been swept in, which wants to deny Arrigo Sacchi, is talking about a return to *catenaccio*. At the moment, the national team is playing with a back five. All they've really done is add a defender and play 5–3–2.' That, of course, was the change Herrera's Inter had made in the 1960s.

One of Hodgson's allies was another future England manager, Sven-Göran Eriksson, who coached Sampdoria and Lazio during this period, and was firmly committed to the flat back four. Indeed, Hodgson had been Eriksson's inspiration during his formative years in Sweden, with Eriksson describing the controversial introduction of zonal marking as 'the greatest ideological battle in Swedish coaching history'. Eriksson graduated from his final coaching course in Sweden – which involved delaying his wedding, not the last time his professional and personal lives would become entwined – by writing a thesis on the advantages of playing 4–4–2, pressing in advanced positions and holding an aggressive defensive line.

Eriksson's early coaching career involved him performing the same job wherever he went. He went to Gothenburg, ditched man-marking, introduced zonal marking and won the Swedish title. He went to Benfica, ditched man-marking, introduced zonal marking and won the Portuguese title twice. He went to Roma, who had already been using a broadly zonal system under his compatriot Nils Liedholm, and therefore struggled to improve the side, but then performed well at Fiorentina, where, once again, he overhauled man-marking. After a second spell at Benfica he moved to Sampdoria, where he achieved modest success and regularly claimed his side played the most attractive football in Serie A. In part, this was because Eriksson favoured attack-minded defenders, an underrated consequence of zonal marking – because defenders were no longer concerned with direct confrontations against forwards, it allowed more technically gifted, intelligent players to be fielded in the backline.

A case in point was Siniša Mihajlović, who had risen to prominence by winning the European Cup for Red Star Belgrade as a commanding central midfielder. He reluctantly played left-back throughout two unhappy years at Roma, and upon signing for Eriksson's Sampdoria was dismayed when he discovered he'd again be deployed at the back. After initially deploying him at left-back,

Eriksson eventually moved Mihajlović into the centre of the back four, a position Mihajlović was so unfamiliar with that he initially refused to play there.

But Mihajlović became outstanding, with Eriksson's skill in drilling a zonal defence ensuring that he coped despite his attacking instincts. He was Serie A's most creative centre-back, demonstrating that defenders could provide the playmaking of *liberos* when deployed in a flat back four. Mihajlović, along with Juan Sebastián Verón and Roberto Mancini, impressed under Eriksson's Sampdoria and later joined him at Lazio, where together they won Lo Scudetto in 2000. In a Lazio shirt, Mihajlović achieved the unique feat of scoring a hat-trick entirely comprising free-kicks with his incredible left foot. His career was somewhat overshadowed by controversies ranging from racism to spitting, and his tendency towards old-school, tough tackling often got him into trouble. But Mihajlović was probably Serie A's best footballing defender during this period, and creative enough to justify his wearing the number 11 shirt.

With Eriksson's Lazio, Mihajlović formed an outstanding central defensive partnership with the classiest Italian defender of this era, Alessandro Nesta. Emerging from the city of Rome at the same time as Francesco Totti, Nesta was a boyhood Lazio supporter who played as a midfielder throughout his youth-team career, before being converted to a full-back and then, because of injuries to first-teamers, switched to a centre-back under Zdeněk Zeman. Nesta was regularly compared to Franco Baresi, naturally a *libero* rather than a stopper, although like Baresi he was also capable of excelling in a flat back four. 'It's great to mark a forward out of the match without using rough methods,' Nesta said. 'That gives me the ultimate thrill.'

Nesta didn't depend on aerial dominance, and managed just one goal in nearly 200 Serie A appearances for Lazio, in somewhat atypical style for a centre-back– acrobatically volleying home against Salernitana in 1999. He was admirably two-footed but left the play-making to others. Nonchalant without being ostentatious, his play-ing style reflected his off-pitch mentality; he once bought himself a Porsche, then immediately sold it because he considered it too flashy. Although Zeman deserves great credit for Nesta's development, Eriksson's coaching converted him into a truly world-class centre-back. 'My two wishes are to play for Lazio forever, and to play for Eriksson forever,' he said during Lazio's title-winning season. Eriksson was sometimes criticised for playing a boring 4–4–2 when others used a *trequartista*, but his preference for a flat back four enabled him to deploy two footballing centre-backs, which was somewhat uncommon in a *catenaccio* system.

It would be unreasonable to suggest all 'zonist' managers were this way inclined, however, and this was arguably Hodgson's downfall at Inter. He famously insisted that attacking left-back Roberto Carlos was a winger rather than a defender, before happily selling him to Real Madrid. In fairness, the Brazilian's defending was haphazard, and his best performances came as a wing-back rather than a full-back. The most pertinent example, in terms of Italy's defensive debate, was Salvatore Fresi.

During the mid-1990s, Fresi was seemingly Italian football's next great *libero*, considered the new Baresi after captaining Cesare Maldini's Italian U21 side to European Championship success. Fresi was an elegant, composed sweeper who anticipated danger and brought the ball forward calmly, excelling for Salernitana and recruited by Inter boss Ottavio Bianchi, a *catenaccio* devotee. But the appointment of Hodgson was disastrous for Fresi – not only did Hodgson deploy a flat back four, he insisted that a ball-player like Fresi belonged in midfield, which harmed his defensive develop-ment. 'I played at the back for a few months,' Fresi remembered of his Inter experience. 'But after they put me in midfield, I was neither fish nor fowl.'

Fresi became the posterboy for believers in the Italian way, with Hodgson quizzed about his positioning at nearly every press conference, and Fresi repeatedly stressing his desire to play as a *libero*, acting as a spokesman for an entire position. 'I'd be lying if I said that I feel comfortable playing in the role that Hodgson gives me,' he admitted in 1997, shortly after Cesare Maldini's appointment as national team manager. 'The *libero* role is my natural position. The future is in the past, or rather in rediscovering the role of the *libero*. Maldini's Italy could be very important, both for me and for reorientating Italian football towards reviving the *libero*.' Sure enough, Fresi was the only newcomer in Maldini's first Italy squad, although he was never capped despite being receiving six call-ups.

In 1998, when Hodgson left Inter for Blackburn Rovers – coincidentally, after Eriksson had reneged on a promise to move to Ewood Park – his replacement was Gigi Simoni, another old-fashioned, devout *catenaccio* follower and another who had played under, and worshipped, Rocco. Simoni immediately switched from a flat back four to a traditional defensive, counter-attacking Italian approach. 'Fresi will be the *libero*, Paganin and Sartor the centre-backs, with Zanetti and Tarantino the wing-backs,' he declared at his first press conference, leaving little doubt about his preference for the Italian way.

And playing the Italian game could still work, as Simoni's Inter demonstrated during their 1998 UEFA Cup Final against Lazio. This was Simoni's *catenaccio* against Eriksson's flat back four, and Inter ran out 3–0 winners, in a contest best remembered for Ronaldo's marvellous goal, putting Lazio goalkeeper Luca Marchegiani on the floor with a succession of stepovers before slotting home. At the other end, Inter played proper old-school Italian football. Taribo

West man-marked Pierluigi Casiraghi and Francesco Colonnese handled Roberto Mancini, both sticking tightly to their specific opponents even when they drifted to opposite flanks. Right-back Aron Winter also man-marked Lazio's Pavel Nedvěd when he drifted inside, while left-sided Javier Zanetti coped with Diego Fuser. On the rare occasions when a Lazio attacker escaped his marker, Fresi stepped in calmly, perfecting his beloved *libero* role. It was his career highlight.

As his fellow Sardinian Gianfranco Zola once told him, Fresi was simply unfortunate to be born in the wrong era. He became a cult figure, his story more mysterious precisely because he was never capped by Italy. In 2013, when Inter were bought by Erick Thohir, the Indonesian gave a knowing nod in Fresi's direction. 'It's easy to speak about the three Germans [Jürgen Klinsmann, Lothar Matthäus, Andreas Brehme], about Roberto Baggio and Ronaldo,' he said. 'But Salvatore Fresi ... maybe most people forget about him, but I remember.' Thohir was outlining his football hipster credentials, namechecking the outcast unappreciated in his own era.

Simoni's love of *catenaccio* ultimately cost him his job. He was dismissed hours after Inter's 2–1 win over Salernitana, and only four days after a 3–1 victory over Real Madrid, because President Massimo Moratti couldn't work out Inter's attacking approach. 'It seemed to me, and to lots of others, that it was evident that Inter simply do not have a game plan and that we haven't been playing well since the beginning of the season. I think that's an important enough reason to take this decision.' When questioned about the peculiar timing of the decision, Moratti hit back. 'Well, it's simply too banal to sack a coach after a couple of defeats.'

At international level Cesare Maldini might not have deployed Fresi as a sweeper, and his defenders played more of a hybrid approach than a strict man-marking system, but it was largely a return to the Italian way – with entirely predictable results. From Maldini's six World Cup qualification games, Italy kept six clean sheets. The problem, though, was that they failed to score in three of these matches – against Poland, Georgia and then, fatally, England – despite Italy boasting arguably the best array of attackers in Europe. Maldini's Italy were simply too defensive. They were forced into a World Cup play-off where they narrowly overcame Russia, partly thanks to brilliant display from 19-year-old debutant goalkeeper Gianluigi Buffon.

At the 1998 World Cup itself, Maldini continued with his traditional Italian system, a blend of 4–4–2 and 3–5–2, with such an obvious 'spare defender' that the system was sometimes termed a 1–3–4–2, recalling Trapattoni's Juventus side of the 1970s and Italy's approach at World Cup 1982, when Maldini was assistant manager. Costacurta played as the *libero* behind Cannavaro and either Nesta or Bergomi. Maldini Jr continued as left-back, while Angelo Di Livio or Francisco Moriero played as a 'returning' right-sided midfielder, effectively a wing-back in a five-man defence. Italy were, of course, defensively excellent, keeping three clean sheets in five matches, but once again attacking failures cost them, and they were eliminated on penalties after a goalless draw with hosts France. Maldini resigned, but the Italian reaction to his side's performance was considerably more favourable than four years previously under Sacchi, even though Italy had been eliminated two rounds earlier.

Sacchi, meanwhile, had returned to Milan for a disastrous spell in the second half of 1996/97, which ended with Milan in 11th place and featured the club's worst-ever Serie A defeat, 6–1 to Juventus. 'It's one of those days when everything you do goes wrong,' Sacchi said afterwards. 'It's an evening to forget in a hurry.' That was an optimistic take; Italy's newspapers were determined to ensure it was never forgotten. 'In another 100 years people will still talk about this result, how Milan conceded six goals and surrendered their league title to their historic rivals,' read the front page of *La Gazzetta dello Sport*. That was pretty much that for Sacchi, in terms of Italian football. He endured a disappointing one-year spell with Atlético Madrid in 1998/99, finishing 13th, and in 2000/01 he took charge of Parma for a month, before resigning because of stress.

Sacchi became a prominent pundit and, inevitably, was a vocal critic of every attempt to reintroduce *catenaccio*. At the start of 1999/2000, the majority of major Serie A clubs had reverted to a three-man defence rather than using a back four, increasingly playing the old Italian way rather than the Sacchi way. 'We're not having a lot of fun,' Sacchi complained. 'My impression is that Italian football has taken a step backwards. There is a lot of conformity. All the teams play the same way, it's difficult to distinguish one team from the other and it's hard to see anything new. Based on the premise that they are using a three-man defence, almost all of the teams actually play with a back five, therefore allowing them to return to the *libero*. We've gone back to the kind of football we used to play 15 years ago.' For many of his colleagues, that was considered a great success.

By this stage Italy's national team manager was Dino Zoff, the goalkeeper from their 1982 World Cup-winning side. Zoff was a curious choice, having enjoyed a relatively unspectacular coaching career with Juventus and then two spells with Lazio – on the second occasion playing 4–4–2 before moving upstairs to become the club's sporting director, working above Eriksson. Zoff was still considered a legendary figure, although it was difficult to work out precisely what he believed in. He began with a 4–4–2, although he explained that his formation 'would depend upon how things go in Serie A – I'll listen to what the club sides are telling me, and obviously, the national team must take account of any tactical indications Serie A is giving me'. This was Italian football's Third Way: Sacchi had insisted on a flat back four, Maldini was committed to the *libero* and Zoff didn't have a preference.

Zoff started the Euro 2000 qualification campaign with a flat four-man defence, and Italy won their first three games. But then things went awry; they drew at home against lowly Belarus, followed an impressive 4–0 win over Wales with a poor display in a goalless draw against Switzerland, collapsed in Naples against Denmark, losing 3–2 having been 2–0 up, and then drew 0–0 away in Belarus. Zoff had stuck with the 4–4–2, and after the bleak display in Minsk was questioned about the popularity of the 3–4–1–2 in Italy. In 1999/2000, 69 per cent of Serie A starting XIs used a back three, including six of the 'seven sisters'. Lazio, the champions, were the exceptions in using a four-man defence, and were also – not coincidentally – the only side with a foreign coach.

Elsewhere, Italian coaches had unequivocally returned to the back three. Juventus's Carlo Ancelotti used Italians Ciro Ferrara – described as the world's best defender by Ronaldo – and Mark Iuliano alongside tough-tackling Uruguayan Paolo Montero. Alberto Zaccheroni's Milan generally featured a trio of Maldini, Costacurta and Roberto Ayala, who never excelled in Serie A despite his brilliance elsewhere. At Inter, Marcello Lippi played the wonderfully gifted Frenchman Laurent Blanc sweeping behind two of Dario Šimić, Christian Panucci and the Colombian Iván Córdoba, who compensated for his diminutive stature with Serie A's most remarkable leap. At Roma, Fabio Capello used Brazilians Aldair and Zago alongside either Amedeo Mangone or Alessandro Rinaldi, while Fiorentina coach Giovanni Trapattoni used Alessandro Pierini alongside the aggressive Czech Tomáš Řepka and Daniele Adani.

The most formidable trio, however, was at Parma, where Nestor Sensini swept up behind Fabio Cannavaro and Lilian Thuram, two all-time great centre-backs who played aggressively and brought the ball forward when required. Cannavaro was a true all-round defender, capable of playing as stopper or sweeper, dispossessing opponents cleanly or through physicality. Thuram was a wonderful footballer, converted from a right-winger into a defender by Arsène Wenger at Monaco, which made him perfect for the right of a three-man defence.

Zoff, as promised, followed Serie A's tactical trend and switched to a 3–4–1–2 for Italy's first friendly after the qualification campaign, a 3–1 defeat to Belgium. He continued with that formation in warm-up matches, although everyone seemed confused about precisely what the attacking plan was. 'It was a weird way of playing – they didn't impose their style but nor was it a counter-attacking system,' said midfielder Paulo Sousa, then of Parma, after Italy had beaten his Portugal side 2–0. 'Italy are the best regarding preparation – tactics, preparation and the study of opponents. But there's no time for the national team to work on all that, and it's making an impact.'

Italian football, which had always prided itself on its tactical sophistication, now felt somewhat out of step with European football trends. In 1999/2000, Serie A clubs' European performance was dreadful; they failed to provide a semi-finalist in either the Champions League or the UEFA Cup, having dominated European competitions throughout the 1990s. Ahead of Euro 2000, Italian football's reputation across the continent was battered. *Corriere dello Sport* ran a front-page headline simply reading 'Stay at home, Azzurri!', with injuries to Buffon, Europe's outstanding goalkeeper, and the world's most expensive player Christian Vieri ruling both out of the tournament and lowering expectations even further.

But Zoff could rely on Europe's most formidable defence. Nesta played as the spare defender between Cannavaro and Iuliano, with Maldini on the left and Gianluca Zambrotta playing the 'returning' role on the right. Italy won all three group-stage matches, defeating

Turkey, Belgium and Sweden, yet their performance was criticised by a familiar figure. 'Italy won by playing Italian-style,' wrote Sacchi in *La Stampa* after the Belgium victory. 'It was a good Italy, in keeping with our habits and our mentality. It was the usual Italy: defensive, opportunist and maybe at times a little boring. We were very good in defence, even if we defended with too many players, always using the same 3–5–1–1 formation.' Every small piece of praise was followed by a criticism – although Sacchi, in fairness, always stuck to tactical analysis rather than the type of personal insults he'd been subjected to.

In the quarter-final Italy overcame Romania 2–0, setting up a semi-final against hosts Holland in Amsterdam. The Dutch were favourites, as after a nervous last-gasp 1–0 victory over the Czech Republic in their opener, they'd subsequently defeated Denmark 3–0, France 3–2 and Yugoslavia 6–1. This was a classic Dutch side offering great width, and the semi-final was Italian defence versus Dutch attack, particularly after Gianluca Zambrotta was dismissed after half an hour for two fouls on winger Boudewijn Zenden, forcing Italy to play with ten men for 90 minutes. Yet Italy stereotypically clung onto a 0–0, eventually winning on penalties with goalkeeper Francesco Toldo the hero. Italy's defending wasn't faultless – Holland missed two penalties in normal time – but they weathered the storm for two hours and didn't concede. The most succinct analysis came from the stands, where Italian supporters held up a banner that simply read, 'Catenaccio!'

Italy narrowly failed to defeat France in the final, conceding a last-minute equaliser to Sylvain Wiltord, before losing to a golden goal from Juventus-bound David Trezeguet. Zoff resigned after the tournament, after criticism from Milan president and then-opposition leader Silvio Berlusconi. 'As a person who loves my country I cannot remain quiet,' Berlusconi fumed. 'Why did Zoff not ensure someone was marking Zidane? You can't allow a player of his ability to do whatever he wants. It was obvious that the final revolved around him, even an amateur could see that. We needed someone with intelligence and a brain, and Zoff has none.'

These remarks were widely dismissed by football pundits, who observed that Zidane had actually been nullified effectively and had endured his quietest game of the tournament. Zoff took the remarks to heart, however, and quit. 'This decision comes as a direct result of Berlusconi's offensive remarks,' he said. 'I feel hurt as a man, and that is the reason I have gone.'

More significant than Zoff's resignation was the identity of his replacement: Trapattoni, who had won seven Serie A titles, all in the 1970s and 1980s, playing the old-school Italian way. 'I thought the system used at the Euros worked well,' he declared at his unveiling. 'I will start from how the team ended their last match, with Zoff's shape and his players. Traditions play a big part in football. We don't have the characteristics to play like Holland or France.' And those nations were the most pertinent comparisons to bookend this Italian era: Dutch dominance had been superseded by Italian ascendancy, but Italy's Euro 2000 Final defeat to France marked the changing of the guard.

# Transition:
# Italy–France

Serie A had dominated European football throughout the 1990s, but the advent of the 21st century saw it dramatically left behind.

The identity of the Champions League quarter-finalists between 2000 and 2002 told the story. Of the 24 places, nine were filled by Spanish sides, seven from England, four from Germany, and one apiece from Italy, Portugal, Greece and Spain. Serie A, once the top dog, was now slumming it with Europe's second-tier leagues. Italy could no longer boast success, and nor did it offer style. The final of Euro 2000 proved the turning point, with French football now taking charge.

France had won the World Cup on home soil in 1998, but it was difficult not to think of them as, stylistically, an Italian side. 'They won because of their goalkeeper, the four defenders and Zinedine Zidane,' blasted eccentric Marseille coach Rolland Courbis, which was a reasonably fair assessment and could pass for a summary of many Juventus performances. France were essentially playing Italian football, simply with more talented players.

The 1998 World Cup quarter-final between France and Italy had produced a 0–0 draw and was described as being 'a match straight out of Serie A – seven of France's starting XI had played there,' by *World Soccer* magazine, while France's players often attributed their eventual success to the influence of Serie A. 'Our generation owes everything to Italian football and what it taught us,' said captain Didier Deschamps. His midfield colleague Zidane indicated that moving to Serie A had taught him about the importance of winning.

Yet France's Euro 2000 Final victory over Italy was framed as good overcoming evil. 'Purists and Parisians alike would have been dismayed had Italy prevailed,' read the *Daily Telegraph*'s report. 'While admiration certainly exists for their ability to plan and then execute such a professional job, the Italian side simply lack the *joie de vivre* which suffuses French football.' Other reports echoed that sentiment. 'Ultimately, Euro 2000 was won by magic, not method,' stated the *Guardian*. France boss Roger Lemerre declared it 'a victory for attacking football'. It was 2000 rather than 1998, when, stylistically, the French era truly began.

France's fruitful period was evidenced by success at major international tournaments, and owed much to the development of world-class players who had all moved overseas, chiefly to Italy, England and Spain. The most influential 'French' club during this period was actually English: Arsenal manager Arsène Wenger became one of the continent's most revered coaches, and sometimes fielded five French players in his starting XI. Ligue 1 remained something of an afterthought, with high tax rates encouraging homegrown products to leave swiftly.

Still, that created room for the next generation to shine in the French top flight before moving on, and nowhere else in Europe produced so many good footballers during this period, partly thanks to the famous Clairefontaine national academy, which provided rival countries with inspiration. France excelled at international tournaments because of talent rather than tactics; at Euro 2000, midfielder

Emmanuel Petit claimed – with some merit – that France had eight of the best eleven players in Europe.

During this period France boasted Europe's most talented play-maker, Zidane, and its most consistent goalscorer, Thierry Henry. Zidane was following in the footsteps of previous great French number 10s, while Henry helped to define the new model for centre-forwards. Meanwhile, France proved adept at producing solid, unspectacular holding midfielders, who protected the defence and allowed the attackers to shine. After a period of Italian conservatism, French footballing flair led the way into the 21st century.

# Part Three

# Foot,
# 2000–04

# 7

# Speed

France's triumphs at the 1998 World Cup and Euro 2000 represented a historic double, but the side's footballing identity had changed dramatically during the intervening period. While the World Cup-winning side depended on a solid defence and lacked inspiration in the final third, the winners of the European Championship played exciting, speedy, positive football. In 1998 France tasted success by playing like an Italian side, but in 2000 they added style and created a true French footballing identity.

The team's evolution is best summarised by assessing France's starting XI for their World Cup Final victory over Brazil, and the starting XI for their Euro 2000 opener against Denmark. Fabien Barthez remained the goalkeeper. The only change in defence owed to Laurent Blanc's suspension from the 1998 final. He naturally retook his place alongside Marcel Desailly, at the expense of Frank Leboeuf, with Lilian Thuram and Bixente Lizarazu continuing at full-back. Didier Deschamps remained in the holding role, with Emmanuel Petit still providing his closest support. Zinedine Zidane and Youri Djorkaeff again provided the creativity. Nine names into the starting XI and this was, save for suspension, the same XI as in 1998.

Then you looked up front. In 1998, France depended on Stéphane Guivarc'h, mercilessly mocked for his clumsiness, his sluggishness and his inability to provide a single goal in France's World Cup triumph – something, incidentally, that Olivier Giroud would replicate 20 years later. After France lifted the trophy, Guivarc'h was retrospectively praised for his selfless running and hold-up play, but he was being damned with faint praise. In their Euro 2000 opener, France fielded two lightning-quick centre-forwards, Thierry Henry and Nicolas Anelka. They belonged to a different universe to Guivarc'h, offering more speed, more technique, more grace. The other player to drop out from the World Cup Final XI, incidentally, was hard-working midfielder Christian Karembeu, indicating France's shift from three cautious midfielders to two, and from three attacking weapons to four.

France also had appointed a new manager. Roger Lemerre had been Aimé Jacquet's assistant for the 1998 triumph and replaced him immediately afterwards, although his impact was widely ignored until France won Euro 2000. Before then he'd been roundly mocked for following his predecessor's template, with satirical takes depicting him as an overpromoted yes-man whose decision-making simply involved imagining what Jacquet would do, which seems remarkable in hindsight given France's development. In fairness, Lemerre's suitability for the job was questionable; his most notable coaching stints were in the 1970s and 1980s, and aside from a brief caretaker spell with Lens in 1997, his only recent managerial experience had come in a decade-long spell in charge of the French army side, winning the World Military Cup in 1995 with a 1–0 final victory over a presumably well-resourced Iran team. It wasn't the usual pathway to managing the full national side.

But, then, that was the general template for French football managers; they were subdued background figures. Whereas Dutch coaches lectured about their philosophy and Italian coaches were studious tacticians, French coaches were, appropriately, more laissez-faire. They weren't ideologists and they weren't grandmasters. Instead they had the mentality of youth coaches, and believed their fundamental job was to guide players and help them to fulfil their potential.

Aside from Jacquet and Lemerre, the other two prominent French managers of this era followed the same template. Gérard Houllier, who enjoyed tremendous success in winning five trophies with Liverpool in 2001, was a former schoolteacher who, after his dramatic failure to guide France to the 1994 World Cup as national team manager, spent the next three years in charge of the U18 and U20 sides, where he coached the likes of Anelka, Henry and David Trezeguet. Arsenal boss Arsène Wenger was another who felt more like a teacher than a manager; he eschewed tactical tinkering and was outstanding at turning talented youngsters into world-class footballers. 'I am, first and foremost, an educator,' he once said. Two players who benefited from Wenger's teachings were France's strikers for that Euro 2000 opener, Anelka and Henry, which means that the Arsenal manager deserves huge credit for the transformation of his country's footballing philosophy. It's also significant that Anelka and Henry had emerged from Clairefontaine, the French national football academy, which became much revered after France's double success. It prompted other major European nations to reconsider their system of youth coaching and draw inspiration from the French model of a central academy. Again, the focus was on player development.

Henry, it should be noted, had been involved at World Cup 1998, scoring against South Africa and twice against Saudi Arabia in the group stage, although he was benched in the knockout stage, and was still considered a winger rather than a striker during an ill-fated six-month stint at Juventus in 1998/99. 'I'm not like Trezeguet. Don't expect bagfuls of goals from me,' he protested upon his arrival in Italy, referring to his close friend and former Monaco strike partner, a pure penalty-box man. Juventus took that advice somewhat literally, often deploying Henry as a wing-back, selling him after six months and then buying Trezeguet the following summer. Henry's poor form meant he dropped down to France's U21 side, despite his role in the 1998 success.

Anelka, meanwhile, had been controversially signed from PSG in 1997 by Wenger, who exploited a loophole in France's system of contracting youngsters and whisked him through the Channel Tunnel, provoking much disgruntlement in his homeland. Anelka was a curious figure, making little attempt to learn English or communicate with teammates, but he proved successful almost immediately because of his electric pace. He scored Arsenal's clinching goal in the 1998 FA Cup Final by streaking away from the Newcastle defence and finishing, and his first hat-trick for the club, in a 5–0 thrashing of Leicester, featured three very similar goals, using his speed to run on to balls played in behind the opposition by Dennis Bergkamp, who named Anelka his favourite strike partner. 'The way Nicolas played suited me perfectly because he was always looking to run forward on goal,' he explained. 'He was focused on heading for goal and scoring, he loved having the ball played to him to run on to and going one-on-one with the keeper.' Anelka, incidentally, had been named in France's provisional squad for 1998 but failed to make the cut, with Henry and Trezeguet preferred.

While Henry was struggling at Juventus, Anelka enjoyed a brilliant campaign for Arsenal in 1998/99, hitting 17 goals, and was fast-tracked into the centre-forward role for France. After he scored both goals in France's 2–0 victory over England at Wembley in 1999, against a backline dominated by his Arsenal teammates, France captain Deschamps excitedly told the press, 'We've found our

Ronaldo!' At the 1998 World Cup France's reputation had suffered due to their lack of a top-class striker, and the aftermath of the final focused on Ronaldo's mysterious illness more than the hosts' victory. Now, France had redressed the balance because they had a genuinely exciting centre-forward.

Make that two. Anelka left Arsenal for Real Madrid in 1999, and Henry replaced him for half the price. It was an astute piece of business from Arsenal, who upgraded in terms of quality while also profiting financially, although Wenger later confessed that among his biggest regrets was never getting to play Anelka and Henry together. Lemerre, though, enjoyed that luxury for the national side, and his strike partnership proved a terrifying prospect for sluggish opposition defenders. Throughout that Euro 2000 opener against Denmark, Henry and Anelka's pace in behind consistently caused problems. There was an early warning sign when Zidane poked a through-ball in behind for Anelka, who rounded Peter Schmeichel and then wastefully shot into the side netting, with Henry fuming that he hadn't squared. The opener came when Anelka was released in the inside-right channel, Schmeichel raced out to block him and the ball rebounded to Blanc, forward on one of his forays from defence, to steer into an empty net.

This pattern continued, France beating Denmark's backline through the speed of their two forwards. Towards the end of the first half, Henry received the ball wide-left, roared through the defence but prodded into the side netting. At the start of the second, Blanc's long diagonal found Henry, who tamely shot wide, with Denmark's defenders waving their arms at each other, unable to cope. Henry scored France's second on the break, receiving the ball on the halfway line and simply sprinting towards goal with no one capable of getting close, before sidefooting past Schmeichel. There was nothing to the goal other than sheer speed: no combination play, no clever assist, no decoy runners. The scoring was completed with yet another through-ball to find two French players breaking past the Danish defence. This time it featured two substitutes, with Henry feeding his Arsenal teammate Patrick Vieira, who squared for Sylvain Wiltord – about to join them at Highbury – to finish. Every goal relied on speed. This was a new-look France.

In France's second game, a 2–1 win over the Czech Republic, Henry opened the scoring in the expected fashion, finishing after a pass in behind, although the goal's genesis was Czech defender Petr Gabriel's woefully underhit back pass. The second came after Djorkaeff lobbed the ball to Henry, again making his classic run into the inside-left channel, and the Arsenal forward played a return pass for Djorkaeff to finish.

Lemerre rotated heavily for the 3–2 defeat to hosts Netherlands in the final group game, with France already through. In the quarter-final against Spain, France lost their way when attempting a different approach to mere speed. Lemerre fielded a 4–2–3–1 with Djorkaeff and Christophe Dugarry on the flanks, drifting inside rather than going in behind. Henry was fielded as the lone striker, a role he disliked, and endured his quietest game of the tournament as France unconvincingly triumphed 2–1.

For France's 2–1 victory over Portugal in the semi-final it was back to basics. When scouting the opposition, Lemerre observed that Portugal's backline wasn't particularly quick. 'That's why he wanted to inject more pace into our play,' recalled winger Robert Pires, yet another Frenchman about to join Arsenal. 'That's why Henry and Anelka started the game. He wanted us to play down the sides because their centre-backs [Fernando Couto and Jorge Costa] were so strong, so good in the air.' The problem, though, was that Portugal defended deeper than France's previous opponents, and therefore playing through-balls wasn't effective. Nevertheless, Anelka, running into the inside-right channel, played a pull-back for Henry's equaliser, before Zidane won it with a penalty late in extra-time. The spot-kick had been won by two substitute strikers: Wiltord and Trezeguet – on for Anelka and Henry – combined, and Wiltord's goalbound shot forced defender Abel Xavier into a goal-line handball.

The impact of these two substitutes foreshadowed the closing stages of the final against Italy. After Lemerre had unsuccessfully reverted to 4–2–3–1 with Henry up front alone, and France found themselves 1–0 down, Djorkaeff and Christophe Dugarry were sacrificed for Wiltord and Trezeguet respectively. With France's last attack of normal time, Barthez's long kick was headed on by Trezeguet towards Wiltord, who steadied himself and struck a low shot past Francesco Toldo. The game went into extra-time, with France now offering more speed and energy than the shellshocked Italians. Lemerre's third substitute also proved crucial. Pires, on for Lizarazu in the dying minutes as Lemerre went all-out attack, produced a change of pace to escape two Italian defenders, then played a cut-back for Trezeguet, who arrowed a left-footed shot into the top of the net, a tournament-winning golden goal. Two years beforehand, France had won the World Cup by keeping clean sheets, but at Euro 2000 they kept only one, in the opening game, and were confident of their ability to outscore the opposition. More than anything else, they were blessed with tremendous depth up front, something unimaginable two years earlier.

The quartet of Anelka, Henry, Wiltord and Trezeguet didn't merely offer plenty of speed and goalscoring ability, but also four different tactical options. Anelka was generally considered an outright centre-forward but preferred playing slightly deeper. Henry was somewhere between a left-winger and a centre-forward, while Wiltord provided a similar option on the opposite flank. Trezeguet was an out-and-out striker who wasn't slow, but thrived on crosses more than the others, which made him something of an outlier. 'People never stop saying how fast players like Henry and Anelka run,' said his father Jorge, a former professional. 'But David thinks quickly. His speed is in his head. I think David has proved in the final that what they do with their legs, he can do mentally in a second.'

But Henry was the main man, and Euro 2000 was arguably the only time he truly took his Arsenal form onto the international stage. 'Thierry gained a lot of confidence in that tournament,' remembered Vieira, his teammate for club and country. 'He attempted a lot of new things. When he played for France I could sense, because I knew him so well, that he held himself back a little bit. With Arsenal he was capable of taking the ball, beating two or three players, then crossing or scoring. For France he didn't feel free enough to do that – but at Euro 2000 he did.'

By the 2002 World Cup, which France started as joint-favourites alongside Marcelo Bielsa's Argentina, Lemerre's striking options were somewhat familiar: Henry, Trezeguet and Wiltord. Anelka, however, was omitted because France had discovered an even quicker striker: Djibril Cissé.

Cissé's rise was fittingly rapid. He'd only made his first Ligue 1 start a month after France's Euro 2000 success, and took until the following spring to establish himself as a regular at Guy Roux's Auxerre. Roux was another French manager renowned for youth development, bringing through the likes of Eric Cantona, Laurent Blanc and Basile Boli during his extraordinary, unprecedented reign as Auxerre manager between 1961 and 2005. Playing up front alongside Guivarc'h, Cissé bagged eight goals in 2000/01 and netted 22 in 2001/02, ending that season as Ligue 1's top goalscorer, but his manager didn't understand the hype. 'He's got a reasonable right foot, a poor left foot and he can't head the ball,' Roux claimed after Cissé had topped the French goalscoring charts. 'So why all the fuss?'

Roux's coolness was probably an attempt to ensure Cissé remained grounded, although there was also some truth to the critique; many questioned whether Cissé was a naturally gifted footballer, and yet his incredible speed meant he was hugely dangerous in this counter-attacking Auxerre side.

Cissé never truly fulfilled his potential, partly because he suffered two broken legs after his move to Liverpool, where he had been signed by Houllier – who also returned to his homeland to complete the signing of two more young French forwards, cousins Anthony Le Tallec and Florent Sinama Pongolle, who had starred together in France's U17 World Championship victory. Young French forwards were all the rage in the Premier League: Arsenal discovered Jérémie Aliadière, Manchester United signed David Bellion. None of this quartet progressed to the French national side, but the desperation to sign French youth strikers revealed the excitement about the country's footballing products.

France had become World Champions without a prolific centre-forward; now, four years later, they travelled to Japan and Korea to defend their title as favourites, with no fewer than three players who had just finished as top goalscorer in a major domestic league: Cissé in France, Henry in England and Trezeguet in Italy. But somehow, France were eliminated in the group stage without scoring a single goal. Even more strangely, the nature of their demise actually enhanced France's reputation for producing quick forwards.

France's downfall came in the opening game, when they suffered a shock 1–0 defeat to World Cup debutants Senegal. The identity of the opposition was significant; Senegal had been patronised beforehand as something of a France B-team, because 21 of their 23-man squad played in France, the only exceptions being the two back-up goalkeepers. It was implied that any Senegalese-born, France-raised player deemed good enough would have declared for the stronger footballing nation, as was the case with Vieira. This was somewhat simplistic, and while the majority of these players moved to France in their teenage years and were developed by French clubs, only two of the squad were born in France rather than Senegal. Their manager was also a Frenchman, the long-haired, charismatic Bruno Metsu, who believed his home country were World Cup favourites, but insisted his adopted nation would compete. 'People are saying we're like a French reserve team,' he acknowledged. 'But we have players good enough to play for France.'

Senegal's greatest weapon was Lens' El-Hadji Diouf, another young forward who relied on speed. His goalscoring record at club level was inconsistent, but he was the reigning African Footballer of the Year after scoring two hat-tricks in World Cup qualification, and had also helped Senegal to the Africa Cup of Nations Final, their best-ever performance. Diouf would become one of football's least popular figures, constantly in trouble for bad behaviour – including several incidents of the ultimate footballing crime, spitting – but going into the 2002 World Cup he was possibly the tournament's most hyped player, and he'd already been snapped up by Liverpool manager Houllier, who suspected that a good World Cup would raise Diouf's price tag considerably, and acted fast.

Before Senegal's contest with France, Metsu showed his players extensive video footage of France's performances, but rather than bothering to outline the strengths of their stars, he highlighted French weaknesses. The reigning champions' major shortcoming was a lack of defensive speed: Thuram was 30, Desailly 33, Leboeuf 34 and Lizarazu 31. Diouf was 21. 'Let's see if the pupils can teach the master a thing or two,' Metsu told his players beforehand.

Senegal's approach was simple: packing the midfield to crowd out France's creative talents, then quickly releasing Diouf with passes in behind. Their dependence on this tactic is illustrated by their lone striker earning a somewhat niche record: in the long history of the World Cup, no one else has been caught offside ten times in 90 minutes, as Diouf managed in this game. But on the rare occasion he timed his run correctly, France couldn't cope. Sprinting into the right channel, he left Desailly hopelessly hacking at thin air, and created an early chance for Auxerre's Khalilou Fadiga. Sprinting into the left channel, he did exactly the same thing to Leboeuf, and this time created the opener for his Lens teammate Papa Bouba Diop, who provided a close-range finish before running away to the corner flag, placing his shirt on the ground and memorably dancing around it with his teammates. That goal was a brilliant demonstration of Senegal's game plan – exploiting Diouf's speed on the break with midfield runners supporting – and was arguably the greatest moment of a somewhat underwhelming World Cup.

France were unfortunate at the other end, with Trezeguet and Henry both hitting the woodwork, but there were no excuses at full-time. 'By concentrating five players in midfield, my friend Metsu concocted a good plan,' admitted Lemerre. 'Individually and collectively we couldn't find a solution. Senegal were better than us.' It was a defeat for France, yet somehow a victory for Ligue 1; Senegal had 11 starters from the French top flight, France only one.

France never really recovered. Henry got himself dismissed for a reckless tackle in the second group game against Uruguay, a dull 0–0, and then was suspended for the final group game against Denmark, in which France were soundly beaten. Zidane returned but was clearly nowhere near fit. France's early elimination was a major shock, although fellow favourites Argentina also went home early in a tournament dominated by underdogs. This was generally blamed on fatigue, and France suffered more than most, having competed at the Confederations Cup the previous summer. But they also appeared unable to cope with the shock of losing to 'France reserves', and

Metsu's side proved the revelation of the World Cup, producing some wonderful counter-attacking football, including one of the goals of the tournament, rounded off by Salif Diao against Denmark. Senegal reached the quarter-final, the joint-best performance of any African side in history. Diouf was clearly their brightest talent, and also uttered the most significant summary, ahead of the quarter-final elimination against Turkey: 'Today we are representing Senegal, Africa, but also France.'

Henry endured a desperately disappointing World Cup, but remained Europe's most revered attacker. During this period no other striker in Europe came close to Henry, who scored 95 league goals between Euro 2000 and Euro 2004. If we exclude Mateja Kežman, who was filling his boots in the somewhat uncompetitive Eredivisie and managed 105 goals, you have to drop down to 83 goals to find Henry's nearest challenger, Portuguese striker Pauleta, of Bordeaux and PSG. Henry was also Europe's most consistent player, regardless of position. While he never won the Ballon d'Or, no one else was voted into the top ten every year between 2000 and 2004. Perhaps what he lacked to win football's ultimate individual award was one truly landmark goal; aside from the Confederations Cup in 2003, Henry never scored in a final, which was something of an anomaly for such a prolific forward.

While Henry had solved France's goalscoring problem up front, and was a consistent goal machine, winning the Premier League's Golden Boot four times and becoming Arsenal's all-time record scorer, the crucial aspect of his game was that he wasn't a pure striker. Henry had taken inspiration from his predecessor at Monaco, George Weah, and the Brazilian duo of Romario and Ronaldo, explaining that they had reinvented the centre-forward position by varying their position, 'disorientating the defenders with their runs, their accelerations and their dribbling'. At club level, Henry perennially battled Manchester United's Dutchman Ruud van Nistelrooy for the Golden Boot award. His rival was a classic goalscorer, yet Henry won this personal battle in four of their five seasons together in England. In the one season Van Nistelrooy triumphed, 2002/03, Henry set a Premier League assists record that still stands today; he was a world-class goalscorer and a world-class creator.

By Euro 2004 France had loaded up further on quick attackers, despite the absence of Cissé and Anelka. Cissé was absent for a peculiar reason. Despite having regularly featured for France's senior side over the previous two years, he'd been slightly cynically shifted down to the U21s to ensure their progress through a qualification play-off against Portugal. Not only were France eliminated, Cissé managed to get himself sent off for violent conduct, his subsequent five-match ban effectively ruling him out of Euro 2004. Anelka, meanwhile, was now at Manchester City and badly out of favour with the new France boss Jacques Santini, who claimed there were '10,000 players' ahead of him in the pecking order. That was a slight exaggeration, but Santini certainly had options, and took no fewer than six forwards to Euro 2004. Alongside Henry, Trezeguet and Wiltord were Sidney Govou, Steve Marlet and Louis Saha.

Govou was another who felt like a sprinter first and a footballer second. Probably the quickest player in France's squad, Govou made his first-team breakthrough at Lyon in 2001, announcing himself on the European stage with two brilliant strikes in the memorable 3–0 thrashing of Bayern Munich. Govou was deployed up front alongside Brazilian powerhouse Sonny Anderson, who had played with Henry at Monaco and was therefore well placed to compare the two. 'He reminds me a lot of Thierry, but Sidney is more explosive,' Anderson ventured. That spoke volumes, not simply about Govou's sheer speed but also about how Henry had become the obvious point of reference for every emerging French striker. In the same way that Argentina were obsessed with finding the new Maradona, France were already searching for the next Henry. He was the role model for the next generation of French forwards, the likes of Anthony Martial and Kylian Mbappé, who both rose to prominence at Henry's first club, Monaco.

Govou, meanwhile, was another who struggled to transform his potential into consistency because of ongoing injury problems. He was a terrifyingly direct dribbler and could sometimes strike from distance, but he was never a natural goalscorer and often panicked in one-on-one situations. Therefore, having previously been considered a promising striker, Govou eventually became a right-winger. This was a common theme among these players – Wiltord ended up on the right for Arsenal, Diouf and Cissé were deployed out wide at Liverpool, and Marlet, originally thought of as a striker on his arrival at Fulham in 2001, was subsequently used wide-right for France after struggling for goals. Henry, of course, had made the reverse journey from the left, switching from a winger into a centre-forward.

At Fulham, Marlet had played up front alongside Saha under the management of their compatriot Jean Tigana, the glorious midfielder from the France side that won the 1984 European Championship. Saha was also considered a winger in his early days and credits Tigana for giving him the confidence to play up front; his prolific form earned him a move to Manchester United, where he would later win the Champions League. Saha was another who suffered from injuries, but on his day was arguably the most complete of these French forwards, combining the speed of Henry with the aerial threat of Trezeguet. He could also finish with both feet, and was another graduate from France's now-fabled Clairefontaine academy, where he'd boarded alongside Anelka and Henry.

The three became close friends, partly because of their shared heritage. 'Our families are from the West Indies, and we used to hang out and speak Creole to each other,' Saha recalled of his Clairefontaine days. 'We shared holidays together at Thierry's parents' home in the Antilles.' This was a common feature of this new breed of French forward, who were all second-generation immigrants with parents generally hailing from the Caribbean. Anelka, Wiltord and Marlet's families were from Martinique, Saha's parents were from neighbouring Guadeloupe, while Henry had one parent from each island. Guadeloupe and Martinique are French overseas departments rather than independent nations, and therefore not members of FIFA. But, as Henry said, 'If there had been an Antillean national team, I would have been on that team, just like someone of Senegalese background wants to play for his colours.' When he scored twice in a 3–1 win over Manchester United, courtesy of two errors from his France teammate Barthez, Henry pulled his shirt over his head to reveal a T-shirt that read, 'For the West Indies'. Meanwhile, Govou's parents were from Benin, Trezeguet's from Argentina (his father was a defender for Estudiantes) and Cissé's from the Ivory Coast (his father captained the national side).

This multiculturalism became the most discussed aspect of the France side, and received extensive coverage in relation to the creeping popularity of far-right politician Jean-Marie Le Pen and his histrionics about the ethnic composition of the squad. The 1998 World Cup victory was widely considered a victory for French multiculturalism. Afterwards, during this period of France dominance, the eight striking options who represented France at a major tournament between 2000 and 2004 – Henry, Anelka, Wiltord, Trezeguet, Saha, Marlet, Govou and Cissé – were all born in mainland France to parents from outside mainland France. Le Pen moaned that these players didn't represent France, but the opposite was the case. These players provided France with the footballing identity it had desperately lacked in 1998.

# 8

# The Number 10

The most celebrated footballer of this French era was, naturally enough, a Frenchman. Zinedine Zidane was crowned Player of the Tournament as France triumphed at Euro 2000, became the world's most expensive footballer the following summer when moving from Juventus to Real Madrid and scored the most memorable goal of this era in 2002, when his majestic left-footed volley won the Champions League Final.

Zidane was a playmaker of poise and grace, worshipped for his unrivalled technical quality. He controlled the ball beautifully, was gloriously two-footed and boasted a range of tricks that showcased his balance and elegance. In particular, there was the move that became known, after Zidane's birthplace, as the 'Marseille turn', where he would perform a double dragback, with the soles of his right foot and then left foot, evading a defender and bringing the ball back around into his path. He was a player who inspired poetry and cinema, was depicted in biographies almost as an abstract concept, and was precisely the type of footballer France had been most desperate to produce.

Post-war French football was effectively a battle between two contrasting ideologies, one that favoured physicality and hard work, the other that placed emphasis on technique and style. The former approach was exemplified by Georges Boulogne, who from 1958 formulated France's coaching curriculum. He believed that French football placed too much emphasis on enjoyment, and used words like 'organisation', 'effort' and 'productivity' to explain his preferred approach. Boulogne became the national coach but performed poorly – France failed to qualify for the World Cups of 1970 and 1974 and the 1972 European Championship – and then acted as France's first national technical director for a decade. No one else influenced French football as much during this period, and while Boulogne deserves credit for his introduction of France's youth academies, his brand of football would not have produced a Zidane.

The best practitioner of the opposite approach was Albert Batteux, the most successful manager in French football history. In the 1950s and 1960s Batteux won five league titles for Reims, steered the national side to third place at the 1958 World Cup and later won a further three league titles with Saint-Étienne. At a time when physical football dominated the French game, Batteux stressed the importance of putting on a show for the supporters with quick passing, direct dribbling and individual brilliance. 'Plan the game so the talent will flourish,' was his grand motto. The key man in his all-conquering Reims side was the legendary Raymond Kopa, who later starred for Real Madrid as a right-sided attacker and won the Ballon d'Or, although Batteux had used him in the number 10 position, dictating play behind two strikers.

Instead, Batteux's right-winger at Reims was Michel Hidalgo, another significant figure, who later became France manager in 1976 and remained a disciple of his former boss. Hildago guided France to the semi-finals at World Cup 1982, only losing to West Germany on penalties after a 3–3 draw that is often considered the greatest

World Cup game ever. Two years later he took France to success on home soil in the European Championship, with Michel Platini their goalscorer extraordinaire, notching nine goals in five games, despite the fact he was a number 10 rather than a striker. This, then, is the lineage that created Zidane: the creative style of football promoted by Batteux and Hildago, combined with the importance of the number 10 role popularised by Kopa and, in particular, Platini. Zidane had big boots to fill, and would follow in the footsteps of both his predecessors, spending five years apiece at Platini's former club Juventus and Kopa's former club Real Madrid.

Platini was his most obvious role model. Even when managers spoke about not typecasting Zidane, they couldn't avoid the comparison. 'You must be careful not to stereotype players, not to lose their charm and talent,' warned Gérard Houllier, France's technical director, when Zidane was first called up to the national side. 'You must have teamwork, and you can have a sophisticated system, but one outstanding player for one moment can bring an added quality. It is what Platini had, it is what Johan Cruyff could do, and Zidane can do that too.' When Zidane first entered the Juventus dressing room he was immediately directed to one particular peg, because that had been Platini's spot.

'It's too heavy a burden to carry,' he complained during his early days at Juventus. 'People have to understand I will never be Platini. I am not a leader of men and never will be.' Platini was one of two players regularly namechecked as Zidane's idol. The other was Uruguayan number 10 Enzo Francescoli, who spent a single season with Zidane's boyhood club Marseille in 1989/90, taking them to the league title and the semi-finals of the European Cup. 'I loved his elegance,' Zidane said. 'When I saw Francescoli play, he was the player I wanted to be. Enzo was like a god.' Zidane's eldest son, who went on to represent France at U19 level, was named Enzo.

While Zidane desperately downplayed the comparisons, Platini enjoyed speaking about Zidane continuing the tradition of the French number 10. Before his stint in football administration, Platini was a self-confessed footballing romantic who seemingly considered himself Europe's official spokesman for his old role. 'The number 10 has always represented certain special gifts in a player,' Platini explained. 'He is the playmaker who can also score goals ... currently in football, there are very few players with Zidane's style. There's Rui Costa in Italy and, in England, the last number 10 I saw in action was Gary McAllister. This type of player is vanishing, and I really want things to work out well for Zidane so managers sign more players like him. Neither Barcelona nor Real Madrid have a real number 10. The last time Rivaldo passed was probably when he was playing schoolboy football.'

Rui Costa wasn't at the 1998 World Cup because Portugal didn't qualify, while McAllister – a slightly more surprising reference – missed out through injury, so Platini claimed that there were only two number 10s at the tournament whose organising committee he chaired: Argentina's Ariel Ortega and, of course, Zidane. Platini was delighted when his compatriot won that year's Ballon d'Or. 'People who love football have to be happy because Zidane's example gives credibility to the number 10 shirt and gives new life to a breed of players who are becoming extinct,' he declared. This was Zidane's only Ballon d'Or, meaning he finished two short of Platini's treble.

Zidane had literally been France's posterboy for their success on home soil, scoring two goals in the 3–0 victory over Brazil in the final. But the World Cup had actually been a disappointment for Zidane until that game. He'd been dismissed in France's 4–0 victory over Saudi Arabia in the group stage for stamping on Fuad Amin and was suspended for two matches, with his absence almost overshadowing France's progress, such was the clamour for their performances to be illuminated by their number 10. He returned for the goalless draw with Italy in the quarter-finals, but was decent rather than decisive, and largely nullified by his Juventus teammate Gianluca Pessotto, who, in typically Italian fashion, was played out of position to nullify France's danger man. Zidane was also relatively quiet in the semi against Croatia, before his crucial impact in the final. His two goals were similar: both headers from corners, hardly a fitting précis of his technical genius.

Zidane's image was beamed on to the Arc de Triomphe as Parisians partied on the Champs-Élysées, but he hadn't been among France's best performers. He'd also flopped two years earlier, at Euro 96, when his involvement in a car crash shortly before the tournament left him short of fitness. Going into Euro 2000, then, Zidane still needed to prove himself on the international stage, despite having scored twice in a World Cup Final, and despite having won the Ballon d'Or. 'We're definitely better than two years ago,' Zidane promised on the eve of the competition. 'Everyone is two years older and has more experience, and we also play in the best European divisions. We now have five attackers with immense quality, which is what we lacked at the World Cup. As for me, at 28 I've matured, and I've reached the summit of my art.'

Few footballers could reasonably refer to their performances with the word 'art', but Zidane's technical quality justified the term, with Euro 2000 providing the perfect canvas. This was a wonderful festival of open, attacking football, in stark contrast to Euro 92, which was dominated by the last days of back pass, and Euro 96, which featured a pitiful 2.06 goals per game. The other semi-finalists all fielded a sublime number 10 as well: Dennis Bergkamp of Holland, Rui Costa of Portugal and Francesco Totti of Italy. But this was Zidane's tournament. France's playmaker was impressive in the group stage, but magnificent in the knockout stage.

In the quarter-final France narrowly defeated Spain 2–1, with Raúl González missing a last-minute penalty. Roger Lemerre deployed a 4–2–3–1 system, with Thierry Henry up front and Zidane flanked by two creative players, Youri Djorkaeff and Christophe Dugarry. They alternated positions and drifted inside to cause Spain problems between the lines. Djorkaeff was nominally playing on the left, but his movement into the centre won the free-kick for France's first goal, which was expertly dispatched by Zidane. Later, Djorkaeff hit France's winner from the right flank, running on to a pass from Patrick Vieira, with France's deployment of multiple attacking playmakers generally causing Spain serious problems.

Djorkaeff, incidentally, was another top-class number 10, and made several vital contributions to France's success over the years. His most significant goal came in 1995, when his late free-kick snatched a draw in a Euro 96 qualifier in Poland, which probably saved Aimé Jacquet's job. For the knockout stages at both Euro 96, where France reached the semi-finals, and the 1998 World Cup success, Jacquet deployed a Christmas tree formation that featured both Zidane and Djorkaeff floating behind a central striker, although Zidane dropped deeper into midfield and Djorkaeff pushed on. Djorkaeff later claimed the system had been his idea, because he was bored of him and Zidane being pitched against one another; there was no reason, he believed, they couldn't co-exist, not least because of France's lack of strikers. That said, he'd also courted controversy when claiming that Zidane should have been substituted after France's Euro 96 semi-final exit on penalties after a goalless draw with the Czech Republic.

'Youri is the type of player you just can't stop,' said France captain Didier Deschamps. 'And he can also score goals.' In 1993/94 Djorkaeff topped the French goalscoring charts with 20 goals, and his three Serie A campaigns with Inter were all more prolific than each of

Zidane's five. In that sense, Djorkaeff, rather than Zidane, was probably the closest thing to Platini, because he timed his runs into the box so effectively.

'The comparison flatters me,' Djorkaeff said when asked about Platini, though he shared his predecessor's belief in the number 10 role. 'Without them, nothing in the game is possible. When Alessandro Del Piero emerged, Platini said that he is a number 9.5, not a number 10. The same goes for Roberto Baggio. I consider myself a number 8 when we are defending and a number 10 when we are attacking. I have realised the importance of being versatile. Today, if a footballer is only able to play in one position, he is dead.' Italian football had trained him well, and Djorkaeff adjusted impressively when fielded wide in a 4–2–3–1.

But when Lemerre switched to 4–3–1–2 for the semi-final victory over Portugal, dropping Djorkaeff and using two speedy forwards, the major beneficiary was Zidane. His movement had been slightly constrained against Spain, but now he found the freedom to drift laterally across the pitch into pockets of space, seemingly playing on the left, the right and through the middle simultaneously, and he produced possibly the finest performance of his international career.

Seemingly every time Zidane collected possession against Portugal he produced something aesthetically remarkable. He received a pass from Bixente Lizarazu, who was briefly in central midfield, held on to the ball precisely long enough to suck in Lizarazu's marker, then backheeled it into the path of his teammate's overlapping run. He received the ball on the run in the centre of midfield, produced a double stepover to escape the attentions of both Costinha and Jorge Costa, poked the ball to Henry, received a return pass and immediately stabbed the ball with the outside of his right foot out to the overlapping Thuram. He received a bouncing ball in midfield and responded with an exaggerated, first-time, over-the-shoulder pass in behind for Nicolas Anelka, which forced Portugal goalkeeper Vítor Baía to dart forward and intercept. He controlled Emmanuel Petit's diagonal ball into Portugal's right-back zone with remarkable calmness, taking the ball on the bounce and changing direction. He also launched a 30-yard drive narrowly over the Portuguese goal.

After half-time Zidane continued his exhibition. Another Petit diagonal, seemingly overhit into Portugal's left-back zone, allowed Zidane to control the ball by effectively chesting it over his own head, pivoting, then immediately controlling the ball on the bounce with the outside of his right foot, sending Portugal defender Dimas the wrong way. His left-footed cross might have produced a goal, but Anelka stumbled.

With five minutes of extra-time remaining, and the score at 1–1 following goals from Nuno Gomes and Henry, Zidane nearly produced his greatest moment yet. He received a pass from Robert Pires deep inside his own half. With his first touch, he managed to jink past both Luís Figo and Paulo Bento, leaving them crashing into one another. With his second touch he poked the ball past the sliding Abel Xavier on one side, before sprinting past on the other. With 30 yards to dribble into, Zidane picked up speed, dropped his shoulder to breeze past Jorge Costa and then, with Portugal's defence completely exposed and Vieira sprinting through for a one-on-one, Zidane bafflingly passed straight to Portugal left-back Rui Jorge, who had been sucked inside and found himself miles out of position. There's no guarantee Vieira would have scored, of course, but it was a desperate shame that the individual performance of the tournament didn't end with an incredible assist.

Even Portugal would have been better off losing in that manner, rather than after their late penalty concession courtesy of Xavier's goal-line handball, because their ensuing protests meant Xavier, Nuno Gomes and João Pinto were all handed at least six-month suspensions from UEFA competitions. Zidane stepped up for his first-ever international penalty, and swept the ball into the top corner. His calmness had been helped by some clever thinking from Pires. As Portugal protested against the penalty award and tried to delay the spot-kick for as long as possible, Pires took the ball, making him the target of Portuguese gamesmanship, allowing Zidane to focus.

This was Zidane's best form at a major tournament, yet he still couldn't escape the Platini comparisons; in fact, his contributions merely underlined the similarity with Platini's vaunted performances at the 1984 European Championship. Zidane had opened the scoring against Spain in the quarter-final with a free-kick, just as Platini had opened the scoring against Spain in the final with a free-kick. Zidane had scored a 117th-minute winner against Portugal in the semi-final, and Platini had scored a 119th-minute winner against Portugal in the semi-final. Zidane would have been fully aware of the latter coincidence, having been a ball boy at Marseille's Stade Vélodrome for the 1984 semi on his 12th birthday.

Despite what Silvio Berlusconi's post-match analysis might suggest, France's number 10 was quieter in the final, dropping deep and leaving France disconnected. After the break he played a couple of good passes through the Italian backline for Henry and Sylvain Wiltord, but he was overshadowed by Totti, who created good opportunities for both Alessandro Del Piero and Marco Delvecchio, who had already scored the opener.

Nevertheless, after France's late comeback, there was little doubt that this was Zidane's tournament, and his teammates were remarkably complimentary about his performances. 'Sometimes you want to stop playing just to watch him,' marvelled Dugarry. 'When we don't know what to do with the ball, we give it to him,' added Lizarazu. 'Zidane dazzled the whole European Championship with his quality,' concluded Petit. It felt like football had entered a new era: the BBC's tournament summary was headlined 'Euro 2000: the re-birth of football'. Euro 2000 was football 2.0, and Zidane was leading the revolution.

Others couldn't avoid the old comparison. 'Zidane is not a Platini,' *World Soccer* magazine's report read, 'but the balance of the individual has changed, and the superstar is now servant to the team, not vice-versa.' Lemerre, however, wanted more from his talisman. 'I feel there is still much more to come from Zidane. He can improve further,' he declared. 'He's phenomenal, on his way to becoming a monument of French football – like Kopa and Platini.'

In truth Zidane didn't improve. Euro 2000 was, as he'd stated before the tournament, when his art peaked. In fact, for all his incredible talent, and his unquestionable thirst for providing decisive moments in the biggest matches, this was a player who suffered badly from inconsistency throughout his club career.

Tactically, Zidane was a slightly confusing player. His best performances generally came as a classic number 10 in a 4–3–1–2, although he didn't define that position in the manner of Platini or Diego Maradona. The purest number 10s are always somewhere between midfielder and forward, capably of exerting influence in deeper positions before pushing forward to provide decisive contributions up front. Zidane's remit was to cover both of those responsibilities and yet he often did neither, which was peculiar for a player of his class.

During his formative years Zidane was considered more of a number 8 than a number 10, with his youth coaches believing his physique enabled him to compete in the midfield battleground. Zidane, somewhat unusually, constantly stressed he had no preference for playing as a defensive midfielder or an attacking midfielder. Although he won the French Player of the Year award for Bordeaux playing in an advanced position, upon his move to Juventus in 1996 he was brought back into a much deeper role, the position Andrea

Pirlo would later define. Zidane initially struggled, and only improved once Marcello Lippi switched his international teammate Didier Deschamps into the defensive role, giving Zidane freedom to push forward.

Gradually, Zidane's attacking tendencies meant Juve's system shifted from 4–4–2 to 4–3–1–2, with the wide players tucking inside to provide defensive support. That suited his style, as he was in essence a creative midfielder who almost sheepishly pushed forward, rather than a footballer born to play as a number 10. In fact, it was only when playing for France that he actually wore that number. At Bordeaux he played in 7, for Juventus he wore 21 and at Real Madrid he surprisingly took the number 5 shirt. In terms of positioning, meanwhile, he was regularly fielded on the left for both Real and France, and asked to drift inside, rather than having the side built around him.

Where Zidane suffered most, in terms of the Platini comparison, was his lack of goals. His predecessor managed an extraordinary rate of 0.52 goals per league game throughout his career, and while expecting Zidane to match that record is somewhat unreasonable, his rate of 0.19 doesn't come close. Their respective half-decade spells at Juventus are particularly telling: Platini played 147 Serie A games and managed 68 goals, whereas Zidane played 151 and managed just 24. To judge Zidane purely on goals would be missing the point. Nevertheless, a more thorough analysis of his decade in Serie A and La Liga suggests he only enjoyed two genuinely outstanding campaigns, with his five-year spells at Juventus and Real Madrid following an almost identical pattern.

Zidane arrived to much fanfare, struggled to adjust in his opening months, before improving and enjoying a broadly impressive first campaign. In his second season for both clubs, 1997/98 for Juventus and 2002/03 at Real Madrid, he won the title and was arguably the division's best player. Then, at both clubs, there was a serious slump for the next two seasons. At Juventus this represented a serious individual decline, whereas at Real Madrid it was the consequence of declining mobility and his side's tactical weakness. Then came an impressive final flourish for both clubs, albeit not on the level of his peak campaigns, meaning that he is remembered fondly in both Italy and Spain. Despite this, Juventus and Real Madrid supporters often speak about Zidane in the same manner, explaining that while he was wonderful to watch, they probably didn't witness his absolute best form. Put those viewpoints together, and it seems that he never quite managed to fulfil expectations on a consistent basis – expectations created on the basis of his international form. Zidane was a France player more than a club player.

His poor form for Juventus from 1998 to 2000 was particularly alarming, because this was theoretically peak Zidane, between a tournament where his goals helped win the World Cup Final, and a tournament where he was the European Championship's best player. In the previous two seasons, Marcello Lippi's side had triumphed in Serie A and reached the Champions League Final, with Zidane in good form, but when Juve's golden boy Alessandro Del Piero suffered a serious knee injury in autumn 1998, expectation fell on Zidane to dominate. He desperately struggled, managing only two goals and three assists as Juve slumped to sixth.

Zidane continued to struggle the following campaign, and when he scored a free-kick against Roma it ended a much-discussed eight-month goalless period. 'The goal released me,' he admitted afterwards. 'I was born to help others score, but my own goal drought was turning into a nightmare. The drought I had suffered since January was becoming a huge burden. Eight goalless months was an inexplicable crisis.' Carlo Ancelotti, who replaced Lippi as Juventus manager, admitted Zidane had suffered from 'a bad one-year period' after that

Roma game, and in the previous weekend's match, a 1–0 victory over relegation-bound Venezia courtesy of a last-minute Antonio Conte goal, Zidane had been jeered by Juventus supporters. 'I didn't like being booed and whistled in the Venezia game, but I took it on the chin, as you have to,' Zidane said. 'I didn't think I played that badly, but I wasn't the same Zidane that played two years ago.'

While Zidane was more of a provider than a goalscorer, he sometimes didn't actually assist much either. In 1999/2000 he created Juve's first Serie A goal of the campaign, scored by Pippo Inzaghi, then didn't manage another assist all season. He scored three free-kicks, but only netted once from open play. The world's most revered footballer, playing as a number 10 for the most dominant side in Italy, managed as many open-play goals as own goals (1), and as many assists as red cards (1). It's remarkable that he suddenly transformed into a world-class player again at Euro 2000, but that was largely the pattern of his career. Juventus owner Gianni Agnelli memorably said that Zidane was 'more entertaining than effective'.

Entertainment, though, was precisely what was demanded at Real Madrid. Zidane's two major transfers, first to Italy and then to Spain, saw his characteristics change to match his new surroundings. Juve turned Zidane from a box of tricks into a more driven player, and in an early interview he explained how he was learning how to play with one or two touches, to dribble as little as possible and to pass at the right moment. 'I learned the winning mentality at Juventus,' Zidane recalled. 'Only there did I understand that winning is an obligation. To be at one of the greatest clubs in the world makes it imperative to get a result.' But after his transfer to Real Madrid in 2001, Zidane's game changed in the opposite manner. Playing for Juventus meant training relentlessly under a demanding manager, before competing in front of a half-empty stadium. Playing for Real Madrid, where power resided with star players rather than the manager, meant relaxed training sessions before being expected to showcase Harlem Globetrotters-style antics under the bright lights of the Bernabéu.

Zidane's compatriot and midfield colleague Claude Makélélé explained the situation at Real: 'Because I understood the Spanish mentality, I was able to explain to him, "Forget Juventus, forget the Italian style. Here you must impose yourself as a true playmaker." That's what Zidane had to get into his head: that here in Real Madrid he was starting again at zero. The worst part was that Zidane's first game was disastrous – we lost 4–2 to Las Palmas and the media blamed him. I realised he was still playing in the Italian style, making an effort to get back into defence. But with Real Madrid it was an open bar. The attackers were there to attack, not to defend ... you do your job in the final third, and I'll stay here to cover you. Don't try to do too much. Everyone has their role.'

The world's most expensive player embraced his newfound liberty. 'I'm freer here, and it's a lot more fun,' Zidane admitted, when asked to compare playing for Juve and Real. The trickery from his street days returned, often producing wonderfully eye-catching moments, but the showboating also slowed Real's attacks. When former Spain manager José Antonio Camacho, a strict disciplinarian, took charge in the summer of 2004, he immediately told Zidane to stop the tricks and start playing one-touch. No chance. Camacho lasted just six matches.

Zidane's regression from an efficient player to a flashy player also affected his international form, in particular his relationship with France's other superstar, Henry. During this period, the national side was based around Zidane rather than Henry, and while the forward wasn't quite as highly revered as the playmaker, Henry arguably deserved to be the main man. Zidane's form oscillated between marvellous and mediocre, whereas Henry was demonstrating unparalleled consistency. Henry was voted French Player of the Year five times, Zidane just twice.

On paper, Zidane and Henry should have worked perfectly: one promised incisive passing, the other offered speed in behind and cool finishes. Yet, despite playing together regularly for France throughout their peak years, Zidane only ever assisted Henry twice. Neither goal, in truth, demonstrated a particular level of understanding. The first, for Henry's sprint into the inside-left channel against Denmark at Euro 2000, featured a simple Zidane forward pass on the halfway line, with Henry doing it all himself. The second, the only goal in France's 2006 World Cup quarter-final victory over Brazil, saw Henry converting a Zidane set-piece.

'They look like two talents repelling each other because they share the same polarity, talent and ego,' wrote Vincent Duluc of *L'Équipe*. Zidane wanted to slow the play, while Henry wanted to speed it up. 'Maybe Titi [Henry] simply doesn't need me,' Zidane suggested when asked about their partnership. 'He brings the ball up from very far back, and he manages to do extraordinary things afterwards. In fact, he starts from so far back that it's easier to work in one–twos with him than to provide him with an assist.'

'The sooner I get the ball, like at Arsenal, where we play without a playmaker, the better it is,' Henry declared in 2004. 'I'm not aiming this at anyone in particular, but sometimes it would be better if the strikers got the ball before the two banks of four opposing defenders closed us down. We should move the ball more quickly.' Henry pretended he wasn't complaining about a specific individual, but the phrase 'where we play without a playmaker' would suggest otherwise.

When Zidane missed the Confederations Cup in both 2001 and 2003, France played quicker football. In Henry's absence, Pires was the side's technical leader in 2001, while Henry returned to assume that role two years later. France won both tournaments, with Pires and Henry voted Player of the Tournament in the two competitions respectively. This was only the Confederations Cup, of course, but considering France's disappointing showings at the 2002 World Cup and Euro 2004, it prompted questions about the team's hierarchy. There was a suspicion, as Philippe Auclair explains in his biography of Henry, that the Arsenal-based players – Henry, Pires, Vieira and Wiltord – formed a cabal intent on making Henry, rather than Zidane, the side's main man, with Arsène Wenger also frustrated that the national side wasn't based around his striker. Amid speculation about a rift between them, Henry felt obliged to phone Zidane and smooth things over.

Ultimately, France won the World Cup and the European Championship with Henry as their top goalscorer, and Zidane either scoring goals in the final or being the competition's best player. But after Euro 2000 France never maximised the benefit of having Europe's best playmaker and Europe's best striker in their ranks. They started both the 2002 World Cup and Euro 2004 as favourites, underlining their status as Europe's dominant football nation, but there were often awkward tactical compromises.

These weren't a factor in France's early elimination from the 2002 World Cup, when suspension and injury meant Henry and Zidane didn't play together in France's early exit. In Euro 2004, though, France encountered tactical problems under Jacques Santini. Although they won Group B, their performances were unconvincing; their opening match, in particular, saw them outplayed by England, and they depended on David Beckham's penalty miss and an extraordinary English defensive collapse to turn a 1–0 deficit going into stoppage time into a 2–1 win. Zidane scored both goals, from a free-kick and a penalty. They subsequently drew with Croatia – 'It was a miracle we didn't lose,' said goalkeeper Fabien Barthez –

and recorded a late win against Switzerland. Then, in the quarter-final, they were eliminated 1–0 by Greece. This doesn't sound quite so scandalous in hindsight, after Greece shocked the rest of Europe to win the competition, but their defeat was a major surprise. 'We were wretched,' said Makélélé. 'It was a total disappointment for the whole country.'

Santini had moved to a formation that suited Henry, a 4–4–2 system with Pires and Zidane drifting inside. Henry played to the left of David Trezeguet, and therefore had licence to link with Pires, with whom he combined so effectively for Arsenal. But others players disliked the system, particularly Zidane, who objected to being fielded on the right, even if he and Pires sometimes switched flanks. After some disappointing performances in pre-tournament friendlies, Zidane and captain Marcel Desailly had spoken to Santini, asking for a return to the 4–3–1–2, but Santini refused to discard two years of work on the 4–4–2. Because it proved unsuccessful, Santini was fired, and Zidane took the disappointment so badly that he announced his international retirement. However, his absence lasted just a year, and he returned after securing a promise that new manager Raymond Domenech would only field him centrally or on the left, never on the right. Henry wasn't entirely pleased with Zidane's return.

By this stage Zidane's Real performances had started to decline, although it's worth reiterating that he often performed fantastically in his first couple of seasons. His winner in the Champions League Final of 2002, Real's 2–1 victory over Bayer Leverkusen, was an absolutely remarkable volley. Rampaging left-back Roberto Carlos had rather speculatively lobbed the ball high into the penalty area, and Zidane found himself in such a perfect spot, in 20 yards of space between the lines with the ball dropping directly to him, that he didn't need to adjust his position. If anything that made the strike harder: running on to a volley like that would be relatively simple for a top-class footballer, but Zidane instead needed to wait and let the ball drop. He then connected perfectly with his left foot, sending it dipping and curling into the net. The fact Zidane had struck with his weaker foot only added to the technical expertise.

Zidane's greatest display for Real came during his best season at the club, 2002/03. In early January, Real faced reigning champions Valencia, who were just two points behind them in the league table, at the Bernabéu. In truth, this game probably shouldn't have been played, as a sudden rainstorm left one flank completely waterlogged. But, amid the chaos, Zidane was unstoppable. He helped create the opener with a wonderful assist that featured a stepover as he received the ball, and a first-time pass through the defence for Ronaldo, who rounded Andrés Palop and rolled it home. Zidane scored the second after a one–two with Raúl, and then Guti made it 3–1.

But this was Zidane's game. In stoppage time he received the ball from the right flank, stepped across the path of the ball with his left leg, letting the ball run between his legs before flicking it into his path with his right foot, evading a challenge in the process, followed by a stepover and a sudden change of direction to beat an opponent, and then, as he approached the defence he paused for one, two, three moments while he waited for the run of substitute Javier Portillo. Then came another stepover, which disguised his subsequent pass through the defence, and Portillo provided the finish. 'He's a magician with the ball,' raved Portillo. 'He did all the hard work and then said to me, "Go get it, kid." It's not easy to understand Zidane, because he's so good he can do anything with the ball. I thought he was going to pass right to Figo, but then he pulled out a brilliant pass from under his hat.' The idea that Zidane was so talented he became difficult for teammates to read was an intriguing, if unintentional, critique.

Zidane's spells with both Juventus and Real Madrid both ended a year sooner than expected. He'd always intended to move to Spain, his wife's home country, but his initial plan was to stay in Italy until 2002. Juve, however, had already lined up Pavel Nedvěd as his replacement, and were keen to move him on. With Real Madrid, meanwhile, Zidane had a contract until 2007 but surprisingly decided to retire in 2006. 'I don't want to start a third year knowing I won't be able to do better than I've done in the past,' he said, when announcing his decision. 'I don't want another year like this one, or even the one two years ago … it's been two years now that I haven't been playing like I want to.'

Just as Zidane's experiences at Juventus and Real Madrid followed a similar pattern, so too both clubs improved after his departure. Juve hadn't won Serie A in Zidane's final three seasons, and subsequently won two Scudettos in a row. Sure enough, Real hadn't won La Liga in Zidane's final three seasons, and subsequently won it twice in a row. In ten seasons in Italy and Spain, Zidane won three league titles, a Champions League and no domestic cups; hardly a disgrace, but not a particularly outstanding list of honours for a player considered the greatest of his era, who joined Juventus and Real Madrid at a time when both were considered the dominant club in Europe, never mind their own country.

Zidane was a throwback, more renowned for his performances in international tournaments than at club level. You picture Zidane in his country's shirt, as you do Pelé and Maradona, whereas you think of the next generation of greats, Leo Messi and Cristiano Ronaldo, in club colours. It was fitting, therefore, that Zidane's final performance came in a France shirt at the World Cup, where he had the opportunity to go out with a bang.

Playing as the number 10 in a 4–2–3–1, Zidane struggled in the group stage of the 2006 World Cup. He was booked in both France's goalless draw with Switzerland and their 1–1 draw with South Korea, which meant he missed the 2–0 win over Togo. He returned for the knockout stage and burst into life with a memorable performance against Spain in a 3–1 second-round win. His free-kick led to Vieira's header to put France ahead, and he completed the scoring in stoppage time by dribbling past Carles Puyol and smashing the ball home. In the quarter-final against Brazil he was unquestionably the game's best performer and provided his second-ever assist for Henry. His next performance was quieter, but he decided the semi-final against Portugal from the penalty spot – just as he'd done in Euro 2000, and just as Platini had done in 1984.

Then came Zidane's final game, and Zidane's final. He opened the scoring against Italy with a chipped 'Panenka' penalty that glanced off the crossbar and bounced down just over the goal line before spinning out again, with Zidane raising his arm, half to celebrate, half appealing for the goal. 'I wanted it to be remembered as a beautiful penalty,' he confessed afterwards. It was, depending on your viewpoint, either a perfectly judged moment of technical brilliance or a slightly fortunate outcome from a self-indulgent gimmick. Marco Materazzi equalised shortly afterwards, and the game eventually reached extra-time. Zidane nearly settled things, as he'd done against Brazil eight years earlier, with his head, but Gianluigi Buffon made a wonderful save. And then, Zidane literally ended things with his head.

Supposedly enraged by Materazzi's abuse of his family, Zidane famously headbutted the Italian defender in the chest, and was dismissed. It was Zidane's 13th red card of his professional career, an incredibly high number for a player whose responsibilities didn't include tackling, and he became only the second player to receive two World Cup red cards. His walk to the dressing room, past the trophy, remains one of football's most iconic images, and it was the last time Zidane was witnessed as a professional footballer – he didn't even return to collect his runners-up medal.

It was an incredibly dramatic final laced with coincidences and symbolism. The goals were scored by Zidane and Materazzi, the two protagonists in the game's other major incident. Zidane's penalty had struck the underside of the crossbar and bounced in, whereas Trezeguet's, the only miss of the shootout, struck the underside of the crossbar and bounced out. Trezeguet had settled the Euro 2000 Final against Italy with a strike into the top-left of the goal; now his miss decided the 2006 World Cup Final against the same opponents, with a shot only a couple of inches higher.

Meanwhile, Zidane was awarded the Golden Ball as the tournament's best player, his second such award, having already won one at Euro 2000. Intriguingly, he had previously declared that he'd never completely stamped his authority on an entire international tournament. 'When I stop playing, I would love people to remember me for my impact on an entire competition. I don't just want to have one good game, or score one important goal. I want to be influential from start to finish,' he explained. 'We all refer to the Pelé World Cup of 1970, the Franz Beckenbauer one of 1974 or the Maradona one of 1986. And we all also talk about the 1976 European Championship of Antonín Panenka, the 1984 one of Michel Platini or the 1988 one of Marco van Basten. I have not yet deserved that special honour – at Euro 2000 I played well but not brilliantly. I did not always shine.' The 2006 World Cup became Zidane's tournament. It wasn't quite the finale he'd imagined, but then Zidane's performances didn't always live up to expectations.

# The Water Carrier

In the couple of years before any World Cup, reports from the host country generally focus on one perennial concern: whether all of the stadiums will be ready. Ahead of the 1998 World Cup in France, however, a different issue arose. There were few problems with the venues, but a serious concern about the supporters supposed to be populating them.

The French public appeared apathetic towards the national side, and therefore towards the tournament itself. France hadn't qualified for either of the previous two World Cups, they lacked competitive matches by virtue of qualifying automatically as hosts and they were performing poorly in friendlies. Meanwhile, Ligue 1 lacked glamour, with the country's stars all playing overseas. French sport, we were told, was about the yellow jersey more than the blue shirt; this was a country obsessed with cycling. But France's success on home soil changed perceptions, and it was significant that the tournament coincided with the ugliest Tour de France in living memory. The 1998 Tour was dominated by the Festina affair, with police raids overshadowing the actual cycling. It was, among stiff competition, the Tour's lowest point in modern times, at precisely the same moment the football side was winning the World Cup in Paris.

The way professional cycling teams operate provides an interesting point of comparison to the manner in which French football sides are structured. The tactical intrigue in cycling stems from its curious position somewhere between a team sport and an individual sport; cyclists compete as a team, but the overall winner is very much an individual. This creates a fascinating dynamic, as there's a clearly designated team leader, with some or all of his teammates riding as 'domestiques', sacrificing their own ambitions for the leader's tactical needs. The domestiques will pace their leader on mountain stages or form a lead-out train for sprinters, they'll relinquish their bike if the leader suffers mechanical problems and they'll ferry water bottles from the team car.

This same sort of structure can be observed in French football sides. No other country so unashamedly supports their star player with a series of unfashionable, limited, no-nonsense holding players behind. In Spain, central midfielders are creators, in England they're expected to cover lots of ground, in Italy they're versatile and capable of playing in wider positions. In France, however, the holding midfielders play purely functional roles, always thinking about their star man. There's always been a delineation between creative attackers and hard-working defensive players, but the tendency to separate the two was particularly overt in French football during this period, in part because of the huge reverence towards Zidane.

This separation had become more extreme since France's success in the European Championship of 1984, when the victorious side boasted perhaps the most vaunted midfield in the history of European football, the famous 'magic square'. Michel Platini was the star play-maker, Jean Tigana surged forward with power and grace, Alain Giresse offered passing quality and could skip past challenges, while Spanish-born Luis Fernández, the final piece of the jigsaw, played in the deepest role, but was a deep-lying playmaker more than a pure holder.

By the time of France's double success in 1998 and 2000, they depended on a solid midfield anchorman, Didier Deschamps, who would later become one of only three men to complete the ultimate footballing double, winning the World Cup as both player and manager. The first was Brazil's Mário Zagallo in 1958 and 1970, next came Germany's Franz Beckenbauer in 1974 and 1990, while Deschamps triumphed in 1998 and 2018. Deschamps is the least celebrated of the trio, considered a limited, workmanlike defensive midfielder and a safety-first manager, but his impact on French football is considerable.

Deschamps was frequently described in patronising terms, generally by juxtaposing him unflatteringly with Zidane, his more illustrious midfield colleague. 'Zidane's role is more difficult than mine was, because I was blessed with teammates who shared my vision of the game,' Michel Platini once said, comparing the France of 2000 with his side of 1984. 'Between Deschamps – who, as we all know, doesn't exactly move crowds, and who deserves praise for reaching the level he's at, given his abilities – and Zidane, there's a fundamental difference.'

Crucially, Deschamps fully understood his limitations. 'I was never going to be as talented as Zidane,' he admitted. 'Instead, I compensated by working a huge amount and helping my team in the best way I could.' Rather than being a fearsome athlete, Deschamps was a small, slight footballer who excelled because of his positional sense and his selflessness. It would be unreasonable to suggest that Deschamps made the anchorman role cool, but he ensured it was considered necessary, at least in his homeland. Alongside Brazil's Dunga, he epitomised the understated, workmanlike, solid defensive midfielder of the 1990s, always working in support of his side's technical talents.

Deschamps had enjoyed a fine footballing education in the famously prolific academy at Nantes, which also produced Marcel Desailly, Christian Karembeu and Claude Makélélé. Desailly and Deschamps won the Champions League together for Marseille in 1993, while all four moved abroad and played as a defensive midfielder in a victorious Champions League Final: Desailly for AC Milan in 1994, Deschamps for Juventus in 1996, Karembeu for Real Madrid in 1998 and Makélélé for the same club four years later. Nantes' academy therefore probably helped to shape the defensive midfield position in modern European football more than any other club, just as Ajax have dominated in terms of ball-playing defenders or Barcelona in terms of deep-lying playmakers.

Nantes might not generally be considered as important as those clubs, but it's also worth acknowledging their remarkable 2000/01 title success, among the most surprising league victories of this century. The club had escaped relegation by a single point the previous season and lost their star man, attacking midfielder Antoine Sibierski, but suddenly launched an unexpected title charge under low-key coach Raynald Denoueix, who had spent his entire playing career at the club and worked in their academy for 15 years before becoming manager. Denoueix is probably the most underrated manager of this era, as he later moved to Real Sociedad and guided them to a hugely impressive second-place La Liga finish in 2002/03.

Denoueix's stint at Nantes was defined by his overwhelming belief in youth, with the majority of the starting XI comprising Nantes academy graduates. The Deschamps role was played by the excellent holding midfielder Mathieu Berson, who, along with the energetic Salomon Olembé, supported the elegant playmaker Eric Carrière. Nantes' success was short-lived, and they spent the following season battling relegation, but any cycling fans recently converted to football would presumably have been comforted to find the yellow jerseys leading the pack.

As a teenager at Nantes, Deschamps had played as an attacking playmaker, and was renowned for his vision and two-footedness. For France's youth sides his intelligence meant he was sometimes deployed as a sweeper, a position he enjoyed because he 'was always facing the play'. More than anything, though, Deschamps was a true captain. He captained his U16 side at the age of 11, he captained Nantes at the age of 19 and became the youngest-ever Champions League-winning captain with Marseille in 1993 at the age of just 24. He was often considered a skipper as much as an actual footballer, more renowned for his tactical intelligence and leadership skills than his dribbling or passing. 'Intelligence is what characterises great players, those who win titles,' said his France teammate Christophe Dugarry. 'I would cite Didier as an example. Here's a guy who, to start with, was limited technically but who succeeded in having an exceptional career, thanks to his incredible ability to adapt. His great quality was his analysis, and self-analysis. He was aware of his qualities, and never tried to over-complicate things. He focused on doing the things he did well, *very* well. He never put his team in danger.'

The common theme with this type of defensive midfielder, however, is that their technical qualities are underplayed. Just because Deschamps wasn't as talented as Zidane, and was happy to play an understated role compared with his illustrious teammate, didn't mean he lacked ability. Daniel Bravo, a young midfielder in the side that won the 1984 European Championship, whose France career briefly overlapped with Deschamps', believed his technical gifts were undersold. 'He has a way of winning the ball and eliminating opponents with a few feints,' he marvelled. 'His way of playing seems simple, but in fact it isn't at all, because he makes incredible technical actions. That's the reason why the opposition rarely take the ball into his zone.'

It was after his move to Juventus, at the age of 25, that Deschamps became truly respected, with his coach Marcello Lippi among his greatest admirers. 'He was already a coach when he was a player,' remembered Lippi. 'He was a leader on the pitch, a reference point for all his teammates and also for me, so I regularly had technical and tactical conversations with him.' Initially fielded out of position in a shuttling role because of Paulo Sousa's presence, from 1996 he became established as Juventus's primary defensive midfielder. This timing was crucial, because Zidane joined that summer, with Deschamps helping him to settle off the pitch and playing a supporting role on it. Together, Deschamps and Zidane would reach two Champions League finals and win two Serie A titles for Juventus. 'We understand each other's game perfectly,' said Deschamps, while Zidane would simply refer to his colleague as 'the boss'.

Aside from their first couple of months at Juventus, Deschamps and Zidane didn't play alongside one another, because there were generally two other midfielders between them in a midfield diamond – but they were unmistakably a double act. 'I've found the best tactic for never having any problems on the pitch,' Deschamps once told Lippi. 'As soon as I get the ball, I give it to Zidane.' That summarised their relationship concisely, and there's a neat parallel in their respective coaching careers. During the period when Deschamps took France to the Euro 2016 Final and then 2018 World Cup success, Zidane was winning three straight Champions League titles with Real Madrid. Sure enough, Deschamps' side was fundamentally cautious, whereas Zidane favoured creativity.

It was another gifted French number 10, however, who uttered the most memorable quote about Deschamps. In early 1995, Manchester United's Eric Cantona was France's captain and main playmaker, but after jumping into the stands at Selhurst Park and kicking a supporter he received an eight-month worldwide football ban. He therefore fell victim to the Deschamps–Zidane axis; the former established himself as France captain, and the latter became the side's star player. Cantona was never selected for the national side again and believed Deschamps had conspired against him. Ahead of a 1996 Champions League tie between United and Juventus, Cantona spoke to journalists for the first time in nearly two years, purely to launch a stinging attack on his compatriot.

'Deschamps gets by because he always gives 100 per cent, but he will never be anything more than a water carrier,' he sneered. 'You can find players like him on every street corner. At present Didier likes to act like a monk and a moralist, but he'll end up wallowing in every kind of vice. The only two decent French players in Italy are Youri Djorkaeff and Zinedine Zidane. The rest are nothing special.'

Deschamps was more bemused than offended. 'I've not had any difficulties with Eric during the five years we've spent together in the French national side, although we have never been mates,' he responded. 'When I see him on Wednesday I'll ask him exactly what he meant. He might believe that I've played a part in him being left out by France, but I've never interfered in team selection.' Deschamps reluctantly embraced his new nickname, which was just as well, because it stuck throughout his career. 'How many players can you find on street corners who have won two Champions Leagues?' he hit back. 'Besides, every team needs its water carriers.' When you consider the comparison to cycling and the work of the domestiques fetching the drinks bottles, 'water carrier' fits perfectly.

For France's 1998 World Cup Final victory, Zidane played with three defensive midfielders behind him: Deschamps, who played the deepest role, plus two others. Emmanuel Petit was a tall, blond, ponytailed midfielder who passed elegantly with his left foot, but he was unquestionably a defensive operator, having been converted from a defender relatively late in his career. At Arsenal, he played alongside Patrick Vieira, who assisted Petit's goal in the 1998 World Cup Final after being introduced as a substitute. To the right was Christian Karembeu, who played various roles throughout his career – defensive midfielder, box-to-box midfielder, right-midfield, right-back – and primarily provided the energy that Deschamps, Petit and Zidane lacked. Karembeu possessed incredible stamina, supposedly because as a youngster in the South Pacific island of New Caledonia, he was one of 14 children, and his job involved running several miles to the nearest town every day before returning to the family home with bread. He was famous for being unbeatable at interval training. In a purely positional sense, Deschamps, Petit, Karembeu and Zidane can be compared to the magic square of 1984, but whereas that quadrilateral had four stars, now there was one obvious leader and three water carriers.

Deschamps' stock fell considerably during the build-up to Euro 2000. Both he and Zidane suffered a World Cup hangover upon their return to Juventus, and Deschamps fell out badly with Lippi having discovering through the press that he'd been dropped ahead of a crucial league game. Lippi departed shortly thereafter, which rather underlined Deschamps' importance – if you lost Deschamps, you'd lost the dressing room. The Frenchman subsequently departed that summer, moving on to Chelsea, where he spent a sole unmemorable season in 1999/2000, winning the FA Cup but suffering from a lack of mobility in big matches. He also struggled to accept being bossed around by Gianluca Vialli, his former Juventus teammate.

Ahead of the European Championship in 2000, Deschamps was widely considered France's weak link, especially as Roger Lemerre had ditched the 4–3–2–1 in favour of a 4–2–3–1, meaning Deschamps had only one, rather than two, fellow water carriers alongside him.

France had been poor since the World Cup and were briefly in danger of not qualifying for Euro 2000, so the French media were campaigning for Lemerre to drop Deschamps and bring in Vieira, who was arguably now Europe's best defensive midfielder and enjoyed a fine relationship with Petit at club level. While his manager Arsène Wenger later fielded a more technical deep playmaker at Arsenal, during this period he was fixated on the French model, deploying two defensive midfielders protecting the defence and leaving the creativity to Dennis Bergkamp, effectively Arsenal's version of Zidane.

Vieira was a fantastic defensive midfielder, and had benefited from a perfect footballing education. He was fast-tracked into the Cannes side by manager Luis Fernández, the holding midfielder from the magic square, and then learned about positional play from Desailly at Milan. Once he broke into the France side, meanwhile, he looked up to Deschamps. 'I wouldn't be able to find a better teacher than Dédé,' he later recalled. 'Certain journalists were saying that he should no longer be playing and I should have taken his place, although I didn't agree with them and the atmosphere was actually very good between us. I have a lot of respect for Dédé; I like him as a guy. Some people rate the player, others don't, but that's another matter … we would talk a lot about positioning, how to cover for each other on the pitch. He likes that: exchanging ideas, talking tactics.' As always, praise for Deschamps was littered with mention of his detractors.

In truth, given Vieira's box-to-box tendencies, his true rival for a starting position was actually Alain Boghossian, a hard-working, up-and-down midfielder who had partnered Deschamps throughout Euro 2000 qualification. 'When "Bogo" was playing rather than me, I found it hard to understand,' Vieira admitted. 'On the other hand, you need someone like Dédé on the pitch. Perhaps I could have brought more to the game than him, because I was better at going forward and had more attacking qualities, but I didn't think I could contribute as much as Dédé when it came to his positional play and his ability to read the game.' Eventually, Vieira sneaked ahead of Boghossian, who missed Euro 2000 through injury in any case, and established himself alongside Deschamps – who, meanwhile, was so angered by the media questioning his ability that he boycotted press conferences before the tournament, with his teammates following suit.

Deschamps' lack of mobility was apparent on a couple of occasions at Euro 2000. He conceded a penalty against the Czech Republic when bringing down Pavel Nedvěd, and wasn't sharp enough in the lead-up to Nuno Gomes's opener in the semi-final. But overall his relationship with Vieira was excellent, and in the semi-final they benefited from the introduction of a third defensive midfielder, Petit. Vieira was named in the official all-star squad for Euro 2000, but Deschamps got the nod in *World Soccer* magazine's best XI. 'Deschamps had been criticised before the tournament as a weak link in the French side, but no one does the simple things as effectively as him,' their explanation read. 'The attacking joie de vivre with which France blew away Italy during extra-time would not have been possible without the uncomplicated endeavour of their captain.'

Euro 2000 success was a fine note upon which Deschamps announced his international retirement, having now won the Champions League, the World Cup and the European Championship, all as captain. He spent a single season at Valencia, although he struggled with La Liga's high-tempo pass-and-move, and he retired in 2001 at the age of just 32. Accustomed to being a very young captain, Deschamps now became a very young manager, taking charge of Monaco, who had just finished mid-table in Ligue 1. Within three years, he'd taken the club to the Champions League Final.

After Deschamps' retirement, France's midfield partnership featured the old Arsenal duo of Petit and Vieira. Petit had since joined Barcelona, where he often played in defence because Pep Guardiola, Xavi Hernández and Phillip Cocu were dominating the midfield roles, and he returned to London in 2001 with Chelsea. Petit struggled for fitness and ended his first campaign back in the Premier League as a defeated finalist in the FA Cup against his old club Arsenal and his close friend, Vieira. 'I purposefully avoided all eye contact during the game, and I'm sure he did the same, and shut out anything that might signal the affection I had for him,' Vieira later confessed. 'It had been bizarre for us that afternoon because we had been teammates, we had been very close.'

Vieira had been devastated by Petit's departure from Arsenal and initially struggled without him; he was sent off in the first two games of 2000/01, earning a five-match ban. His most regular partner for the next couple of seasons at Arsenal was the box-to-box midfielder Ray Parlour, whose long-range opener turned that FA Cup Final in favour of Arsenal, but Vieira was better suited to playing alongside Gilles Grimandi, another French holding midfielder. Grimandi had arrived at Arsenal in 1997, moving from Monaco at the same time as Petit, and was more of a centre-back than a central midfielder, a physically and technically unremarkable footballer. But it was Grimandi who regularly played alongside Vieira in 2000/01, arguably the latter's most individually dominant campaign at Arsenal, despite the club's lack of honours. Grimandi freed Vieira to push into attack, and while Grimandi wasn't in the same class as Petit, he was the classic domestique, happy to do the unfashionable jobs in support of the side's stars, which perfectly suited Vieira, always more of an all-rounder than a pure holding midfielder.

After the 2002 World Cup disaster Petit's career wound down, first for country and then for club. His Chelsea career was unexceptional, although he was impressive towards the end of 2002/03, helping Chelsea qualify for the Champions League, which in turn ensured they were bought by Roman Abramovich. The Russian's most significant purchase in his first summer was another French water carrier: Claude Makélélé.

Makélélé had risen through the ranks at Nantes as a speedy right-sided midfielder and had struck up a fine relationship with Karembeu, then an overlapping right-back. It was, in hindsight, a curious right-sided combination considering that Karembeu would win the World Cup in 1998 and Makélélé would reach the World Cup Final in 2006, both as central midfielders.

Just as Deschamps had moved from Nantes to Marseille in 1989, Makélélé followed in his footsteps in 1997, and his move to Celta Vigo the following season transformed him into a top-class midfielder, as he played alongside World Cup winner Mazinho, who had featured beside the aforementioned Dunga for Brazil. 'Mazinho taught me how to move and what to do, and gave me great tactical knowledge about managing the game and moving at speed,' explained Makélélé. 'He opened up the spirit of this new role. I spent hours working with him, learning the correct positions to take up, when to play one touch and two touch.' Together they formed a superb central midfield duo and helped Celta record some remarkable results in European competition, defeating Jupp Heynckes' Benfica 7–0 and Lippi's Juventus 4–0. Makélélé scored in both thrashings, indicating that he hadn't yet developed into a purely defensive midfielder. Then, in 2000, Makélélé moved to Real Madrid to replace Fernando Redondo. Real had also bought Flavio Conceição and Albert Celades, two other cautious central midfielders, but it was Makélélé who would become regarded as Real's most important player, largely because of Real's tactical naivety.

During this stage Real were embarking on their *galáctico* era. President Florentino Pérez was intent on creating the world's greatest roster of attackers, and signed one superstar every summer: Luís Figo in 2000, Zidane in 2001, Ronaldo in 2002. With the golden boy Raúl still undroppable, Real were increasingly creating an imbalanced starting XI, featuring too many players who demanded a free role. The defence was almost entirely ignored; the fifth *galáctico* was left-back Roberto Carlos, but he was eternally rampaging forward on the overlap.

Behind this mass of attacking intent, Makélélé became the side's key man. Vicente del Bosque, who guided Real to the Champions League in 2002, explained that Makélélé's all-round footballing ability meant he could act as 'the first defender and the first attacking midfielder', and he occupied a position at the base of midfield. Makélélé covered for everyone, and protected the centre-back partnership of Fernando Hierro and Iván Helguera, two converted central midfielders.

'My role as Real gave me true pleasure,' Makélélé said after his departure. 'I was prepared to do the defensive work; I enjoyed stopping my opponents scoring as much as helping my teammates to make the breakthrough. What's most important is to provide protection behind those in front of me. Zidane, Figo, Raúl and Ronaldo were sensational because they could get forward in the knowledge I would stay in front of the defence to cover for them. Some believed I played the role of a servant, that I did the hard work to allow the "true" stars to express themselves, but I didn't see things that way. I consider my role to be crucial for the balance of the team. I thought of myself as the true boss of the midfield, the one that sets the tempo and gives confidence to the group. Other players thought the same.'

Inevitably, Makélélé was frequently compared to Deschamps and called the new water carrier of French football; and just as Deschamps eventually embraced the nickname, Makélélé welcomed the comparison. 'In many ways, we water carriers are the new number 10s. We are the ones dictating the tempo and bossing the play. Didier was a very important figure, and his trophy cabinet shows how successful he was.'

This was the key to Makélélé's success; he might not have been the most creative or spectacular player, but like Deschamps he was a fine analyst, studying the opposition two days before the match, focusing on the qualities of the opposition's best player and how to effectively nullify him. This type of tactical intelligence meant Makélélé became another ambassador for the holding midfield position. 'You know what your role is, how you have to move, how your teammates move and what they need from you at every moment,' he outlined. 'It is a silent leadership and is something that must be protected because it is important ... all coaches would like to have that kind of player, a midfielder who always thinks about the balance of the team. It requires a quality that not all players have.'

Real Madrid's superstars regularly declared Makélélé the side's most important player, a recognition of his tactical contribution but also, perhaps, a judgement made out of sympathy because Makélélé was constantly struggling to be granted a new contract with wages that justified his importance. Usually, their compliments featured some form of metaphor. 'When people look at a Porsche, they are admiring the body of the car,' suggested Roberto Carlos. 'But what is it that really makes it so special? It's the engine. And our engine is Claude.'

Pérez didn't agree, and in 2003 he sold Makélélé to Chelsea, while effectively replacing him with another *galáctico*, David Beckham, who provided more attacking qualities while lacking Makélélé's ball-winning ability. Considered together, this remains among the most widely ridiculed transfer moves of the modern era, not least because of Pérez's dismissive comments towards the departing Frenchman: 'He wasn't a header of the ball and he rarely passed the ball more than three metres ... he wanted half of what Zidane is earning, and that was not possible.'

But Zidane knew, more than anyone, the importance of a holding player to bring out his own talents, and repeated Roberto Carlos's analogy when asked about Real ditching Makélélé in favour of Beckham. 'Why put another layer of gold paint on the Bentley when you are losing the entire engine?' Manager Carlos Queiroz went slightly off-message. 'I said at the time, that a Ferrari without a wheel would have problems.'

Just like Deschamps, Makélélé's quality in possession was underrated. Petit, his teammate for both Chelsea and France, referred to him in the same breath as two more greatly revered footballers. 'Pep Guardiola, Fernando Redondo and Makélélé started to show something else as holding midfield players,' he explained. 'It used to be all about fighting and tackling, but football started to change with that type of player in central midfield – it wasn't all about fighting spirit and winning the ball. Of course, they are important, but mainly it was about how you control the game, and it was done by controlling the ball.'

Makélélé agreed, believing that he revolutionised the holding role because of his attacking, rather than defensive, abilities. 'I am perhaps better technically and tactically than the holding defensive midfielders of the 1980s and 1990s, like Luis Fernández, Franck Sauzée or Didier Deschamps, but I don't do anything radically different to what they did. I am simply a more complete footballer,' he said. 'I think that the game has changed, and that, to be a top-level player in any position, you now have to know how to keep the ball, give precise passes and contribute to each phase of a move.'

It was only after Petit's international retirement in 2002 that Makélélé became a France regular. It was curiously late in his career; he was already 30, but then his retreat into the holding midfield position was a long, slow process. He holds something of a grudge about his belated international recognition. 'It's hard for me to reconcile the fact that I was part of the same generation as Zidane, Petit, Barthez, Thuram, Pires and Djorkaeff, but I never won anything with Les Bleus,' he admitted. Makélélé had missed Euro 96 because he was asked to play at the Olympics, missed the 1998 World Cup because he'd been playing wing-back at Marseille, and said his omission from the Euro 2000 squad was because he played at Celta Vigo, an unglamorous club. He even missed the 2001 and 2003 Confederations Cup triumphs because the La Liga season finished late, while in 2002 he was in France's squad, but only started the final group game. For Euro 2004, however, Makélélé played alongside Vieira in a fearsome defensive midfield combination that looked impressive until the surprise quarter-final defeat to Greece. This same partnership also excelled as France reached the World Cup Final in 2006.

It was Makélélé's success in the Premier League, though, that solidified his reputation as the new French water carrier. He played as the deepest midfielder in a 4–3–3 formation, largely under José Mourinho, and Chelsea's success inspired others to replicate that shape, removing a centre-forward and playing a cautious defensive midfielder. Makélélé's performances earned him the ultimate honour, the holding role becoming known, in England, as simply the 'Makélélé role'.

The legacy of these French water carriers would become clear much later. When France fell at the final hurdle on home soil at Euro 2016, it was arguably because Deschamps, now in charge of the national side, couldn't find a role for defensive midfielder N'Golo Kanté, instead preferring a combination of two box-to-box midfielders, Paul Pogba and Blaise Matuidi. Two years later, for France's 2018 World Cup success, Matuidi was pushed wide and Pogba was partnered by Kanté, who was a more energetic iteration of Deschamps or Makélélé but shared many of the same qualities: selflessness, positional discipline and ball-winning ability.

'Kanté doesn't stop running,' said Makélélé. 'He's undoubtedly one of the best central midfielders in the world … some players are meant to be superstars, but some, like N'Golo and myself, must be happy making other people look good.' No other European nation understood that as much as France, who always found the right balance between the revered team leader and the humble water carrier.

# Transition: France–Portugal

France had enjoyed tremendous success at international level, and were producing more top-class players than any other European nation. Their club sides, however, still weren't succeeding in Europe.

The record of Ligue 1 clubs in European competition has always been dreadful. Marseille's Champions League victory in 1993 was the country's first-ever European club trophy, and even that was over-shadowed by a matchfixing conviction that stripped them of that season's domestic title. PSG's Cup Winners' Cup success three years later is Ligue 1's only other triumph, a record that puts them behind Belgium and Ukraine in terms of European club trophies.

There was nearly a third French success in 2004, courtesy of a familiar face. Didier Deschamps had taken charge of Monaco imme-diately after his retirement in 2001, and following a troublesome first season spent battling relegation, Monaco qualified for the Champions League at the end of his second campaign. In his third, they battled through to the Champions League Final with memorable victories over Real Madrid and Chelsea.

In the final, Deschamps' Monaco met José Mourinho's Porto, who had won the UEFA Cup the previous season. Both clubs were surprise finalists, both hailed from relatively minor leagues, and their managers were 35 and 41 respectively. In a match played at the unusually unglamorous destination of Gelsenkirchen, this was either a complete anomaly or the start of a new era.

The final was also billed as a play-off to decide the next manager of Europe's most up-and-coming club, newly monied Chelsea. It was either Deschamps or Mourinho, and as a former Chelsea player the Frenchman appeared to hold an obvious advantage. In hindsight, it appears Roman Abramovich had already made his decision, but Porto's victory nevertheless confirmed Mourinho's status as Europe's hottest young managerial talent, and marked the end of the French era and the beginning of the Portuguese era.

Three weeks after Porto won the Champions League, its home stadium hosted the opening match of Euro 2004. Merely hosting the tournament was a huge achievement for a country of Portugal's relatively modest resources, especially as their bid had surprisingly defeated their neighbours Spain, who had turned down Portugal's offer of hosting the tournament jointly to go it alone. Voting patterns revealed that the Portuguese bid won because it attracted almost universal support from UEFA's smaller nations. Portugal was representing the underdogs, and constructed the most ambitious, spectacular set of new stadiums of any European Championship. While some became white elephants, the 'Big Three' of Benfica, Sporting and Porto were now playing in world-class arenas. 'We have invested in the modernisation of Portuguese football,' declared Gilberto Madail, President of the Portuguese Football Federation and in charge of organising Euro 2004. 'We have built new stadiums and training facilities, which will in turn create a new mentality. It will all be because of 2004.'

Portugal enjoyed a superb run on home soil, reaching the final of Euro 2004 before falling to Greece. While international success would have to wait until 2016, Portugal were now a serious force;

they were the only nation to reach at least the quarter-finals at Euro 2004, the 2006 World Cup and Euro 2008, which represented a huge improvement when you consider Portugal had only qualified for three major tournaments in the whole of the 20th century.

While Mourinho established himself as the most dominant coach of this period at Chelsea, his compatriot Cristiano Ronaldo became Europe's greatest player, winning the Ballon d'Or in 2008.

So during this period Portugal boasted a Champions League-winning side, the most consistent national team in Europe, the continent's most vaunted manager and its most celebrated player. The Portuguese top flight remained somewhat peripheral, like Ligue 1 before it, but this was nevertheless the Portuguese era.

Part Four

# Futebol, 2004–08

# 10
# Structure

Even José Mourinho didn't truly believe Porto could win the Champions League in 2004.

The previous season, Mourinho had taken the club to UEFA Cup success with a dramatic 3–2 victory over Celtic, but his ambition for the Champions League was modest. Mourinho had two targets: he wanted to qualify for the knockout stage, and he wanted to inflict defeat on one of the continent's big clubs, putting Porto – or, more likely, himself – on the map, which explains why he celebrated Porto's victory over Manchester United in the second round more jubilantly than any subsequent win.

'We can do some nice things,' Mourinho said ahead of his first Champions League adventure. 'But I don't think we can win it. Only the sharks who can afford to spend £40 million on one player can do that.' Porto had barely strengthened in the transfer market during the summer following their UEFA Cup win. Apart from centre-forward Hélder Postiga departing for Tottenham, to be replaced by Benni McCarthy, it was an identical side to the one that had defeated Celtic. But Porto's cohesion helped them to the most unlikely triumph of the Champions League era.

2003/04 was arguably the competition's greatest season, because it was completely dominated by underdogs. Some explain this by pointing to the lack of outstanding sides, but nothing could be further from the truth. This was Arsenal's Invincible season. It was the only season in which Carlo Ancelotti's AC Milan, the dominant Champions League side of the era, won Serie A. It was when Lyon, midway through their run of seven straight titles, were probably at their strongest.

But the quarter-finals produced four unlikely results. Arsenal were defeated by cross-town rivals Chelsea with a late Wayne Bridge goal at Highbury. Milan lost in remarkable circumstances; having won the first leg 4–1 against Deportivo, they lost 4–0 in La Coruña. Porto defeated Lyon 4–2 on aggregate in an enthralling tie, while Monaco's victory over Real Madrid's *galácticos* was even more eventful – Didier Deschamps' side won on away goals after a 5–5 draw. All four semi-finalists felt like outsiders, and the biggest outsiders won: Porto, the side from the most modest country, the side of unknowns plucked from mid-table Primeira Liga teams. Their experience of European success proved decisive, and they also boasted the continent's most impressive young manager. Mourinho would later become renowned as a defensive coach, but during his period in Portugal he was committed to high-tempo, proactive possession play.

Mourinho's first taste of top-level football came when working as an interpreter for Bobby Robson at Sporting Lisbon and Porto, before following him to Barcelona, by which point he'd become Robson's assistant. Mourinho gained a reputation for translating Robson's press conference answers with extra tactical detail, and also constantly talked himself into trouble because he was more aggressive than Robson towards players, referees and journalists. 'Mourinho put people's backs up from the very first day,' wrote Enric Bañeres, a columnist for Barcelona-based newspaper *La Vanguardia*. 'It's one thing being haughty and arrogant if you're Johan Cruyff, quite another if you're a nobody. Robson would have been far better off if he'd had a number two who was familiar with the club and the players, someone with a deft touch at handling people.' Mourinho's attitude during that period in Barcelona would prove significant many years later.

When Robson was moved upstairs to be replaced by Louis van Gaal, Mourinho continued as an assistant. His role under the two managers differed hugely. Robson was a hands-on training-ground coach, who focused on attacking. Mourinho's job was therefore twofold: about taking a step back and planning the nature of training practices, and, in Mourinho's words, 'Whilst maintaining the primacy of attacking football, I tried to organise it better, and this organisation stems directly from the defence.' Van Gaal, on the other hand, focused on planning, then delegated the training practices to Mourinho and other assistants, who were charged with implementing Van Gaal's typically Dutch possession drills. 'Back then we spoke the same language, we believed in the same things,' Xavi Hernández recalled of Mourinho. 'We worked within Barca's philosophy.'

Once you consider that experience, Mourinho's declarations on his appointment at Porto manager in 2002 are unsurprising. 'I promise that I intend to play on the attack,' he said. 'I promise that we will work towards that goal every day, until we reach a perfectly systematic and automatic model. When that day comes, I promise you attacking football, and until then, I promise that I deliberately intend to attack … with players of the stature of Porto's, it would not make sense to transform an attacking philosophy into a more defensive model. The very characteristics of these players set us on a specific path, which will never include a defensive way of playing.'

The phrase 'perfectly systematic and automatic model' could have been borrowed from Van Gaal, but this approach is also typically Portuguese, and Porto were a good representation of this footballing identity. Portuguese football has long considered the game in systematic terms, taking a wider view and implementing the fundamental principles of the game in a studious manner.

This tendency can be traced back to the inter-war years, and the influence of Cândido de Oliveira, who coached Sporting, Porto and also the national side in three separate spells. After his first stint coaching Portugal in the 1920s, Oliveira travelled to London to participate in a coaching course run by the English FA, and effectively worked as an intern at Arsenal, where Herbert Chapman had revolutionised football with his WM formation.

Oliveira subsequently wrote an influential book in 1936 entitled *Football: técnica e tática* (*Football: Techniques and Tactics*), a deconstruction of the WM formation, which he'd introduced during his second stint with Portugal, well before many other established footballing nations employed the system. The book was widely read by his contemporaries, and promoted a particularly theoretical approach towards football. After working as a secret agent for Allied forces during the Second World War, monitoring Nazi Germany's movements in Portugal, Oliveira subsequently wrote another significant book, *Evolução táctica no futebol* (*The Evolution of Football Tactics*), in 1949. He was also joint founder of the sports newspaper *A Bola* in 1945, still popular today. Oliveira was insistent that sport journalists must not solely inform and entertain, but educate as well. He was a hugely significant figure in the development of Portuguese football, and the country's 'super cup' trophy is named after him.

Portuguese football was also greatly influenced by the legendary Béla Guttmann, who took charge of Benfica during their glory days of the 1960s. While famous for his declaration that 'the third year is fatal' for a football coach and for the so-called 'curse' he placed on Benfica in European finals after his departure, Guttmann's true legacy was about promoting attacking football, playing with direct wingers and stressing the importance of the system over individual brilliance.

The third crucial figure was José Maria Pedroto, who inspired Porto's rise in the late 1970s, partly as a result of his use of a statistical analyst, José Neto. They met when Pedroto was coaching Vitória de Guimarães and also lecturing part-time. As a student, Neto attended once of Pedroto's classes and asked him a seemingly simple question: 'What is the importance of the game in relation to organising training?' This prompted a lengthy discussion and a follow-up meeting in Pedroto's office, and Neto subsequently provided Pedroto with a complete statistical analysis of a recent Vitória game, considered the first such study in Portugal. Pedroto later returned to Porto, brought in Neto as his analyst and repeatedly stressed the importance of his work. 'More than the titles that he won with Porto,' Neto later said of his mentor, 'it's his doctrine that's the greatest legacy for Portuguese football.'

Mourinho, then, fitted the template for a Portuguese coach: a studious tactician who believed in the primacy of the system. 'For me, the most important aspect in my teams is to have a game model, a set of principles that provides organisation, and from the first day of training, our attention is dedicated to that,' he explained. While Mourinho is often accused of not evolving football tactics in any comparable way to contemporaries like Pep Guardiola or Jürgen Klopp, this overlooks Mourinho's revolutionary approach to match preparation, which inspired almost every other top-level coach over the next decade. He was the most significant practitioner of the coaching approach known as 'tactical periodisation', which originated in Porto.

Its inventor was Vitór Frade, a professor of physical education and philosophy at the University of Porto. During the late 1980s and 1990s, Frade created a programme to 'universalise' football training, which, in practice, meant the complete rejection of the idea that training the physical, technical, tactical and mental elements of football should be carried out separately. Frade's philosophy required every single training exercise to incorporate all four factors, and therefore overhauled the previous established approach, which would feature, for example, draining physical training sessions that were solely about running or tactical sessions in which defensive shape was practised at walking pace without the ball. There remains a belief among many Portuguese coaches that you simply cannot fully understand tactical periodisation – sometimes called 'the training process' – unless you've studied under Frade, who became Porto's 'director of methodology' during Mourinho's spell in charge. Upon his appointment, Mourinho claimed that he wanted to 'Portuguesify' the side in terms of players' nationalities, and by focusing on a clear playing structure and a distinct training methodology, he also Portuguesified Porto in a wider sense.

Mourinho first met Frade when working with the academy at Vitória de Setúbal, his hometown club, in the early 1990s, and they remained in close contact throughout the next decade. When Mourinho was appointed manager of Leiria in summer 2001, the club's president informed him that he'd identified a wonderful location for pre-season training in the picturesque Portuguese countryside, with a backdrop of rolling hills that would be perfect for cross-country running. Mourinho, to his surprise, said there would be no running exercises whatsoever. All his work would be concentrated on the training pitch – always involving the ball to improve technique, always involving positional considerations to work on strategy, and always involving a level of complexity to ensure that players remained focused.

'I do not believe in practising skills separately, shooting, dribbling and tackling,' Mourinho explained at a coaching seminar in Tel Aviv in 2005. 'A boy can practise passing the ball brilliantly, but in a game it's different. The "universal" activity is crucial – you have to put together all these aspects in a match situation. Many clubs do fitness work separately, sending players for 45 minutes with a fitness coach, but I don't believe in this, because there are exercises that can improve your physical qualities using the ball. I make the players play a simple, small-sided game of football, but they can only cross the halfway line if they are sprinting. Players don't enjoy working without the ball, so why take it away from them? A great pianist doesn't run around the piano or do push-ups with the tips of his fingers; to be great he plays the piano. The best way to become a great player is to play football.'

Mourinho's sessions always lasted 90 minutes – or 120 minutes if he was preparing his squad for a match that might involve extra-time. He also introduced the mandatory use of shin pads in training, which might sound like a minor detail but was actually a telling sign of his new approach. Previously, players would practise technical drills in isolation, and any small-sided matches were played in a reserved manner – you didn't tackle a teammate in training as you would an opponent on matchday. But Mourinho's training sessions accurately replicated match situations, and therefore shin pads were necessary. His assistant, Rui Faria, had studied physical education under Frade and was an expert in tactical periodisation. Elsewhere, he would have been considered a side's fitness coach – but since there were no specific fitness activities, Mourinho refused to consider him in such specific terms. 'Our daily concerns are directed to make operational our game model,' said Mourinho. 'However, the structure of the training session is related not only to tactical objectives, but also with the physical fitness component prioritised.' Again, a Portuguese coach was concerned with the concept of structure.

Porto's fitness levels proved particularly important throughout their run to Champions League success, because they depended far more on pressing than any of Mourinho's later sides. Porto pressed aggressively high up the pitch and used a very advanced defensive line, based around the central pairing of Jorge Costa and Ricardo Carvalho. Costa had fallen out with Mourinho's predecessor Octávio Machado and had been loaned out to Charlton despite being club captain, but was astutely brought back into the squad by Mourinho. Carvalho, meanwhile, was a Porto academy product who became one of Europe's best centre-backs under Mourinho, capable of defending with brain or brawn. The full-backs were Paulo Ferreira, who was converted from a right-midfielder by Mourinho, and performed excellently in the Champions League against left-wingers like Ryan Giggs and Jérôme Rothen, while left-back Nuno Valente followed Mourinho to Porto having played under him at Leiria.

As a quartet they had a brilliant relationship when stepping up to catch the opposition offside, although there was something curious about this aspect of Porto's game plan. Throughout their Champions League run, opposition strikers would consistently be flagged offside incorrectly, when replays showed they were actually onside. The most notorious example came in the second round at Old Trafford, when Manchester United's Paul Scholes had a goal wrongly disallowed. This happened with such regularity throughout the competition that it felt like more than good fortune; Porto's defenders were somehow so convincing at acting like they'd caught opponents offside, even when they hadn't, that assistant referees repeatedly fell for it. Against Deportivo in the semi-final, Porto won four offsides, of which one was clearly incorrect and denied Depor a one-on-one chance. In the final against Monaco, Porto won an incredible 12 offsides, of which three were incorrect, two of which would have presented a Monaco striker with a clear goalscoring opportunity. Instead, Deschamps' side didn't manage a single shot on target. Mourinho's Porto were also highly effective at collecting bookings without facing suspensions. They went into the second leg of the semi-final in La Coruña with six players a yellow card away from being suspended. A further two players were booked during the game, yet all eight players successfully walked the tightrope and were available for the final against Monaco.

In that final, Porto's high defensive line kept Monaco target man Fernando Morientes away from the box and meant his flick-ons came to nothing. Costa and Carvalho also positioned themselves intelligently to intercept through-balls, while goalkeeper Vítor Baía swept outside his box effectively. Although Porto's 4–3–1–2 formation theoretically allowed Monaco full-backs Patrice Evra and Hugo Ibarra (on loan from Porto, peculiarly) time on the ball, Porto pressed them towards the touchlines. The forward duo of Carlos Alberto and Derlei covered a flank each, while the players on the outside of the midfield diamond, Pedro Mendes and Maniche, pushed out wide to further crowd them. Costinha, meanwhile, played the holding role expertly and sometimes acted as an extra centre-back. Mourinho described Costinha as his 'coach on the field', the man who would come across to the touchline and receive tactical instructions before transmitting them to teammates.

Porto started slowly and were fortunate when Ludovic Giuly, Monaco's elusive attacking midfielder, was forced to depart through injury midway through the first half. His replacement, Dado Pršo, was a second target man and Porto's high defensive line coped easily. Mourinho's side went ahead out of the blue, shortly before half-time, through striker Carlos Alberto. He miscontrolled a Ferreira cross, the ball bounced against a defender, but then the Brazilian instinctively pivoted and volleyed home. It was his only major contribution to the final and, in truth, the only memorable moment of his career – a highly rated 19-year-old Brazilian international at this stage, he managed fewer than 40 professional goals.

Indeed, Carlos Alberto's substitution prompted the spell that confirmed Porto's triumph. Mourinho introduced the speedy attacking midfielder Dmitri Alenichev, who played on the left of Porto's diamond, with Maniche pushing higher alongside Deco, Porto's number 10 and star man. Now Porto played on the break, with Alenichev particularly crucial. Midway through the second half Deco brought the ball through midfield and found Alenichev on the left, before receiving the return pass on the edge of the box, shaping as if to bend the ball into the right corner, before cutting it back into the left corner, sending goalkeeper Flavio Roma the wrong way. It was a remarkably calm finish. 'I breathed in and isolated what was happening; it was just me, the goalkeeper and the centre-backs,' Deco related afterwards. 'I was able to make the play without even thinking, as if I'd been playing in the park with my friends. If I'd thought about everything surrounding that moment, about it being the decisive goal in the final of the Champions League, the most normal reaction would have been to hit it as hard as I could.'

Then Alenichev scored the third, running through on to a deflected through-ball and smashing home. The nature of these two goals gave the impression that Porto were a counter-attacking side, but their default approach was considerably more proactive.

Such was Porto's emphasis on pressing, Mourinho encouraged his players to conserve their energy when in possession. 'It's what I call "resting with the ball",' Mourinho stated in his biography. 'With the pace of play that we impose, it's necessary to rest, otherwise no one will make it to the end of the match. It's about alternating moments of great intensity and pressure with periods of rest with the ball, which is nothing more than possession for possession's sake.'

This 'resting with the ball' meant Mourinho's Porto dominated possession in 10 of their 13 Champions League matches that season, including home and away against Real Madrid, Manchester United and Deportivo. The only exceptions came against three French sides: away at Marseille in a 3–2 group stage win, in the second leg of their 4–2 aggregate win over Lyon and in the final against Monaco. On each occasion Porto were ahead for a long period, and the opposition felt compelled to push forward and take charge. Otherwise, Porto dominated possession.

The diamond midfield, meanwhile, wasn't Mourinho's first-choice system. In general he favoured the 4–3–3 that was common throughout Portuguese football, although a combination of injuries to his wingers and the need to strengthen the midfield to enforce possession dominance against strong European opposition meant he turned to 4–3–1–2. Porto were highly organised in both formations because Mourinho drilled his players in two systems, and two systems alone. Switching between two structures became his default approach; it was 4–3–3 and 4–3–1–2 again with Chelsea, 4–2–3–1 and 4–3–1–2 with Inter, and then, broadly speaking, 4–2–3–1 and 4–3–3 for the rest of his career to date. Mourinho trained Porto to switch between the formations on the basis of subtle hand gestures, leaving the opposition perplexed. In both systems Porto were almost mechanically synchronised in their movements, always retaining an extremely clear structure regardless of whether they were in or out of possession.

After Porto's Champions League success, Mourinho moved to Chelsea and won the Premier League in his first campaign. In England he became renowned as a purely defensive manager; in his first season, Chelsea kept 25 clean sheets in 38 games, conceding just 15 goals, although Mourinho insisted he wanted to play more positively. 'I would like to have more control of the game in terms of possession,' he said. 'In five years in Portugal I never had a match where my team has had less possession than the opponents. Never, never. We could play Real Madrid, Deportivo, Manchester United, and we always had a bigger percentage. So we could have more possession, and that takes time, but we are going in the right direction.' Mourinho's statistics weren't entirely correct, as detailed above, but the general thrust of his argument was fair, and Porto had indeed dominated against the three specific opponents he named.

In the Premier League Mourinho's newfound emphasis on counter-attacking meant more focus on the concept of the transition, which was something of an unfamiliar notion in England. Although not an approach unique to them, the Portuguese focus on the transition was another way in which the country looked at the game structurally. It broke football down into four separate periods, which flowed in a continuous cycle: a team went from the possession phase, to transitioning to out of possession, to the out-of-possession phase, before transitioning back to the possession phase. Because a side's formation would differ significantly according to whether or not they had possession, there were opportunities to exploit the opposition's sluggishness at transitions. This, incidentally, was another major part of Frade's thinking. 'There is no attacking football or defensive football,' he argued. 'When you have the ball, you have to think about what will happen when you lose it. When you do not have it, you need to know what you will do when you get it back.' Mourinho's Chelsea excelled in this respect.

'Mourinho was big on transitions,' remembered Damien Duff, who played as a winger on either flank in Mourinho's 4–3–3 at Chelsea. 'It was probably the first time I'd heard it. If you lose the ball, it's transitioning from attack to defence, running back quickly, recovery runs or sprints – on the other hand, if you win the ball it's transitioning from defence, exploding forward quickly. When you win the ball back, that's when teams are most vulnerable because they're not in a defensive shape and boom, you're gone. We steamrolled teams that year by having that down to a T. I could go through, off the top of my head, 30 or 40 goals when it was: win the ball back and go within four or five seconds. He was probably the first [to talk about transitions]. I don't remember having that from any other coaches.' Mourinho also brought the Portuguese concept of tactical periodisation to Chelsea, which surprised striker Didier Drogba, who arrived at pre-season training with running shoes, only to be told by Mourinho that there wouldn't be any running drills.

Another example of Mourinho's studious, methodical approach was evident in his emphasis on opposition scouting. He had initially impressed as an opposition scout, wowing Robson with his methodical approach to analysing matches and summarising opposition game plans. 'He'd come back and hand me a dossier that was absolutely first class,' Robson remembered. 'As good as anything I'd ever received. Here he was, in his early thirties, never been a player, never been a coach to speak of either, giving me reports as good as anything I ever got from the top professional people I'd brought in to scout for me at World Cups. There would be the way the teams played in the match he'd been sent to – both teams – with defence and attack covered very well, patterns of play, nicely set out with diagrams and a different colour for each team, all clear as a bell.'

Mourinho expected to be provided with dossiers of similar quality. Early in his coaching career he found himself unimpressed with the analysis department in a brief stint at Benfica. He subsequently refused to use their analysis and instead hired an old university classmate at his own expense, such was the importance he placed on researching the opposition properly. He also instructed scouts to spy on opposition training sessions, reporting back with a likely starting XI.

When he returned to Porto as manager in 2002 Mourinho could count on another bright young Portuguese coach as his opposition analyst: André Villas-Boas, who was another Robson protégé. During

Robson's spell in charge of Porto, a 16-year-old Villas-Boas found himself living in the same apartment complex. He posted a letter through Robson's door questioning his decision to omit Domingos Paciência, a popular striker, from the side. When Robson challenged him to outline his arguments, Villas-Boas followed up with an extensive statistical analysis, which is reminiscent of how José Neto had wowed José Maria Pedroto in the 1970s. Robson was impressed, arranged for Villas-Boas to attend a coaching course with the English FA despite his protégé being too young, and then employed him at Porto. There, Villas-Boas worked closely with Mourinho, who subsequently used him as his opposition analyst upon his return as manager.

'Because José knew me well from his time as Bobby's assistant, he asked me to create the Opponent Observation Department,' Villas-Boas later explained. 'It takes me four days to put an entire file together, so it is very comprehensive. The reports are given to all the players as well as the manager. The idea is that when the players go out on the pitch, they are totally prepared, so there can be very few surprises during the game. My work enables José to know exactly when a player from the opposition team is likely to be at his best or his weakest. I will travel to training grounds, often incognito, and then look at our opponents' mental and physical state before drawing my conclusions and presenting a full dossier to José.'

When planning his strategy for a particular match, Mourinho considered the opposition as much as his own side. When talking about the challenge of facing Real Madrid's *galácticos*, he made a humorous – but revealing – remark. 'A strange thing happened as my technical team and I were preparing for the game,' he said. 'When we put pen to paper to draw up the plan, we realised we would need 13 players to beat Real ... I needed a player to mark Fernando Morientes and a free midfielder close behind, another player to mark Luís Figo and another in the area he frees up with his diagonal passes. I'd need a player for marking Zinedine Zidane, but as he plays out of his zone a great deal, I'd have to play a right-back to occupy that space. Finally, as I always play with three forwards, I'd need to keep them. If we added it up, including the other players I usually play with, we would need 13 players in order to beat Real Madrid. As the referee didn't allow this, we only played with 11 players and lost 1–0.' It's difficult to imagine many other successful coaches considering the game in this manner, effectively working backwards from the opposition.

Mourinho believed researching the opposition was so fundamental to match preparation that he turned it into a group activity. For pre-season friendlies, he would sometimes make 11 changes at half-time, with the first-half XI tasked with providing feedback to the second-half XI about their opponents. Ahead of the final against Monaco, Villas-Boas's department prepared a personalised DVD for each player, highlighting the approach of each specific opponent. The players watched the footage at home and then Mourinho chaired a meeting where the information was shared. He didn't simply have an opposition analyst, he quite literally had a team of opposition analysts.

And just as Mourinho studied the characteristics of the opposition, he often attempted to hide his own side's characteristics from the opposition. Before the triumphant Champions League Final, Porto faced Benfica in the Portuguese cup final. There was no particular need for Mourinho to rotate his side, because there were ten days between the games, but he made changes solely to trick Monaco. 'I knew that Monaco's coach would be observing us at the match and so I didn't play what I considered to be my best team at the time,' Mourinho said. 'Benni McCarthy played instead of Carlos Alberto and this change, in terms of strategy, altered everything. I sought to hide from Didier Deschamps the way I would play in the Champions League Final, and thus surprise him.' Porto lost the first final 2–1 in extra-time, but at least Mourinho hadn't given away his game plan for the more important contest.

Villas-Boas, incidentally, would follow Mourinho to Chelsea and Inter, before embarking on his own managerial career. He took Porto to an unbeaten title-winning campaign in 2010/11 while also matching Mourinho's achievement of winning the UEFA Cup, now rebranded as the Europa League. Coincidentally, Porto's victory in the final came against fellow Portuguese side Braga, now managed by Domingos Paciência – the subject of Villas-Boas's letter that had started his coaching career. His Porto played a 4–3–3 system with an aggressive defensive line, and the integrated nature of their movement was very deliberate, very systematic. Villas-Boas then replicated Mourinho's move to Chelsea, where he had less success; he wasn't adept at man-management and was often denounced as a 'laptop manager', such was his focus on the methodical aspects of football.

But in Portugal a studious approach to the game is respected. Throughout his managerial career Mourinho has consistently updated a document illustrating his coaching philosophy, which 'contains the objectives and methodologies for my practice, and how to achieve these … nothing more than the systematic setting down of my ideas. If I had to give it a title, it would be "The evolution of my training concepts"'. Mourinho insists it will never be published, but this document is essentially the textbook for Portuguese football coaching. The next generation of Portuguese coaches, like Villas-Boas and Paulo Fonseca, often claim their approach is more similar to Pep Guardiola's than Mourinho's. But then Mourinho's Porto template was more similar to that of Guardiola's sides than it was to Mourinho's later sides, who were considerably more defensive.

Porto, meanwhile, struggled badly after Mourinho's departure. His successor Gigi Delneri had been appointed after performing impressively in Serie A with an attack-minded Chievo side. But Delneri was sacked before he'd taken charge of a single competitive game. Mourinho – still in contact with his former players – suggested it was because Delneri didn't follow the principles of tactical periodisation.

'In the same way that I had to follow an Italian manager [Claudio Ranieri] at Chelsea, it was not easy for an Italian manager to follow me at Porto,' Mourinho told *World Soccer*. 'We have completely different concepts of training. For example, at Chelsea, the way they used to develop aerobic condition was putting players through 12 sprints of 100 metres. The way I develop aerobic condition is three against three, man to man, in a 20-metre by 20-metre square. It's completely different, and I imagine it was the same for Delneri. The Porto players were with me for two and a half years, they believed in me, in my methods, in the way we do it. The next day I leave, and a manager arrives who works completely differently. You can see the problem.' Porto's players were insistent on training in what was, at this stage, an approach very particular to Portugal.

# 11

# The First Port of Call

Having stated his intention to 'Portuguesify' Porto upon his appointment in 2002, José Mourinho had largely accomplished this by his final game – up to a particular point on the pitch. For Porto's Champions League Final victory in 2004, their goalkeeper was Portuguese international Vítor Baía. The four defenders – Paulo Ferreira, Jorge Costa, Ricardo Carvalho and Nuno Valente – were all Portuguese. In midfield, the trio of Costinha, Pedro Mendes and Maniche were also all Portuguese.

In the final third, however, the situation was different, because strikers Carlos Alberto and Derlei were both Brazilian. Meanwhile, the player tasked with linking the Portuguese eight and the Brazilian pairing, as the sole attacking midfielder in Mourinho's 4–3–1–2, was Deco. Fittingly, he was a Portugal international who had switched allegiance from Brazil.

In the mid-1990s Ajax and Holland relied on the likes of Edgar Davids and Clarence Seedorf, born in the former Dutch colony of Suriname in South America. At the turn of the century France's reliance on Thierry Henry and Nicolas Anelka, sons of parents from French overseas territories in the Caribbean, became clear. The impact of Argentines in Spain was also significant, but it was Portugal whose style has been most heavily influenced by those born in former colonies or outside the mainland.

The national side's top two scorers hail from the two Autonomous Regions of Portugal, both situated thousands of miles off the country's west coast: Cristiano Ronaldo was born in Madeira, while Pauleta, who never competed in the Portuguese top flight, was from the Azores. Carlos Queiroz, the coach responsible for developing Portugal's 'golden generation' in the early 1990s, was born in the former Portuguese colony of Mozambique, as was Portugal's most legendary player – before Ronaldo, at least – Eusebio, the hero of the all-conquering Benfica side of the 1960s. Rui Jordão, Portugal's top scorer at Euro 1984, was from Angola. There have also been several Portuguese internationals of Cape Verdean descent, including Nani, Jorge Andrade and Silvestre Varela.

But it was inevitably Brazil, the world's most successful football nation, that proved the most significant link. Brazil became independent from Portugal in 1822, after a period during which the two countries were so closely linked that the capital of the Portuguese Empire was briefly Rio de Janeiro rather than Lisbon. Cultural links between the two countries remain close, and one of the conditions of Portuguese citizenship is a good command of the language, which clearly gives Brazilians an advantage.

Portugal's evolution into a serious football nation in the 1950s and 1960s owed much to the influence of a Brazilian coach. Otto Glória was born in Brazil to Portuguese parents, and enjoyed brief stints in charge of Botafogo and Vasco da Gama. Upon moving to Benfica in 1953 he won the Portuguese league title three times, and after subsequent stints with Porto and Sporting, became the national side's manager ahead of the 1966 World Cup, their first appearance at the tournament. He made significant advancements in terms of diet, physiology and tactics, and focused on discipline and organisation while also encouraging his attackers to be creative and free-spirited. 'He revolutionised Portuguese football,' remembered Eusebio.

Four decades passed before Portugal appointed another foreign coach, ahead of Euro 2004 on home soil. It was another Brazilian: Luiz Felipe Scolari, who had won World Cup 2002 with his home country, and he took charge of Portugal the following year, his first experience of European football. It was a controversial appointment, not merely because Scolari was foreign, but also because his salary was far higher than anything his predecessors had earned. The Portuguese Football Federation, however, felt compelled to push the boat out and recruit someone with a track record of international success, ahead of the biggest tournament in the history of Portuguese football. Scolari was the obvious choice.

But Scolari's tactical approach didn't fit the stereotype of how Brazilians play football. As Brazil coach he declared the days of *joga bonito* – the beautiful game – were over; he liked tactical discipline, encouraged tactical fouling and packed his side with defensive-minded players. 'In Sao Paulo or Rio de Janeiro, people are used to technical, skilled football, but in Rio Grande do Sul, where I am from, the emphasis is on physical play,' he explained. 'Because of that, my teams may not play beautifully, but they are organised and productive.' He did, however, win the World Cup with a three-man attack comprising Ronaldo, Rivaldo and Ronaldinho. Much like his compatriot Glória, Scolari combined strict tactical instructions with a love of individual flair, and therefore inevitably felt drawn to Deco.

Throughout the previous decade Portugal's undisputed number 10 was Rui Costa. At his peak he was the equal of any European playmaker, capable of dribbling purposefully and sliding delicate through-balls between defenders. He also contributed in terms of goalscoring at international level, although he suffered a drought at AC Milan, where he'd lost his status as first-choice attacking midfielder to the outstanding Kaká, who offered a similar level of dribbling and passing ability, but also scored prolifically. Rui Costa graciously accepted his reduced status at club level, helping Kaká's development, but the last thing he expected was to lose his place in the national side as well – to another Brazilian.

Deco's performances for Mourinho's Porto were hugely impressive. He could play as a number 10 in the 4–3–1–2 or retreat to the left-centre midfield role in a 4–3–3. He was primarily renowned for his composure in possession, particularly his ability to receive the ball in tight situations with his head up and pausing for a second before playing an incisive pass. But, significantly, he was also constantly praised for his work rate, aggressive pressing and tracking back. 'Deco is a truly world-class player,' said Mourinho. 'Not only does he produce great individual brilliance, he offers so much more to the team. He is a superb passer and has a competitive personality, and he will naturally tackle and chase back for the good of the team.' In Porto's 2002/03 league campaign, Deco was booked 15 times in 30 games.

When UEFA's technical director Andy Roxburgh discussed the possibility of teams lining up without a striker in 2008, he identified Deco as the shining example of an all-round midfielder for the next tactical era. 'The six players in midfield all could rotate, attack and defend,' he said. 'But you'd need to have six Decos in midfield; he doesn't just attack, he runs, tackles and covers all over the pitch.' That gave Deco an edge over Rui Costa, who was more of an old-school, languid number 10, and he also had the advantage of playing regularly alongside Costinha and Maniche, Portugal's deep-midfield pairing at Euro 2004.

Scolari could therefore attempt to re-create the spine of the Porto side, and shortly after his appointment as Portugal manager he had a lengthy meeting with Mourinho. 'I enjoyed speaking to him a great deal – he was very friendly and open,' Mourinho later said. 'We basically talked about my players – Scolari wanted to know everything about them, and I was at his entire disposal to answer all his questions and doubts. We analysed each man, from his height to his characteristics. We also touched on the Deco case, and he told me that he was completely in favour of having him in the Portugal team.'

But Deco wasn't Portuguese, had no family links to the country and was therefore only eligible for citizenship once he'd lived in Portugal for six years. It was something of an anomaly that he'd never been selected by Brazil, even if his development into a top-class footballer came relatively late. He had been selected for Brazil's Olympic squad in 2000 but was forced to withdraw through injury. Deco later confirmed he'd been in discussions with Portugal 'for two or three years' before he was granted citizenship in 2003, somewhat speedily after the sixth anniversary of his arrival in the country.

His decision proved controversial, with the two leading lights of the golden generation voicing their displeasure at his selection. 'There's a reason they call it the national team of Portugal,' said Rui Costa. Luís Figo, the team captain, agreed. 'It's something that distorts team spirit and I don't agree with it,' he declared. 'If you're born Chinese, well, you have to play for China. I have nothing against those that do it, but it's superficial.'

Even Mourinho, the manager who had developed Deco into a world-class player, was opposed to his selection. 'When, one day, I'm a national coach, I will only take players born in my country, that's for sure,' he said. 'Or if not born in my country, then with parents with a big connection with the country. I will never take a player just because he has a passport from my country, just because he might make my team better.' He repeated the statement many years later. 'If one day I coach Portugal, I'll go with the Portuguese. The national team is Portugal, it's not "Portugal and friends". Portugal is for the Portuguese.'

But Scolari was insistent. 'I'm the one that decides the national team, not the players,' he responded. 'I don't give in to pressure from anybody. Those who disagree have the option not to play.' Of course, Scolari's own nationality merely fuelled the controversy; this wasn't simply a Brazilian being selected for Portugal, but a Brazilian being selected for Portugal by a Brazilian.

Deco, for his part, was always particularly complimentary about his adopted nation. 'Portugal has been my home for seven years,' he said ahead of Euro 2004. 'It's where I have established myself as a player, I owe everything to Portuguese football and am honoured to play for them … I adore Brazil but when I go back there, it's only like going on holiday now. Portugal is home.'

Deco made his Portugal debut in March 2003 at Porto's home ground – against Brazil. He was introduced as a substitute after an hour, in place of winger Sergio Conceição, and with ten minutes remaining Portugal won a free-kick 25 yards from goal. Deco stepped up, and struck a shot through the wall and past Brazilian goalkeeper Marcos. He didn't quite know how to react, awkwardly throwing his arms into the air and clapping himself. It finished 2–1, with a Brazilian player having handed a Brazilian coach his first Portugal victory, against Brazil. Incidentally, Portugal hadn't defeated Brazil since the 1966 World Cup, under the management of another Brazilian, Glória.

In spite of the inevitable complaints that Scolari couldn't feel the same passion as a Portuguese coach, his South American attitude boosted national spirit across his adopted country. Upon his arrival Scolari said felt the Portugal squad was 'depressed' after failing to reach the knockout stage of the 2002 World Cup, and he introduced a Brazilian professor of psychology, Regina Brandão, to improve the mood in the camp. 'We have different attitudes, I am South American and I like my players to be happy and joking,' he acknowledged. 'The

Portuguese players weren't used to that; they are used to angry faces. In Portugal I find everyone gets serious about every game. You need balance.' He repeatedly spoke about the importance of harmony in the 'group', which became something of a buzzword, later copied by his fellow moustachioed World Cup-winning coach Vicente del Bosque.

Scolari also changed the mentality of Portugal's supporters. Ahead of Euro 2004 Scolari announced he wanted to see 'a Portuguese flag in every window' across the country – to a somewhat muted reaction, because this type of overt, patriotic flag-waving simply wasn't part of the culture in Portugal, a reserved country. But, after initial scepticism, the Portuguese public responded positively. 'He brought the Portuguese people together and urged us to have pride in our flag,' remembered goalkeeper Ricardo, quoted in Tom Kundert's *The Thirteenth Chapter*. 'We didn't have the culture of the flag beforehand – that's typically South American, like you find in Argentina and Brazil.' Defender Fernando Meira agreed. 'Scolari played a fundamental role for the Portugal team and Portuguese football, because he managed to revolutionise and unite our football like never before. It was amazing how Scolari managed to unite our *seleção*, to get the entire country and all the Portuguese communities around the world to cheer on the national team in a completely different way. I remember Euro 2004 and the flags in all the windows of Portuguese homes up and down the country. It was something he asked for, and that made a difference in Portugal.'

Scolari had a difficult task ahead of Euro 2004. Portugal had spent a decade praying that the 'golden generation' – the original version, before that moniker would be used for other national sides – would eventually come good and win Portugal's first major championship. But as the tournament approached there was suddenly a new generation, those who had just taken Porto to Champions League success, many of whom were on the fringes of the national side the previous year – and Cristiano Ronaldo. Scolari was forced to select a side that balanced the two generations, with Rui Costa versus Deco the main debate, even if both agreed they could play together.

While Figo remained opposed to the use of Deco, Rui Costa became more welcoming. 'At the beginning we were not in agreement with Deco's incorporation into the team, myself included,' he admitted. 'Not necessarily because he is Deco, it is just a question of principle. But I must admit he has given us additional quality, and I believe he will be a regular in the Portugal squad for many years to come.' With Deco on the bench, Rui Costa started Portugal's opener, a shock 2–1 defeat to Greece, with the hosts' consolation goal coming in stoppage time, a header from substitute Ronaldo. Portugal's players admitted they felt under enormous pressure, but there were also tactical problems. In particular, Portugal's possession football was far too ponderous to penetrate Greece, with Rui Costa often slowing the play.

Therefore, for Portugal's second game, against Russia – which Scolari described as 'life or death' – he brought three more Porto players into the side. He introduced defenders Nuno Valente and Ricardo Carvalho, but also included Deco in the number 10 role, meaning Rui Costa dropped to the bench. It proved a good decision, as Deco was the star, assisting the opener. He received a pass from Maniche in an inside-right position and confidently let the ball run across his body before skipping past the challenge of Andrei Karyaka. He dribbled towards the edge of the box, feinting as if to whip in a cross, before driving a low return pass into Maniche, now on the penalty spot, who finished smartly.

In the second half, Deco was joined by Rui Costa, brought on in place of winger Simão. He played some wonderful passes, and two minutes from full-time settled the game. Now wearing the captain's armband after Ronaldo had replaced Figo, Rui Costa received the ball inside his own half, purposefully drove forward 50 yards in possession before prodding the ball through the defence to Ronaldo on the left, running into the box and converting Ronaldo's excellent outside-of-the-boot cross. The Estádio da Luz exploded, and there was a lengthy embrace between Rui Costa and Deco, Portugal play-makers old and new. Scolari had brought the group together and united the generations. 'We were playing in a different way from normal, making quick passes and moving the ball out wide,' a relieved Scolari said afterwards. Deco had accelerated Portugal's attacks.

The final group game was one of the most famous victories in Portugal's history, their first-ever competitive win over fierce rivals Spain. Two of Scolari's changes proved crucial. First, Nuno Gomes replaced Pauleta in a like-for-like change up front. Second, Scolari decided to switch Deco and Figo, moving the former to an unfamil-iar wide position, allowing Figo to operate centrally. These switches brought the game's only goal. Receiving possession between the lines, Figo flicked the ball on to Nuno Gomes, who held up play and waited for Figo's run, and with the Spanish defence anticipating a return pass, Gomes spun and smashed the ball into the far corner. Portugal had qualified, Spain were out.

In the quarter-final against England, Scolari again demonstrated his ability to alter the game from the bench. With Portugal 1–0 behind after Michael Owen's early strike, Scolari made three attack-minded changes. First, holding midfielder Costinha was replaced by a winger, Simão, with Figo again moving inside. Next, Figo himself was replaced – to his obvious disgust – by Hélder Postiga, a second striker. Finally, right-back Miguel departed and on came Rui Costa. To borrow a Portuguese expression, Scolari had put all the meat on the barbecue.

The changes worked magnificently. With seven minutes of normal time remaining, Simão delivered an inswinging left-wing cross that was headed home by his fellow substitute Postiga. 1–1. Into extra-time, and now Portugal needed to play another 30 minutes with an absurdly forward-thinking XI featuring six attacking players – Deco, Rui Costa, Simão, Ronaldo, Postiga and Nuno Gomes. Scolari solved the problem by playing 4–2–4, with Rui Costa alongside Maniche in midfield – and Deco at right-back. The playmaker who had just orchestrated a Champions League victory, and who would finish second in the Ballon d'Or that year, was able to play in defence because of his tenacity and work rate. It summarised his all-round qualities, and Rui Costa was seen giving him a motivational talk before extra-time.

This allowed Rui Costa to push forward, and he took full advantage. At the start of the second period, he received possession in the centre circle and stormed through the centre of the pitch. Phil Neville attempted to haul him down but merely toppled over himself and then, from an inside-left position just outside the box, Rui Costa checked back onto his right foot and smashed a superb drive in off the crossbar. It produced the biggest roar of the tournament.

Alas, it wasn't the winner. Frank Lampard equalised shortly after-wards, and the game went into penalties. It was a dramatic shootout that featured David Beckham blazing his penalty miles over the crossbar, Rui Costa doing the same, and Postiga scoring with an incredibly delicate Panenka, when a miss would have eliminated the host nation. With an emotional Eusébio bellowing instructions from the sidelines, the shootout went into sudden death, and at that point Portuguese goalkeeper Ricardo bizarrely decided to remove his gloves.

'We had prepared for penalties in training, and I had watched some DVDs looking at where England players had shot,' he explained in Ben Lyttleton's *Twelve Yards*. 'But when I saw Darius Vassell coming towards me, I thought, "Bloody hell. I have seen every player score a penalty on this DVD but not this guy. Nothing. Has he even taken one before?" I looked at my hands. I had to do something. So I ripped off my gloves. Vassell looked at me, and he looked at the referee, who said, "That's fine." To this day I still don't know why I did it.'

Somehow, it worked. Ricardo saved from Vassell with his bare hands, then was so pumped up that he shooed Nuno Valente away and smashed home the winning penalty himself. 'The emotions were too strong in this game and I want to give my sincere thanks to all the Portuguese for the way they have been supporting the players and the national team,' Scolari roared. 'I also want to thank my players,' he added, almost as an afterthought.

The semi-final victory over Holland was less memorable than the wins over Spain and England, finishing 2–1 courtesy of Ronaldo's second header of the tournament and Maniche's stunning drive from a short corner, which was so unexpected that it was missed by the television director, who was still showing a replay. Scolari had a familiar message. 'Congratulations to the Portuguese people, as their support was fantastic,' he said, before announcing that he'd signed a two-year contract extension, to great public approval.

4 July 2004 should have been the greatest day in Portuguese football history – their first-ever major tournament final, in Lisbon, with only Greece standing in their way. But having shocked Portugal in the opening game, Otto Rehhagel's side bookended the tournament with a second victory over the hosts, with Angelos Charisteas heading in the only goal thanks to some questionable positioning by Ricardo. Portugal struggled to create chances for the first hour, although Rui Costa, in his final game for Portugal, was fantastic when introduced in place of Costinha. He ran the show and created Portugal's two best chances, both with through-balls for Ronaldo, who didn't take full advantage.

'We ask for forgiveness from the Portuguese people,' pleaded Scolari. Yet the players were heroes, and to many supporters the defeat felt natural. It fitted the sad, mournful character of the Portuguese form of singing *fado* – which is part of 'the three Fs' that supposedly define Portugal, alongside Fátima, the city famous for apparitions of the Virgin Mary, and, of course, *futebol*. Incidentally, goalkeeper Ricardo had a second opportunity to clinch a European title on home soil the following summer, when Sporting reached the UEFA Cup Final, played at their own stadium. They lost 3–1.

With Rui Costa retired, Deco was now Portugal's undisputed midfield leader for the 2006 World Cup, where Scolari was attempting to win the tournament for the second time in a row. Portugal's results from this tournament felt somewhat familiar. After progressing into the knockout stage comfortably, they defeated Holland with a Maniche winner, just like in Euro 2004, although the game is remembered primarily for its sixteen yellow cards and four red cards, the highest tally in World Cup history. Then came a repeat of the Euro 2004 quarter-final, a victory over England on penalties, before the semi-final, which was a throwback to Euro 2000, with a defeat to France courtesy of Zinedine Zidane's spot-kick. Portugal were considered somewhat boring, as they went six hours without scoring between Maniche's goal against Holland in the second round and Nuno Gomes's late consolation in the third-place play-off defeat to Germany. Yet this was only the second time Portugal had progressed past the group phase, after Glória's side of 1966.

Deco, meanwhile, continued to shine after his 2004 switch to Barcelona. At a time when Xavi Hernández and Andrés Iniesta were still trying to demonstrate their quality, Deco was often Barcelona's chief midfield creator, including for the 2006 Champions League Final victory over Arsenal, where he became one of a small group of players to win the Champions League with two sides. Maintaining his reputation as a hard-working player, the history section of Barcelona's official website profiles him as 'a complete footballer who combined commitment and hard work with the great technical skill often found among Brazilians. He was able to make the final pass, to create and score, but also to commit tactical fouls when necessary', which seems an odd, if telling, compliment from a club obsessed with midfield passing. He stayed at the Camp Nou for four years before joining Chelsea, where he became the first signing of the club's new manager, his old ally Scolari.

Deco was the symbol of the modern South American influence in Portugal, as it became common for Benfica, Sporting and Porto to field twice as many players from that continent as Portuguese nationals. Much later, in 2017, Vitória de Guimarães made history by becoming the first side to field no Europeans in a European competition; their side for a Europa League draw with Red Bull Salzburg featured four Brazilians, two Colombians, a Venezuelan, a Uruguayan, a Peruvian, a Ghanaian and an Ivorian. This was an extreme example, but Portuguese clubs had successfully marketed themselves as, almost literally, the first port of call for South Americans looking to make it in Europe. That reputation wasn't merely due to language or geography, but also because of one particular man. By 2008, not only did Portugal boast Europe's most celebrated player, Cristiano Ronaldo, and its most revered manager, José Mourinho, but also its most influential agent. Jorge Mendes was seemingly involved in every major European transfer, and was often described as the most powerful man in football.

In his youth Mendes unsuccessfully tried to become a professional footballer, before launching his business career by setting up a video rental store, a beach bar and a nightclub. His introduction to football agency came when he befriended Nuno Espírito Santo, a Portugal

U21 goalkeeper who hailed from the former Portuguese colony of São Tomé and Príncipe, off the west coast of Africa. Mendes brokered Espírito Santo's transfer from Vitória de Guimarães to Deportivo, and later took him to Mourinho's Porto. Mendes's reputation soared when he arranged Cristiano Ronaldo's transfer from Sporting to Manchester United in 2003 and Mourinho's move from Porto to Chelsea the following year. Gradually, Mendes's Gestifute agency came to represent almost every major figure in Portuguese football – the vast majority of national team players, as well as Scolari and his replacement as coach, Carlos Queiroz. Gestifute claims that, during the period between 2001 and 2010, it was responsible for 78 per cent of transfer revenue earned by Sporting Lisbon, 70 per cent earned by Porto and 51 per cent earned by Benfica.

Mendes contributed to Portugal's mass importing of South American talent, partly through the concept of third-party ownership. In some countries, this was illegal and a Europe-wide ban on the practice would be introduced in 2015. But beforehand, in many countries including Portugal, a percentage of a player's registration rights could be owned by a private investment company, in the expectation that he would subsequently be transferred for a large fee, thus bringing a windfall.

Therefore, in addition to representing several young South American players and bringing them to Portugal, Gestifute also bought part of their registration rights. A classic example was Anderson, a talented young Brazilian midfielder. In June 2005 Gestifute purchased 70 per cent of his economic rights from the Brazilian side Grêmio. The following week Anderson signed a pre-contract agreement with Porto, which led to a €7 million transfer, with the Portuguese club assuming responsibility for Grêmio's rights and also purchasing part of Gestifute's share. Anderson completed the transfer in January 2006 and spent 18 months in the

Portuguese top flight, before moving on to Manchester United, who bought him for €30 million.

Because third-party ownership was illegal in England, United needed to buy out Gestifute's share, which reportedly earned Mendes around €5 million. By this stage Anderson had only played 19 league games in Brazil and 18 league games in Portugal. His rapid rise demonstrated the value of being represented by Mendes and the value of joining a Portuguese club. Moving to Porto, Benfica or Sporting meant a gentle introduction to Europe in a reasonably competitive league, often playing under a good coach, usually with the bonus of Champions League football.

Other Brazilians, meanwhile, replicated Deco's decision to represent Portugal. One example was Pepe, who had moved to Portugal in 2001 at the age of 18, playing for Marítimo and Porto. In 2006 Brazil manager Dunga attempted to select him for the national team, but the player declined, declaring that he was waiting for Portuguese citizenship. 'Nobody in Brazil knew me ... this is my way to repay Portugal,' he explained. He became eligible in 2007, and then immediately left Porto for Real Madrid, as if he'd deliberately stayed precisely long enough to represent Portugal. Initially he was deployed as a rampaging midfielder for Portugal, dribbling forward to score their opening goal of Euro 2008, before later switching to his customary centre-back role and winning over 100 caps. He would occasionally, and memorably, be deployed in midfield by José Mourinho at Real Madrid.

In 2009, meanwhile, Portugal were boosted by the decision of Liédson, a Brazilian striker who had banged in 100 league goals since joining Sporting in 2003, to take up Portuguese citizenship. 'I have felt Portuguese for a long time now,' he said. 'I will never stop being Brazilian. I love my country like I love Portugal, it's just that the competition in my position is bigger.'

Portugal's professional footballers' union, the SJPF, publicly objected to Liédson's decision. The union's chairman Joaquim Evangelista melodramatically claimed Portuguese footballers were 'in danger of extinction', and said selecting Brazilians like Liédson could 'lead to the loss of the national team's identity'. In one sense, he was right – Portugal weren't accustomed to producing prolific goalscorers.

## 12

# Wingers

Foolproof confirmation that a country possesses a defined football-ing identity is the existence of a well-worn cliché for their national side. Ahead of a major international tournament, TV pundits are often forced to talk about national sides they haven't watched over the previous two – or four – years, but they can nevertheless always fall back on the old caricatures.

So, just as Italy were always 'slow starters', Germany were always 'efficient' and Holland always played well before being eliminated because their players had begun arguing, Portugal now had their own stereotype – they played great football but they lacked a clinical striker. And more so than the aforementioned clichés, it was a view promoted by the Portuguese themselves.

Portugal's famous golden generation had won both the 1989 and 1991 U20 World Cups, the latter on home soil in Lisbon with a penalty shoot-out victory over Brazil in front of 127,000 fans. The manager for those triumphs was Carlos Queiroz, a typically academic product of the Portuguese coaching school.

Queiroz had a modest playing career as a goalkeeper in his home country of Mozambique, before moving to Portugal in his twenties. There, he studied at the Technical University of Lisbon, and in 1982 became the first student to graduate from the institution with a master's degree in football. 'This was almost a revolution,' he later told *El País*. 'I battled to the last drop of my blood to do a masters in football training methodology. I was the first, and with that I opened many possibilities in the intellectual field as a coach.'

Queiroz believed that top-level football would become strikerless – teams would instead need their centre-forward to drop deep, contribute to build-up play and drag defenders out of position to create space for teammates. For the U20 1991 success, João Pinto started up front but drifted around to allow Toni, Luís Figo and Rui Costa to break forward. Queiroz became the national coach immediately afterwards, and his vision became Portugal's template.

After Portugal impressed en route to the Euro 96 quarter-finals, prompting Chelsea player-manager and part-time TV pundit Ruud Gullit to memorably declare that they played 'sexy football', they were defeated by the Czech Republic, courtesy of Karel Poborský's scooped finish. 'Portuguese football doesn't seem to produce out-and-out strikers any more,' Luís Figo admitted afterwards. 'It's especially hard when Benfica and Sporting tend to buy foreign forwards. Paulo Alves is the only player who is a traditional striker – Domingos and João Pinto like to drop back, get involved in the build-up and run at defences from deep. Still, our strength is that we attack in numbers.' *World Soccer* magazine's tournament review opined that, 'While modern football demands gifted, mobile players, Portugal possessed too many in Rui Costa, Luís Figo and João Pinto. They were almost too mobile for their own good.'

Despite Portugal failure to qualify for the 1998 World Cup, expectations ran high ahead of Euro 2000, although the side's stars expressed similar concerns. 'We lack a true centre-forward,' complained Rui Costa. 'In Italy I notice so many excellent attacking players who can't get into the national team. But we, through nobody's fault, haven't even got one. It's a great shame. How many goals would a striker like Christian Vieri score if he had Figo and Sergio Conceição on the wings?' Midfielder Paulo Bento agreed: 'We create so many opportunities but get it wrong in front of goal. It's been the same formula for years, a problem with forwards. We pass ten times before we get the ball into a shooting position. We need a real striker.'

At Euro 2000 Portugal unexpectedly were able to field one of the competition's most prolific strikers. Nuno Gomes found himself in the starting XI at short notice when Ricardo Sá Pinto dropped out injured, and he scored four goals, including three in the knockout phase. He was so impressive that Fiorentina signed him to replace Roma-bound Gabriel Batistuta. But that goalscoring return was something of an anomaly for Nuno Gomes, who was useful rather than deadly. In the mould of many Portuguese strikers, his game was more about creating space for midfield runners.

'I'm a striker who has always looked at how Pippo Inzaghi moves, hoping to steal some of his secrets, even if I play in a different way, a lot further from the goal,' Nuno Gomes said. 'That's the way I help the team – and that's the most important aspect.' Inzaghi's movement made him a prolific poacher, but Nuno Gomes's movement was merely intended to disrupt defences. Peculiarly, 'Gomes' isn't actually part of his real name. He is Nuno Miguel Soares Pereira Ribeiro, and received the extra name in tribute to Fernando Gomes, an unusually prolific Portuguese striker who twice won the European Golden Shoe in the 1980s. Portugal were desperate to find a 'new Gomes', so they literally created one.

Nuno Gomes spent much of his Portugal career competing with Pauleta, who scored regularly during eight seasons in France and became Portugal's record goalscorer with 47 goals. Only four of these, however, came in major tournaments: a hat-trick against

Poland at the 2002 World Cup and the winner against Angola four years later, his final international strike. But while Portugal lacked a regular striker, they were producing several speedy, direct, two-footed attackers who could score. They simply all preferred playing out wide.

The obvious example was Luís Figo, the true superstar of Portugal's golden generation and the world's most revered player at the turn of the century. His transfer from Barcelona to arch-rivals Real Madrid in 2000 for a then world-record fee remains unequalled in modern times for the controversy it provoked, and he was later awarded that year's Ballon d'Or, the first Portuguese player to be crowned Europe's best player since Eusébio in 1965.

Figo grew up in Lisbon and joined Sporting at the age of 11, becoming the perfect template for the type of player the club would consistently produce over the next couple of decades. He was a true winger, capable of operating on either flank because he was gloriously two-footed and bamboozling opposition full-backs because of his ability to dribble past them on either side. Figo was tricky without trying tricks – he was focused, efficient and ruthless. 'He could do a thousand different things: go outside, go inside, he could pass the ball and go,' remembered Albert Ferrer, who played behind him on Barcelona's right flank. Iván Córdoba, a teammate at Inter, remembered something similar. 'He would change direction ten times when running at the full-back,' he laughed.

Rui Costa, the other symbol of the golden generation, said Figo was 'possibly the best winger I've ever seen, for his ability in one-on-one situations, his crossing. He wasn't a winger that just stayed wide, because he would come inside and create chances.' At Sporting and Barcelona, Figo was a classic winger in a 4–3–3, but drifted around more for Real Madrid when allowed positional freedom, and later played more centrally for Inter. Had Figo developed in a different environment, he might have become a number 10 or a speedy striker. But Sporting had a habit of producing wingers. Portugal's most talented player of the 1980s, Paulo Futre, was a wonderfully talented dribbler often compared to Maradona, but while he would latterly find himself playing as a number 10 in Italy and England, at Sporting he was developed into a winger. Figo, though, was on a different level. 'He was our Cristiano Ronaldo,' said Nuno Gomes.

A variety of factors were responsible for Sporting's tendency to specialise in wingers. The use of a 4–3–3 system throughout their academy certainly helped; Rinus Michels boasted that few countries produce 'true flank players' like the Netherlands and Ajax, but Portugal and Sporting are their obvious rivals in that respect, and the similarity in formation is difficult to ignore. There was also a fundamental belief in letting players express themselves, to demonstrate skills and attempt trickery at the Sporting academy, with wide players particularly indulged. 'We've always specialised in wingers here,' one of the academy's coaches, Miguel Miranda, told the *Guardian* in 2017. 'Coaches limit touches for central players, who are encouraged to spread the ball wide into wingers, who have unlimited touches to create chances from wide.' But equally important for the next generation of Sporting talent was the fact that Figo was their role model. Just as Thierry Henry created the template for future French forwards, Portuguese youngsters grew up wanting to wear number 7, rather than number 9, and become the new Figo.

After Figo left in 1995, the next talented winger out of Sporting's academy was Simão Sabrosa, a similar player who was capable of operating on either flank. He was less powerful but technically excellent, and particularly prolific from free-kicks. Such was the likeness, Simão replicated Figo's switch to Barca in 1999, then under the management of Louis van Gaal, who loved proper wingers. Simão, inevitably, found himself as Figo's understudy and omitted from matchday squads until Figo was out injured, at which point he started three games in a row. In 2000 Figo decamped to Real Madrid and Simão was expected to step up. He started 15 of Barca's first 17 games in the following campaign, and seemed to confirm his newfound seniority with the second goal in the 2–0 victory over Real in Figo's stormy return. But then Simão picked up an injury and never re-established himself in the first team again. In 2001 he returned to Lisbon, joining Sporting's rivals Benfica and thereby, albeit indirectly, crossing Portugal's greatest divide, just as Figo had done in Spain.

During this period Simão's game improved exponentially, particularly in terms of his goal return. During his second season back in Portugal Simão finished joint-top goalscorer in the Portuguese top flight with 18 goals, a remarkable total considering, for example, that Figo managed just 16 in his four complete seasons at Sporting combined. Now the club's captain, Simão had developed into the player Barcelona thought they were signing. In 2003/04 he denied José Mourinho's Porto a historic Treble by heading the winner in the Portuguese cup final, ending Benfica's eight-year silverware drought – an almost unthinkably disastrous period for Portugal's most successful club. Simão was now a true Benfica hero. Meanwhile, his former club Sporting had already produced another two incredibly exciting young wingers, and no one could decide which would enjoy the more successful career. On one flank, there was Ricardo Quaresma; on the other, Cristiano Ronaldo.

Quaresma and Ronaldo didn't get along. Although Quaresma was a year older than Ronaldo, the latter's prodigious talent meant they often played together for Sporting's U18 and B sides; reluctant to pass to one another, each attempted to outshine his rival with trickery. During their formative years, Quaresma and Ronaldo's approaches were almost identical: both were absolutely obsessed with quickfire stepovers, and their coaches regularly preached the importance of end product. 'From an early age I've heard criticism that I always try to do too much on my own,' a young Quaresma admitted. 'But I'm just playing my natural game. Ever since I was young I've loved inventing tricks with the ball.' Ronaldo said something similar: 'Dribbling and dodging is the way I play. I've played that way since I was little. I love dodging and feinting, getting past the opponent. I know that people get annoyed, but I'm not trying to make fun of my opponents. That's just my style.'

If anything it was Quaresma who offered more end product. Generally fielded on the right flank, Quaresma would use his stepovers to go down the line and whip crosses into the box with his right foot. When he found himself with a goalscoring opportunity he would hammer the ball towards goal with the outside of his right foot, often surprising goalkeepers with the dramatic swerve he achieved. This manner of striking the ball, known as the *trivela* in Portugal, would become Quaresma's trademark, and he would repeatedly attempt it throughout his career. 'The key thing to remember is to slice your foot through and under the outside of the ball,' he explained. 'So connecting with the bottom left-hand corner with your right foot. This will give it the right spin.'

Quaresma contributed heavily to Sporting's title victory in 2001/02, before Ronaldo had made his debut. At times he was unstoppable, scoring a brilliant long-range effort in a 5–1 thrashing of Salguerois in November. The following month he opened the scoring against Varzim in the first minute with a classic *trivela*, then assisted two goals for Mário Jardel with a right-footed cross and a left-footed cross before he dribbled down the outside, jumped over the left-back's tackle and squared for João Pinto to tap in – 4–0 before half-time. In a 4–1 thrashing of Leiria, Quaresma collected possession on the halfway line, attracted the attention of four defenders, dribbled to the corner of the box and then unleashed a brilliant shot that hit the crossbar, rebounded onto the post and bounced in. But he was primarily about assists, and contributed heavily to Jardel's ludicrous tally of 42 goals in 30 league games.

Quaresma also focused on enjoying himself, and he was briefly nicknamed 'The Harry Potter of the Alvalade', Sporting's stadium. There was no doubt about his idol. 'I really admire Luís Figo, because he started out at Sporting with the youth team,' Quaresma said. 'Then he went to Barcelona, achieved what he did there, and then went to Real Madrid. That inspired me to follow in his footsteps.' That's precisely what happened; just like Figo in 1995 and Simão in 1999, Quaresma kept the four-year cycle going by leaving Sporting for Barcelona in 2003, after a slightly underwhelming second season in the Portuguese top flight. Barca could also have signed Sporting's other young winger that summer, but instead tried to negotiate a pre-contract agreement – and therefore missed out on Ronaldo.

While Figo and Quaresma grew up in Lisbon, Ronaldo's decision to join Sporting's academy was somewhat more complex. He was from the island of Madeira, playing for Nacional, but at the age of 12 was invited on a trial by Sporting, who subsequently asked him to join their youth system. 'When I was a kid, Figo was my hero, so it was wonderful to be able to play for his old club,' said Ronaldo, who inherited his affection for Figo and Sporting from his mother rather than his father, who supported Benfica. But joining Sporting meant moving 600 miles across the Atlantic just as he was entering his teen-age years, and while Ronaldo was technically moving within his home country, the similarity to Leo Messi's experience is obvious. While Messi benefited from relocating with his family, Ronaldo was alone in Lisbon, and, like Messi, was mocked by his new teammates because of his unusual accent. He was also nicknamed 'The Noodle' because of his thin frame and was frequently criticised for being too selfish in possession. Nevertheless, his rise was remarkable, and he became the first player to play for Sporting's U16, U17, U18, reserves and first-team sides in the same year.

But there remained major concerns about his all-round game. In 2002, the year of his senior debut, Sporting's first-team coach László Bölöni compiled a progress report on Ronaldo. According to Guillem Balague's biography, Bölöni noted that Ronaldo's aerial game was poor, he didn't work hard enough to improve his technique, his defensive discipline was questionable, he wasn't strong enough, he was selfish and lacked mental strength, and had 'no tactical awareness as an individual or a team player'. Considering these issues, he hasn't done badly. Despite these reservations, Bölöni introduced him to the first team, and at the start of 2002/03 announced to the Portuguese press that Ronaldo 'will be better than Eusébio and Figo', Portugal's two Ballon d'Or winners. It was quite the claim.

Ronaldo debuted in October 2002 against Moreirense, scoring twice. His first goal was a direct dribble from the halfway line, during which he rode a cynical challenge, threw a stepover with his left foot to tease the last defender before bypassing him onto his right foot and dinking over the goalkeeper. It was an outstanding debut goal. The second was a close-range header. Ronaldo only made another ten starts that season, managing one more goal. But his potential was obvious, and like Quaresma he produced some amazing moments of trickery.

The interesting aspect of Ronaldo's development at Sporting, however, is that throughout his youth-team days he was often deployed as a centre-forward or a second striker, rather than as a pure winger, and Jose Mourinho compared him to a classic goalscorer. 'The first time I saw him, I thought, "That's the son of Marco Van Basten." He was a striker, but a very elegant player.' When Sir Alex Ferguson sent one of his assistants, Jim Ryan, to scout Ronaldo in Portugal, the resulting report read, 'I think he's a winger, but he's playing as a central striker in the youth team.' Arsenal were also in negotiations to sign Ronaldo, and Arsène Wenger had promised him the club's number 9 shirt.

It was Manchester United, however, who were victorious in the battle to sign Ronaldo, something that can be attributed to both the existing Portuguese connection at the club, and, indirectly, to Portugal's hosting of Euro 2004. The previous summer, Ferguson had appointed Carlos Queiroz as his assistant manager, and he was aware of Ronaldo. Queiroz also knew of Sporting's reputation for producing young talent, advising Ferguson to sign both Ronaldo and Quaresma, and formulating an informal agreement between Sporting and United, based on sharing youth-coaching expertise. Sporting, meanwhile, wanted a big club to play at the inauguration of their new stadium, built ahead of Euro 2004, and therefore as part of the deal United travelled to Lisbon in summer 2003. They were exhausted from a draining pre-season tour of the USA, and had a Community Shield clash with Arsenal three days later. The trip was something of an inconvenience, useful neither in terms of commercial revenue nor fitness. But the game proved crucial in regard to Ronaldo's future.

In Sporting's first match at the Estádio José Alvalade, Ronaldo played his last match in their colours. He was sensational against United, starting wide-left and repeatedly beating John O'Shea with a series of stepovers before going down the outside, or checking inside and shooting with his right foot. When O'Shea stood off, Ronaldo picked up speed and breezed past him. When O'Shea stuck tight, he ended up fouling Ronaldo. After the break Ronaldo showed his versatility by switching to the right and running in behind, and United couldn't stop him on that flank either.

After the game United's players implored Ferguson to sign Ronaldo, and five days later the deal was complete. 'We have been negotiating for Cristiano for quite some time, but the interest in him from other clubs accelerated in the last few weeks so we had to move quickly to get him,' Ferguson said. 'It was only through our association with Sporting that they honoured our agreement of months ago,' he added. When Ronaldo was introduced to O'Shea at United's training ground, the Irishman joked that he deserved a share of the signing-on fee, as his inability to cope with the winger convinced United to act fast.

Upon Ronaldo's unveiling, Ferguson also speculated about Ronaldo's position at United. 'He's an extremely talented footballer, a two-footed attacker who can play anywhere up front: right, left or through the middle,' he said. 'He's one of the most exciting young players I've ever seen.' In a half-hour cameo appearance on debut against Bolton on the opening day of the season, Ronaldo was again phenomenal. He started on the left, bamboozled right-back Nicky Hunt and won a penalty off Kevin Nolan, before once again switching to the right and getting Ricardo Gardner booked for a frustrated late tackle. He was already a fan favourite. Four days later he made his international debut – fittingly, introduced as a substitute in place of Luís Figo. 'Keep calm, and play the way you do for your club,' was Figo's advice.

'Of all the players I coached while at Portugal, there was one that was especially important for Cristiano Ronaldo. That was Luís Figo,' Luiz Felipe Scolari later recalled. 'When Ronaldo started with the national team, the first one to help him was Figo. He was the first player to challenge Ronaldo to dribble and shoot, to score goals, to play his own game, to keep working all the time and become a better footballer.'

Ronaldo's initial progress at United was disappointing. He looked underdeveloped physically and became a figure of fun because of his obsession with tricks, routinely throwing his leg over the ball two or three times every time he dribbled towards the opposition full-back.

He regularly played *rabona* crosses by swinging his right foot behind his left leg. He would sometimes pass the ball to an overlapping right-back by backheeling the ball against his other foot, rebounding perfectly into his teammate's path, or receive the ball on the touch-line and toy with full-backs, rolling his studs over the top of the ball with one foot, while performing more stepovers with the other.

Of course, Premier League full-backs responded to this showboating by booting him up in the air, as did his teammates in training. 'When he came over here, his first thought was to entertain,' said Rio Ferdinand. 'We wanted to win. We knew that if he had an end product, we had a far better chance of being successful. For want of a better word, we were kicking it out of him, the entertainment factor, to get us goals and assists.' Ronaldo managed only four league goals in his first season, although he also headed the opener in the FA Cup Final victory over Millwall. His two goals at that summer's European Championship on home soil were also both headers. Quaresma, meanwhile, endured a disappointing sole season at Barcelona, managing only one goal. Lke Simão before him, Quaresma returned to Portugal, moving to Porto as part of the deal that took Deco to the Camp Nou.

In 2004/05, Ronaldo continued on Manchester United's right flank and scored five goals in all competitions, including two in a memorable 4–2 victory at Arsenal. In 2005/06 he scored nine times, yet he was still very inconsistent: he started the season with one goal in 15 games, then scored seven in seven, then went 11 matches without scoring before netting on the final day, a 4–0 victory over Charlton. That game proved significant; Sir Alex Ferguson omitted a furious Ruud van Nistelrooy from the matchday squad, and he never played again for United. The Dutch poacher, who had dominated United's attack for the previous five seasons, had also constantly squabbled with Ronaldo, repeatedly barracking him for not crossing enough.

Having impressed throughout qualification, Ronaldo's 2006 World Cup was slightly underwhelming. He usually played from the left, with Figo on the right – although, as always, the Portuguese wingers swapped flanks. His contribution to the knockout stage was hampered by injury, after a truly dreadful tackle in the second-round victory over Holland. Right-back Khalid Boulahrouz, nicknamed 'The Cannibal', put an early reducer on Ronaldo with an extremely high challenge, thrusting his studs against Ronaldo's thigh when battling for a bouncing ball. It should have brought a red card, and set the tone for the rest of the famously violent contest.

Ronaldo's tournament was most memorable for his reaction after his Manchester United teammate Wayne Rooney stamped on Ricardo Carvalho as they tangled for the ball. Ronaldo raced over to the referee to draw attention to Rooney's transgression and was caught winking towards the dugout after Rooney was sent off. Ronaldo was now regarded as the devil by the English press, who blamed him for the red card. Ronaldo and Rooney smoothed things over after the game, but the situation became so serious that Ronaldo stated his intention to leave Manchester United. But Ferguson and Queiroz, in particular, convinced him to stay, and this summer proved the making of Ronaldo. At international level, Figo's retirement meant he was now Portugal's key attacker, and he soon inherited the captaincy too. At club level, Van Nistelrooy's departure meant he was now United's most important attacker.

He returned to the Premier League for 2006/07 a completely different beast. 'I remember when he came back from the 2006 World Cup after all that controversy with the Wayne Rooney red card,' Gary Neville recalled. 'He walked into the dressing room and I thought: "Jeez, what has happened to him over the summer?" When he had come to the club he was this thin, wiry boy. Now he was a light heavyweight. He'd been on the weights over the summer and it was like watching someone grow up in a matter of weeks. What ensued for the next two years was astonishing.'

Without Van Nistelrooy, Ronaldo and Rooney dominated a Manchester United side based around counter-attacking speed. Queiroz, who had set the template for Portuguese football with his strikerless approach, exerted a major influence over United's tactics, and Ferguson didn't attempt to sign a replacement for Van Nistelrooy. Now it was about multiple attackers bursting forward in turn, with Ronaldo the star.

He had completely changed his approach, and was obsessed with goalscoring. The only noticeable trick he retained was his 'chop', where he dribbled on the outside of the left-back before suddenly jumping and backheeling the ball behind his other leg, surprising his opponent with his change of direction and allowing him to cut inside towards goal. He'd also learned the physical side of the game. In a trip to Blackburn Rovers, which United won 1–0, the home fans started by booing Ronaldo for his World Cup antics. Then he was poleaxed by a dreadful tackle from Sergio Peter, but rather than exaggerating his pain and trying to get his opponent dismissed, Ronaldo picked himself up and played on, the same fans giving him a standing ovation on his substitution. He was more driven, more focused, more efficient and more prolific. He also spent more time on the left flank, cutting inside to shoot with his right foot, such as his memorable solo effort for the 88th-minute winner at Fulham, and he regularly arrived late at the back post to head home. Suddenly Ronaldo was the complete attacker, and he was voted the Premier League's Player of the Year. Having managed 18 goals in his first three Premier League campaigns combined, he now bagged 17 in a single season.

Yet Ronaldo continued to improve, and his 2007/08 campaign was possibly the best individual campaign the Premier League has ever witnessed. Manchester United coach René Meulensteen had challenged him to reach 40 goals for the season in all competitions and spent hours with Ronaldo on the training ground, encouraging him to score scrappier efforts, rather than always looking to score the perfect goal. Together they worked on visualisation techniques that involved drawing diagrams, splitting the goal into different sections and assigning colours to each corner of the net. Generally, when players are asked about their approach in front of goal, they deliver a stock answer along the lines of, 'There's no real trick, you just have to remain calm and focused.' But when Ronaldo was asked, he said something entirely different: 'My goalscoring technique is a secret I'll never divulge.'

In 2007/08 Ronaldo's position was impossible to define, although he now rarely started on the right because he loved cutting inside and shooting with his right foot. But Ferguson increasingly deployed him up front. The most memorable example came in a famous 2–0 victory away at Roma, where Ronaldo was tasked with continually running in behind the opposition, stretching the play as United countered quickly. He opened the scoring with a towering header, when Paul Scholes clipped the ball into the box from the right, and Ronaldo, starting his run from well outside the penalty box, sprinted forward, soared into the air and powered a downward header into the bottom corner. This was the single moment that confirmed Ronaldo's ability to become a proper centre-forward, and probably confirmed his status as the world's best player too.

In keeping with Queiroz's long-standing beliefs, sometimes United played without a forward, and sometimes they appeared to have three, with Rooney and Carlos Tevez in support. Ronaldo effectively played wherever he wanted in an ultra-fluid United system. If the opposition's left-back was poor defensively, he'd play down the right; if the centre-backs were slow, he'd play through the middle. For the 2008 Champions League Final in Moscow, Ferguson suspected that

Chelsea's makeshift right-back Michael Essien was vulnerable in the air. So Ronaldo, having been used up front in the two-legged semi-final win over Barcelona, was now on the left – and, sure enough, he opened the scoring by outjumping Essien and producing another towering header. Ronaldo missed his penalty in the shoot-out, but United recovered to triumph. In 2007/08, Ronaldo won the Champions League, European Player of the Year and the European Golden Shoe. The final award was probably the most significant for Portuguese football, indicating that their lack of a traditional number 9 was of little concern.

One of the Manchester United players who successfully converted their spot-kick in Moscow, incidentally, was Nani. He grew up playing on the streets of Lisbon, and was snapped up by Sporting. There he developed into yet another outstanding winger, like Figo, like Simão, like Quaresma, like Ronaldo. After following in Ronaldo's footsteps from Sporting to Manchester United in 2007 he suffered from one of Ronaldo's previous 'problems': he showboated excessively. In United's 4–0 thrashing of Arsenal in February 2008, Nani infuriated several opponents by performing a 'seal dribble', juggling the ball with his head while running towards his own goal, away from opponents. 'We were incensed and most rightly so,' complained Arsène Wenger. 'It is difficult enough to swallow when you are three or four goals down. You do not want to be teased or humiliated.'

'In Portugal I have done this many times, but it is only because it is an entertaining spectacle and not because I disrespect my rivals,' Nani responded, while confessing that his manager, somewhat unusually, agreed with Wenger. 'I am a professional and am always very respectful with all the opposing players, but I do appreciate now that it may have looked bad. After the match the manager spoke to me and demanded that I do not repeat it.' Nani clearly modelled himself on Ronaldo, with whom he lived during his first year at

Manchester United, but it was only after Ronaldo's departure that Nani fulfilled his potential, and he enjoyed a particularly impressive 2010. He was arguably the most two-footed of all these Portuguese wingers. Generally playing from the right, he could cross expertly with his right foot, or cut inside and shoot powerfully with his left.

Figo continued to shine after his international retirement in 2006. He moved to Inter, with whom he won four straight Serie A titles – the last coming under José Mourinho – until he retired in 2009. His successor in Inter's number 7 shirt was a familiar face: Quaresma, whom Mourinho never truly appreciated because of his lack of defensive work. 'I am sure he'll change and become more tactically disciplined,' Mourinho said in Quaresma's early days. 'Right now he likes kicking the ball with the outside of his foot.' He never truly improved his tactical discipline, and he certainly never stopped kicking the ball with the outside of his foot.

Before joining Inter, Quaresma enjoyed a return to form at Porto and had regained his place in the Portugal squad. His first goal for the national side was classic Quaresma, coming in March 2007 in a 4–0 victory over Belgium in qualification for the 2008 Euros. Wide on the right flank, he received a pass from Ronaldo, chopped his way inside to the edge of the box before producing an extravagant, outside-of-the-boot *trivela* that curved majestically into the far corner, a goal that he reproduced with his stunning strike in the 2018 World Cup group-phase match against Iran.

In a world of inverted wingers like Ronaldo, who now favoured the left flank because it allowed him to cut inside and shoot, Quaresma was almost an inverted-inverted winger, a right-footer whose insistence on using the outside of his foot meant he was more of a goal threat from the right, and more of a crossing threat from the left, making him almost unique in the modern game. While never succeeding in a major league, flopping with both Barca and Inter,

Quaresma remains a cult hero in Portugal and Turkey, the two countries where he has spent the majority of his career.

Among all these talented wingers, Portugal never managed to improve their production of proper centre-forwards. Between Euro 2008 and the 2014 World Cup they relied on either Hugo Almeida, a tall, physical centre-forward who was used in the expectation that he'd hold up the ball and create goalscoring chances for Ronaldo, or Hélder Postiga, a more mobile player in his younger days but increasingly a static decoy option too. Neither player scored regularly, while Liédson's stint with the national side was brief, in part because he preferred to run in behind and didn't combine well with Ronaldo.

Fast-forward to Euro 2016, by which point Ronaldo had scored over 350 goals in seven seasons with Real Madrid and was really a forward rather than a winger, while Nani and Quaresma were playing in Turkey for Fenerbahçe and Beşiktaş respectively. After decades during which Portugal had played 4–3–3 or 4–2–3–1 with two speedy wingers and a non-goalscoring striker, manager Fernando Santos made a major decision – he simply wasn't going to bother with a pure striker anymore, instead deploying an extra central midfielder, with Ronaldo and Nani playing up front together. Ronaldo cut inside from the right, Nani cut inside from the left, in a system that was essentially a fluid version of a 4–4–2 with a diamond midfield. On one occasion Santos reverted to 4–3–3, for the goalless draw against Austria in the group phase, with Quaresma joining his fellow ex-Sporting wingers, although this system was soon ditched and Quaresma returned to his customary role on the bench.

After Portugal scraped through their group with three draws, they defeated Croatia 1–0 in extra-time with a 116th-minute goal. It featured their three wingers, after Quaresma had been introduced in place of midfielder João Mário. Nani received the ball on the left flank, toe-punted a low ball across the box for Ronaldo, whose shot was saved, which allowed Quaresma to nod the rebound into an empty net. After squeezing past Poland on penalties, Portugal defeated Wales 2–0 in the semi-final, with a Ronaldo header from a corner, and then a Nani goal as he diverted Ronaldo's scuffed shot over the line.

In the final, Portugal finally won their first-ever tournament, avenging the disaster of the Euro 2004 Final in Lisbon by defeating France in Paris. Ronaldo, sadly, limped out of the match early, to be replaced by his old Sporting teammate and rival Quaresma, who played up front alongside Nani. For extra-time, however, Santos introduced a proper striker, Guinea-Bissau-born Eder. He'd played just 13 minutes in the tournament, was coming off a poor campaign at club level and had never scored a competitive goal for Portugal. But somehow he scored the winner, receiving the ball with his back to goal, then turning and firing a low, long-range drive into the net. It was entirely unexpected, and entirely out of keeping with the story of Portugal's style over the past couple of decades. Ronaldo, meanwhile, was limping up and down the technical area, shouting more instructions than Santos.

But Eder, of course, had only been Portugal's Plan C. Portugal didn't use a proper centre-forward from the outset, and when Ronaldo limped off injured it was Quaresma who was considered his natural replacement. Santos had placed his faith in Ronaldo, Nani and Quaresma, the three products of Sporting's academy, the most prolific birthplace of wingers anywhere in Europe. Their development owed much to the inspiration provided by Figo, and Portugal's tactical approach was partly the result of Queiroz's doctrine 25 years beforehand.

By this point it was increasingly common to see the likes of Spain and Germany playing without a proper goalscoring centre-forward in an attempt to surprise the opposition with the speed and mobility of multiple attackers. But it was Portugal who had originally championed this approach, and it was only right that – eventually – they had their moment of glory.

# Transition:
# Portugal–Spain

In summer 2008, after a long and difficult campaign, Barcelona parted ways with manager Frank Rijkaard. Barca were evidently at the end of an era, lacking the tactical discipline of Europe's elite sides and reliant on a couple of ageing superstars. However, with a talented squad and a host of promising youth products on the verge of a breakthrough, managing Barca was an extremely coveted job, and their next appointment would be the most significant in modern European football.

Eventually, Barcelona's board decided to appoint the man who had previously been coaching the club's B team, Pep Guardiola. Equally significant, however, was who they didn't appoint, José Mourinho, which was briefly a distinct possibility. Mourinho had left Chelsea early in 2007/08, and with Barca struggling under Rijkaard, he met with vice-president Marc Ingla and sporting director Txiki Begiristain in Lisbon, delivering a PowerPoint presentation explaining how he'd reformat Barcelona, as part of a three-hour pitch for the job.

Mourinho made a strong case, and was an outstanding candidate; he had created two highly successful sides at Porto and Chelsea, had previously worked at Barca under Bobby Robson and Louis van Gaal, and favoured the 4–3–3 system that was fundamental to the club's approach. Mourinho promised to adapt his methods and play more expansive football, and even suggested having Guardiola – with whom he'd enjoyed working at Barca – as his assistant.

But Johan Cruyff raised concerns about Mourinho's defensive mindset, Begiristain thought his aggressive attitude in press conferences would cause problems, while Ingla simply said he didn't like him. Barcelona therefore turned down Europe's most revered coach and instead plumped for the entirely inexperienced Guardiola, a novice who had been considered a mere potential assistant by Mourinho and who possessed just a year's experience in the fourth tier. It was a snub from which Mourinho would never recover, and a decision that shaped the next four years of European football.

Barcelona had not opted for Portuguese, but for Spanish. Or, as they would prefer to consider it, Catalan. Guardiola was a home-grown Barcelona boy who would initially concentrate on restoring the philosophy of Johan Cruyff, and then would evolve Barcelona and become the most innovative tactician Europe had witnessed in many years. He would stay at the Camp Nou for four years, winning three La Liga titles and two Champions Leagues.

This four-year period also coincided with Spain's dominance of international football. Following a long spell during which they were regarded as Europe's greatest underachievers, they became the first side to win three consecutive major international tournaments: Euro 2008, the 2010 World Cup and Euro 2012.

Spain's ascendancy transformed the European game. After an era in which top-level football was predominantly defensive, counter-attacking and played with relatively little regard for technique and entertainment, Barcelona and Spain completely reversed that trend. Suddenly, football seemingly became a battle to see who could dominate possession, and the Spanish approach spread across the continent.

This Spanish success popularised the use of slightly built, technically gifted footballers. Spain produced a huge number of playmakers, to the extent that they started deploying them up front too, which changed perceptions about the nature of centre-forwards. Meanwhile, the country's ultimate showpiece game, *El Clásico* between Barca and Real Madrid, became more intense than ever – particularly after Mourinho was appointed as Real's manager in 2010, prompting a two-year war between him and Guardiola.

By virtue of achievements at both club and international level, and because of the presence of the modern era's greatest two footballers, Leo Messi and Cristiano Ronaldo, there has never been a period quite like that in Spanish football between 2008 and 2012. It was an incredible four-year spell, one that had an unparalleled impact on the rest of the continent.

Part Five

# Fútbol, 2008–12

## 13

# Tiki-taka

On one hand, Pep Guardiola cannot take responsibility for the advent of Spanish football's possession-based dominance, because by the time he took charge of his first Barcelona game in August 2008, the ball was already rolling. Spain's Euro 2008 triumph meant neutrals were already drooling over the mesmeric passing combinations orchestrated by Xavi Hernández and Andrés Iniesta, the two pillars of this era.

On the other hand, Guardiola's influence was already considerable. When Xavi and Iniesta rose through La Masia, Barcelona's academy, they were instructed to watch and learn from Barcelona's number 4, the slow, slight but supremely intelligent Guardiola. Despite the presence of so many superstars at the Camp Nou throughout the 1990s, no other footballer was so inextricably associated with the 'Barcelona way'. He was the role model for Barça's next generation, and therefore when appointed manager in 2008 Guardiola inherited a generation of midfielders who had been taught to play like him.

As a teenager, Guardiola had been plucked from Barcelona's reserve side and chucked into the first team by Johan Cruyff, who insisted on a methodical playmaker, rather than a defensive ball-winner, at the base of midfield. Guardiola was defined by his conservative positioning and his calm, understated distribution. 'My job was to move the ball around for my teammates to finish off,' he modestly explained. He was Cruyff's on-field leader, the player who received instructions from the dugout and dictated Barcelona's play, while Louis van Gaal marvelled about how, even as a player, Guardiola 'could speak like a coach'. Yet, partly because of these qualities, Guardiola was always regarded as a mysterious figure who over-analysed performances and distanced himself from teammates. He spoke about his interest in politics and poetry, and was therefore considered something of an outsider.

Guardiola's departure from Barcelona in 2001 at the age of just 30 effectively marked the end of his top-level playing career. He enjoyed a brief spell in Qatar, presumably to boost his pension pot, but also played in Serie A for Brescia and Roma, then in Mexico. These experiences were largely preparation for his coaching career. In Rome, Guardiola learned about defensive positioning from Fabio Capello, and in Mexico played under Juanma Lillo, a cult figure who is sometimes regarded as the inventor of the 4–2–3–1 formation, and is an inspiration for many Spanish coaches.

It was a curious way for this highly esteemed player to finish his career, but at this point Guardiola had few options. Despite being such an experienced, successful and influential footballer, deep-lying playmakers simply weren't valued during the mid-2000s. 'I think players like me have become extinct because the game has become more tactical and physical,' he told *The Times* in 2004. 'At most clubs, players are given specific roles and creativity can only exist within those parameters. I haven't changed, my skills haven't declined. It's just that football has changed, it's a lot more physical. To play in front of the defence right now, you have to be a ball-winner. If I were a 20-year-old at Barcelona, I'd never make it.' Guardiola's mission was to reverse that trend, and his incredible success at Barcelona was achieved thanks to three midfielders in his mould.

During Spain's period of dominance, possession football was epitomised by Xavi, a physically unspectacular footballer who played straightforward passes, but boasted the sharpest footballing mind of his generation and an unparalleled ability to understand every facet of the tactical battle unfolding around him, positioning himself to drag opponents out of position before prodding the ball past them. Xavi was, like Guardiola, a proud Catalan, a complete football obsessive, a relentless analyst and an ideologue in regard to possession play. His nickname at Barcelona was 'The Machine', a phrase used in other countries to highlight physical attributes, but in Xavi's case referring to his brain. 'I am, basically, a passer,' he said. 'I get the ball, I pass the ball. I get the ball, I pass the ball. I get the ball, I pass the ball.' And repeat.

Xavi was always a talented midfielder, but he struggled to impose himself in Barcelona's first team at the turn of the millennium, for one major reason: Guardiola. Xavi's debut in 1998 was greeted with praise from his then-teammate and future manager, who complimented his awareness and maturity, before nervously adding that he wasn't quite ready to give up his place. Van Gaal repeatedly compared the two, and Xavi only established himself after Guardiola's departure. 'The lucky break came for me when Pep left,' Xavi later admitted. 'As a player, I needed him to go – but then I loved it when he returned as manager.'

By the time Guardiola took charge, Xavi had already been shifted into a more advanced position, the right-centre-midfield role in Barcelona's 4–3–3. But in those early days, Barcelona were so obsessed with Xavi being Guardiola's replacement that he was repeatedly fielded in the holding role. 'Until Frank Rijkaard arrived, I was a "pivot" for six or seven years,' Xavi explained. 'They asked me to get up and down, and provide assists, but it's difficult from that position. Ten or 15 metres further up the pitch makes it much easier for me.' Indeed, Rijkaard had a difficult job convincing Xavi of this positional switch, after he'd spent his teenage years being typecast as 'a pivot', 'a number 4', or, more simply, 'a Guardiola'.

Even more revealing is the development of his long-time teammate Iniesta, who was naturally a very different player. He offered something extra – the change of speed to escape challenges, particularly when combined with his trademark *croqueta*, rapidly playing the ball from one foot against the other to slalom past opposition challenges. Iniesta was therefore capable of playing in tighter spaces in more advanced positions, but at La Masia he was fielded in the deepest midfield role, such was Barça's obsession with turning creative midfielders into Guardiola clones. Iniesta's father believes this positional deployment hampered his son. 'When he was little he scored lots of goals,' José Antonio said. 'He always dribbled well; he would see the move a second before everyone else and he accelerated quickly. He got in the box too. At youth team level he could do everything, he had it all … but everything changed when he got to Barça B at 16 and they made him play as a number 4. A deep midfielder, like Guardiola, Luis Milla, Xavi, Albert Celades, Iván de la Peña … that distanced him from goal. I remembered people telling him he was the new Guardiola. They made him play in a manner that didn't entirely suit his characteristics.'

Iniesta's first direct contact with Guardiola was at the Nike Cup, effectively an U15 club world championships that Barcelona won at the Camp Nou. In the final, Iniesta assisted the equaliser, then scored the winner and was later presented with the trophy by Guardiola, who told him, 'In ten years' time, I'll be watching you play here every week.' Later, Barça's B team coach, Josep Maria Gonzalvo, realised that Iniesta looked more comfortable in an advanced role and pushed him forward, only for Lorenzo Serra Ferrer, Barca's coach in 2000/01, to instruct Iniesta to model himself on Guardiola again. During this period, when other top European clubs demanded strength and tackling from deep midfielders, Barcelona was the only club in which Iniesta would have been considered in that position, and he was regularly deployed there in his formative first-team years. In a 2–0 victory over Benfica in the 2006 Champions League quarter-finals, for example, a 21-year old Iniesta played the Guardiola role, with the tough-tackling Mark van Bommel fielded in the left-centre position Iniesta coveted.

Another promising La Masia graduate was Cesc Fàbregas. Playing in the same Barca youth side as Gerard Piqué and Lionel Messi, Fàbregas was another capable of playing higher up the pitch, yet was generally fielded in the number 4 role at La Masia. 'Guardiola has always been my idol since childhood,' he said. Fàbregas, like Iniesta, also enjoyed personal encouragement from Guardiola. Aged 13, and suffering from personal problems because his parents had separated, Fàbregas was presented with a signed number 4 shirt by a Barcelona youth coach, with the message, 'To Francesc Fàbregas. Waiting a couple of years to see you wear the number 4 shirt at Camp Nou. Good luck, Pep Guardiola.' Upon realising the level of competition for a central midfield slot at Barcelona, Fàbregas departed for Arsenal, where he was initially viewed in the Guardiola mould, but was increasingly pushed forward to become an attacking midfielder. Again, only Barcelona would have considered deploying that type of footballer in front of the defence.

Finally, there was the most literal Guardiola clone of all, Sergio Busquets. A tall and commanding player, he was naturally suited to protecting the defence despite playing up front in his younger days. Although Busquets only joined Barca at 16, long after Guardiola had departed as a player, his dad Carles was one of Cruyff's sweeper-keepers in the Dream Team days, and Busquets had therefore been schooled in the Barca way. Busquets was also the first of this quartet to play under Guardiola, for Barca's B team in 2007/08, the season before Guardiola was promoted to the top job. Xavi, Iniesta and Fàbregas incorporated the Guardiola influence into more advanced roles, but Busquets simply played the classic Guardiola role. 'If I could come back and play as any player, it would be Sergio Busquets,' said the man himself. Therefore, both the Spanish national side from 2009, when Busquets made his international debut, and Barcelona from 2011, when Fàbregas returned, would often deploy four players who had modelled themselves on Guardiola. His impact on Spanish football was enormous, before even considering his impact as a coach.

At Euro 2008, prior to Busquets' involvement, Xavi, Iniesta and Fàbregas featured alongside other hugely talented playmakers: Liverpool's deep-lying passer Xabi Alonso, renowned for his long diagonal passes, Valencia's David Silva, a quick-witted between-the-lines creator, and Villarreal's Santi Cazorla, an elusive, two-footed player in the Iniesta mould. Both Alonso and Silva, incidentally, would peak many years later with Bayern Munich and Manchester City respectively, the former adding penetrative, line-breaking passes to his armoury and the latter operating slightly deeper and dictating play. On both occasions their manager was Guardiola.

Spain's array of playmakers was widely remarked on even before Euro 2008, simply because it was so unusual. Germany hadn't yet undergone their stylistic revolution and France eschewed genuine creators. There were some playmakers in the tournament – Portugal's Deco, Holland's Wesley Sneijder, Italy's Andrea Pirlo – but they were largely supported by foot-soldiers, whereas Spain won the final with Xavi, Iniesta, Fàbregas and Silva together, with naturalized Brazilian Marcos Senna protecting the defence. Beforehand, the term 'tiki-taka' had already been used to describe Spain's style, as had '*jugones*', essentially meaning 'playmakers', revealing the extent to which Spain were now football's technical leaders. Although doubts still remained about their ability to convert raw talent into success, these would not last for long.

The most surprising aspect of Spain's evolution into pass masters at Euro 2008 was the identity of their coach, the seemingly anti-quated Luis Aragonés, renowned as a defensive tactician. The 69-year-old's only La Liga triumph had arrived fully 31 years earlier with a physical Atlético Madrid side depicted as 1–3–1–3–2, with a sweeper behind the defence and a defensive midfielder ahead of it. His Barcelona reign in 1987/88, just before the arrival of Johan Cruyff, featured technical players, but he'd subsequently reverted to less attractive football, often with impressive results, taking Valencia to second place in 1995/96 and unfancied Mallorca to third in 2000/01 through counter-attacking.

Most significant was Aragonés's 1998 rant about Spain's shift away from the style of '*La Furia Roja*' ('The Red Fury'), as the national team was once known. 'Every country has its way of living football and that is the way to act,' he said. 'Italy has won three World Cups with *catenaccio*, the Argentines and Brazilians never waver from their football idiosyncrasies. Spain has ours too. Spanish football has never been exquisite and we should not try to go against our DNA. *La Furia* was not just a nickname, it was not used to sell tickets, it's a philosophy that the national team needs to recapture. We have dedi-cated ourselves to this idea that we all need to be brilliant on the ball, but no, we are not that kind of a football team. Right now, we have a crop of 10 or 12 players who have a terrific touch on the ball, but they can't all play together.'

However, when appointed Spain manager and presented with so many classy playmakers, Aragonés crammed them all together to produce some wonderful performances at Euro 2008, an overwhelmingly positive, attack-minded tournament. 'It was,' *World Soccer* editor Gavin Hamilton wrote in his post-tournament analysis, 'as if Euro 2004 had never happened.'

Aragonés's Spain played a modification of 4–4–2. With Senna sitting deep and David Villa dropping off Fernando Torres, it was more strictly 4–1–3–1–1, and that trio of Iniesta, Xavi and Silva were crucial, with Aragonés sacrificing width to deploy three playmakers together. Nevertheless, Spain's progress wasn't entirely about tiki-taka – at least, not as it would later be understood. Their opening goal of the tournament, in a 4–1 victory over Russia, was remarkably direct; when left-back Joan Capdevila intercepted a pass midway inside his own half, Spain had no players in central-midfield positions – there was a gaping 40-yard space in the middle of the pitch. Capdevila therefore thumped the ball downfield for Torres, who outwitted the last defender and knocked the ball past the goalkeeper for David Villa to roll into an empty net. Spain had bypassed midfield completely. Spain's second goal was a counter-attack, rounded off by Villa, with Capdevila once more the catalyst, his powerful dribble swiftly turning defence into attack. Villa completed his hat-trick on 75 minutes after a more typical slick passing move, then Fàbregas wrapped up the scoring with a close-range diving header after a quick break. 'We like to counter-attack,' said Aragonés afterwards. But in later years, counter-attack would be considered the antithesis of the Spanish style.

Spain won their second group game 2–1, against Sweden. After Torres converted in the aftermath of a set-piece, their stoppage-time winner came from another direct Capdevila pass: his 50-yard ball was intended for Torres but ran through to Villa, who tucked the ball home. It wasn't quite Route One, but it wasn't tiki-taka either. After a 2–1 victory over Greece with a heavily rotated side, Spain overcame

Italy in the quarter-finals, but only on penalties after a frustrating goalless draw. Spain were superior but far from fluent against an Italy side lacking their suspended midfield duo of Andrea Pirlo and Rino Gattuso.

Spain defeated Russia 3–0 in the semi-final, but this time Aragonés complained about the lack of tiki-taka. 'We started playing the kind of football that Russia like – long passes,' he moaned. But after a poor opening 15 minutes, Spain started playing proper possession football. All three goals came in the second half, and it was becoming clear that Spain's possession play was exhausting opponents. Their semi-final performance was particularly attack-minded; when Iniesta teed up Xavi for his volleyed opener, Spain had five players in the box, and they eventually recorded 11 shots on target. Silva and substitute Dani Güiza completed the scoring, both converting passes from Fàbregas, whose contribution to Spain's treble success is often overlooked.

Spain completely outplayed Germany in the final, creating a succession of chances and scoring the winner after half an hour through Torres, who latched on to Xavi's through-ball and dinked home. Ten minutes from time, Senna – the man protecting the defence to allow others forward – dribbled past two challenges, played a forward pass and stormed into the box for the return ball, and was inches away from making it 2–0. This was Spain's holding midfielder, desperately attempting to increase the margin of victory. Xabi Alonso, theoretically introduced to provide extra midfield discipline, went on a similarly ambitious run in stoppage-time. Spain's tiki-taka was combined with all-out-attack.

'I think all football lovers want people to make good combinations, to get into the penalty area and to score goals,' said Aragonés, taking charge of his final game as Spain coach. The 69-year-old, having spent his career renowned – or derided – as a defensive manager, was now associated with proactive pass-and-move football. 'Now we will start expecting to win on this sort of stage,' he said. 'I just hope Spain carry on in this way, and have many more victories.'

This style and a similar level of success were reproduced at club level. Guardiola's debut season as Barcelona coach, 2008/09, was among the most impressive club campaigns in history. Barca won the Treble for the first time, while playing the most attractive football Europe had witnessed for years, drawing comparisons with Rinus Michels' Holland and Arrigo Sacchi's AC Milan. Guardiola proved a revolutionary whose impact was notable in every aspect of Barcelona's play: an aggressive sweeper-keeper, an advanced defensive line, and, later, integrated pressing and the absence of a conventional centre-forward. More than anything else, however, Guardiola was concerned with dominating midfield through possession play.

He took charge of Barcelona when they were a shambles, with previous manager Frank Rijkaard exhausted and the team's star players badly out of shape. It was only two years since Barcelona had lifted the European Cup, but in that 2–1 victory over Arsenal in 2006, Rijkaard left Xavi and Iniesta on the bench, instead playing a midfield trio featuring one playmaker, Deco, alongside converted centre-back Edmílson and the aforementioned Van Bommel, a defensive midfielder who tended to play man rather than ball. Granted, there were fitness concerns about both Spanish midfielders, but Rijkaard often preferred strength to skill, and his side was built around attacking talents rather than the midfield trio. For all La Masia's emphasis on promoting Guardiola-style players, the first team didn't always field them.

At this stage there was a genuine debate about whether Xavi and Iniesta could play together. It wasn't an unreasonable concern, considering they'd been developed to perform in the same positions, and the best midfields generally feature three distinct footballers playing different roles and fulfilling different responsibilities. Under other coaches, Xavi and Iniesta wouldn't have co-existed. "'We can't play together!' When you look back on that debate now, you think, "My God!"' remembered Xavi years later. 'They had said the same about Pep when I first came through ... they said we didn't defend, we didn't fit in the same midfield, blah blah blah.' To Guardiola, it wasn't Xavi or Iniesta, it was Xavi *and* Iniesta. Oh, and Busquets too. He'd only previously played in the fourth division with Guardiola's Barcelona B, but was soon playing in La Liga.

Guardiola made an inauspicious start. Barcelona began with a 1–0 defeat away at Numancia, and their first home match was a 1–1 draw against Racing Santander, with the Camp Nou just over half-full. One man was impressed, however: Johan Cruyff. 'I saw one of the best Barcelona performances for years,' he said, to some bemusement. But, as always, Cruyff was proved right, and Barcelona's fortunes changed in their third game.

For the first time Guardiola started Busquets, Xavi and Iniesta together, and Barça completely dominated throughout a 6–1 victory away at Sporting Gijón. The opener was significant, with Iniesta typically slaloming inside from the left and dinking the ball into the box for Xavi to head home, the two embracing warmly afterwards. Barça's next two goals came from Xavi corners, before Leo Messi assisted Iniesta, than Iniesta repaid the favour for Messi, and then, in the final minute, Xavi assisted Messi. Ninety minutes that were the next four seasons in miniature: Xavi and Iniesta dictating the play, then teeing up Messi. Barcelona had clicked, and collected a staggering 58 points from their next 20 games.

La Liga is hardly unaccustomed to large victories over its minnows, but Barcelona reserved their best displays for top-half sides, beating second-placed Real Madrid 6–2, third-placed Sevilla 4–0, fourth-placed Atlético 6–1, sixth-placed Valencia 4–0, seventh-placed Deportivo 5–0 and eighth-placed Málaga 6–0. Only fifth-placed Villarreal, probably the closest side to Barcelona stylistically at this stage, competed well. The Málaga victory in March was the best example of Xavi's influence: he scored the opener, then laid on assists for the front three – Messi, Thierry Henry and Samuel Eto'o – all before half-time.

The Champions League victory in Guardiola's debut campaign was slightly unconvincing. Barca were fortunate to squeeze past Chelsea in the semi-finals courtesy of Iniesta's famous late strike, and while they were eventually dominant in a 2–0 final victory over Manchester United in Rome, they'd been battered for the opening ten minutes, relying on desperate last-ditch blocks, before an Eto'o breakaway goal changed the match. The contest was more memorable for the closing stages, when Sir Alex Ferguson introduced two extra attackers, effectively switched to 4–2–4, and Barcelona had the freedom of midfield to retain possession and kill the game. The final moments of Barcelona's most successful season were therefore spent simply playing keep-ball, which neatly summed up their approach. Guardiola had faith in both the midfield (the zone of the pitch) and in midfielders (the type of player).

Ferguson's analysis of Barcelona concentrated on the former. 'If you put three in the middle, they'll put four. If you put four, they'll put five,' he said. Guardiola consistently instructed players from other positions to overload the centre in big games, often with Iniesta fielded wide-left but drifting inside. Guardiola's second season, meanwhile, was dominated by the increasing use of Lionel Messi as a false 9, which became Barcelona's first-choice system by Guardiola's third season, 2010/11. Messi's popularisation of that role is covered extensively in the following chapter, but a crucial benefit was that he acted as a number 10 ahead of the existing three-man midfield, another way of overloading the opposition in the centre by forming a diamond.

Guardiola's faith in midfielders involved using them elsewhere on the pitch. Barcelona constantly needed another centre-back to cover for injuries, yet Guardiola's preference was redeploying midfielders at the heart of defence. Yaya Touré deputised there in the 2009 Champions League Final, Sergio Busquets often slotted in comfortably, while Javier Mascherano practically became a permanent centre-back upon his signing from Liverpool. 'Midfielders are intelligent players who have to think about the team as a whole,' Guardiola explained. 'They're selfless players who understand the game better than anyone and the more midfielders you have, the easier it is to slot them into other positions. That's how they become versatile and that helps us to have smaller squads.' Guardiola was attempting to create a side featuring as many midfielders as possible.

Guardiola's fourth and final season with Barcelona was his least successful, the only year he failed to win La Liga. But it proved tactically fascinating, as he increasingly tried new formations to keep opponents guessing – and to boost the number of midfielders in his side. In a 3–2 victory at Milan in November 2011 Guardiola used a 3–3–1–3 straight out of the Ajax playbook, and played six midfielders down the spine: Javier Mascherano in the middle of defence, a midfield quartet of Busquets, Xavi, Seydou Keïta and Thiago Alcántara, with Fàbregas up front.

His most extreme experiments were reserved for two Supercopa matches. Barcelona beat Porto 2–0 in the European version, and ended with a centre-back partnership featuring two midfielders, Busquets and Mascherano, plus Xavi, Keïta, Iniesta and Fàbregas. In the FIFA World Club Cup Final later that year, a 4–0 win over Santos, Guardiola crowded the midfield even further, fielding the usual trio of Busquets, Xavi and Iniesta, but with Fàbregas and Thiago drifting inside from the flanks, and Messi as a false 9. With Dani Alves pushed forward to become a right-winger, Barcelona were playing 3–7–0. Santos simply couldn't cope. 'They invented a new formation,' gasped their coach Muricy Ramalho. His players were equally stunned. 'You can't play if you haven't got the ball, and getting it back from these guys is almost impossible,' said their stylish number 10 Ganso, while future Barca forward Neymar couldn't believe his eyes. 'We have to learn how to play football from them,' he declared. 'I saw the best players in the world today: Messi and Xavi.'

But Barcelona were always most comfortable in the classic 4–3–3, with Busquets sitting deep and protecting the defence, Xavi controlling play to his right, and Iniesta shuttling forward to link midfield and attack. These three La Masia products, inspired by Guardiola as youngsters and now peaking under his management, dominated every big match in which they played together throughout these four years. Sometimes Barcelona were leaky at the back, sometimes they struggled to convert chances, but they were never found wanting in midfield. 'People refer to that midfield as Xavi–Iniesta–Busquets,' said Xavi. 'That midfield will be eternal and remembered forever, for the way it played, and for what it won.'

Vicente del Bosque, who replaced Aragonés as Spain's national team coach in 2008, made no attempt to replicate Barcelona's midfield structure, despite overwhelming similarities in personnel. At the 2010 World Cup, after plenty of chopping and changing up front, Del Bosque settled on Barca-bound David Villa and Barca's wide forward Pedro Rodríguez as his most advanced players, while Busquets, Xavi and Iniesta were regulars too. Therefore, five of the 'front six' were identical to those from Guardiola's best Barcelona side. But rather than fielding someone in Messi's role to completely mimic the template, Del Bosque instead selected Xabi Alonso, a deep-lying midfielder, meaning that Spain retained the ball for longer but struggled to penetrate the opposition.

This line-up required a different formation, 4-2-3-1. Busquets and Alonso formed the deep midfield duo, while Xavi was pushed forward into the number 10 position, where he looked uncomfortable receiving the ball with his back to goal, but dominated play by dropping deep. Iniesta, meanwhile, was a wide attacker with licence to drift inside, often creating an off-centre diamond with the three conventional midfielders. All three Barca players remained impressive, and Iniesta was more prominent for Spain, with the absence of Messi allowing him more attacking freedom. Yet the redeployment of these players felt like a waste of Barca's cohesion, and Del Bosque's Spain lacked the passing patterns that were second nature to the Spanish champions. Spain's triumphs were marred by a frustrating sense that they could have been more adventurous, more entertaining, more '2008' – and, more than anything, a bit better.

Such a negative assessment of arguably the greatest international side of all-time might seem harsh, but these criticisms were coming from key figures in Spanish football. The most notable critic was Del Bosque's predecessor, Aragonés. 'Xavi is being played out of position,' he complained midway through the 2010 World Cup, claiming that the midfielder needed to be fielded deeper. Xavi agreed, privately petitioning the coaching staff to change the midfield stricture and play with a single pivot, Busquets, allowing Xavi to replicate his Barcelona role. But Del Bosque wilfully stuck to 4-2-3-1, with his stubbornness influenced by the need to select the side politically, balancing the contributions of Barcelona and Real Madrid players.

After all, Del Bosque was a Real Madrid legend, having made over 500 appearances for the club as an outstanding deep midfielder in the 1970s, when he was renowned for his intelligence and selflessness in possession. He subsequently spent nearly his entire coaching career with Real too, so switching to the Barcelona system, which meant dropping Real's Alonso, would have risked upsetting the squad, the press and a large section of the public. Hailing from Salamanca, a city renowned for its academic rather than footballing pedigree, Del Bosque was a classic Castilian: impressively moustachioed, unfailingly polite, a committed family man, and determined to simply keep everyone happy. He repeatedly spoke about the importance of 'the group', the overall atmosphere in the travelling party, and considered this more crucial than tactical nuances. Indeed, for a squad primarily comprising players from two rival clubs that were enduring an extremely bitter war, everything was incredibly harmonious – Sergio Ramos and Gerard Piqué's feud would only arise later.

Del Bosque was a highly successful coach, having taken Real Madrid to two league titles and two Champions Leagues in a four-year spell from 1999, although he was unceremoniously sacked in 2003 after 'only' winning the league that season, as President Florentino Pérez demanded European success too. Pérez subsequently explained that 'Del Bosque's profile is a traditional one – we are looking for someone with more emphasis upon tactics, strategy and physical preparation.' Del Bosque is a mild-mannered man, but was genuinely incensed at the allegation that he wasn't modern enough.

Nevertheless, the caricature was exaggerated rather than misleading, and he remained a calm father figure, more similar to Arsène Wenger than Guardiola: he wasn't about tactical tinkering, but had a firm belief in possession-based football. 'I always want midfielders in my team, as many as possible. I'd love everyone to be a midfielder,' he declared. He also said something very similar to Guardiola: 'If I were a player, I would be like Busquets.' Barca and Spain were coached by two former deep-lying passers. 'There are more similarities between Guardiola and Del Bosque than people think,' said Xavi.

Del Bosque's pre-match team-talks, sometimes lasting a minute but often as short as 15 seconds, were primarily about repeating Spain's philosophy. 'Keep on playing the way we know how, be loyal to our style,' he calmly told his players before the World Cup Final, according to Graham Hunter's account in *Spain*. He wasn't as revolutionary as Guardiola, but his approach was even more singular – keep the ball.

The major difference between Guardiola's Barcelona and Del Bosque's Spain was the purpose of possession play. Whereas Guardiola's Barcelona and Aragonés's Spain were thrilling, attack-minded sides based around moving the ball forward, Del Bosque's Spain were defined by their goals-against tally, using possession play to starve the opposition of chances. They conceded just three goals from their 13 games at the 2010 World Cup and Euro 2012 combined, and the most pertinent statistic from Spain's run of success is their clean sheets record: a perfect 10 from 10 knockout games at Euro 2008, the 2010 World Cup and Euro 2012.

But Del Bosque's Spain were rarely convincing going forward. At the 2010 World Cup they started dreadfully – a 1–0 defeat against Switzerland in which Del Bosque used Iniesta and Silva on the flanks, both drifting inside into Xavi's zone, while Xavi dropped back to his natural position, too close to Busquets and Alonso. Spain regularly had five midfielders located in the space where Barcelona would have coped with three, which sacrificed width and allowed the opposition defence to remain narrow. This packing of the centre was a very different approach to Guardiola's Barcelona, who generally used two wide forwards to stretch play and create gaps in the opposition defence in keeping with the Dutch model.

After that Swiss defeat, a senior committee of players met with Del Bosque, emphasising that they believed in his philosophy. But the approach now changed – Silva was dropped and Spain played with at least one attacker offering width and forward running. Sometimes Villa started in a wide-left position, sometimes Jesús Navas, a genuine touchline-hugging dribbler, played on the right, while eventually Del Bosque used Pedro in his Barcelona role, running in behind from wide.

Throughout the 2010 World Cup, Spain's matches followed a very similar pattern, essentially a three-card trick. First, they played tentatively at 0–0, retaining possession for long periods without creating chances, simply moving the ball across midfield to maintain control and draining the opposition. 'You see the other side getting desperate. They run and run for very little of the ball,' explained Juan Mata, yet another playmaker in Spain's squad. 'That wears them down bit by bit.'

Second, after around an hour Del Bosque would introduce substitutes who offered more penetration, which resulted in late goals. Spain won all four 2010 World Cup knockout matches 1–0, against Portugal, Paraguay, Germany and Holland, with winners in the 63rd, 83rd, 73rd and, finally, the 116th minute. Powerful central striker Fernando Llorente was a crucial Plan B against Portugal, Fàbregas and Pedro provided extra forward thrust against Paraguay, while Fàbregas and Navas were decisive in the final against Holland.

Finally, having gone 1–0 ahead, Spain would revert to retaining the ball in deep positions, killing the game slowly – in stark contrast to their Euro 2008 approach, when they kept on attacking.

Their most typical performance came in the semi-final victory over Germany. Jogi Löw's counter-attacking side were completely different from two years beforehand, boasting a young, fresh and relatively unknown generation of players who had already beaten

England 4–1 and Argentina 4–0 after going ahead early and being afforded space to sprint into.

This was the greatest stylistic contrast of the World Cup: Spain's possession against Germany's counter-attack – and possession prevailed. Busquets kept Mesut Özil quiet, Spain pressed effectively, and after they steadily increased the pressure in the second half Carles Puyol powered home a header from Xavi's corner. In the 17 remaining minutes Spain's possession play was more effective than ever. Germany's counter-attacking, which involved sitting deep to draw the opposition onto them, now proved useless because Spain retained the ball in midfield, held their positions and refused to push forward.

'When we eventually did get the ball back we were exhausted from chasing it for so long,' admitted Germany striker Miroslav Klose, while his manager outlined the difference between Aragonés's Spain and Del Bosque's Spain. 'It's extraordinarily difficult to win the ball back if you lose it to Spain,' said Löw. 'In 2008 they won the European Championship in a spectacular way, totally convincing, but in the last couple of years they have evolved, introduced some changes and they now play as if they were on automatic. This team has a unique ability to dominate you and control you.'

Then came the World Cup Final, in which Spain were pitched against the country to whose football they owed so much, the Netherlands. Pre-match discussion focused on the connection between the two footballing nations, primarily through the Ajax influence on Barcelona: Rinus Michels, Louis van Gaal, Frank Rijkaard and, more than anyone else, Johan Cruyff. 'I'm going to watch this game with a few Spanish friends,' Cruyff announced. 'And I take the view that no matter which team wins, I can't lose.'

But the final wasn't an extravaganza of positive football. Holland, having decided they weren't capable of outplaying Spain in a possession-based contest, resorted to an antiquated, aggressive and outright brutal approach. It finished 8–5 to Holland – in terms of bookings. The most infamous foul was Nigel de Jong's karate kick into the chest of Xabi Alonso, with the ball only vaguely in the picture. De Jong was shown a yellow card, but referee Howard Webb later admitted it should have been red. Equally reprehensible, albeit less blatant, was the conduct of pantomime villain Van Bommel, who over the course of his career had steadily descended into the role of hatchet man, targeting the opposition's most talented player. Here he sought out Iniesta, a sensitive clash considering he'd kept Iniesta out of the side for Barcelona's Champions League Final victory in 2006. 'It wasn't a nice game of pretty football,' Van Bommel admitted. 'But which final is?'

Holland's approach nearly succeeded. Their only attacking tactic was getting right-winger Arjen Robben in behind the Spain defence with through-balls, but it worked twice – first Robben was denied by a fine Iker Casillas save, then he uncharacteristically elected to remain on his feet under pressure from Puyol and lost the goalscoring opportunity.

In fairness, both managers attempted to win the contest, and the game opened out in the second half and into extra-time. Del Bosque summoned the attack-minded Fàbregas in place of Alonso, with Xavi happily dropping deep alongside Busquets. Meanwhile, Holland manager Bert van Marwijk introduced playmaker Rafael van der Vaart for De Jong, so the Dutch conceded more space in front of their defence, allowing Iniesta and Fàbregas to shine. Iniesta created a one-on-one chance for Fàbregas at the start of extra-time, but he shot straight at keeper Maarten Stekelenburg.

Iniesta was the matchwinner. In the 109th minute his quick burst forced Johnny Heitinga to pull him down, bringing a red card and leaving Holland undermanned in defence. Seven minutes later, he charged through on goal again, assisted by a delicate Fàbregas chip. Goalscoring is Iniesta's major weakness, and he'd previously wasted two presentable chances by not shooting quickly enough. 'You'd never imagine that it will be Andrés who scores in the World Cup Final,' laughed Guardiola years later. 'You could do a poll, "Who's going to score?" and you wouldn't even put Andrés on the list.' But this time he steadied himself, waited for the ball to drop, then smashed home the most important goal in Spanish football history.

Spain were popular champions, given the conduct of the Dutch – even for a disgusted Cruyff. 'They didn't want the ball,' he complained of his compatriots. 'This ugly, vulgar, hard, style – yes, it served the Dutch to unsettle Spain. If they got satisfaction from that, fine, but they ended up losing. They were playing anti-football.' Dutch football would no longer be held in such high esteem, especially considering that Spain was now the unrivalled home of possession football. The only man who refused to criticise the Dutch was Del Bosque. 'The final was all about attacking football,' he proclaimed, ever the diplomatic statesman. 'Both sides tried to play the game the way it should be played.' Which was plainly nonsense.

Two years later, at Euro 2012, Spain became even more possession-based. The personnel available in midfield and attack was similar, but Del Bosque moved closer to his dream of fielding a team of midfielders, using no fewer than six: Busquets and Alonso still deep, Xavi still the number 10, Silva and Iniesta notionally wide midfielders but crowding the centre of the pitch, and Fàbregas leading the line. This was peak tiki-taka.

Again, their attacking threat was often questionable. In the group stage they thrashed a poor Ireland side 4–0, but in a 1–1 draw with Italy and a 1–0 win over Croatia they struggled to create chances. Of course, the commitment to possession play ensured their defensive record remained excellent. At the quarter-final stage they dispatched

France 2–0, with Xabi Alonso commanding the midfield and scoring both goals on his 100th cap, the first time he'd overshadowed his Barcelona-based teammates in a tournament game.

In Spain's semi-final clash with Portugal they nearly regretted their lack of penetration. In a contest that felt like Barcelona against Real Madrid, with Portugal boasting Cristiano Ronaldo, Pepe and Fabio Coentrão, Paulo Bento's side pressed excellently and played on the counter-attack. Del Bosque ended up using the closest thing to a Barcelona-style frontline, with Pedro and Navas breaking in behind from wide, and Fàbregas the false 9. Spain again struggled to create clear chances, and Portugal nearly won the game in the final minute of normal time, but Raul Meireles's poor pass on a counter-attack forced Ronaldo wide. It finished 0–0, and Spain won on penalties.

A third straight final, and yet now Spain were widely criticised for being so overwhelmingly cautious. 'Spain's play is like love without the sex,' said former France left-back Bixente Lizarazu. The most notable critic was Arsène Wenger, a lover of possession football who had spent the previous few years marvelling at how Barcelona had 'turned football into an art', yet found Spain's ultra-tiki-taka significantly less entertaining. 'They have betrayed their philosophy and turned it into something more negative,' he complained, attending the tournament as a pundit. 'Originally they wanted possession in order to attack and win the game; now it seems to be first and foremost a way not to lose. They have become more conservative, and they don't want to give the ball up because they don't want to give you a chance to score. That's the impression you get from Euro 2012. Yes, it can be hard to break down defensive opponents, but this is a challenge that confronts every successful team. They are still absolutely outstanding, but they have less penetration than before.' It was an entirely reasonable critique, and Wenger was merely mirroring the feelings of many. But Spain's players predictably defended their honour. 'Those people who think we are playing boring football, in my opinion they don't understand the game,' said Fàbregas. 'If people think it is boring that Spain always win, that is fantastic for us,' added Xavi.

Then came the final, where Spain produced unquestionably their greatest performance under Del Bosque, demolishing Italy 4–0. Their opening two goals were hugely different, but both brilliant. The first was a superb piece of intricate combination play flowing from Xavi, to Iniesta, to Fàbregas, to Silva, who headed in. The second was also a passing move, but much more direct; Xavi collected the ball in midfield and waited for the speedy run of left-back Jordi Alba, who darted through the Italian defence, collected Xavi's through-ball and fired home. 2–0 at half-time and surely game over. As we'd previously learned, once Spain were ahead they didn't allow the opposition a chance. Cesare Prandelli, the unusually forward-thinking Italy coach who considered Spain's possession football his side's template, ended up using all three of his substitutes by the 57th minute, partly because of injury, partly in a desperate attempt to get back into the game. But this proved fatal: Thiago Motta, the Brazilian-born, Barca-schooled Italy midfielder, was Prandelli's final substitute but lasted barely five minutes before hobbling off. Italy played the final half-hour with ten men.

In every other knockout game under Del Bosque, Spain had played ultra-conservatively having gone ahead. But now this was an opportunity for Spain to prove their critics wrong. Boring football, you say? OK, have some of this. All three of Del Bosque's substitutions introduced extra goal threats: Pedro for Silva, Torres for Fàbregas, Mata for Iniesta. Both Torres and Mata helped themselves to goals. Neutrals had spent Spain's previous matches imploring them to keep possession less and attack more, yet now were begging for Spain to have mercy on this Italian side, who were playing their most proactive, entertaining football for decades and who were undeserving of this humiliation. But Spain were ruthless, and this 4–0 victory will always be used to refute any suggestion Spain were boring. 'That was the real Spain,' declared Gerard Piqué afterwards. Yet, in truth, Spain had gone four years without playing this way at a major tournament, despite always dominating possession.

The final's outstanding player, fittingly, was Xavi. Throughout this period his unparalleled ability to dominate matches made him the single greatest example of the Spanish passing style that had spread across Europe. Xavi wasn't particularly popular until Euro 2008, when he was already 28, but then his short-passing style became the inspiration for midfielders across Europe. 'Winning has served to make people re-evaluate our style, my style,' Xavi said. 'It's not just about recognition, it's about more than that. Honestly, I am very happy because, from an egotistical perspective, six years ago I was extinct as a player. Footballers like me were in danger of dying out.' Now, footballers like him were more revered than ever.

## 14

# False 9s & Argentines

By 2012 the concept of the false 9 had become established across Europe. But to demonstrate Spanish football's shift away from conventional centre-forwards it's worth recalling Spain's starting XI for their final match at a major tournament before their period of dominance began.

For Spain's 3–1 second-round defeat to France at the 2006 World Cup, Luis Aragonés fielded three centre-forwards together: Raúl González, David Villa and Fernando Torres. Raúl was Spain's captain, Villa was La Liga's most consistent goalscorer and Torres was the new kid on the block. But the decision to field all three backfired: Raúl and Villa were substituted ten minutes into the second half, replaced by two wide midfielders in Luis García and Joaquín, as Spain attempted to gain control. They eventually lost 3–1, and it was the same old Spain: technically proficient but ultimately underwhelming.

Aragonés's determination to cram all three into Spain's starting XI, however, was understandable. Spain were entirely unaccustomed to such riches up front, demonstrated by the fact that this trio would eventually occupy the top three slots in Spain's all-time goalscorer list: Villa finished his international career on 59 goals, Raúl managed

44 and Torres 38. Indeed, Spain's traditional lack of prolific centre-forwards was so stark that their previous all-time leading goalscorer was centre-back Fernando Hierro. Yes, Hierro took penalties and was sometimes deployed in midfield, but the statistic nevertheless highlights a traditional shortcoming up front.

Before the generation of Raúl, Villa and Torres, Spain's most prolific goalscorers belonged to a bygone era. Pichichi, the 1920s Athletic Bilbao striker, scored so regularly that La Liga's top-goalscorer award was named after him, the award's record winner being Telmo Zarra, another Athletic striker, who triumphed six times in the 1940s and 1950s. The legendary Alfredo Di Stéfano took the Pichichi five times in the 1950s but was more an all-rounder than a striker and was Argentine rather than Spanish. The diminutive Quini won five times for Sporting Gijón and Barcelona in the 1970s and 1980s but only managed eight international goals. Later, Mexican bicycle-kick specialist Hugo Sánchez won five times in the 1980s. Only Sánchez's teammate at Real Madrid Emilio Butragueño can be considered a genuinely top-class Spanish centre-forward in the second half of the 20th century, and even he wasn't prolific, only once managing more than 15 goals in a league campaign. Spain simply lacked a classic goal poacher in the mould of Germany's Gerd Müller or England's Gary Lineker.

So, while Aragonés was overjoyed at suddenly having three world-class goalscorers at his disposal, the situation was completely atypical. Italian sides, for example, were accustomed to fielding three central attackers, but Spain were not, and they would increasingly move away from using any strikers whatsoever. This was inspired by a Spain-based – but not Spanish – footballer popularising the false 9 role.

Leo Messi's incredible stint as the world's greatest footballer has stretched well beyond this particular era, but 2008–2012 witnessed his explosion from a promising wide attacker into a devastatingly effective centre-forward. Before 2008/09 Messi had scored 42 goals for Barcelona. By the end of 2011/12 he was on 253 and had become the club's all-time top goalscorer.

It was fitting that Spain's perceptions of a centre-forward were changed by an Argentine. While Dutch football is unquestionably the major contemporary influence on Spain's footballing identity, the country's links with Argentina are also important. The connection can be traced back to 1921, when a Spanish side comprising primarily Basque players exuding *La Furia Roja* toured Argentina, Uruguay and Brazil, and were completely overwhelmed by the attractive, patient, possession-based approach of their hosts, which started the Spanish reverence towards Latin American football.

Later, there was a hugely influential tour of Spain by the all-conquering 1947 San Lorenzo side, who outplayed Spanish opposition with technical, skilful football. The Argentine champions defeated Spain's biggest clubs before thrashing the national side by an aggregate score of 13–6 over two matches. 'There was a before and after in Spanish football, delineated by the San Lorenzo visit,' said Jaume Olive, a Barcelona youth coach, quoted in Jimmy Burns's *La Roja*. 'The Argentine champions left a deep imprint, an elaborate football of short passes, of triangulation, in contrast to the more direct football of Spain, where to talk about tactics was regarded as heresy. The Argentines believed in making the best use of the ball and strategy, and the Spaniards could only respond with *La Furia* and improvisation.'

In principle, this Argentine influence should have faded when foreign players were banned in La Liga from 1962, a hasty response to Spain finishing bottom of their World Cup group. Instead, the ban had the opposite effect because *oriundos*, foreigners with Spanish roots, were still permitted, and most hailed from Argentina. An investigation later discovered that over 75 per cent of these imports actually had no genuine family connection to Spain and that falsifying papers had become commonplace, so the ban was lifted in 1973 – which prompted Cruyff's arrival. But during that 11-year period, Spain effectively banned footballers from elsewhere in Europe, but was awash with Argentines.

The key figure was Alfredo Di Stéfano, who was signed by Real Madrid from under the nose of Barcelona in 1953, subsequently won two Ballons d'Or and was Real's outstanding player during their run of five straight European Cups won between 1956 and 1960. In the days before switching allegiance was prohibited, Di Stéfano played for Argentina, Colombia and Spain, reflecting where he was playing his club football at the time, but while the majority of his international appearances came for Spain, his style was unmistakeably South American.

'He revolutionised the concepts we had in Spain about the game,' said his Real teammate Vicente Miera, quoted in Ian Hawkey's biography of Di Stéfano. 'We were used to football being thought of in distinct segments: defenders concerned with marking strikers, a midfield organiser without much right to get involved in creative play, a centre-forward waiting for the ball to come to him. Alfredo was all-terrain, and had the capacity to finish as well. When he arrived it was as a number 9. We thought he was going to always be up front, expecting passes. No. We very soon saw he would be coming deep, exchanging passes, contributing to the organisation of the team. It was really striking the different things he did, the way he thought.'

In later years, Spain's affection for Argentine football was largely because the South Americans were simply a more successful footballing nation. Between 1978 and 1990 Argentina won the World Cup twice and were runners-up once, while Spain managed a lone quarter-final appearance. It was only natural that a more successful

Spanish-speaking country that constantly exported players to Spain became so admired. Meanwhile, Argentine midfielder Jorge Valdano, who starred for and managed Real Madrid, became Spanish football's grand philosopher, a hugely respected, idealistic football thinker who steadfastly endorsed attractive football. Compatriot César Luis Menotti, the coach who symbolised attack-minded coaching in Argentina, and managed Barcelona and Atlético Madrid in the 1980s, was another famous footballing ideologue. He, like Valdano, espoused the importance of individual expression and a positive footballing identity.

There was also Diego Maradona, the greatest footballer of the 1980s, who joined Barcelona in 1982 for a world-record fee and spent a couple of eventful years at the Camp Nou before being transferred to Napoli for another world-record fee. Maradona's performances at Barca were mixed, but his influence on world football world was enormous. The reverence for his number 10 shirt and his role (the *enganche*, meaning hook) is greater in Argentina than anywhere else in the world. The importance of the *enganche* has defined Argentine football, which was historically concerned with creating a playing style distinct from that of both their Spanish colonial masters and the English, who introduced the game to Argentina. While European football was considered heavily systematised, Argentines prided themselves on individualism and spontaneity; in his history of Argentine football, Jonathan Wilson traces this back to 'the explosion of cultural self-confidence and creativity in the 1920s, which also inspired the rise of the tango'. Typically, the number 10 was a *pibe*, a scruffy, lower-class kid who developed his skills playing street football and refused to allow his natural instincts to be compromised by coaches. He needed to be a natural genius rather than a learned scholar, and ideally he was physically underdeveloped, a brilliant dribbler and left-footed.

This image was cultivated long before the emergence of Maradona, who didn't create the stereotype but fulfilled it perfectly. Maradona is held in such affection in Argentina not simply because he was the world's best footballer, but because he was so stereotypically Argentine, so perfect for their interpretation of the number 10, and because he bolstered the legend of the *enganche* for the next generation to follow. In the 1990s and early 2000s, Argentine football's desperation to discover a 'new Maradona' was matched by Spanish football's determination to import him. Every serious contender for that tag headed to La Liga: Ariel Ortega and Pablo Aimar to Valencia, Javier Saviola and Juan Román Riquelme to Barcelona. And then, of course, there was Messi.

Messi's move from Rosario to Barcelona has become, with good reason, the most fabled story in modern football. Messi was an outstandingly gifted youngster, but was diagnosed with a growth-hormone deficiency that required medical treatment costing thousands of pounds per month for him to stand a chance of becoming a professional. His hometown club, Newell's Old Boys, decided they couldn't justify the outlay and, in the midst of Argentina's financial crisis, the Messi family looked abroad. Barcelona heard about Messi's potential and, after the club's directors hesitated over the decision, Barça's first-team director Charly Rexach unilaterally signed Messi, with his contract hastily written on a restaurant napkin. At 13, Messi belonged to Barcelona.

Nevertheless, Messi remained Argentine. He didn't reside with other Barcelona academy players at La Masia, but instead with his family, who had emigrated from Argentina. His future wife Antonella was a childhood friend from Rosario, and the sizeable Argentine community in Barcelona played a significant role in his upbringing. His diet was typically Argentine, consisting largely of red meat, and his closest companions in his formative days in Barcelona's first team were Latin Americans rather than Spaniards. And, while the Spanish national side were inevitably interested in securing his services, Messi never wavered from his commitment to *La Albiceleste* rather than *La Roja*.

In footballing terms, too, Messi was a classic Argentine, utterly obsessed with playing as a number 10, and whereas other Barcelona youngsters were taught to idolise Guardiola, Messi idolised Maradona. He'd witnessed his hero in the flesh at the age of six – attending Maradona's 1993 debut for Newell's Old Boys, where Messi entertained spectators with half-time keepie-uppies. Maradona had everything: he was a ruthless goalscorer, a direct dribbler and a prolific provider all rolled into one, and demanded to be used between the lines of midfield and attack. That's precisely how Messi wanted to play.

Upon his arrival at Barcelona Messi was already introducing new concepts. Rodolfo Borrell, an influential youth coach at Barcelona who later worked at Liverpool and joined Pep Guardiola at Manchester City, remembers his introduction to Messi was a photo-copy of an Argentine newspaper report that used the common Argentine footballing words *gambeta*, meaning dribbling, and *enganche*. Tellingly, Argentine football had developed words for skills and positions that were not yet familiar in Spain, and Messi would later teach Spanish football the value of both concepts.

Messi was a shy member of Barcelona's youth sides, only speaking when he was asked a question. And when the question was 'Which position do you play?', his response was always '*enganche*', a word that baffled his teammates. There was also a tactical problem; Barcelona's youth sides generally used a 4–3–3 system that offered no place to a number 10, so Messi was fielded out wide. He hated being used wide-left, but tolerated wide-right because he could drift inside on to his favoured left foot. Curiously, even when Barcelona's youth coaches switched to 3–4–3 with a diamond midfield, opening up the possibility of Messi playing as a number 10, a young Cesc Fàbregas was often fielded there instead. The first youth coach to deploy Messi centrally was Tito Vilanova – later Pep Guardiola's assistant, and then his replacement – when the Argentine was 15 years old. However, Vilanova deployed Messi as the number 9, foreshadowing his future position under Guardiola.

Significantly, when representing Argentina's youth sides Messi was routinely played in his favoured number 10 position. That, to Argentines, was his obvious role – he was unquestionably an *enganche*, and despite the fact he'd been coached in Europe and was quicker than archetypal number 10s like Riquelme, he remained stylistically Argentine. The crucial evidence was his incessant dribbling, learned on the streets of Rosario rather than the training pitches of La Masia. 'For me, it was difficult to pass the ball. I kept forgetting to do it,' he recalled of his early La Masia days in an interview with Argentine magazine *El Gráfico*. 'Gradually I managed to play more for the team, but I didn't make it easy for them, because I have always been very stubborn. Barcelona showed me lots of things, but they never tried to change my style.'

Messi became Barcelona's youngest-ever player in October 2004, and their youngest-ever goalscorer in October 2005. His debut goal was assisted by Ronaldinho – minutes after an identical combination between the two had resulted in a Messi goal being wrongly disallowed for offside – and the world's greatest player become Messi's mentor, despite the Argentina–Brazil rivalry. Ronaldinho, like Messi (and Rivaldo before them), was a natural number 10 shifted out wide within Barca's 4–3–3, and Messi essentially became his mirror image, playing on the right flank while the Brazilian dominated the left. Messi became a regular in 2005/06, and already started to intimate, privately, that he wanted a central role. 'I'm not saying, or suggesting, or agreeing with the statement that we have before us the new Maradona,' said his manager Frank Rijkaard in 2005. 'I prefer to say that we have before us the new Messi ... he has an innate class that allows him to play in a number of positions, even though he believes that, ultimately, he will play in the hole.' That would have to wait, however, and Messi ended 2005/06 on a disappointing note, missing the Champions League Final because Rijkaard didn't think he'd fully recovered from injury.

In 2006/07 Messi made serious progress, scoring a brilliant hat-trick in a 3–3 *El Clásico* draw, and then replicated his hero's two most legendary goals within the space of two months, first copying Maradona's famous dribble through the England defence with a memorable solo effort against Getafe, then imitating his infamous 'Hand of God' goal in the derby against Espanyol. Curiously it was this handball, as much as his incredible dribbling ability and increased goalscoring threat, that suggested Argentina had finally found the new Maradona. Indicating a changing of the guard, Argentine journalists now started to search for the 'new Messi'.

But 2007/08 was an underwhelming campaign, marred by niggling injuries, concerns about Messi's diet and a sense that the increasingly ill-disciplined Ronaldinho, who lived three doors down the road from Messi, had become a negative influence. There was, however, a significant development in Barca's 1–1 draw at Sevilla in February, when Messi was deployed centrally for the first time in Barcelona's attacking trio, with Thierry Henry wide-left and Giovani dos Santos on the right. Messi played well but Barcelona didn't, and the experiment wasn't repeated under Rijkaard.

Meanwhile, Spain's national side were still using conventional strikers, but now only two rather than three, after a significant development. Raúl, Spain's golden boy for a decade and captain for the previous four years, was ditched by Luis Aragonés after a shock 3–2 loss to Northern Ireland in September 2006. Spain supporters were angry at the defeat, but even more furious about Raúl's subsequent departure from the squad, and despite Spain qualifying relatively comfortably for Euro 2008, the issue remained contentious. Aragonés's house was covered in pro-Raúl graffiti, and when the Spain squad arrived at Málaga station for a friendly with France they were met by a group of supporters chanting Raúl's name and waving his number 7 shirt. But Raúl, still performing well for Real Madrid, would never again play for Spain. The national team had moved on, and Aragonés started Euro 2008 with a 4–4–2 formation featuring Villa dropping off Torres.

In truth, even a two-striker system still felt unnatural for Spain, whose players were accustomed to playing in 4–2–3–1 or 4–3–3 formations at club level. Torres and Villa, however, maintained an excellent relationship – they'd played together since the Spanish U21 side, and their wives were good friends. When Spain thrashed Russia 4–1 in their opening game of Euro 2008, Villa scored a hat-trick and made a point of celebrating all his goals with Torres – even his third, after Torres had been substituted and was sitting in the dugout. They were in it together, and both were on target in the 2–1 win against Sweden, albeit in a disappointing performance. Against Italy in the quarter-final, Aragonés started both together up front, but Italy were largely comfortable and the game ended goalless, with Spain going through on penalties.

There was a major blessing in disguise 34 minutes into Spain's semi-final, another meeting with Russia, when Villa limped off on 34 minutes. It might sound ludicrous to suggest that a tournament-ending injury to Euro 2008's Golden Boot winner improved Spain's chances of success, but the enforced substitution transformed their passing, and they completely controlled the game after Villa was replaced by Fàbregas, who grabbed two assists in a 3–0 win. 'Villa is injured and I don't know whether he'll play in the final,' said Aragonés after that semi-final victory. 'But in any case, tonight we played better with one forward than two.' That was the moment of realisation. Villa missed the final, so Fàbregas continued in an attacking midfield role. Torres, who was forced to peel off to the wings when playing alongside Villa, now led the line solo as he did expertly with Liverpool, enjoying greater freedom to sprint into the channels, and he scored the winner against Germany from the inside-right position. Throughout Euro 2008 Spain looked more effective, and indeed more Spanish, with one up front. Never mind simply controlling the game better; they scored every 75 minutes with a two-man strike force, but every 34 minutes with a lone striker.

Meanwhile, Guardiola had been appointed Barcelona coach and immediately sold Ronaldinho, with Messi inheriting his number 10 shirt. But Messi and Guardiola had a curious relationship. Messi, unlike the other La Masia graduates, was not predisposed to Guardiola. To him he was just another coach, although Guardiola got Messi on board when intervening in his dispute with Barcelona's board over his participation in the 2008 Olympics. Messi was desperate to play in China, Barca weren't obliged to release him and rejected Argentina's request, but Guardiola – remembering his own Olympics experience in 1992 – took the player's side. Messi played in a fearsome front four alongside Juan Román Riquelme, Ángel Di María and Sergio Agüero, winning gold in Beijing. More importantly, Guardiola had won his trust.

While Guardiola immediately recognised Messi's talent, he wasn't an archetypal Guardiola player, primarily because he dribbled so frequently. Messi's dribbling was classic dribbling, weaving past opponents towards goal. Guardiola's recommended manner of dribbling was subtler, carrying the ball into parts of the pitch that drew opponents out of position, thereby opening up gaps to pass into.

Guardiola, for example, believed Messi's famous goal against Getafe, when he dribbled past half the opposition, was the consequence of poor attacking play; Messi received the ball too deep, drove towards goal too directly and his teammates were in poor positions and unable to offer support. In his book *Barça*, Graham Hunter recalls Guardiola shouting instructions to Barça's B team in 2007/08: 'I don't want you all trying to dribble like Messi! Pass it, pass it and pass it again. Pass precisely, move well, pass again!' But Messi was largely uncoachable, playing his own way. 'He's a purely intuitive player, which is why you have to give him freedom,' Guardiola conceded.

His decision to move Messi into a false 9 role is generally considered to have been made ahead of Barcelona's trip to the Bernabéu in the final month of Guardiola's first campaign. In reality, it actually happened in Barça's first victory under Guardiola, the 6–1 thrashing of Sporting Gijón on matchday three. As was to become customary, Samuel Eto'o started up front and Messi began in his usual right-sided position, but they swapped positions ten minutes into the game, confusing the Sporting defence and running riot. It was peculiar, then, that Guardiola decided to deploy Eto'o up front and Messi on the right for much of 2008/09. Seemingly, he preferred to keep that trick up his sleeve for season-defining matches.

The trip to Real Madrid, eight months after the trip to Gijón, certainly fell into that category: Barça were four points ahead of Real, with five games remaining. A Real victory, and it was game on; a Barcelona victory, and the title was basically decided. Guardiola, studying the videos of Real's immobile centre-back pairing of Fabio Cannavaro and Christoph Metzelder the night before the game, suddenly decided it was time to unleash Messi in a central role. This was clearly a last-minute decision. Barcelona hadn't trained in that system, and Guardiola phoned Messi and told him to come to his room to watch clips of Real's defence. Messi, supposedly, laughed at Guardiola's suggestion of playing him through the middle. Guardiola believes this is because Messi thought it was would be too risky and he'd be too isolated, although you suspect that it was actually because Messi thought the move was obvious and should have happened long ago.

Either way, that was the plan. Before the game Guardiola gathered together Xavi, Iniesta and Messi, instructing them to dominate by creating a three-against-two situation around Lassana Diarra and Fernando Gago. That's exactly what happened. In a 6–2 victory that effectively clinched the league title, Messi scored two, created another for Henry from his position between the lines, and helped to give Barcelona total dominance in the centre. Real's centre-backs had no idea how to stop him. 'It's just not in our game to follow him into midfield,' said a baffled Metzelder afterwards. Messi was doing to Real Madrid what Di Stéfano had once done for Real Madrid.

This tactic wasn't witnessed again until the Champions League Final against Manchester United later that month. Again, Guardiola started with Messi on the right and Eto'o up front, but there was a pre-arranged tactic to switch them after ten minutes, to confuse United. It worked perfectly in Barça's 2–0 victory; Eto'o opened the scoring when cutting inside from the right, and Messi confirmed the win with a header from a classic centre-forward position. 'In the finals, Andrés, Xavi, Busquets and I have always come together to give us a numerical advantage, to control the ball and the game,' explained Messi. He was a midfielder as much as a forward, a proper number 10 as he'd always wanted.

Guardiola was credited for this tactical innovation, but the praise deserves to be shared. His assistant, Vilanova, had fielded Messi up front during his youth-team days. His predecessor, Rijkaard, had experimented with him centrally. Various Argentina managers used him as a number 10. And, most significantly, Messi himself had continually insisted that his future lay in a central role. Playing him as the central forward in Barca's 4–3–3, with Henry and Eto'o wide, was effectively the same as Messi playing as an *enganche* in an Argentina-style 4–3–1–2, simply with the strikers playing wider. To Europeans he was a false 9, to South Americans he was a true 10.

That, you might think, was that – Messi had found his long-term position. But Guardiola still considered this nothing more than a useful tactical alternative, because immediately after Barcelona's Treble success he made the most controversial signing of his managerial career, Zlatan Ibrahimović. The transfer fee wasn't simply a club record £59 million, but also involved Eto'o moving to Inter Milan in a part-exchange deal. Many questioned whether Ibrahimović was a better striker than Eto'o at all, let alone £59 million better, but more significant than the comparison of abilities was the comparison in style; Eto'o was a speedy attacker with the mobility to play wide, whereas Ibrahimović was a proper striker. Guardiola's intention was to play not with a false 9 but a classic 9, or, in his description of Ibrahimović, an 'inverted pivot'.

With Messi returning to the right, Ibrahimović's Barcelona career started excellently. He became the first Barca player to score in his first five matches, including two headers that underlined Barca's potential to play more directly. He was briefly sidelined with a thigh injury, then returned as a substitute in *El Clásico*, volleying home the winner after six minutes on the pitch. In the second half of Ibrahimović's sole Barcelona campaign, however, things went dramatically downhill, his relationship with Guardiola souring to the extent that they weren't on speaking terms. Media coverage focused on the personal nature of their squabble, helped by Ibrahimović's rather fancifully ghost-written autobiography referring to Guardiola as 'my enemy' and 'a spineless coward'.

In truth, the problems stemmed from tactical concerns and, more specifically, Messi's demands to have the side constructed around him. The Argentine first registered his concerns with Guardiola by texting him on the coach journey back from an away trip, and while different sources suggest slightly different wordings, it's widely agreed that the thrust of Messi's message was, 'Well, I see I'm not important to the team anymore.' Later, he spoke to Guardiola personally and explicitly demanded to play centrally, telling his coach to 'stick the others out wide'.

This had inevitable consequences for Ibrahimović, and created a problem Guardiola couldn't solve. Now determined to placate Messi, he tried everything to get Ibrahimović into the side; he tried a 4–2–3–1 formation with Messi behind the Swede, which hampered Barcelona's traditional midfield passing patterns, so then briefly fielded Ibrahimović wide-right in a 4–3–3, which plainly didn't suit him.

The obvious compromise was returning Messi to the right, with Ibrahimović up front, and that's what Guardiola did for both legs of Barca's notorious Champions League semi-final defeat to José Mourinho's Inter, probably his starkest tactical error during four years at Barca. Inter's ageing centre-back pairing of Walter Samuel and Lúcio would have been terrified by the prospect of Messi playing as a false 9, flanked by quick runners in Pedro Rodríguez and Bojan Krkić. Instead, they were comfortable against Ibrahimović, who endured two miserable games against his former side. The sight of Guardiola beckoning the Swede over to the touchline to offer tactical guidance, with Mourinho heckling from the adjacent technical area, is the abiding image of Ibrahimović's time at Barca. 'I didn't have a relationship with the coach,' Ibrahimović said after his departure to Milan. 'He hardly looked at me. Messi wanted to play centre-forward and got his way.'

Ibrahimović's departure in 2010 was compensated for by the arrival of Villa, who spent that summer combining with Xavi, Iniesta, Busquets and Pedro in Spain's successful World Cup-winning side. For the second tournament in a row, however, it became obvious that Spain were more dangerous with one striker rather than two. Vicente del Bosque had recognised the problem with a conventional strike partnership, but still wanted to accommodate both Torres and Villa, to play the latter wide-left in a 4–2–3–1.

The problem here, though, was personnel rather than tactics. Torres had missed much of the preceding season through injury, and was still carrying a meniscus problem going into the tournament. He never looked sharp enough, playing a part in each of Spain's seven matches without completing 90 minutes, or contributing any goals or assists. Later, in a documentary about Spain's World Cup win, Torres admitted he took painkilling injections to be fit for the tournament, despite being warned that they could hamper the rest of his career. This appears a significant revelation, because Torres was a shadow of his former self afterwards, never recovering his speed or confidence. Having hit 56 league goals in the three seasons leading up to the 2010 World Cup, he managed just 57 in the rest of his European career, spanning eight campaigns. Nevertheless, Del Bosque persisted with him until the semi-final stage, before turning to wide-forward Pedro, meaning Villa could move up front. Spain produced their best performance of the World Cup against Germany, and for the second consecutive tournament, a semi-final switch to one up front, albeit with Villa rather than Torres, helped Spain over the line.

At Barcelona, having played with his new teammates successfully at international level, Villa was inevitably a more natural fit than Ibrahimović. But the problem, if such a thing can ever be considered a problem, was the presence of Messi. When Villa signed for

Barcelona he was told his position would be up front. He was deployed there on debut, scoring in a 3–0 win over Racing Santander, and alternated with Bojan between the wide-left and centre-forward roles in his second game. But that was a shock 2–0 home defeat to newly promoted Hércules, during which Villa appeared uncomfortable playing with his back to goal against a deep defence.

Guardiola needed to reformat his side, and therefore for Barca's next game, a Champions League game against Panathinaikos, he deployed his 'MVP' forward line for the first time: Messi, Villa and Pedro. Messi returned to the false 9 position, with Villa cutting inside from the left and Pedro on the right. Barcelona won 5–1, and Messi ran the game from his central position. He scored twice and should have had more, hitting both posts and the crossbar, and missing a penalty. His second goal was the best possible demonstration of his false 9 role. Receiving the ball 30 yards out, with Panathinaikos parking ten players on the edge of the box, Messi stormed forward, played one–twos with first Xavi, then Pedro, and fired home. Classic Barcelona one-touch football, combined with Messi providing directness through the middle.

Barcelona's forward trio played this way in their next league game, a 2–1 victory at Atlético Madrid, one of Barca's most tactically significant victories under Guardiola. He wanted a spare defender against Atlético's dangerous duo of Diego Forlán and Sergio Agüero, so Busquets dropped in and played as a third centre-back. Messi's ability to drift deep, therefore, meant he became the third midfielder to ensure Barca dominated the centre. Depending on the positioning of Busquets and the full-backs, Barca shifted between systems that looked like 4–3–1–2 and 3–4–1–2, the two systems that dominated Argentine football, both based around an *enganche*. Barcelona's optimum system now appeared obvious, with Messi playing centrally, so Villa was forced into a left-sided position, rather than the central role he'd been promised. Messi's advice about 'sticking the others out wide' had been followed perfectly; just like Henry, Eto'o and Ibrahimović before him, Villa had been denied his favoured central role.

Barcelona's most entertaining contest in 2010/11 was the 3–1 home victory over Villarreal in November. The wonderfully fluid Villarreal were arguably the only side to arrive at Camp Nou that season with the intention of outpassing Barca, which made for an enthralling, high-tempo and tactically fascinating game, partly because Villarreal also played a strikerless system. Although 4–4–2 on paper, the mobile forwards Giuseppe Rossi and Nilmar continually drifted out to opposite flanks, inviting the notional wide midfielders, Santi Cazorla and Cani, to move into the centre. It was an alternative method of playing without a fixed striker, and Villarreal's football that night, and throughout the season, earned plenty of praise from Barcelona's players. 'I don't remember a game that was that intense, playing against an opponent that is as strong as Villarreal,' remarked Guardiola afterwards. 'They're a gem of a team … the way they play, the way they press, they're the team that has made us suffer the most.'

Villarreal still lost, however, and Barcelona's second goal was another extraordinary Messi double-one–two, this time even simpler, but even more brilliant, than against Panathinaikos. Receiving the ball outside the box, with seven Villarreal players between him and the goal – and only one teammate, Pedro – Messi suddenly darted towards goal while producing two lightning-quick one–twos: Messi pass, Pedro return, Messi pass, Pedro return, Messi finish, dinked over the goalkeeper, from a tight angle, with his weaker right foot. Pedro hadn't moved, playing the two most literal wall-passes you'll ever witness, while Messi's three touches were played from three different zones: in front of the Villarreal midfield, then between Villarreal's midfield and defence, then in behind Villarreal's defence.

Messi started the move, linked the move and finished the move: a number 8, a number 10 and a number 9 within seconds, almost defying tactical description.

Messi was now the complete all-round attacker. There are essentially only three things a player can do when collecting possession: he can dribble, shoot or pass, and Messi excelled in all three respects. In 2010/11 his dribbling statistics were incredible, successfully beating opponents on 186 occasions, over 100 times more than anyone else in La Liga, demonstrating the extent to which dribbling was almost a foreign concept. He remained prolific, scoring 31 goals from 31 starts, but his biggest improvement after moving centrally was in terms of creativity. Messi managed 18 assists, the most in La Liga, and more tellingly, 11 of those assists came from through-balls slid between defenders for onrushing teammates. No one else in La Liga managed more than four.

This became Barcelona's classic move: Messi receiving the ball between the lines, tempting the centre-backs forward, and then slipping the ball through for Villa or Pedro, breaking in from wide to receive the ball in behind. In the famous 5–0 *El Clásico* victory he assisted Villa twice in this manner, happily playing a backseat role and ending a run of nine consecutive matches on the scoresheet. His relationship with Villa and Pedro was excellent: they might not have been as individually gifted as Henry, Eto'o or Ibrahimović beforehand, or Alexis Sánchez, Neymar or Luis Suárez afterwards, but they worked perfectly with Messi in Barcelona's system.

Barca rounded off 2010/11 with a 3–1 Champions League victory over Manchester United, a win that was far more convincing than their 2–0 win in the final two years earlier, with Messi giving Barca total control. 'We had to decide how to play tactically against Barcelona because of Villa and Pedro and the way they penetrated, and the fact they had no central striker made it hard to plan,' said

Ferguson. 'The two wide players were big improvements on Henry and Eto'o in terms of penetration.'

Messi's teammates, to a certain extent, attempted to claim him as a true Barcelona product. 'He's from Argentina, but it's like he's from here,' declared Xavi. Gerard Piqué offered a more balanced summary: 'He came with a very individual game to which Barcelona added the team game.' But the more intriguing story is not about Barca's influence on Messi, but about Messi's influence on Barca. It's obvious that his promotion of Argentine concepts, the *enganche* and *gambeta*, played a significant part in shaping Barcelona's style.

Barca struggled in 2011/12, with Villa injured, Pedro struggling for form, and newcomers Fàbregas and Sánchez unable to grasp Guardiola's tactics. But Messi enjoyed his best-ever goalscoring return, managing a scarcely believable 73 goals in 60 games. Barcelona's most thrilling and tactically fascinating football came at the start of the campaign, particularly when Guardiola deployed Fàbregas close to Messi in something approaching a 3–3–4, the duo taking it in turns to play number 9 and 10, linking seamlessly thanks to their rapport from their youth-team days. Barcelona were effectively deploying two false 9s.

Spain manager Del Bosque, meanwhile, suddenly found himself with a dilemma up front ahead of Euro 2012, with Villa out injured. He selected the out-of-form Torres, Athletic Bilbao's Fernando Llorente and Sevilla's Álvaro Negredo, with the latter detailing their styles neatly. 'Torres is very quick and mobile,' Negredo said, 'Llorente is big and strong … and I try and link well with my teammates and be in the right place at the right time.' Three distinct centre-forward options for Del Bosque to choose from: a sprinter, a target man, a link-up-man-cum-poacher.

But Messi's success at Barcelona had redefined football, to the extent that it was now entirely acceptable to play without a centre-forward. Ahead of Spain's opening Euro 2012 contest, Del Bosque suspected that Italy's old-school defenders would prefer a physical battle against a conventional striker, and therefore left out Torres, Llorente and Negredo, and instead played Fàbregas in the false 9 position he'd played for Barcelona on occasion. He sometimes alternated with David Silva, who started on the right of the 4–3–3.

Spain hadn't trained in that system, so the decision came as a shock to the players, and rather predictably they played in front of Italy rather than penetrating them. Silva played short backwards passes in positions where Messi would have turned and dribbled, while Fàbregas played too deep. But Spain's equaliser was a good example of their intentions: Silva, finding himself as Spain's most advanced player, received the ball between the lines, poked a left-footed pass through for the onrushing Fàbregas, who was making the type of out-to-in run usually associated with Villa or Pedro, and he finished smartly. It was a stereotypical false 9 goal, with the fact that a 'stereotypical false 9 goal' even existed saying much about Messi's influence.

Torres started the next two matches, victories over Ireland and Croatia, but Fàbregas returned for the 2–0 quarter-final win over France, with Spain's movement in the final third more integrated, and more effective at penetrating the opposition defence despite the lack of a striker. 'We are playing with three forwards,' Del Bosque insisted after that win. 'Iniesta, Fàbregas and Silva.' These clearly weren't forwards – they were midfielders – but in Spain the definition had changed.

Negredo was a surprise starter against Portugal in the semi-final, but was ineffective and replaced by Fàbregas ten minutes into the second half, prompting an improvement in Spain's passing. And therefore, just like in Euro 2008, Fàbregas's impact as a substitute in the semi-final meant he started the final, leading the line in Spain's famous 4–0 victory over Italy. He played more advanced than in previous matches, stretching the opposition defence with runs into the channels rather than continually coming short; he wasn't really a false 9, merely a midfielder deployed up front and instructed to go in behind. 'They may not play with a recognised striker,' rued Italy coach Cesare Prandelli, 'but they still cause a hell of a lot of problems.'

Playing in this manner marked the logical climax of Spain's increasing shift away from centre-forwards. They'd tried three when exiting the 2006 World Cup, generally used two at Euro 2008, switched to just one at the 2010 World Cup and finished Euro 2012 with none. Messi's influence on Spanish football was entirely contradictory. He smashed goalscoring records – while inspiring Spain, and others, to play without a goalscorer.

## 15

# El Clásico

It might sound peculiar to consider a single fixture a fundamental part of a country's footballing identity, but *El Clásico* was, during the Spanish era, the definitive concept in European football, a match that encapsulated every major footballing debate.

It was Pep versus José, Messi versus Ronaldo, possession versus counter-attack. And, just as Spanish football popularised possession play and a false 9, it also promoted this model of one grand occasion between a country's two biggest clubs. Suddenly, German observers referred to Bayern Munich versus Borussia Dortmund as *Der Klassiker*, France rebranded PSG versus Marseille as *Le Classique*. In truth, nothing came close to the original, which consistently attracted the world's largest TV audience for a football match.

In part, this was because no other major European footballing nation is so dominated by two clubs. It's not simply that 33 per cent of Spanish fans support Real and 26 per cent Barcelona – with no one else boasting more than 5 per cent – it's also that almost everyone who doesn't support Barca or Real nevertheless has a favourite between them. When surveyed, only 11 per cent of all Spanish fans expressed no preference.

But *El Clásico* in its current form, as the ultimate season-defining occasion, is a relatively modern concept. Tensions between the clubs originated in the pre-war years, and became particularly heated after Real captured Alfredo Di Stéfano from under Barca's noses in 1953. However, between 1960 and 1990, Barcelona won La Liga just twice; fewer than Atlético Madrid, then considered Real's fiercest rivals, and the same number as Athletic Bilbao and Real Sociedad. Barca were merely one of many challengers to Real. But between 2008 and 2012, before Atlético's resurgence, La Liga was unquestionable a duopoly, partly because of the scandalously uneven distribution of TV money in Spain. In 2011/12, depressingly, third-placed Valencia were actually closer to relegation than the big two, 20 points clear of the drop zone, but 30 points behind second place.

Of course, Barcelona versus Real Madrid always offered extra significance because of political tensions. Barca are not the sole representatives of Catalan independence, and Catalonia is not the only Spanish region boasting nationalist sentiments. But rebellious political feeling has become a defining part of Barca's identity, along-side their commitment to passing football, and even a casual observer will hear the chants for 'independència' when the Camp Nou's match clock displays 17:14 (representing the year the Army of Catalonia were defeated in the Siege of Barcelona) and notice the banners declaring that 'Catalonia is not Spain'.

In that respect, football created an interesting situation, because Catalonia *was* Spain – or, rather, Spain was Catalan. The national side was no longer dominated by *La Furia* or Basque clubs, or based around star individuals in the manner of Real Madrid. Instead, between 2008 and 2012 it was about the patient possession play epit-omised by Xavi Hernández, Sergio Busquets, Cesc Fàbregas, Gerard Piqué, Carles Puyol, Jordi Alba, Andrés Iniesta, David Villa and Pedro Rodríguez – nine crucial players who represented Barcelona, the first six of whom were also Catalan. Spain established themselves as Europe's best national side, and Barcelona established themselves as Europe's greatest club side, by using the same philosophy and the same players.

This was difficult for Real Madrid: the club of royalty, the club of the capital, the club of Spain. As Jimmy Burns outlined in *La Roja*, his history of Spanish football, throughout the national side's years of underachievement Real Madrid had 'helped promote an image of Spanish success overseas, converting itself into Franco's most important export ... Real Madrid were *the* representative of Spanish football at its best ... playing creative, offensive football in a way no other club in the world could match.'

But now what? These two clubs, as Xavi once outlined, are always 'on the two sides of the scale', and just as Barca had responded to Real's technical superiority in the 1960s by playing strong, fast, physical football, that's exactly what Real did here. In moving away from technical football, Spain's biggest club became less Spanish.

It is remarkable how quickly Barcelona's dominance became established. In 2007/08, Real had won their second straight league title in a dominant season that included two victories over Barcelona, particularly memorable for the pre-game 'guard of honour' Barca's players were forced to give their rivals at the Bernabéu. Samuel Eto'o and Deco had, conveniently, previously collected bookings to earn a suspension and therefore avoided the humiliation, but the others had no escape. Barca applauded Real on to the pitch, then lost 4–1. Puyol, Barcelona's captain, described it as the worst moment of his career. In summer 2008, Barcelona appointed Pep Guardiola. But more important, in the context of *El Clásico* rivalry, was who they didn't appoint: José Mourinho.

The first *Clásico* during this era of Spanish dominance, in December 2008, was most memorable for an event that occurred a week beforehand. While Guardiola's Barcelona streaked away at the top, Real Madrid were on a terrible run of form, losing three matches in a four-game spell, the only exception an unconvincing 1–0 win over relegation-bound Recreativo de Huelva. After the third defeat, 4–3 to Sevilla, Real's German coach Bernd Schuster made an extraordinary admission when asked about the following weekend's trip to Barcelona. 'I am less worried about that game than any other,' he explained. 'Winning at Camp Nou is impossible. Barcelona are rolling over everyone. It's impossible to beat them – it's their year.' Real were clearly underdogs, but describing a must-win game as a cannot-win game was suicidal. Schuster was sacked.

Real surprisingly appointed Juande Ramos – who had recently been dismissed by Tottenham Hotspur, bottom of the Premier League – then travelled to Barcelona and lost 2–0. Yet they performed surprisingly well, with Dutch winger Royston Drenthe missing a one-on-one at 0–0, and Barca's goals, scored by Eto'o and Leo Messi, only arriving in the final seven minutes. 'Considering the situation, we're satisfied,' said captain Raúl González, which was understandable but also underlined Real's inferiority. Ramos was evidently not a long-term appointment, but his recovery job was hugely impressive: after that Barcelona defeat, Real won 17 of their next 18 games, only failing in a 1–1 derby draw against Atlético. Real were therefore just four points behind as they welcomed Barcelona to the Bernabéu, an awkwardly timed contest for Guardiola's side, sandwiched between two tight Champions League semi-final legs against Chelsea. It was game on.

Ramos attempted to nullify Barcelona's strengths. Using a 4–2–3–1 formation to match Guardiola's midfield triangle, he effectively fielded two left-backs: Gabriel Heinze, a converted centre-back tasked with tracking Messi, and Marcelo, deployed as a defensive-minded winger to halt Dani Alves's overlapping runs.

But this was, of course, 'the Messi game', his first deployment as a false 9 since Guardiola's debut victory. He scored twice, and Real simply couldn't cope. Thierry Henry also bagged a brace, and centre-backs Puyol and Piqué bagged one apiece in a 6–2 victory, the first time either side had scored six in *El Clásico*. Barcelona effectively won La Liga that night, as they were seven points clear with four games remaining. Neither side won another league game: Real gave up, Barca concentrated on the cup competitions to complete the Treble, and were already considered an all-time great side.

Real's new sporting director, Jorge Valdano, summarised the club's situation. 'We must put Real back where they belong – we have to try and remove Barcelona from their dominant position,' he said. It was less about winning and more about toppling Barca, and Real responded in typical fashion. The architect of their previous *galácticos* policy, Florentino Pérez, was elected president for a second stint, and immediately splurged on superstars. Real broke their own world transfer record, set eight years beforehand when signing Zinedine Zidane, by recruiting Kaká from AC Milan. They waited fully two days before breaking the record again, for Manchester United's Cristiano Ronaldo. Pérez also spent huge sums on Lyon's Karim Benzema and Liverpool's Xabi Alonso, considered an important signing to help preserve Real's identity as a good Spanish footballing side. Álvaro Arbeloa, Álvaro Negredo, Raúl Albiol and Esteban Granero followed. It was, at the time, the most expensive transfer window in history.

Barcelona, in fairness, also spent big on Zlatan Ibrahimović, plus Maxwell and Dmytro Chygrynskiy, but benefited more from the promotion of Pedro, and Guardiola's decision to play Busquets rather than Yaya Touré. Pedro and Busquets had cost Barcelona nothing, which prompted Catalan journalists to creatively redefine this rivalry as *cantera* (youth academy) versus *cartera* (wallet). It was a simplification, but not entirely inaccurate – Real were essentially a collection of expensive individuals, whereas Barcelona were a cohesive unit.

'Barcelona play better football,' Ronaldo conceded. 'But only because they have been together for longer.'

Amid all this spending, it almost went unnoticed that Real also appointed Manuel Pellegrini, formerly of Villarreal, as their manager – but then Real were historically defined by players rather than coach. Real started Pellegrini's first *Clásico*, in November 2009, one point ahead of Barca at the top. This was largely billed as a meeting between Ronaldo and Ibrahimović, both making their first appearance in the fixture, but both were suffering from injuries, which meant Ronaldo was limited to playing for the first 65 minutes at the Camp Nou and Ibrahimović for the last 40. Ronaldo had a fine chance midway through the first half after outstanding work by Kaká – Real's two record-breaking signings combining – but his low shot was saved by Víctor Valdés's feet. Ibrahimović's volley proved the winner, with Real failing to score despite playing against ten men for 30 minutes after Busquets' red card.

For the second year running, Real were content with a brave defeat at the Camp Nou, almost reducing themselves to plucky underdogs. Pellegrini boasted that he'd 'never seen Barca create so little', sporting director Valdano claimed Real were 'leaving here satisfied' and Real-supporting newspaper *Marca* suggested it 'tasted like a victory'. It was a curious attitude considering that Real had lost the game, and with it the leadership of La Liga.

For the second *Clásico* of 2009/10, in April, the teams started level on points – and Real had a 100 per cent home record. The title race was 50:50, and therefore, just like the previous campaign, it was time for Guardiola to spring a tactical surprise. He was wary of Marcelo blunting Alves's overlapping bursts again, so used the Brazilian as a right-sided forward in Barca's 4–3–3, with Ibrahimović's absence meaning Messi played as a false 9, with Pedro wide-left. Pellegrini, meanwhile, attempted to dominate the centre with a diamond midfield: Alonso played behind Fernando Gago and Marcelo, while Rafael van der Vaart linked midfield and the forwards, Ronaldo and Gonzalo Higuaín. But despite Barcelona theoretically being overrun in midfield four against three, they managed to dominate that zone. The key, once again, was Messi, who typically dropped into a midfield position to occupy Alonso. Meanwhile, Real were startled by Alves playing as a right-sided forward, and rather than left-back Arbeloa marking him, Marcelo – on the left of the diamond – tracked him. That meant no one was in a position to stop Xavi, and he once again dominated this fixture. The opener came in telling fashion, when Messi dropped into midfield, played a sideways pass to Xavi – in fully 20 yards of space between the lines – and he chipped a return pass over the defence, allowing Messi to collect the ball and fire home.

At half-time Guardiola reformatted his side and returned Alves to right-back, so Marcelo played further forward. But it was still unclear who was supposed to be tracking Xavi, and ten minutes into the second half he collected the ball in oceans of space on the halfway line, waited for Pedro to make a run in behind, slipped the ball through the defence and Pedro finished with typical precision. 2–0, game over, and Barcelona were now clear title favourites. It might have been a greater margin of victory, as Xavi twice played superb passes in behind for Messi, who was thwarted by Iker Casillas both times. Xavi could have recorded four assists at the Bernabéu for the second year running.

Despite taking Real to a club record 96 points, Pellegrini was sacked after a single campaign having consistently been subjected to astonishingly strong criticism in the pages of *Marca*. Pérez wanted an upgrade, and there was one obvious candidate: Mourinho. Real fans had already started supporting him; Mourinho's Inter Milan had defeated Barcelona in the Champions League semi-finals with notoriously negative tactics that involved 'deliberately giving the ball away', in Mourinho's words, which denied Barca the opportunity to become the first club to retain the trophy in its modern format. Moreover, that year's final was at the Bernabéu, and Real supporters couldn't stomach the thought of Barcelona celebrating a historic achievement in their own backyard. Mourinho, winding up Barcelona while predisposing himself to his future employers, constantly talked about Barca's 'obsession' with winning the Champions League at the Bernabéu. He was still fuming from his snub two years earlier, and now framed himself as the anti-Barca coach, which is precisely why Real were so seduced.

After all, Real don't generally appreciate intense, demanding, all-powerful managers like Mourinho, preferring more easy-going figures like Vicente del Bosque beforehand, or Carlo Ancelotti and Zinedine Zidane afterwards. Power at Real traditionally resides with the club's president and the players; the manager is almost a disposable middleman. But this was different. Mourinho demanded power over almost every aspect of the club, which Pérez granted him. 'This year's *galáctico* is José Mourinho,' Real's president announced.

Mourinho's appointment marked another departure for Real, a club traditionally concerned with attractive football. He was now renowned as a defensive manager after his stints with Chelsea and Inter, and while he promised his outlook would be more positive to keep the supporters happy, he didn't personally care about whether his side's football was entertaining – to him, football was solely about winning, and he had absolutely no time for the Spanish possession obsession. Cruyff would later criticise Mourinho for being 'a titles coach, not a football coach', to which Mourinho responded with a simple, 'Thank you. I like that.'

Mourinho's arrival immediately made Real less cultured, less possession-based and less Spanish. They waved farewell to two players who had been at the Bernabéu for 15 years: illustrious forward

Raúl, considered too slow to counter-attack, and languid playmaker Guti. Real recruited two Germans who had impressed on the break at the World Cup: the wonderfully elusive playmaker Mesut Özil and powerful box-to-box midfielder Sami Khedira. There was also Ángel Di María, a hard-working wide midfielder, speedy right-winger Pedro León and centre-back Ricardo Carvalho, who had played under Mourinho at both Porto and Chelsea. Barcelona had popularised patience and technique, but Mourinho prioritised physicality and speed. Now Real, once that great symbol of Spanish football, would effectively become Portuguese: their manager was Mourinho, their star was Ronaldo, while the player who would personify their style in *Clásicos* was Pepe.

Whereas Portuguese football had previously been considered exciting, attack-minded and technical, it was now viewed in a more negative light, partly thanks to Mourinho's ultra-cautious tactics during Inter's Treble-winning campaign of 2009/10. It was Mourinho who had introduced the phrase 'park the bus' in 2004, mocking a rival's ultra-defensive tactics. Now he personified that approach. Portugal's 2010 World Cup campaign under Carlos Quieroz was also largely negative – in four matches they kept three clean sheets, but also failed to score three times before being eliminated by Spain. Portugal were now, more than ever, the anti-Spain.

For their part, Barcelona appeared genuinely enthused by the challenge of Mourinho. Xavi said his arrival would 'motivate us more', and Guardiola believed that Mourinho 'will make me a better manager – it is important that he works in Spain because he is one of the best in the world. He will make us all better.' Everyone was prepared for a titanic battle between Guardiola's Barcelona and Mourinho's Real, with Arrigo Sacchi describing the situation as 'like having two Picassos in the same period'. Spain were now the world champions, La Liga was the centre of the footballing world, and the intensity of *El Clásico* had stepped up a notch. 'It doesn't matter if you're 10, 50 or 100,' declared *El País*. 'You've never lived anything like the moment you're living now.'

The battle lines were drawn. Barcelona's midfielders were instructed to actively slow down breaks with prolonged build-up play, so their players could organise themselves into the correct positional structure. Real thrived on the counter-attack, were compact and excellent at transitions without being overwhelmingly negative, the perfect hybrid between Mourinho's preferred style and the approach favoured by Real's supporters. More importantly, Real started with ten wins and two draws in the league, and arrived at the Camp Nou in November for Mourinho's first *Clásico* one point ahead of Barca. Mourinho instructed his players to let Barca dominate possession but keep a relatively high defensive line; they weren't trying to fully compete or entirely retreat. This halfway house, however, resulted in the biggest humiliation of Mourinho's career: Barcelona 5–0 Real Madrid.

Mourinho, like Pellegrini before him, was terrified of Alves's overlapping runs, and therefore swapped his wingers. Ronaldo couldn't be trusted to track back, so moved to the right, and the disciplined Di María attempted to stop Alves, although this hampered Real's usual understanding on the counter-attack. It was another familiar problem, however, that cost Real: how to stop Xavi. It was widely expected that Mourinho would drop Özil in favour of an extra defensive midfielder, but he continued with the creative option, while also asking Özil to man-mark Xavi. This was plainly not Özil's speciality, and Xavi demonstrated his intelligence by pushing high up the pitch, where he knew Özil would be uncomfortable following, to the extent that he scored Barca's opener from a centre-forward position. Pedro made it 2–0, and then Mourinho reversed his two major pre-match decisions. First, Ronaldo reverted to the left, from where he was more threatening. Then Özil was sacrificed and the destructive Lassana Diarra took his place. This was Mourinho's admission that he'd got his starting tactics wrong.

Mourinho knew his side couldn't drop deep, because Barcelona would happily play keep-ball in midfield. Real therefore took an even higher defensive line, but this exposed them further, and from his now-customary false 9 position, Messi created two goals for Villa with pinpoint through-balls. The scoring was completed in almost mocking fashion in stoppage time, by a completely obscure player, Venezuelan-born winger Jeffrén Suárez, who looked so surprised that at first he didn't quite know how to celebrate. But Gerard Piqué, the Barcelona boy whose grandfather was once Barcelona's vice-president, certainly did.

As his teammates huddled by the dugouts, Piqué held up five fingers to the supporters, and the supporters held up five fingers back. This was *La Manita*, the little hand, a reference to the way Barcelona had celebrated after their 5–0 victory over Real Madrid in 1994. 'That gesture strung more than the 5–0 itself,' wrote Real-supporting *Marca*.

In fact, this was the third time in living memory that Barcelona had defeated Real by five goals, when added to the 5–0 win in 1973 shortly after Cruyff's arrival as a player and the 5–0 win in 1994 under Cruyff's management. A 4–0 win over Mourinho's Real would have been merely famous, but a 5–0 win made it unforgettable, era-defining, part of the hat-trick: the Michels–Cruyff side, the Cruyff–Guardiola side and now the Guardiola–Xavi side, tracing Barca's greatest influences through the generations. 'Stay humble,' Guardiola told his players after they'd returned to the dressing room, trying to disguise his delight. 'But what you've just done is fucking spectacular.' Real's president, Pérez, described it as 'the worst game in the history of Real Madrid'.

Luckily for Mourinho he had four months to prepare for his next meeting with Barcelona, but it was merely the first of four fixtures between the sides in 18 incredible, intense, action-packed days. The 16th of April: the return fixture in La Liga; 20 April: the Copa del Rey final; 27 April: the Champions League semi-final first leg; 3 May: the second leg. In the previous eight seasons, Real and Barca hadn't met in any cup competitions at all, only playing twice per season in the league. Now they faced four matches in 18 days, in a highly tactical series that would essentially decide all three major trophies. 'When you play many times against each other, it becomes like the basketball play-offs,' explained Guardiola, in Guillem Balague's biography. 'You do one thing, they respond with another, you answer in another way … the guessing, the changing, the preparing, the switches during games, guessing what formation they will play, how we can surprise them – that is what makes everything enjoyable, what gives meaning to everything.' It was a head-to-head clash between the world's two most revered tacticians.

The opening contest of the series, the league encounter at the Bernabéu, was an appetiser before the main course. Barcelona were eight points ahead of Real and, despite playing against ten men throughout the second half after Raúl Albiol's dismissal, were happy with the 1–1 draw, with Messi and Ronaldo both scoring penalties. Most significant, however, was Mourinho's midfield selection; this time he omitted Özil and used what he described as his 'high-pressure triangle', with Pepe as a holding midfielder behind Khedira and Alonso. While Pepe had played that position for Portugal, he was principally a centre-back, so this was Mourinho unashamedly injecting extra physicality into midfield. Pepe was the game's best performer, sitting solidly in front of the defence and denying Messi the freedom he'd enjoyed in the 5–0. Barcelona essentially confirmed the title with this draw, but it felt like Mourinho had already conceded

La Liga and was using this contest purely as preparation for the following three *Clásicos*.

Four days later, the sides reconvened in Valencia for the first cup final *Clásico* for 21 years. Mourinho again used a 4–3–3 system, but this time Ronaldo moved up front, with Di María and Özil, magnificent upon his return, out wide. The midfield trio again comprised Pepe, Alonso and Khedira. But, crucially, Mourinho deployed them in a different formation; Pepe was no longer merely screening the defence, but playing a box-to-box role, allowing Alonso to sit deep and spray diagonal passes. Pepe was handed the task of pressing Xavi, Real's major tormentor in past *Clásicos*, and he also pushed forward to become a goal threat, heading against the post. Once again, Pepe was the game's key player: a one-man, marauding pressing machine and the antithesis to the Spanish philosophy of cramming multiple playmakers into midfield.

The two sides were employing utterly contrasting tactics, and the game's two 'goals' summarised everything. Barcelona thought they'd won it with a classic move, with Messi receiving the ball in a false 9 position, slaloming past two challenges and threading a pass into Pedro, who made a typical out-to-in run and finished coolly – but the linesman flagged for offside, and the match remained goalless. Then, in extra-time, Real scored the winner with an attack typical of their approach: a quick ball out wide, a cross into the box and a powerful header from Ronaldo. It was, literally and symbolically, an anti-Barca goal. Real had clinched the Copa del Rey – which ended up badly damaged after Real's celebratory bus parade through Madrid, when Sergio Ramos dropped it from the open-top and the driver ran it over. 'Parking the bus' jokes ensued.

Suddenly, momentum was with Real, and Mourinho felt emboldened. He claimed Barcelona looked 'psychologically tired' in the cup final, and strongly outlined his objections to the Spanish style. 'Here, people think that good football is just about having possession. They're limited thinkers. I believe there are many other ways of playing well, like defensive organisation, solidarity, the ability to withstand pressure and to close down spaces while preparing a counter-attack at the same time. In my opinion, tonight Real played a great match because they demonstrated all those qualities.'

Now, the tension between Mourinho and Guardiola turned to outright hostility. In the aftermath of the Copa defeat, Guardiola mentioned Pedro's offside goal and how matches are decided by fine margins. He wasn't actually arguing with the decision, but in a press conference shortly before the Champions League first leg at the Bernabéu, Mourinho mocked Barca's coach for complaining about a correct decision. This infuriated Barca's manager, who hit back later with a famous press-conference rant. 'Tomorrow at 8:45 we are going to face one another on the pitch,' Guardiola ranted. 'He has already won the off-pitch battle, he has been winning all season ... in this press room, he is the fucking chief, the fucking boss. I don't want to compete with him in this arena, not even for a second.'

Barcelona's players later said they thought Guardiola's response was brilliant, although had they lost the subsequent game it might have been considered his Kevin Keegan moment. In the grand scheme of things it probably had minimal impact on the Champions League game, but it confirmed that Mourinho had seriously rattled Guardiola, who was privately speaking about quitting at the end of the season. He wasn't enjoying this *Clásico* series, which he would later describe as 'tremendously hard, with a lot of tension – very intense and very tiring'.

The first leg at the Bernabéu was a dirty game of attrition, with both sides spending longer fouling – and complaining about fouls – than playing football. Real Madrid pressed less than in the cup victory, which enraged Ronaldo, again playing as a lone striker. He frantically attempted to close down three Barcelona players on his own, realised no one was backing up his press, and threw a melodramatic strop midway through the game. Real concentrated on sitting deep and blocking Barcelona's route to goal, which involved the towering figure of Pepe again performing a man-marking job on Xavi, and with Iniesta out injured, Barcelona offered little invention. The first half finished goalless.

The game's crucial incident occurred after an hour and involved the key man in Real's game plan: Pepe. He steamed in front of Pedro to win a loose ball, then his momentum carried him furiously into a challenge on Alves, whom he tackled both high and late. He was shown a straight red card. On the touchline Mourinho gave the fourth official a sarcastic wink and a thumbs-up, mouthing 'Well done' to him, and he was also dismissed. Now down to ten men, Real's game plan collapsed because Xavi was no longer marked and Real's 4–4–1 system meant that they were outnumbered in midfield. Barcelona piled on the pressure, and Messi converted substitute Ibrahim Afellay's cross for the opener.

Messi, in truth, had been unusually quiet in this sequence of *Clásicos*, but then three minutes from time he provided the outstanding moment of this otherwise petulant, scrappy series with a truly magnificent solo run, collecting the ball between the lines, beating four Real players and rolling the ball home with his right foot. It was an incredible goal, yet surely wouldn't have happened if Real had still had eleven men on the pitch; the space between their defensive and midfield quartets was huge, because they'd previously been accustomed to playing with a defensive midfielder between them. Pepe's departure had cost Real dearly, but his red card felt like an inevitable consequence of Mourinho's instructions, which involved Pepe taking his battering-ram act to every corner of the pitch.

By this stage, the on-field proceedings were discussed less than the manager's press-conference rants, and this game was followed by Mourinho's famous '*Por qué?*' speech in which he claimed that Barcelona were consistently getting favourable refereeing decisions. More intriguing was his suggestion that 'The strategy I implemented wouldn't have allowed us to lose.' His certainty was unconvincing, but having been utterly destroyed in the 5–0 at Camp Nou just four months earlier, it increasingly felt like he understood how to blunt Barca.

At 2–0 down and with Pepe suspended, Real had little chance in the return fixture. The game finished 1–1 and was uneventful; Pedro opened the scoring, Marcelo equalised and Real rarely looking like mounting a comeback. The first leg had decided the tie, according to most observers – including Mourinho. Indeed, this game had a wider significance, providing the title for *Prepárense para peder* (*Prepare to Lose*), a stunning exposé of Mourinho's Real regime by the *El País* journalist Diego Torres. In his book, Torres claims that Mourinho gathered his players ahead of the second leg and, despite Real Madrid being 2–0 down, encouraged them to play defensively and take a 0–0 draw. That way Mourinho could attribute the aggregate defeat purely to refereeing decisions. It split Real's players; some understood his thinking, others were infuriated. Zinedine Zidane, part of Real's backroom staff and close to many of the players, contradicted the coach, suggesting Real's players 'should try to beat Barcelona – we are Real Madrid and Real Madrid always go out to win'. There were now serious problems in Real's dressing room. Ronaldo was becoming increasingly frustrated by Mourinho's tactics; in two years at Real he'd only won a sole Copa del Rey.

That cup triumph meant that Real faced Barcelona in the two-legged Supercopa, which kicked off Spanish football's dramatic 2011/12 campaign. In the first leg, at the Bernabéu, Mourinho used the same starting XI as in the 5–0, as if he'd spent the intervening four matches gradually correcting tactical errors and was now confident enough to demonstrate that his initial approach could work. Real were bold and proactive; Karim Benzema kept running in behind, Ronaldo played wide-left and caused Alves serious problems. Real dominated, and only excellent individual goals from Villa and Messi saved Barca. It finished 2–2.

Barcelona won the Supercopa in the second leg with a 3–2 victory over Real, in a game utterly dominated by Messi. He provided the assist for Iniesta's opener on 15 minutes, collecting the ball deep, easing past a couple of challenges and providing a perfect through-ball. Ronaldo flicked in a clever equaliser five minutes later, but just before half-time Messi played a one–two with Piqué, and cleverly dinked the ball home. Ten minutes from time, Benzema made it 4–4 on aggregate with a scrappy goal after a set-piece, but Messi hit a late winner after another one–two, swapping passes with newcomer Adriano and thumping in a left-footed volley to spark the wildest celebrations you'll witness at a semi-competitive game. No match between these two is ever less than full-blooded.

Real were furious at their late concession, which prompted the single biggest flashpoint throughout these increasingly bitter *Clásicos*, when Marcelo made an atrocious two-footed tackle on Cesc Fàbregas, directly in front of the dugouts. The Brazilian was dismissed and disappeared down the tunnel, leaving an utterly chaotic scene behind him: a mass brawl that featured all 21 remaining players, most of the substitutes, several of the coaching staff and a couple of unidentified, smartly dressed men who happened to be nearby. The referee waded through the melee finding others to dismiss; Villa was one, Barcelona's substitute goalkeeper José Pinto another, and the fourth player sent off was Özil, escorted down the tunnel by Marcelo, who had generously returned to the pitch in an attempt to calm the mess he'd created. 'They're not to blame,' said Gerard Piqué. 'They're just following orders.' The most serious incident in the melee was Mourinho taking the opportunity to stroll across the turf towards Barcelona's assistant coach Tito Vilanova, approaching him from the side and poking his finger into Vilanova's eye. It was a completely unprovoked, cowardly act, and it took Mourinho a year to apologise.

By now, tensions between Real and Barcelona players – and in particular those who played together for Spain – were at their peak. Vicente del Bosque was seriously concerned, particularly by the sight of Xavi and Casillas, long-term friends who had brought the Spain squad together, furiously arguing on the pitch. Casillas later phoned Xavi to apologise for his part in the ruckus, admitting he hadn't realised how bad Marcelo's tackle had been. Their close friendship, incidentally, infuriated Mourinho, who fell out with his goalkeeper to the extent that he later dropped 167-cap Casillas in favour of one-cap Diego López. The senior members of Spain's national team just about held everything together, although Barcelona's players were surprised that Xabi Alonso became so unsporting throughout their running battles, and had reservations about Álvaro Arbeloa, the most ardent Mourinho loyalist in Real's dressing room.

There was a long wait for the first league *Clásico* of the 2011/12 season, in mid-December, which saw arguably Guardiola's most advanced tactical plan of his four-year spell, resulting in a 3–1 victory for Barca. The win was particularly impressive considering Barcelona had gone 1–0 down within 30 seconds, when Real pressed heavily, goalkeeper Víctor Valdés got his pass wrong and Benzema fired in the quickest goal in *El Clásico* history.

Guardiola had a plan that involved – as with many of his game plans in big matches – switching shape after ten minutes. Barca lined up in something approaching their usual 4–3–3 system, with Iniesta playing wide-left, Messi in a right-sided role and newcomer Alexis Sánchez up front. But suddenly they changed formation dramatically. Messi became a number 10, which caused a knock-on effect throughout the side; Alves pushed forward from right-back to become the right-winger, so right-sided centre-back Puyol became right-back, Piqué moved across to follow him and – most impressively – Busquets dropped into a peculiar hybrid role that saw him playing as half-midfielder, half-defender.

There were several benefits. Busquets found space away from Özil and fed balls into midfield, while also closing down the German when required. Ronaldo, playing on Real's left, was now facing both Puyol and Piqué when he attempted to dribble towards goal. Alves offered a huge threat from the right and created Barca's crucial third goal, a Fàbregas header, after earlier goals from Sánchez and Xavi. This was a genuine tactical masterclass, Barca winning away at the Bernabéu with an almost indecipherable system. This was the only time Real failed to win, however, during a 22-game spell midway through the season. They were in command of La Liga, yet were still struggling to defeat Barcelona.

There were two 'bonus' *Clásicos* when the sides were almost inevitably drawn together for a two-legged Copa del Rey quarter-final in January. It was a strange tie. Real again opened the scoring early at the Bernabéu, this time through Ronaldo, and competed well in open play, but they struggled badly at defending set-pieces and conceded goals to Puyol and Abidal in a 2–1 defeat. They felt compelled to attack in the return leg and dominated the first half, again pressing excellently but missing chances. Pedro scored on the break and then Alves slammed in an incredible long-range strike to make it 4–1 to Barca on aggregate. Real hit back, scoring two second-half goals through Ronaldo and Benzema to leave themselves only one goal away from winning the tie. It didn't come, yet Real had dominated proceedings and were now confident of taking the game to Barcelona.

Three months later, Real returned to the Camp Nou for the title showdown, four points ahead of Barcelona. Guardiola believed his side needed to win – a draw was not enough because Barca surely wouldn't claw back four points from Real in the subsequent four matches. For Barca it was win or bust; for Real a draw was enough. And when a draw is enough, Mourinho usually plays for – and achieves – that draw.

But in a different sense a draw wasn't enough. Granted, it would put Real on course for the league title, but it would also ensure that from six *Clásicos* in 2011/12 – two each in league, cup and Supercopa – Real wouldn't have defeated Barcelona once. And Mourinho's mission in Madrid wasn't solely about Real winning – it was about beating Barca, not just in the league table but also on the pitch. Without a victory over Barcelona, Real would be accused of merely being flat-track bullies.

Barcelona, by this stage, were unravelling dramatically. Guardiola had fallen out with several players, most notably Fàbregas and Piqué, and for this crucial *Clásico* he put faith in two young La Masia graduates, Thiago Alcántara and Cristian Tello, in 3–3–1–3 formation – a shape, as Guardiola admitted, that is highly risky unless you control the entire game, something Barcelona were finding increasingly difficult.

Mourinho deployed his default 4–2–3–1. Özil, often omitted from *Clásicos* or shunted out wide, played his favoured number 10 role. Ronaldo, often moved up front because of concerns about his defensive indiscipline out wide, played in his preferred left-sided role. After pressing in the early stages, Real dropped off – but not to the extent of Mourinho's Inter two years earlier. Instead they continued to hold an aggressive offside line as in their 5–0 defeat, but here

Barcelona lacked penetrative runs. Alves was fielded as a winger but offered little goal threat, while Tello's movement was good but his finishing woeful. Messi was contained; one of Real's centre-backs, either Pepe or Sergio Ramos, could follow him into deep positions, and the other would cover, without any Barca player exploiting the space created.

Throughout Guardiola's time at Barcelona his side were considered vulnerable to two types of attack: set-pieces and counter-attacks. That's where Real's goals came from here, making it the definitive, textbook anti-Barcelona victory. Khedira scrambled in a scruffy opener from a corner on the right, and Real led for the majority of the match. Then substitute Alexis Sánchez scored an even scrappier equaliser for Barcelona, but two minutes later Real confirmed their victory with a classic direct move; Özil drifted right to receive a pass and then played a through-ball into the path of Ronaldo, who shifted the ball to the side of Valdés, steadied himself, and then fired home. Barcelona were defeated – in the title fight, and on the pitch.

That was essentially the end of Guardiola's Barcelona. Three days later, Barca were beaten in the Champions League semi-final by Mourinho's former club Chelsea, who unashamedly copied the approach of his Inter in 2010. Three days after that, Guardiola announced he would leave Barcelona at the end of the campaign, a decision greeted with genuine sadness within Spain and across the football world. Guardiola was utterly drained after four years in charge, and in particular after two years of fighting an ugly war against Mourinho's Real, which Guardiola believed he'd lost. Pictures of Guardiola upon his appointment and his resignation are startling – he'd aged a decade and his demeanour was drastically gloomier. He hadn't enjoyed his final season at Barca and declared he had 'mostly bad memories' of the *Clásicos*, despite the incredible 6–2, despite the glorious 5–0, despite winning 3–1 with the most daring tactical system of his managerial career.

Everyone pointed the finger at Mourinho for Guardiola's departure, which was considered a blow not merely to Barcelona but to Spanish football as a whole. 'Mourinho did more harm than good; he damaged Spanish football,' said Iniesta. That, of course, was music to the ears of Mourinho. 'Yes, I damaged Spanish football,' he said. 'By being the manager that broke Barcelona's dominance.'

# Transition: Spain–Germany

For the first few international tournaments of the 21st century, Germany arrived with an uninspiring squad and a defensive approach, and either crashed out early with little sympathy or reached the final stages amid praise for their resilience and toughness. The Bundesliga, meanwhile, was considered among Europe's second-tier leagues.

Then suddenly it all changed. At the 2010 World Cup Germany were the most thrilling side in the competition, putting four goals past Australia, England and Argentina. They were defeated by eventual champions Spain in the semi-final, but scored twice as many goals as Vicente del Bosque's side in the competition. This was a new, young, exciting Germany side, and almost immediately the footballing world speculated that Euro 2012 would be their tournament: once their young squad had a couple more years' top-level experience, Germany would supersede Spain.

A few weeks beforehand, meanwhile, Bayern Munich had reached the Champions League Final, dominating José Mourinho's Inter but losing 2–0. After the defeat, Bayern president Uli Hoeneß looked to the future. 'We mustn't fret,' he said. 'After all, Munich will host the Champions League Final in 2012, so there's plenty to dream of.'

From two years out, 2012 was earmarked as the start of German dominance.

It didn't happen so smoothly. Bayern battled through to the Champions League Final in their home stadium, and then were almost inexplicably defeated by Chelsea, despite managing 35 shots to Chelsea's nine, and 20 corners to Chelsea's one. Germany, meanwhile, seemed set for another crack at Spain in the Euro 2012 final, but then surprisingly exited at the semi-final stage against Italy.

We therefore had to wait until the following season, 2012/13, for the moment when Germany's ascendency became clear. The turning point came over two midweek evenings in late April, in the Champions League semi-finals. On the Tuesday Bayern recorded an incredible 4–0 victory over Barcelona, the side that had utterly dominated European football for the previous four seasons. 'The Torch Passes to Bayern Munich,' read the *New York Times* headline. On the Wednesday Borussia Dortmund inflicted a 4–1 defeat on Real Madrid. It was 'more evidence of a shift towards German dominance of Europe', according to the BBC.

The German league leaders had thrashed the Spanish league leaders, and then the reigning German champions had thrashed the reigning Spanish champions. 'Germany 8, Spain 1: Bayern and Dortmund have overrun all of Europe!' screamed *Bild*. 'Bayern Munich and Borussia Dortmund have handed out first-class business cards for German football,' said German Football Association president Wolfgang Niersbach, which itself felt like a very German metaphor. 'Everyone saw Germany as a top football address in Europe. This applies to the Bundesliga, the individual clubs and, of course, the national team. We can now dream of an all-German final at Wembley.' Both sides completed the job in Spain, and the Champions League Final was Bayern versus Dortmund.

Now, for the first time in the modern era, German club football became genuinely admired for its on-pitch quality. Previously, positive coverage focused on fan-owned clubs, cheap tickets and brilliant atmospheres, but now the football itself took centre-stage. Germany had the infrastructure to develop top-class technical talent and the coaching to outwit Europe's best. Bayern defeated Dortmund at Wembley to complete the Treble, and then appointed Pep Guardiola, Europe's most revered coach, suggesting they would dominate for the next few years.

A year later, at the 2014 World Cup, Spain were eliminated at the group stage. Germany recorded perhaps the most momentous result in World Cup history, defeating hosts Brazil 7–1 in the semi-final, and then lifted the trophy, having overcome Argentina. The rest of Europe now sought its inspiration from Germany, a footballing landscape dominated by quick attacking, aggressive pressing and the complete reinvention of what 'German football' meant.

Part Six

# Fußball, 2012–16

# 16

# Verticality

For decades Germany arrived at international tournaments and pundits used the same old cliché to describe them: efficient. It essentially referred to the national side's ability to reach the knockout stages in a ruthless, mechanical manner; they weren't the most technically gifted team, but they always found a way.

The modern Germany side was very different: skilful, technical, likeable. But somehow the old cliché still worked. Amid growing frustration at Spain's determination to retain possession without providing penetration, Germany offered similar levels of technical quality, but their use of the ball was simply more ... efficient. Germany's 1–0 defeat to Spain at the 2010 World Cup showcased the style of Europe's new dominant footballing nations – it was tiki-taka versus counter-attack.

That said, it would be unreasonable to suggest that German football represented the opposite of Spanish football. This wasn't a comparable situation to defensive Italian football superseding attack-minded Dutch football in the mid-1990s, for example, because German players and coaches considered Spanish football their inspiration. 'Spain are always our role model,' Germany manager Jogi Löw explained to German magazine *11 Freunde* in 2012. 'I am totally convinced that one can no longer win titles by playing ugly football. In recent years, we have made huge progress in our play, and now we have a quickness and a creativity that allows us to be on a par with Brazil or Spain in terms of playing style. We used to have to compensate for that with guts and willpower.' Midfielders like Mesut Özil and Toni Kroos boasted comparable technical quality to their Spanish equivalents, and both moved to Real Madrid having been constantly linked with Barcelona. Xavi Hernández said that Kroos offered 'a way of playing that reminds me a lot of myself – he is like my successor on the field'.

Yet within the sphere of technically proficient football, the stereotypical Spanish and German schools were very different. Xavi's Barcelona would noticeably decline counter-attacking opportunities when they won the ball, preferring to retain possession. Pep Guardiola spoke about a golden '15-pass rule', explaining that such a lengthy sequence was necessary for his players to organise themselves in the correct positional structure.

Instead, German football was about transitions. Almost every Bundesliga side was capable of winning the ball in a deep position and pouncing quickly on the counter, speedily turning defence into attack. Statistics from Opta demonstrate that there were significantly more counter-attacking goals in Germany than in Spain; between 2012 and 2016, a sample of 100 games from the Bundesliga and La Liga would, on average, produce 32 and 19 'fast-break' goals respectively. These figures only accounted for when counter-attacks were directly finished, of course. Other goals were scored from set-pieces won through counter-attacking, or when a side successfully pressed to win the ball quickly, having initially driven forward on a counter.

German football's love of counter-attacking became particularly apparent in Bayern's famous 7–0 aggregate victory over Barcelona in 2013. That season, Jupp Heynckes' side had recorded ball-retention

statistics second only to Barca across Europe, and pre-match speculation focused on whether Barcelona would finally record less than
50 per cent of possession, having not fallen below that mark for over
300 games stretching back to May 2008, just before Guardiola's
appointment. In the end, it wasn't a factor. Barcelona recorded 63 per
cent of possession in Germany, and 57 per cent back in Spain,
because Bayern didn't even attempt to out-pass them, instead dominating in the areas where Barcelona were stereotypically, if rarely,
exposed: physicality, set-pieces and counter-attacking. Bayern were
capable of outpassing almost anyone, but against Barcelona they
were harder, better, faster, stronger. Heynckes' team didn't perfect
one particular style as gracefully as Barcelona, but they were true
all-rounders, capable of winning matches in different ways.

Bayern's first two goals in Munich came from set-pieces, finished
by powerful forwards Thomas Müller and Mario Gómez. As
Barcelona increasingly pushed forward in search of an away goal,
they played into the hands of Bayern, who ruthlessly attacked
through the speedy wide duo of Arjen Robben and Franck Ribéry.
The Dutchman added the third goal from the right, surprising
Barcelona by dribbling down the outside before finishing with his
left foot, while Müller rounded off a break down the left for the
fourth. 'They were physically very strong,' said Xavi afterwards. 'In
fact, they were superior. We didn't create chances. It's a dreadful
result.'

Heynckes, meanwhile, was delighted by his side's strategic intelligence. 'The decisive factors were the organisation of the team and the
tactical discipline,' he said. 'We did so well defensively, every player
was really happy to stay back ... we can do this and attack, because
we have a lot of creativity and quality going forward. If we have the
spaces, then we use them.' Bayern's attacking players, particularly
Ribéry and Robben, were content to defend for long periods, then

delighted to burst into space. In Munich, Bayern had drawn Barcelona on to them and then attacked in behind, and they executed the same approach at the Camp Nou. Robben collected a long diagonal pass from David Alaba, cut inside as usual and curled the ball into the far corner, before Ribéry took charge, twice dribbling down the left and crossing, with first Gerard Piqué slashing into his own net, and then Müller providing a trademark far-post header. 7–0 over the two matches.

Ribéry and Robben were old-school wingers, proper dribblers, the type Barcelona had eschewed in favour of a false 9 and wide forwards making off-the-ball runs. They typified Bayern's approach throughout this period, right from Robben's debut as a half-time substitute in a 3–0 victory over Wolfsburg in 2009. The Dutchman scored two goals, both on the counter-attack, both assisted by Ribéry, both celebrated by pointing to his new wing partner. Their second goal was particularly memorable, with the attack starting on the edge of Bayern's own area, and featuring the two wingers swapping passes at breakneck speed, with Wolfsburg defenders struggling to keep up – and Bayern teammates not even trying. It was an ominous warning sign; Bayern would attack predominantly through these two players, in this fashion, for the next decade. The two brilliant counter-attackers had bounced around various clubs beforehand, frustrating managers and struggling to fulfil their potential, but German football suited Ribéry more than France or Turkey, and suited Robben more than England or Spain.

As a side focusing on possession play, Bayern were an anomaly in the Bundesliga. They recorded a pass-completion rate of 87 per cent in their Treble-winning season, whereas every other Bundesliga side managed somewhere between 71 per cent and 81 per cent. Bayern were the counter-attacking side when they played Barcelona, but every domestic opponent became the counter-attacking side when they played Bayern, which demonstrated the difference between the Spanish style that had dominated for the previous four years, and the German style that was becoming increasingly influential.

Bayern's major rivals during this period were Borussia Dortmund, who had enjoyed a two-year spell of Bundesliga dominance under Jürgen Klopp. They were a very different side. Whereas Bayern's fondness for superstars and squabbles led to them to being nick-named 'FC Hollywood' in the 1990s, Dortmund were cast as an old-school working-class club reliant on their fighting spirit and a raucous atmosphere. While Bayern could sign ready-made super-stars, including cherry-picking Dortmund's best players, Klopp's side was populated by modest homegrown talents like Marcel Schmelzer and Mario Götze, alongside clever signings from lesser leagues like Shinji Kagawa and Robert Lewandowski. They were greater than the sum of their parts, thanks to Klopp's tactical intelligence and ability to galvanise supporters and players alike.

The most fundamental part of Klopp's philosophy was his so-called 'gegenpressing' – more on that later – but Dortmund's counter-attack-ing was also sensational, and their transformation from finishing fifth in 2009/10 to winning the title the following season was about added directness: *Vertikalspiel*, as the German press described it. 'We've started putting a much, much greater focus on vertical passes,' Klopp acknowledged midway through his first title-winning campaign.

The difference between Bayern and Dortmund was typified by the nature of the wide players. Ribéry and Robben were genuine world-beaters, whereas Dortmund's Kevin Großkreutz and Jakub Błaszczykowski were more workmanlike, known more for their energy than their technical quality. In Klopp's system they acted as wide midfielders rather than wingers, and tucked inside close to the central players. Although both were capable of dribbling, they were more focused on off-the-ball sprints into spaces vacated by the opposition full-backs, creating vertical passing options and making good decisions on the run. 'We're tactically very disciplined, trying to get the ball forward from a structured base,' explained centre-back Mats Hummels. 'But that's just what most teams are trying to do. What we've got is genuine passion. We're properly up for it.'

Concepts like these – motivation, passion, desire – are sometimes considered an alternative to a tactical approach. But Klopp ensured such concepts enhanced his tactical approach, and his animated presence on the touchline came to symbolise Dortmund, who did everything with tremendous energy and commitment. 'It's about making the crowd happy, about producing games with a recognisable style,' Klopp declared on his unveiling at Dortmund. He stuck to his word. Journalists spoke about heavy metal football, about full-throttle football, finding any metaphor that involved speed, noise and organised chaos.

Whereas Bayern were openly modelling themselves on the Barcelona model, Klopp positioned himself as the alternative. 'Barcelona's team of the last four years, with their serenity ... sorry, that's not enough for me,' he laughed. 'If Barcelona's team of the last four years had been the first one that I saw play when I was four, I would have played tennis instead. I like fighting football, not serenity football; rainy day, heavy pitch, everybody has a dirty face, and then they go home and can't play football for the next four weeks. That's what Borussia are all about.' Klopp would later speak admiringly about Barcelona's pressing game, but in possession he wanted something different. It was Dortmund rather than Bayern who represented modern German football, and their archetypal counter-attacking performance came with a legendary 5–2 win over Bayern in the German cup final of 2012.

The cup final was a scrappy affair, characterised by defensive mistakes. Bayern goalkeeper Manuel Neuer had a particularly poor game, and both sides scored penalties after clumsy, needless fouls. But the cup final victory was pure Dortmund, with Lewandowski leading the line, Kagawa drifting laterally into pockets of space to prompt counter-attacks, and Großkreutz and Błaszczykowski roaring forward out wide. Later, Klopp would find himself forced into tactical tweaks to surprise Bayern, and the arrival of the speedy goalscoring winger Marco Reus and development of Mario Götze would offer more star quality. But, like every great heavy metal act, Dortmund's earliest material was their best.

Dortmund's cup final victory perfectly demonstrated the concept of the transition, a term that had come into popular usage a few years beforehand but was a particularly fundamental part of German football ideology. The offensive transition is the moment when a side goes from not having possession to having possession, and the defensive transition is the reverse. Dortmund were particularly adept at the former.

Großkreutz and Błaszczykowski played important roles at these offensive transitions. Bayern dominated possession, and so for the majority of the game Dortmund's wide midfielders were deep inside their own third, helping their full-backs by doubling up against Ribéry and Robben. And then, when Bayern's passing moves broke down and Dortmund won possession, they would suddenly break. Both wide players were excellent at sensing when a transition was imminent, and would start their attacking movements before Bayern's full-backs had sensed the danger, sprinting into gaps and encouraging vertical passes. Kagawa, meanwhile, perfected the number 10 role, making arced runs into the channels.

Two of Dortmund's goals were particularly memorable. With Klopp's side already 2–1 up, Robben attempted a crossfield pass to Ribéry, which was intercepted by Dortmund right-back Łukasz Piszczek. Others might have simply cleared the ball upfield, but

Piszczek calmly nodded it to Błaszczykowski, collected the return pass and played a long ball towards Lewandowski, who knocked it down for Kagawa, continued his run to collect the Japanese play-maker's through-ball, then finished past Neuer. In the space of 12 seconds, Dortmund had gone from an interception deep inside their own half, to scoring, courtesy of a one–two, a vertical pass, another one–two and a first-time finish.

The goal that effectively ended the final, putting Dortmund 4–1 up, was another fast break. This time Großkreutz blocked a Bastian Schweinsteiger shot and the ball bounced to Sebastian Kehl. He fed Kagawa, who was already on the run behind Bayern's midfield pairing, attacking Bayern's two centre-backs, who had been exposed by the advanced positioning of their full-backs. Kagawa sprinted forward with the ball, slowed his dribble slightly to allow Großkreutz to advance down the left before slipping him in, and then, with Lewandowski intelligently shifting his run to occupy the opposite channel and ensure that Dortmund were exploiting the space on both sides of Bayern's centre-back pairing, Großkreutz found the Pole, who blasted into the far corner. Dortmund's game plan was carried out flawlessly, and Lewandowski subsequently completed his hat-trick.

Bayern couldn't get their heads around the result. Heynckes protested that Dortmund didn't have many chances, Philipp Lahm insisted Bayern had been superior until half-time. But Dortmund captain Kehl's analysis was fairer, explaining how his side 'waited for our chances on the break, and ended up deserving to win'. Klopp was, unusually, almost lost for what to say. 'We were ice-cool and scored some great goals,' he managed. 'I simply don't have the words for what the team did today, to describe my feelings. We will see in the years to come whether anyone will be able to outperform our achievements of this season.' Dortmund had clinched the

Double, having already won the Bundesliga with a record points tally.

In terms of individual players, German football's brightest talent during this period was also renowned for his counter-attacking incision. Germany's run to the 2010 World Cup semi-finals had been illuminated by the performances of the extraordinarily gifted Mesut Özil, a footballer who was unlike anything Germany had produced for years, but also, perhaps more significantly, unlike anything Spanish football offered either. Özil was not a deep-lying playmaker like Xavi or a between-the-lines ball-hoarder like David Silva, but a counter-attacking creator who excelled when receiving the ball on the run, much like Kagawa in the role Klopp created for him at Dortmund.

Özil had been particularly bright at the 2010 World Cup when Germany were already leading matches, with the opposition coming on to them and leaving space to break into. Significantly, his three assists at the tournament were for the fourth goal in a 4–0 win against Australia, the fourth goal in a 4–1 win against England and the fourth goal in a 4–0 win against Argentina. All three came after Özil ran into the inside-left channel, before squaring for a tap-in. Özil was the new face of German football: young, quick, technical and from an immigrant background. Although Özil had been born in Germany, he had spoken only Turkish until the age of four and only had a Turkish passport until his decision to play for Germany, which divided opinion in his family. He himself acknowledged that his creative, technical qualities weren't entirely typical for German players. 'My technique and feeling for the ball is the Turkish side to my game,' he explained. 'The discipline, attitude and always-give-your-all is the German part.'

Özil's excellent off-the-ball running was partly explained by his positioning at Werder Bremen, where he played as a number 10 at the top of a midfield diamond, and provided width by drifting towards the channels, rotating positions with Aaron Hunt and Marko Marin. He carried that style into his performances for the national team, and to Real Madrid, whom he joined in 2010. José Mourinho is sometimes criticised for not appreciating flair players, but just as he got the best from Deco at Porto and Wesley Sneijder at Inter, Özil's best spell came under Mourinho at Real.

While he was sometimes shoved wide or dropped for *Clásicos*, Özil was a fundamental part of Real's 4–2–3–1, regularly supplying assists for Cristiano Ronaldo and beloved by Mourinho precisely because he was so dangerous on the break. It was his counter-attacking through-ball for Ronaldo at Camp Nou in 2012 that effectively wrapped up Mourinho's only league title in Spain, while his lateral movement constantly pulled opposition holding midfielders out of position and opened up space for his compatriot Sami Khedira – another German midfielder signed by Real on the back of his 2010 World Cup performances – to burst into. In fact, Real's midfield under Mourinho illustrated the Germany versus Spain contrast nicely; Germans Özil and Khedira were naturals on the break, with Spaniard Xabi Alonso sitting deeper and providing the patient passing. With back-up Lassana Diarra a defensive-minded French water carrier, they ticked all the boxes.

Although Özil continued to record fine assist statistics after his move to Arsenal in 2013, he was never entirely as effective, in part because Arsenal's build-up play was slower. But Özil's international form remained excellent, and he was voted the German national team's player of the year in 2011, 2012, 2013, 2015 and 2016 – the one missing year underlining the fact his best form didn't coincide with the national team's triumph in Brazil. He was effectively a Germany regular from his debut in 2009 until the 2018 World Cup, when he quit the national side because, 'In the eyes of [German FA president

Reinhard] Grindel and his supporters, I am German when we win, but I am an immigrant when we lose.' In response Grindel, admitted, 'I could have taken a clearer position at some points and stood by Mesut Özil. I should have been clear with my words. Such attacks are completely unacceptable.'

Özil's international career was played solely under Löw, a manager who immediately recognised that Özil was perfect for his type of football, which was based around forward-thinking, direct attacking. Löw was often described as being heavily influenced by his time with Stuttgart, where speed and vertical passing were prioritised. 'I have developed an offensive style, a combination between passing and running, regaining possession of the ball and rapid counter-attack,' he said.

In 2010 Löw declared that football was a sport 'defined by a succession of sprints', a very different interpretation to the dominant Spanish approach. When asked at Euro 2012 whether he still believed that statement, Löw outlined his philosophy more thoroughly. 'It is like that now, more than ever before,' he explained. 'The tempo of the game has increased. Players do an awful lot of running now and the way that has traditionally been interpreted is to say that the team who runs more wins the game. Our analysis, though, has shown that that view is too superficial. Our focus now is on what kind of sprints players make, where they do it, how they do it and in what direction. Emotionally speaking, sprints forward have much better connotations than running back. If you are going forward, you forget how much you have run and how fast you have done. It doesn't hurt as much to sprint forwards.' His Germany side were blessed with yet more players who loved sprinting forward, with Borussia Mönchengladbach's terrifyingly quick Marco Reus and Bayer Leverkusen's ultra-direct André Schürrle providing more attacking options.

Germany's performances at Euro 2012 were more balanced than at the 2010 World Cup, partly because opponents sat deeper and prevented them from counter-attacking. In the group stage they overcame Portugal 1–0 with a header from old-school forward Mario Gómez, who also scored both goals in a 2–1 victory over the Netherlands, when Germany dominated by overloading the centre and rotating their midfield trio intelligently.

Their winner in the final group game, a 2–1 victory over Denmark, was more typical. Lars Bender, a midfielder deployed at right-back on his first international start, won a tackle on the edge of his own box and then sprinted 80 yards. Germany combined in perfect fashion, with Gómez, his back to goal, feeding Khedira, who carried the ball 20 yards. Özil, who had started in the inside-right channel, made one of his typical lateral runs into the inside-left channel, simultaneously creating the passing angle for his Real Madrid teammate Khedira and opening up space for Bender's sprint. Özil supplied one of his classic low assists from the left and Bender converted. That was German football: a quick counter-attack, based around ball-winning, sprinting, clever movement and vertical passes.

Germany's 4–2 quarter-final victory over Greece was more about possession play, and then the 2–1 semi-final defeat to Italy prompted questions about Löw's tactics, after he dramatically altered his system in an attempt to contain the wonderful Andrea Pirlo, an approach that backfired. But Germany were on the right track. Özil's interview with German newspaper *Die Welt* after the Italy defeat was particularly telling. He rejected complaints about the players' lack of motivation, denied that the side lacked leaders, rubbished criticism of Germany's training base and laughed off speculation about Löw's future. Germany knew they were on to something good, and proved it two years later in Brazil.

That said, it wasn't all smooth sailing for Germany at the 2014

World Cup. They went into the tournament with various injury problems, including the complete absence of their most dangerous attacker, Reus. Löw was seemingly unsure of his side's optimum structure and made some significant alterations as the tournament continued. There was a major scare in the 2–1 extra-time victory over Algeria in the second round, when Germany's backline looked sluggish and vulnerable to counter-attacks, and even in the 1–0 extra-time victory in the final, Argentina created better chances. All that is largely forgotten, though, because of two facts. First, Germany lifted the trophy. Second, they beat hosts Brazil 7–1.

Germany's coaching staff had acknowledged before the tournament that possession play and heavy pressing would be difficult in Brazil because of the sweltering conditions, and considered that a counter-attacking approach was therefore preferable. 'We knew Brazil's defence would be disorganised quickly,' Löw explained in Raphael Honigstein's *Das Reboot*. 'We wanted to do well defensively,' added his captain Lahm, 'either by winning the ball quickly or breaking through their first wave of attack, because Brazil would then often split into two: attack and defence. Opportunities would arise that way.' It worked out perfectly.

Germany's 5–0 half-time advantage had arisen almost entirely by breaking into one particular zone, in behind Brazil left-back Marcelo. It only took four minutes for these opportunities to become evident, when Marcelo pushed forward to close down Müller at a throw-in, and then switched off twice in the same move, as both Khedira and Müller raced in behind, although Klose miscontrolled and couldn't find Müller. Three minutes later, Marcelo found himself too high up the pitch as Germany launched another attack, which saw Müller cross to Özil, who teed up Khedira, but his shot hit his teammate Kroos.

Four minutes after that, Marcelo tried a stepover in the opposition third and was dispossessed by Müller, who again sprinted forward alongside Khedira down the right. Here, Marcelo actually made an excellent recovery run to tackle both players, then raised his hand to acknowledge his mistake. From the resulting corner, however, Germany opened the scoring. It recalled their 2010 displays against England and Argentina, where breakthroughs had come from set-pieces finished by Klose and Müller respectively. Those two again proved crucial; Klose blocked off David Luiz, which created space for Müller to volley home.

It was Klose, who overtook Ronaldo as the World Cup's all-time top goalscorer at this tournament, and Müller, the winner of the World Cup Golden Boot in 2010, who represented the old German efficiency. Neither were particularly elegant, but both boasted an unquestionably brilliant international goalscoring record. Klose was decent over the course of a season but excelled himself at tournaments; Müller was a confusingly clumsy player but also devastating on the biggest occasions. Germany married the old and new efficiencies.

Although Marcelo provided one moment of danger in the opposition box, forcing Lahm into a sliding tackle, he was continually caught out of position at transitions. After 14 minutes he cynically blocked off Müller, who had played a one–two with Khedira. After 19 minutes he conceded possession and Germany launched another break, but Kroos's pass towards Müller was overhit. 'The spaces were bigger than against defensive teams,' Müller diplomatically explained afterwards, and no one was better at breaking into space than Germany.

After 22 minutes Marcelo was again caught too high at a transition, and on the counter-attack Müller's near-post cross was cleared for a throw-in, down Germany's right. From this throw-in Germany worked a passing combination, and Marcelo dropped too deep, playing Müller onside. The familiar combination worked again, with Müller backheeling for Klose to finish.

Now the floodgates opened. Özil, starting on the left of the front three, sensed all the space was on the opposite flank, so drifted to the right, launched a break with the overlapping right-back Lahm, and his cross found Kroos, who thumped it home. 3–0. 'The Brazilian team were in shock after we scored the second and third goals,' recalled Löw. 'You could really feel that on the pitch.' Now Germany could repeatedly break through the middle. Khedira teed up Kroos, 4–0. Then Özil teed up Khedira, 5–0.

At half-time Germany felt sorry for Brazil. They had little appetite for embarrassing their hosts further, and the starting XI were content to conserve their energy for the final, so defended in numbers and only half-heartedly attacked. 'We just made it clear that we had to stay focused and not try to humiliate them,' recalled centre-back Mats Hummels.

But after an hour Löw substituted 36-year-old Klose and introduced André Schürrle, who had been arguably the Bundesliga's most devastating counter-attacker during a tremendous 2012/13 campaign with Leverkusen, before a less successful season at Chelsea. While his teammates were content with five goals, Schürrle sensed an opportunity to play himself into the side for the final, and smashed in the sixth and seventh, before Oscar scored a not particularly consolatory consolation goal. It was the most embarrassing World Cup defeat of all time for the hosts, but it was also a German counter-attacking triumph. Brazil had dominated in terms of possession, territory and shots, while Germany had sat back and sprinted into space. It was almost too efficient. Özil apologised to David Luiz at full-time for the margin of victory, while Bastian Schweinsteiger said he would have preferred to have won 2–0.

Schürrle also provided a key contribution as a substitute in the final, his sudden sprint and cross assisting Mario Götze's winner against Leo Messi's Argentina, clinching Germany's fourth World Cup title. It's the 7–1, though, that will go down in history.

In the Bundesliga, meanwhile, Germany's football culture was being challenged by the appointment of Pep Guardiola as Bayern manager in 2013. Taking charge immediately after Bayern had wrapped up the Treble under Heynckes, Guardiola's appointment was evidence of German football's sudden lofty reputation, but also prompted questions about Bayern's future footballing philosophy. Guardiola was widely regarded as an ideologue who only knew how to tiki-taka. Everyone expected Bayern to shift from 4–2–3–1 to 4–3–3, and it seemed Guardiola would struggle to incorporate Ribéry and Robben, as his Spanish model favoured wide forwards making off-the-ball runs rather than dribbling wingers. The truth was somewhat more complex.

Having studied German football intently throughout his year-long sabbatical in New York, Guardiola arrived in Munich obsessed with the counter-attacking threat posed by nearly every Bundesliga side. His approach with Barcelona had always depended on structured positional play in possession, but in Germany he became even stricter and repeatedly emphasised that Bayern needed to hold on to possession to assemble in the correct formation, which would prevent leaving gaps for opponents to break into. His Barca side hadn't been defeated often, but the losses usually came when their defence was exposed to quick counters. 'I just want them to start off moving forward together for a few metres so that, if we lose the ball, the opposition can't take advantage of our lack of unity,' he explained in pre-season. 'Every team in Germany is capable of mounting a counter-attack before you've had the chance to even breathe, and if we lose our unity it gives them a chance to break through and make chances.' He jokingly referring to Germany as 'Kontaland', the land of counters.

This was a theme Guardiola would repeatedly return to. In *Pep Confidential*, Martí Perarnau's inside look at Guardiola's first season in Bavaria, the most common reason given for his tactical tinkering was to prevent opposition breaks. After a victory over Hannover, Guardiola was informed that their coach, Mirko Slomka, had declared that any German side was capable of perfecting a counter-attack in 11 seconds. Guardiola disagreed. 'I think it's even quicker than Mirko says. This league is remarkable in terms of counter-attacks. In Spain there are great sides that hit you with good counters, but I've never seen anywhere to equal the Bundesliga for the number of teams who can hit you with so many effective, massively quick counter-attacks.' Guardiola's golden 15-pass rule became more fundamental than ever, and he increasingly experimented with unusual defensive structures to ensure his side were always prepared for a speedy defensive transition. In that sense, the German obsession with counter-attacking only reinforced Guardiola's preference for Spanish possession play.

In a different way, however, Guardiola's approach changed significantly. He initially attempted to transfer his Barcelona template onto his new charges, and his two summer signings underlined that endeavour. The first was Götze, controversially signed from Dortmund and earmarked to play Leo Messi's false 9 role; the other was a Barcelona midfielder, Thiago Alcántara, who had risen through La Masia and played for the first team semi-regularly, including in the victory over Santos, Guardiola's favourite win with Barca because of the unusual 3–7–0 formation he'd used. These two appeared set to dominate the new-look Bayern, but both suffered from injury problems during their first year. Götze completed 90 minutes in the league on nine occasions, Thiago only on eight. The two players intended to be the symbols of Bayern's evolution under Guardiola were therefore largely peripheral.

With Götze generally unavailable, Bayern depended more than Guardiola had expected on Mario Mandžukić, an old-fashioned, workmanlike centre-forward renowned for his aerial ability. Guardiola had never played with a striker in that mould at Barcelona, aside from his unsuccessful dalliance with Zlatan Ibrahimović, who was considerably more creative anyway. There was also a surprisingly prominent role for 35-year-old veteran Claudio Pizarro, another target man, who managed ten Bundesliga goals.

Thomas Müller, meanwhile, had been used as a midfielder in pre-season, but after Guardiola was left unconvinced by his positional discipline he was redeployed as a forward. Mandžukić departed after a single season and was replaced by Dortmund's Lewandowski, a silkier link-up player, but also a towering striker who thrived on crosses, and the big Pole scored 13 headers during his two seasons under Guardiola. As a result Bayern routinely played with a big man up front, meaning Guardiola had moved away from the Spanish model he'd popularised. 'When I first arrived in Munich I thought I could more or less transfer Barca's game to Bayern, but what I actually did was marry the two,' Guardiola admitted. 'I brought the Barcelona philosophy and adapted it to Bayern.'

The shift was obvious from Guardiola's first Bundesliga game, a comfortable if largely uninspiring 3–1 victory over Borussia Mönchengladbach, which ended with Guardiola complaining about Bayern's sluggish defensive transitions. 'We didn't always press well, we gave Gladbach too much time, their counter-attacks weren't controlled and when we lost the ball, we didn't always get back into position straight away,' he complained. But more surprising was Bayern's approach in possession. Although the centre-backs, Jérôme Boateng and Dante, attempted to play out from goal-kicks, they thumped a surprising number of long balls downfield towards Mandžukić. They also regularly hit diagonals to the wings, as Bayern attempted to find Ribéry and Robben as quickly as possible. These two, along with Lahm, were Bayern's best players that evening, which foreshadowed their performances under Guardiola for the next three seasons.

Ribéry and Robben were not, as some had anticipated, ostracised under Guardiola. Instead they dominated his team. 'Who are our unstoppable guys? The wide guys, Ribéry and Robben,' Guardiola explained in Perarnau's book. Rather than them starting deep and roaring forward on the counter-attack, however, Guardiola wanted his side positioned higher, ensuring the wingers' accelerations lasted no more than four or five seconds. 'If we set a really high defensive line and establish our central defenders where the midfield would normally be, then it will limit our opponents' scope to double up on the wingers. We will convert each play into a one-versus-one situation, where our guys are the very best. They can also cross excellently and we've got top-quality finishers to convert those chances. At Barca, Messi did the destroying down the centre of the pitch. At Bayern it will be Ribéry and Robben, from the wings.'

This marked a significant shift in Guardiola's thinking. He'd previously stressed that dribbling was largely inefficient, and best utilised to tempt opponents out of position, before passing past them. The emphasis on crossing was also somewhat unexpected, but this was the new Guardiola. 'I have to adapt to Bayern, but Bayern has to adapt to my work too,' he said. Together, they created a distinct brand of football that felt, entirely logically, like a hybrid of the Spanish and German models. Guardiola's general instruction was that Bayern should be patient when working the ball into midfield, and then more direct in the final third. Spanish at first, then German.

Bayern retained their Bundesliga title in Guardiola's first season, finishing 19 points ahead of Dortmund, but they failed to successfully defend the Champions League. They were troubled by counter-attacking in Europe, wobbling in the opening stages of the second round match against Arsenal when Özil, typically, ripped through their lines, and found themselves surprisingly vulnerable to Danny Welbeck's speed in the quarter-final against a dreadful Manchester United side who finished only seventh that season. Then came disaster in the semi-final, where they were thrashed by Real Madrid 5–0 on aggregate, again being exposed on the break. Karim Benzema rounded off a direct passing move to score the only goal in a 1–0 win in Madrid. 'Possession is meaningless if you give away chances,' complained Bayern legend Franz Beckenbauer, working as a pundit at the game. 'We should be happy Real only managed to score once.'

Then Bayern capitulated in the home leg. Guardiola named an aggressive 4–2–4 system and literally told his players beforehand, 'You are German, so be German and attack!', but Bayern were thrashed 4–0. In fact, they lost 4–0 to Real Madrid in an almost exactly the same manner they'd beaten Barcelona 4–0 the previous year. Two set-pieces, both nodded in by Sergio Ramos, started the rout, before Cristiano Ronaldo and Gareth Bale streaked away on a counter-attack for a third, and Ronaldo fired a free-kick under the wall for the fourth.

In terms of identity, Real Madrid 5–0 Bayern, on aggregate, was slightly confusing. The Spanish side had beaten the German side – but Bayern were playing broadly Spanish football under Guardiola, while Real were still considered the anti-Barcelona, the counter-attacking kings, and their football was almost more German in style. Bayern's 7–0 win over Barcelona the previous year, and now Real's 5–0 win over Bayern this year, furthered the belief that counter-attacking football had the upper hand over tiki-taka, regardless of whether Bayern had won or lost. Guardiola's approach was now openly questioned. 'I understand that this style of game is not part of

German football culture,' Guardiola told Perarnau afterwards. 'I do understand. In Germany clubs like to play a style of football that's very different from my own, and no doubt people prefer Madrid or Dortmund's game.' That sentence was significant, putting Madrid alongside Dortmund in terms of style.

In his second season Guardiola was able to field an all-Spanish midfield – Javi Martínez remained at the club, Thiago showed some flashes of brilliance when fit, while Xabi Alonso arrived from Real Madrid to play the role Guardiola had perfected during his playing days. Toni Kroos made the reverse journey, moving to Real Madrid, while Bastian Schweinsteiger was sold to Manchester United a year later. Two homegrown World Cup-winning midfielders had left. One banner, erected outside Bayern's training ground, complained that the club's identity was being destroyed, while Guardiola's predecessor Heynckes pointedly remarked that Bayern needed to ensure German 'remained the team's main language'.

Yet the Spaniards fully embraced their new surroundings and were determined to adapt themselves to the Bundesliga. 'I came here to become German,' Thiago explained. 'I need to toughen up and become more resilient.' Alonso spoke about how he enjoyed the German style of football, which was quicker and more physical than La Liga, and reminded him of his Premier League days. At Real Madrid he was renowned for diagonal passing, but with Bayern he concentrated more on arrowing line-breaking vertical passes into the forwards. Once again Bayern won the Bundesliga, but once again they were eliminated in the Champions League semi-finals – this time by Guardiola's former club Barcelona. For once it wasn't such a clash of styles. At Camp Nou Leo Messi scored two wonderful goals to put Barca 2–0 up, and as Bayern pushed forward in search of an away goal, Neymar streaked away on a counter-attack to effectively wrap up the tie.

In Guardiola's third and final season in Munich, Bayern were no longer competing against the Dortmund of Klopp, but against the Dortmund of Thomas Tuchel. He'd established himself as a hugely promising coach at Mainz, Klopp's former club, and his impact on Dortmund was considerable. Tuchel represented the cross-pollination between Spain and Germany better than anyone; he borrowed heavily from Guardiola's emphasis on positional play in possession, but continued Dortmund's all-action, intense, high-energy approach that he'd inherited from Klopp.

The first meeting between Guardiola's Bayern and Tuchel's Dortmund was a fascinating tactical encounter that eventually ended with Bayern winning 5–1. It was a game all about pressing, and notable for that fact that both teams used a midfield diamond: Bayern 3–3–1–3 and Dortmund 4–3–1–2. It was a very German game, all about remaining compact and pressing aggressively in midfield. Neither side could gain an advantage in that zone, and it therefore became about long balls to bypass the pressure. Dortmund's Hummels started attempting long diagonals towards Pierre-Emerick Aubameyang, and gradually Bayern realised that this tactic would be their best approach too.

Bayern's problem was that Dortmund's strikers were closing down David Alaba and Jérôme Boateng, their two most creative defenders, and leaving Javi Martínez, playing between them, free. Guardiola therefore switched two defenders: Martínez and Boateng. The latter was capable of thumping direct passes into attack, and now it was him, rather than Martínez, who was getting time on the ball.

Boateng used his newfound freedom perfectly, by launching an enormous pass over the top for Thomas Müller, who opened the scoring. Boateng played an almost identical ball in the first minute of the second half, this time for a Lewandowski finish, which made it 3–1 and meant Tuchel's side had no way back. It was a remarkable situation: a Guardiola side effectively playing route one football and prospering because their deepest centre-back was firing passes over the top for big strikers. It was, of course, the absolute epitome of vertical football. Did Guardiola ever expect to make a tactical change by switching two centre-backs to play long-ball football more effectively? Probably not, but then he had become a very different manager in Germany.

Forty-eight hours after Bayern's win over Dortmund, Guardiola dined with Tuchel, just the two of them together in a restaurant, analysing the match and discussing tactical ideas. That, in itself, felt very German: cooperation between rivals for mutual benefit. The conversation represented the synthesis of the Spanish and German models. Guardiola had made German football's approach more technical, but German football had made Guardiola's approach more vertical.

# 17

# Gegenpressing

As counter-attacking was such a fundamental part of German football, Bundesliga sides were constantly evaluated in terms of their speed in transitioning from defence to attack and their speed in transitioning from attack to defence. The concept of the transition itself, though, had become considerably more complex because of the importance placed on the hottest new concept in European football: gegenpressing. Essentially, this meant attempting to win possession quickly after it had been squandered, although there were several variations.

To appreciate the rise of gegenpressing, first you must consider the nature of the traditional style of football in Germany, the only country more fixated than Italy on the concept of strict man-marking and a sweeper. Germany's all-time greatest player is Franz Beckenbauer, credited with pioneering the attack-minded sweeper role, having started as a midfielder and then dropped back into defence to conduct attacks from deep. The Italian sweeper was, initially, purely a defender, whereas the German sweeper used his freedom to push forward and attack from a position where he was difficult to mark. Beckenbauer was the genius in an otherwise functional, joyless German machine.

The 1974 World Cup Final pitted Beckenbauer, the 1972 Ballon d'Or winner, against Johan Cruyff, the 1973 Ballon d'Or winner. The two captains were the world's two best footballers and essentially dictated their nation's footballing approach for the next couple of decades: Germany's man-marking with a sweeper versus Holland's pressing with an offside trap. Germany, and Beckenbauer, emerged victorious, so while others fell in love with Holland's Total Football style, Germany continued with their own.

In the modern era, Germany's star player was usually their sweeper. Lothar Matthäus was converted from a midfielder into a sweeper for the 1994 World Cup, while Matthias Sammer's outstanding performances throughout Germany's Euro 96 triumph two years later ensured he was voted Player of the Tournament and won the Ballon d'Or. Sammer's injury problems meant Matthäus resumed the role at the 1998 World Cup, and then played awkwardly as something between a defender and midfielder at Euro 2000 at the age of 39. This wasn't progressive football. Leverkusen's Jens Nowotny was a classic German sweeper at the turn of the century, although he was another who suffered from injuries, which meant club teammate Carsten Ramelow essentially played as a sweeper during Germany's run to the final of the 2002 World Cup. Even the brilliant goalscoring midfielder Michael Ballack, by far Germany's best player of the 2000s, had started as a sweeper, and was frequently tipped to end his career there too. By his latter days, however, Germany had finally moved away from that model.

Because of their dogged commitment to playing with a sweeper throughout the 1990s, the German approach was the most tactically distinct – or tactically antiquated – in Europe. 'The league that differs from all the others is the German league,' said Inter manager Roy Hodgson in 1997. 'If you took two teams from England, Italy, Spain or France, didn't know what countries they were from, couldn't hear the language and played the game in Venezuela, you wouldn't know who the English were, who the Italians were, who the French were and who the Spanish were. You might know if you had a German team, as they play a distinctive style; they still play man-to-man with a sweeper.' As Italian football during that period demonstrated, playing zonally with an offside trap was necessary to press in advanced positions and dominate the game.

When a trio of Bundesliga sides reached the Champions League quarter-finals in 1998, all three used man-marking and a sweeper, in contrast to the other five sides, who all played a back four and defended zonally. The best modern demonstration of the classic German game was Greece's sensational triumph at Euro 2004, when old-school German coach Otto Rehhagel used the old German system, in stark contrast to the other 15 sides who used a flat back four. 'The Greeks created a major surprise by turning back the footballing clock and recycling lost arts,' read UEFA's technical report. 'It remains to be seen whether Rehhagel has pointed us back to the future.' But ultimately Greece's unlikely success came over a short, six-game period, and their ultra-defensive approach was loathed across the continent. Meanwhile, German football was undergoing a significant tactical revolution.

German football histories often trace the rise of the four-man defence, zonal marking and pressing back to an episode of football programme *Das aktuelle Sport-Studio* in December 1998 that featured Ralf Rangnick, the manager of exciting, upwardly mobile second-tier side Ulm. Rangnick proceeded to explain the merits of his zonal system, which in turn enabled his side to press aggressively. He was widely slammed by prominent German football figures, either for acting as if his coaching colleagues were Luddites or for placing too much focus on tactics. 'All this talk about the system is nonsense,' said Beckenbauer. 'Other players can do more with the ball, ours cannot. Four at the back, with zonal marking or a sweeper, it doesn't matter.'

But Rangnick helped to popularise a counter-cultural movement within German football. Within a few years, the majority of Bundesliga sides – and the national side – were playing a flat back four and defending zonally. Rangnick's coaching career has been inconsistent, and more notable for his ability to get second-tier sides promoted rather than his work in the Bundesliga. But then, that's not the point. As Raphael Honigstein observes in *Das Reboot*, 'Rangnick may never have won the championship, but he has won the argument.' Such was his influence, Rangnick regrets revealing his coaching secrets so candidly.

Germany's other major proponent of pressing was Jürgen Klopp. His coaching approach was shaped by his experience playing for second-tier Mainz in the mid-1990s under Wolfgang Frank – like Rangnick, another rare German disciple of Sacchi – whose influence would only become apparent when many of his players enjoyed successful coaching careers. 'We watched this very boring video, 500 times, of Sacchi doing defensive drills, using sticks and without the ball, with Paolo Maldini, Franco Baresi and Demetrio Albertini,' Klopp recalled. 'We used to think that if the other players are better, you have to lose. After that we learned anything is possible; you can beat better teams by using tactics.'

Frank coached Mainz between 1995 and 1997 with great success. They then struggled without him when reverting to old-school German tactics, so re-appointed him in 1998 for another two-year spell. When they again suffered a dip in form after his second departure, the club asked Klopp, still playing in defence, to immediately take charge. Klopp focused on re-installing Frank's system of zonal marking and pressing, and enjoyed a memorable seven-year stint with Mainz. He earned promotion to the Bundesliga, but then suffered relegation back to the second division and departed after being unable to gain promotion for a second time. But Klopp's reputation had steadily risen, partly because of his excellent work as a TV pundit, and in the summer of 2008 he was appointed by cash-strapped Dortmund, a fallen giant who had just finished 13th out of 18 sides and conceded the most goals in the Bundesliga. Within three years they were champions.

Klopp's Dortmund were a young, energetic side capable of shutting down opponents with terrifying intensity. They played a high defensive line, with 19-year-old duo Mats Hummels and Neven Subotić immediately installed as the centre-back partnership in a system described as 4–2–3–1, although without possession it was essentially 4–4–2, which Klopp considered 'the most effective system to play without the ball, and the easiest system to implement because the running lines are the simplest'. The emphasis on running was crucial.

This was the period when Europe had fallen in love with the possession play of Pep Guardiola's Barcelona, but, as previously outlined, Klopp found their passing game somewhat tedious. What Klopp admired was Barca's commitment to winning the ball. 'It's extraordinary how high up the pitch this team is when they win the ball back,' he marvelled. 'And the reason they do that is because every player presses. I think Leo Messi wins the ball back the most when he loses possession. If he loses it, he's right back there the moment the opposition player takes a touch, to win the ball back. The players press like there's no tomorrow, as if the most enjoyable thing about football is when the other team has the ball. And what that does for them is, for me, the biggest achievement of them all, the best example that I've ever seen in football.' It summarised the German obsession with transitions; everyone else loved how Barcelona kept possession, but Klopp studied what they did the moment they lost it.

Focusing on regaining possession immediately changed the way transition football was considered. As outlined above in Chapter 10 in the discussion about the Portuguese focus on the transition, coaching courses usually explain modern football as a series of four situations, flowing continuously in a circle: the possession phase; the transition from possession to out-of-possession; the out-of-possession phase; and then the transition to possession. And repeat. But now, the defensive transition was about regaining the ball quickly and returning immediately to the possession phase, effectively short-circuiting the way football was considered. Sometimes you could watch Barcelona for an entire half and not witness their out-of-possession structure.

Klopp borrowed from this approach and spoke about it with a specific term: 'gegenpressing', which translates as counter-pressing. It's sometimes misunderstood, however. Counter-pressing isn't to pressing what counter-attacking is to attacking. It's not necessarily countering a press, but pressing a counter.

There were two significant differences between Guardiola's approach and Klopp's approach that mean the Dortmund manager should be considered a genuine revolutionary. First, Guardiola's Barcelona pressed quickly simply because they didn't want to spend any time in their out-of-possession phase. 'Without the ball, we are a disastrous team, a horrible team, so we need the ball,' explained Guardiola. It was a defensive tactic, merely a proactive way of defending, so they didn't have to defend in the traditional sense. Barcelona would recover the ball and then retain possession for long periods, organising themselves in their positional structure.

Klopp's Dortmund were very different. They were perfectly solid without possession, and defending deep actually suited their counter-attacking. But they gegenpressed because Klopp believed it was a valuable attacking tactic. 'Think about the passes you have to make to get a player in a number 10 role into a position where he can play the genius pass,' Klopp later urged. 'Gegenpressing lets you win back the ball nearer to the goal. It's only one pass away from a really good opportunity. No playmaker in the world can be as good as a good gegenpressing situation, and that's why it's so important.' Barcelona and Dortmund both attempted to regain the ball quickly, but for completely different reasons.

Second, while Guardiola's players would press intelligently, with one man pressuring the opponent on the ball and others cutting off passing angles into opponents, Klopp's side were less calculating and more extreme. They piled players into the immediate vicinity of the player in possession, almost crowding him out through intimidation. It explained why Klopp's wide midfielders, usually Kevin Großkreutz and Jakub Błaszczykowski, tucked inside – their structure was geared towards gegenpressing, which was only possible when compressing space quickly. While other teams were focusing on vertical compactness, Klopp was also concerned with horizontal compactness, and Dortmund frequently regained possession by boxing in teams towards the touchline.

This gegenpressing was often combined with more conventional pressing as the opposition attempted to play out from the back. Most typically, Dortmund would use a medium block, standing off the opposition centre-backs, before pressing once the ball was played into the full-backs or midfielders. Dortmund rarely used a full-pitch press, because doing so encouraged the opposition to kick the ball long. Although that served to disrupt their opponents' build-up play, Klopp really wanted the opposition to play their way into trouble, and Dortmund's mix of pressing, counter-pressing and counter-attacking was essentially how they overcame Bayern to win the Bundesliga in 2011 and 2012.

The classic example came in Dortmund's 3–1 momentous victory over Bayern in February 2011, the result that transformed Dortmund into almost sure-fire champions. From a Bayern goal-kick, centre-back Holger Badstuber received the ball, turned and played it into midfielder Bastian Schweinsteiger. But as soon as Schweinsteiger received possession, he was pressured on both sides by Dortmund duo Großkreutz and Robert Lewandowski, forcing him to panic. He attempted to offload first-time but completely missed the ball. It bounced off his standing leg and fell to Großkreutz, who stormed forward and slipped in striker Lucas Barrios, who sidefooted home. Schweinsteiger had a disastrous game, and if Germany's most revered midfielder couldn't cope with Dortmund's energy, what chance did other Bundesliga players have?

For a more specific instance of gegenpressing, a classic Dortmund goal came in a 2–1 Champions League victory at Arsenal in 2013. Marco Reus dribbled down the left and attempted to pass inside to Lewandowski, but he miscued straight to Arsenal skipper Mikel Arteta on the edge of his own box. Arteta passed first-time to midfield colleague Aaron Ramsey, and Dortmund stormed into battle. Lewandowski closed down Ramsey from the front, Reus did so from behind, while Henrikh Mkhitaryan moved inside from the opposite flank to congest the play, with Dortmund's midfielders pushing forward to impose further pressure. Ramsey suddenly found himself swarmed by three yellow-and-black shirts: Reus, Lewandowski and Mkhitaryan. Reus slid in from behind to dispossess the Welshman, while Lewandowski collected the loose ball and flicked it right to Mkhitaryan, who slammed home.

In just six seconds Dortmund managed to lose possession, regain possession and score, with their three most dangerous attackers combining on the edge of the box. Three of Arsenal's defenders had already started their offensive transition and began pushing up the pitch before suddenly finding themselves out of position, and

Mkhitaryan's shot was struck from precisely the position left-back Kieran Gibbs had been occupying six seconds beforehand. The left-back, having expected an Arsenal counter, found himself too wide, but Dortmund had pressed the counter; they'd counter-pressed. 'The best moment to win the ball is immediately after your team just lost it,' Klopp reiterated. 'The opponent is still looking for orientation where to pass the ball. He will have taken his eyes off the game to make his tackle or interception and he will have expended energy. Both make him vulnerable.'

The combination of Dortmund's compression of the opposition at turnovers and their energy meant they sometimes appeared to have an extra man on the pitch, and in that game at the Emirates this sense was supported by the 'distance-covered' statistics. Arsenal's players ran 106.3km combined, while Dortmund's covered 117.8km. The difference of 11.5km was exactly the distance covered by Dortmund right-back Großkreutz, who constantly found himself unmarked on the overlap.

Dortmund's distance-covered statistics were often remarked on, because this was a side with seemingly limitless energy resources. In their victory over Marseille on the previous Champions League matchday, Klopp had said, 'We had to put in a lot of effort and if we'd run just a few kilometres less today, we would have struggled.' He had previously given his players a target: if they covered more than 118km collectively in nine out of ten matches, they'd be rewarded with three extra days off during their winter break. The players missed the target, but Klopp generously granted them the extra rest anyway because of their efforts. Later, Klopp would suggest that his players improved when running less, and their increased emphasis on possession play made them less frantic. The running statistics themselves were a bit of a sideshow, but after a few years of Spanish dominance and all the attention paid to possession statistics, German dominance meant that the focus was now on how much ground the players were covering.

Klopp's Dortmund, however, were a victim of their own success. Their brand of pressing and gegenpressing was so overwhelmingly effective, with Dortmund's back-to-back title victories earning respect from supporters across the country and inspiring other coaches, that many Bundesliga sides increasingly incorporated Dortmund's principles into their own play. Bundesliga matches became even more frantic, because more sides attempted to engage the opposition in advanced positions.

Most problematically for Dortmund, one side inspired by their approach was Bayern Munich. While Bayern managed to pinch Mario Götze, Robert Lewandowski and Mats Hummels from Dortmund, perhaps their most decisive steal was the concept of pressing and gegenpressing itself, after Jupp Heynckes and his coaching staff concluded it was the major difference between the two sides. Having found themselves overwhelmed by the energy and ball-winning ability of Dortmund in 2010/11 and 2011/12, Bayern hit back in 2012/13 to win the Treble, and won every subsequent league title during this period of German dominance. Klopp openly complained that his theories had been replicated so blatantly. 'They have done to us what the Chinese do in industry,' Klopp moaned, referring to factory closures in the Ruhr. 'They see what others are doing, copy it, and then go down the same route with more money.'

This became particularly notable in 2012/13, the season the two sides met in the Champions League Final, because Bayern's pressing had become considerably more intense. Leading the line was Mario Mandžukić, not only a powerful, physical centre-forward but also extremely hard-working, supported closely by Toni Kroos, who boasted great technical quality, was six foot tall and powerful. They would close down the opposition defence with tremendous tenacity, backed up by Schweinsteiger and Javi Martínez.

Bayern's gegenpressing was different to that of Barcelona and Dortmund, not based around passing lanes or piling players into one specific area but more about man-marking in advanced positions. They were a physical side, and often won possession quickly through physical confrontations and tackles rather than interceptions. The wide duo of Franck Ribéry and Arjen Robben would also contribute, and just as Messi set the example for his Barca teammates, Bayern's aggression was most notable when their supposedly flakey wingers got involved. 'When I win the ball, nobody's interested,' Schweinsteiger told Ribéry. 'But when you dive into a tackle, the whole stadium celebrates.' Both sides' pressing played a crucial role in their runs to the Champions League Final in 2013.

In the first knockout round Bayern travelled to Arsenal for the first leg and pressed relentlessly. An early high press forced Arsenal to hopefully hoof the ball long; Bayern won the second ball and launched an attack that ended with an unmarked Kroos firing home from the edge of the box to open the scoring in a 3–1 victory.

In the quarter-finals Bayern met Italian champions Juventus, and again pressing proved crucial in the opening stages. Bayern went ahead within 30 seconds, courtesy of a fortunate, deflected long-range David Alaba strike, but they had already twice pressed to win possession inside the Juventus half. Mandžukić was a one-man pressing machine, tearing after Juve's three centre-backs before dropping back to keep Bayern compact. His energy allowed Bayern's midfielders to concentrate on crowding Andrea Pirlo, who looked hurried and flustered throughout Bayern's 2–0 win. 'I'm the first to say I'm not satisfied with my performance,' admitted Pirlo afterwards. 'I made many mistakes in such an important match, which is disappointing. We now have to analyse why we had so many misplaced passes.' The analysis would have been simple: Juventus weren't prepared for the intensity of Bayern's press. Notably, in the return leg, Juventus started at a much higher tempo and introduced a more aggressive press, troubling Bayern in the opening stages. But Heynckes' side rode out the storm and won 2–0 in Turin.

Then came that famous 7–0 aggregate semi-final victory over Barcelona, where Bayern's counter-attacking and set-piece threat accompanied their tenacious, man-orientated press when Barcelona played out from goal-kicks. Bayern's star performer in this respect was a Spaniard: Javi Martínez, considered an elegant, deep-lying passer during his time with Athletic Bilbao, but who had transformed into a physical, all-action monster during his first season at Bayern. 'I am the most German of all Spanish footballers,' joked Bayern's number 8.

In the first leg Martínez pushed up on to Andrés Iniesta and repeatedly won possession, making the game's most tackles and twice as many fouls as anyone else. 'Javi has a spectacular physical potential,' a shell-shocked Sergio Busquets said afterwards. 'He gets all around the pitch and wins back possession everywhere. He's the lungs of the team.' The closing stages featured Iniesta cynically hacking down Martínez as his compatriot stormed past, which showed how desperate Barcelona had become, how they'd been physically overwhelmed.

Dortmund's run to the final was less convincing. Klopp's overcame Shakhtar Donetsk in the second round, before struggling badly against Manuel Pellegrini's Málaga, drawing 0–0 away from home, then relying on two stoppage time goals from centre-backs in the return leg to win 3–2. Again, however, the most impressive part of Dortmund's game was their pressing, and they were unfortunate not to win in Andalusia.

Next was the semi-final meeting with Real Madrid, whom Dortmund had already faced twice in the competition. Their first group-phase meeting, a 2–1 Dortmund victory, had been a perfect demonstration of Dortmund's advantage over Real. José Mourinho's side didn't press and they couldn't cope with Dortmund's harrying, which typically involved standing off Real's centre-backs and closing down on the first pass into midfield. Dortmund's opener was typical; Pepe moved forward with the ball, tried to pass into Özil but miscued, and Sebastian Kehl, pushing up to intercept, played a first-time ball into Lewandowski, who streaked away behind the out-of-position Pepe and scored. Real equalised immediately with a direct goal that featured Mesut Özil playing the ball in behind for Cristiano Ronaldo, but Dortmund left-back Marcel Schmelzer fired home from the edge of the box for the winner. Klopp's side should have won by more. It was notable that Real struggled after the first-half departure of Sami Khedira, who had started impressively, and from then on Özil was the one Real player who looked capable of coping with Dortmund's tempo. Of Real's players, only the two German players appeared well suited to this type of frantic contest. Dortmund appeared set to triumph 2–1 in Madrid too, until Özil curled in a wonderful last-minute free-kick, a rare occasion on which he found himself ahead of Ronaldo in the queue.

Real, then, had been given plenty of preparation for playing against Dortmund's intensity, yet still found themselves absolutely blown away when they met again in the semi-final. Within the first minute at the Westfalenstadion Ronaldo had dribbled the ball over the left touchline because he was being pursued by two Dortmund players, Luka Modrić had been tackled and conceded possession, and Xabi Alonso spooned the ball out of play under pressure. Real looked terrified, hitting hopeful long passes in the vague direction of striker Gonzalo Higuaín, while Mourinho gestured for his players to calm down. Eight minutes in, Lewandowski turned in a left-wing Mario Götze cross, although Real equalised just before half-time, when Hummels underhit a back pass, allowing Higuaín to square for Ronaldo.

The pattern of the game was very clear, with the energy of Klopp's side enabling them to take control at the start of both halves, before they gradually tired and Real fought back. Dortmund's spell at the start of the second half resulted in three further goals from Lewandowski, in the 50th, 55th and 67th minutes, effectively wrapping up the tie. Lewandowski's four-goal haul must be considered among the greatest Champions League performances of modern times, although midfielder İlkay Gündoğan was equally crucial in dictating Dortmund's play that night. Pushing up aggressively to press, regaining possession and then driving forward into attack, he typified the German approach. Like Martínez the previous evening for Bayern, Gündoğan was wearing the number 8 shirt, and this felt like a specialist German position, a modern iteration of the box-to-box midfielder, the role that Khedira – who was overshadowed here – played for the national side.

Real rallied late on but couldn't reduce the deficit, and it remained 4–1. 'It was an unbelievable display from my team,' grinned Klopp afterwards. 'For the first 25 minutes we were great, then we lost our way a bit and let them back into the match. At half-time we spoke and I urged the players to start playing the way we had early on, which we did, and we were much better.'

'They were the better side by far,' admitted Mourinho. 'They won their individual battles. They were better organised than us, they were better physically and better mentally. The game went from 1–1 to 4–1 in such a short space of time ... we lost possession easily and couldn't cope with their transitions and speed on the break.' You'll rarely find two managers providing such a concise summary; Klopp described the flow, Mourinho explained the specifics. Klopp's side wobbled in the second leg, losing 2–0 in Madrid, but Dortmund progressed to set up an all-German final at Wembley.

Dortmund were widely considered the neutral's favourites, especially after news broke that Bayern were set to sign Götze from them in the summer. He, conveniently, was out injured for the match. Klopp played up his side's status as the popular choice. 'It depends on which kind of story the neutral fan wants to hear,' he said. 'If he respects the story of Bayern, and how much they have won since the 1970s, he can support them. But if he wants the new story, the special story, it must be Dortmund. I think, in this moment in the football world, you have to be on our side.' It was probably over the top and a little arrogant, but it was very Klopp. And many agreed.

European matches between two teams from the same country are often slow, attritional affairs. But with both Dortmund and Bayern now accustomed to pressing heavily and playing at a high tempo, this was an energetic, fast-paced, end-to-end final. It was essentially played like a Bundesliga game, and ranks among the best Champions League finals.

Just like against Real Madrid, Klopp's side started extremely well, attempting the game's first six shots and forcing Manuel Neuer into a couple of excellent saves. Their press meant Bayern were unable to work the ball forward from defence, with centre-backs Jérôme Boateng and Dante merely swapping sideways passes. Dortmund were on top, but couldn't make their advantage count, and then typically faded after the first 25 minutes. Bayern improved towards the end of the first half, mainly threatening from set-pieces.

Once again, Dortmund provided a burst of energy at the start of the second period, but in the latter stages Bayern increasingly dominated. Robben, who had started in his usual right-wing position, switched places with centre-forward Müller and used his speed to exploit Dortmund's high defensive line. Bayern got in behind six times during the second half, each time involving Robben, and on one of these occasions he assisted Mandžukić for the opener.

Dortmund equalised through Gündoğan's penalty after Dante's clumsy foul on Reus, but Bayern, and Robben, kept on coming. Müller rounded Dortmund goalkeeper Roman Weidenfeller and squared towards Robben, but Neven Subotić made a miraculous last-ditch clearance.

A Bayern goal was coming, and in the 89th minute Robben finally supplied the major goal his career had previously lacked, collecting a loose ball on the edge of the box after Ribéry had backheeled, before weaving through the Dortmund defence and rolling the ball home. 'In the end we were a little tired and Bayern took advantage,' admitted Dortmund centre-back Hummels. Klopp agreed. 'From the 75th minute it was very hard for us after a tough season.'

That was the inevitable problem with such a high-energy game – it was exhausting. As Jonathan Wilson outlines in *Inverting the Pyramid*, legendary pressing sides often only excel for a three-year period: Viktor Maslov's Dynamo Kiev in the 1960s, Rinus Michels and Ştefan Kovács's Ajax in the 1970s, and Sacchi's Milan in the 1980s were the three classic examples. You can add Guardiola's Barcelona, who won three league titles and two Champions Leagues but then slumped in his fourth season, and also Klopp's Dortmund, whose ultra-intense pressing had really begun in 2010, brought two league titles and this run to the Champions League Final before things went downhill afterwards. Dortmund tired towards the end of matches, towards the end of seasons and towards the end of Klopp's reign.

They performed competently the following season, 2013/14, finishing second to Guardiola's Bayern and reaching the Champions League quarter-finals. But 2014/15 was truly disastrous, with Dortmund languishing in the relegation zone at the midway point, and while they recovered to finish seventh, Klopp departed at the end of the campaign. Nevertheless, his influence on German football because of his promotion of gegenpressing was considerable, as later outlined by Rangnick, he of the TV punditry that arguably started the German obsession with pressing. 'The extreme transition game has come into play, in which teams rush forward after having won the ball, and after having lost it, many teams try to switch immediately to counter-pressing,' he explained. 'This has led to a lot more sprinting. The number of fast runs or sprints in a match has increased dramatically. In terms of athleticism and dynamics, football has become a completely different game.'

Bayern, meanwhile, pressed even more aggressively under Guardiola. He shifted the defensive line still further up the pitch and drilled his players in automatically moving forwards, rather than backwards, when possession was lost, asking for a four-second gegenpress before they started to return to a deeper block. He was particularly impressed with the work ethic of Mandžukić and Müller, his two main forwards. 'Their pressing is brutal,' he gasped in his first season in Bavaria. 'If you ask Müller to make a 40-metre diagonal run to the other wing, he'll do it at full speed, regain his position, and do it a hundred times more if necessary.'

In a league in which heavy pressing was now commonplace, Guardiola also developed tactics to counteract it. Dropping the holding midfielder into defence to play around the opposition forwards three against two was an approach he'd used at Barcelona with Sergio Busquets, and the approach became even more indispensable in Germany. It was sometimes difficult to decipher whether Bayern were playing with a back three or a back four, such was the ability of Philipp Lahm and later Xabi Alonso to drop in smoothly.

Guardiola's first Bundesliga meeting with Dortmund, a 3–0 Bayern win, saw Bayern start midfielder-cum-defender Javi Martínez in a second striker role. Bayern hit long balls towards him and Mandžukić to avoid their early problems in the Champions League Final, when they couldn't play through Dortmund's press. Instead they bypassed the press altogether. This was a surprising approach from Guardiola, and later his Bayern side would attempt to pass through the press more stylishly, especially after the arrival of Alonso.

The national side, of course, played in a similar fashion. Jürgen Klinsmann, who effectively kickstarted Germany's new approach when taking charge ahead of the 2006 World Cup, spoke frequently about 'immediate ball recovery', while his former assistant and successor Joachim Löw often used the phrase 'active ball-winning'. Germany didn't press aggressively throughout the 2014 World Cup, but the tactic was nevertheless crucial on occasion. The most significant example came in the 7–1 victory over Brazil, for Germany's fourth goal. Barely a minute after Kroos had hammered in the third, Brazil attempted to play out from the back, and from his starting position on the halfway line, Kroos sprinted 25 yards forward to rob Fernandinho, swapped passes with Khedira and fired home.

Over the next couple of years pressing and gegenpressing became more widespread at club level across Europe, but at international tournaments they remained relatively rare. Euro 2016 was a dull, flat tournament in which the majority of sides dropped back into their own half and waited to soak up pressure. Germany, however, bucked the trend. Their quarter-final game against Italy, which Löw's side won on penalties, saw them switching system in order to press Italy's defence three against three. Germany also engaged France in advanced positions in the semi-final and therefore dominated, although they lost 2–0 because of individual defensive errors.

2015/16 was the first Bundesliga season after Klopp's departure from Dortmund. Although he was soon appointed Liverpool manager and took gegenpressing to the Premier League, there was no less pressing in German football. Klopp's fellow revolutionary Rangnick was now in charge of RB Leipzig, Germany's most upwardly mobile club, and gained promotion to the Bundesliga with a particularly aggressive, high-tempo style. They then finished second in their debut campaign in the top flight under Ralph Hasenhüttl, after Rangnick reverted to his position as sporting director.

Klopp's influence was now obvious in the approach of most Bundesliga sides. 'Gegenpressing has become a German institution, and Klopp a model for countless coaches,' wrote Tobias Escher in his history of German football tactics, *Vom Libero zur Doppelsechs*. 'Nowadays, every Bundesliga team uses gegenpressing ... Klopp developed the new standard that we witness on almost every Bundesliga pitch. In 2015/16, at least ten of the 18 Bundesliga teams played Klopp football.'

Klopp's greatest legacy is that the German word '*Gegenpressing*', rather than its obvious translation as 'counter-pressing', is now widely used across Europe. Everyone is therefore aware of the concept's origins and the fact that, for the first time since Beckenbauer re-defined the role of sweeper, German football has been responsible for genuine tactical innovation.

# 18

# Reinvention

Unlike their previous World Cup-winning sides, which generally featured one dominant individual, Germany's class of 2014 was an egalitarian, harmonious group. Selecting one particular hero proved difficult.

In the aftermath of the final there were probably six candidates. The headline writers namechecked Mario Götze, who volleyed in the winner, while the most prominent figure in photographs was captain Philipp Lahm, who lifted the trophy. The true leader in the final was Bastian Schweinsteiger, who largely nullified Lionel Messi's influence between the lines. Overall, Toni Kroos was Germany's most consistent player in Brazil, while up front Thomas Müller was the side's top scorer with five goals. Meanwhile, goalkeeper Manuel Neuer was voted third in the Ballon d'Or, behind the perennial duo of Messi and Cristiano Ronaldo.

There were two notable things linking these six German stars, one of which was obvious: Götze, Lahm, Schweinsteiger, Kroos, Müller and Neuer all played for Bayern Munich. But there was also something more stylistically significant. Germany's success at World Cup 2014 was a triumph for the country's reinvention as a footballing force; they banished their reputation as boring and mechanical by playing inventive, expansive football, and these six individuals were masters of reinvention.

This was the second straight World Cup in which Pep Guardiola exerted a key influence on the victorious squad. Back in 2010 six of Spain's starting XI in the final had played for Guardiola's Barcelona the previous season. In 2014 six of Germany's starting XI in the final had played for Guardiola's Bayern the previous season. Under his leadership many of Bayern's regulars found their careers transformed. German boss Jogi Löw was an astute tactician who formulated clever solutions to strategic problems, but limited time on the training ground with his squad meant he couldn't transform players in the manner of a club manager like Guardiola. Because his Bayern team won three Bundesliga titles at a canter, Guardiola could attempt ambitious tactical experiments, which subsequently provided the national side with more options, often because key players suddenly found themselves comfortable in an entirely different position. Not all of the national team's positional redeployment owed to Guardiola's tinkering, but his impact was undeniable.

Germany defeated Argentina in the final despite suffering from a succession of midfield injury problems, starting when Sami Khedira was ruled out shortly before kick-off. He was replaced by Christoph Kramer, a youngster whose Germany debut had been in a pre-tournament friendly and was now starting his first-ever competitive international. Kramer didn't make it to half-time, having sustained a serious head injury in a collision with Argentina centre-back Ezequiel Garay after 15 minutes. He was allowed to continue despite the seriousness of the collision, and the extent of his problems was only revealed when, after a further 15 minutes, he shouted to referee Nicola Rizzoli, 'Ref, is this the final?' Rizzoli informed Schweinsteiger, and following consultation with Germany's bench Kramer was removed.

His replacement was wide forward André Schürrle, so Germany had to reshape. Mesut Özil shifted into a central role alongside Schweinsteiger and Toni Kroos, which meant Germany were without the physicality and energy provided by Khedira and Kramer – or indeed, by the Bender twins, Lars and Sven, who both missed the tournament through injury. Meanwhile, the normally excellent Kroos endured a difficult game and was fortunate that his disastrous headed back pass, intended for Neuer, was blasted wide by Gonzalo Higuaín under absolutely no pressure. With things falling apart around him, it was time for Schweinsteiger to be the all-action, physical leader.

The Bayern midfielder, the first of the six German heroes, was outstanding. He bossed the game, completing more passes than any other player, and made two crucial interventions to stop Messi, first intercepting a cut-back and then stopping his pass towards Ezequiel Lavezzi. He dominated the zone in front of the defence despite being harshly cautioned in the first half-hour, with his influence forcing Messi to search for the ball out wide or in behind. Schweinsteiger ended the final bloodied after an aerial collision with Sergio Agüero, but this only served to amplify his heroism. It would have been difficult to imagine such a performance at his first World Cup, on home soil in 2006.

Schweinsteiger used to be thought of very differently. During his first years as a professional he was a frustrating talent, with little interest in training hard or taking football seriously; reports about his clothes, haircuts and choice of car overshadowed his performances. He was an inconsistent winger, generally fielded on the right for Bayern, often on the left for Germany, who occasionally provided good deliveries into the box, but exerted little dominance on matches and seemed unlikely to fulfil his potential.

Everything completely changed after Bayern's appointment of Louis van Gaal in 2009/10. Van Gaal wanted proper wingers out wide, but believed in Schweinsteiger's ability, so redeployed him as a central midfielder alongside the tough-tackling Mark van Bommel. Schweinsteiger's game was transformed; he read the game impressively, he positioned himself intelligently and he dictated play. 'The biggest change for me is that finally I've been allowed to play in my best position,' he explained at the time. 'I'd always had a hard time before with coaches feeling that other players – like Jens Jeremies, Niko Kovač, Owen Hargreaves and Michael Ballack – had a better claim on that position. So I'm grateful to Van Gaal.' The absence of Michael Ballack from the 2010 World Cup through injury meant Schweinsteiger became Germany's key central midfielder, forming a fine partnership with Khedira. Löw referred to Schweinsteiger as the side's 'emotional leader'.

His change in position coincided with a change in attitude; with more responsibility on the pitch came more responsibility off it. Some, only half-jokingly, attributed this to German Chancellor Angela Merkel, who sat beside a suspended Schweinsteiger in the stands at Euro 2008. 'She told me that I shouldn't do the same stupid things again,' he said, referring to his red card against Croatia. 'When Frau Chancellor says you have to do something, you have to do it.' German newspaper *Die Zeit* ran a series of cartoons depicting the two exchanging wistful love letters, and the duo shared a warm embrace after the World Cup Final success.

It was Löw, however, who had originally deployed Schweinsteiger in the middle. Back in 2007 Löw shocked supporters by fielding him centrally in a Euro 2008 qualifier against Wales. In a somewhat mediocre quartet also featuring Marcell Jansen, Thomas Hitzlsperger and Roberto Hilbert, he was man of the match, pulling the strings from midfield. It took Schweinsteiger a couple of years to replicate that switch at club level, but it was Löw's decision in 2007 that marked the beginning of his maturing into one of the world's best central midfielders. A positional redeployment had changed everything, and while this occurred a few years before Germany's era of dominance, it meant their 'emotional leader' became a role model for his teammates as someone who had reinvented himself.

But some of Schweinsteiger's teammates weren't just reinventing themselves – they were reinventing their entire position. En route to World Cup success, Germany's nerviest contest came, somewhat surprisingly, in the second round against Algeria, who boasted sound defensive organisation, integrated pressing and speed up front. Against Germany they performed excellently by using an intelligent and nearly decisive counter-attacking strategy.

Algeria closed down the German midfielders in packs before hitting long balls in behind for lone striker Islam Slimani, who consistently beat centre-backs Shkodran Mustafi and Per Mertesacker for speed. What Algeria didn't expect, though, was that goalkeeper Manuel Neuer would produce one of the most memorable goalkeeping performances in World Cup history, despite barely making a save. Neuer's key contributions all came when sweeping; in total, he had 20 touches outside his box. He was Germany's second World Cup hero.

Previous examples of such extravagant ball-playing goalkeeping at World Cups felt ostentatious; Colombian René Higuita's embarrassing error against Cameroon at the 1990 World Cup springs to mind. But while Neuer was often dangerously close to being bypassed and leaving his goal exposed, ultimately his decision-making was flawless. Afterwards, he was told about the expression 'sweeper-keeper', and laughed because he'd never previously encountered the English-language, conveniently rhyming term, but he was now the poster boy for that role.

German goalkeepers have rarely been innovative. Sepp Maier, the outstanding Bayern keeper of the 1960s and 1970s, had started out as a forward and was comfortable in possession, but the most memorable instance of a Germany goalkeeper finding himself on the edge of the box was Harald Schumacher's infamous challenge on France's Patrick Battiston at the 1982 World Cup. Otherwise, German goalkeepers reflected their country's overall footballing style: solid, functional and old-school.

The turning point came ahead of the 2006 World Cup, when manager Jürgen Klinsmann had a choice between Bayern's Oliver Kahn and Arsenal's Jens Lehmann, both 36. Kahn had been a Bayern regular for a decade, had won the Golden Ball as the World Cup's best player four years beforehand (although he was culpable for Ronaldo's opener in the final) and had won 84 caps. Lehmann had just 29 caps, had bounced around various European clubs and was considered error-prone. It was a bitter rivalry. The legendary Maier, Germany's goalkeeping coach, came out in support of Kahn. This angered Klinsmann, who replaced Maier with Andreas Köpke, Germany's goalkeeper for their Euro 96 triumph. That proved telling; Köpke, Klinsmann and Löw settled on Lehmann, rather than Kahn, with Köpke explaining it was primarily a tactical decision. 'Both goalkeepers have extraordinary ability, but we are convinced that Lehmann fits better with our playing philosophy,' he said. Lehmann was better at sweeping, whereas Kahn stayed on his line.

'Kahn once said that in order to concentrate, he began to look just at the ball during a game,' Lehmann recalled. 'It was then that I understood why Kahn had not seen and dealt with so many situations more quickly. Anyone just looking at the ball only knows where it is, not where it will be.' Germany were changing from being reactive to proactive, and Lehmann was therefore their man. He was among Germany's 2006 World Cup stars after his decisive shootout save from Argentina's Esteban Cambiasso in a memorable quarter-final.

Kahn promptly retired from international duty, which meant Lehmann kept his place for Germany's run to the Euro 2008 final. Then, from the 2010 World Cup onwards, Germany's number 1 was Neuer.

This was a smooth transition, because Lehmann had been Schalke's number 1 when Neuer was rising through the club's youth ranks. 'I always looked up to Jens,' Neuer declared. 'He played for Schalke, and I was always impressed by his way of playing and his charisma. He is an attacking goalkeeper. I used to arrive early at home games to watch Jens warm up – he was quite innovative and did exercises I hadn't seen before.' Later, he said Lehmann was 'a bit of a goalkeeping revolutionary', and had 'the most modern goalkeeping style in Europe'. His other role model was, of course, Edwin van der Sar, the modern era's first true sweeper-keeper.

Neuer spent five years as Schalke's number 1, impressing in their run to the Champions League semi-finals in 2011 before moving to Bayern. This is a divide that few players cross, and around 6,000 Bayern supporters protested against his signing at the Allianz Arena, holding up 'Koan Neuer' ('No Neuer') signs. But he quickly won over supporters with his starring performances – between the posts and, increasingly, outside the box.

While always regarded as an aggressive goalkeeper, it was the arrival of Guardiola for the 2013/14 season that allowed Neuer to become still more proactive. Bayern's defensive line played even higher, on average 43.5m from their goal rather than 36m as in the previous season, which itself had been a very aggressive line. As Bayern built their passing moves in the opposition half, Neuer was always adjusting his position in relation to the ball and the defensive line, moving back and forward in unison with his defence. Sometimes his starting position would be 15 yards out of his penalty box, and his confidence in possession produced some remarkable moments.

In one match against Hertha Berlin, Neuer swept up by heading the ball over an attacker, before letting the ball bounce and nodding it calmly to Jérôme Boateng. In another match against the same opposition, Neuer found himself in a position to take a quick throw-in after a Hertha long ball bounced out of play. He regularly showcased Cruyff turns under pressure from opponents, and memorably produced an extraordinary touch in 2014 against Eintracht Frankfurt, when left-back Juan Bernat knocked a waist-high back pass to him, prompting Neuer to pivot and instinctively respond with a volleyed backheel to Xabi Alonso. Neuer was no ordinary goalkeeper. Löw said he could easily play in midfield; Miroslav Klose said he could play up front in the second division, although Neuer himself reckoned the fourth tier was more realistic.

Neuer wasn't immune to mistakes, and sometimes his style looked perilous. In Bayern's 4–0 defeat to Real Madrid in 2014 he twice misjudged when sweeping, allowing both Gareth Bale and Cristiano Ronaldo free shots at an open goal from 40 yards – Bale's attempt went over, Ronaldo's bounced just wide. Another similar incident against Wolfsburg resulted in Josuha Guilavogui hitting the post from the halfway line, with Neuer stranded in the opposition half. But he usually managed to get away with it.

That 2014 World Cup performance against Algeria remains Neuer's most famous, and there were four particularly decisive moments. In the opening stages, Algeria hit a long ball into the left-hand channel for Slimani. Neuer, from a starting position outside his box, raced out to meet him, but Slimani's first touch took the ball past Germany's goalkeeper. As the striker shot from a tight angle, Neuer recovered enough ground to make a sliding block with his feet, still well outside his area.

This set the tone. Later, when Mertesacker desperately tackled Slimani and the ball ran loose, Neuer again sprinted outside his box straight towards Algeria midfielder Sofiane Feghouli and Boateng, both racing full-tilt to get the ball, and produced a slide-tackle to put it into touch. Later, a diagonal ball in behind for Slimani produced another Neuer dash forward and a spectacular diving header, and he made a similar clearance two minutes from the end of normal time, once again denying the onrushing Feghouli.

The concept of a goalkeeper sweeping outside his penalty area was hardly new, but Neuer interpreted his role particularly liberally. The early sliding block on Slimani, in particular, saw Neuer running back towards his own goal, and was therefore classic last-ditch defending rather than the usual, forward-facing contribution of an aggressive goalkeeper. 'For years my goalkeeping style is the one I employ today,' he explained after Germany's triumph. 'It was just the global attention that comes with the World Cup gave it a completely different platform. Our match against Algeria sticks in the memory because I had to come out of my area to act like an outfield player so many times.' Neuer also indicated that his positioning was appropriate because Germany's centre-backs, Mertesacker and Mustafi, weren't particularly quick, and that a wet pitch worked in his favour, as long passes skidded through to him.

'If a team tries to play high, and the defenders are moving up high, this means you have to go into the opponent's half and it's obvious the goalkeeper has to move up too,' Löw said. 'If a player can hit a 60-yard pass on the counter-attack you need a goalkeeper who can move higher. Neuer has the same technical skills as the others. He has a feeling for the field and a feeling for distances.'

While German football didn't have a particularly grand history of sweeper-keepers, it was arguably a more significant development in Germany than anywhere else. After all, this was a country previously fixated on the playmaking sweeper, which was now extinct as teams deployed a flat defence and an offside trap. Köpke, Germany's goalkeeping coach, was asked whether he'd witnessed anyone better at clearing up behind the defence. 'Perhaps only Beckenbauer,' he responded. One German newspaper, in the aftermath of the Algeria game, published a front page with Neuer and Beckenbauer's faces fused together. Neuer's aggressive positioning, then, should be considered as much the reinvention of the sweeper as the reinvention of the goalkeeper.

Beckenbauer himself was less enthusiastic. 'I wouldn't say that he's a better sweeper than me,' he responded grumpily. 'Yes, Neuer saved us in some situations, as an outfield player would do. But he threw caution to the wind. Twice he was lucky that he met the ball at exactly the right time. If he had come in too late, he could have been sent off. I would prefer that he remains in goal against France.' It was a reminder of the old, conservative approach that Germany had left behind. Later, many felt that Neuer was fortunate not to be penalised for colliding with Gonzalo Higuaín in the final, when sweeping to the corner of the box and punching the ball clear.

Neuer's sweeping became such a fundamental part of his side's approach that it influenced his manager's choice of formation at club level. As a general rule, against dangerous forwards Guardiola felt most comfortable deploying an extra defender: a back three against a dangerous strike partnership, a back four against a front three. This changed because of Neuer. In his second season Guardiola travelled to his former club Barcelona for the Champions League semi-final, and started with an incredibly bold system. Against Europe's most fearsome front three of Leo Messi, Luis Suárez and Neymar, Guardiola fielded a back three of Boateng, Rafinha and Medhi Benatia.

In previous years Guardiola would unquestionably have used a back four in that situation. But now he considered Neuer sufficient enough an insurance policy, allowing Bayern to press seven against seven higher up the pitch in the opening stages. Barca played an unusual number of long balls, and Neuer was twice called on to sweep outside his box. Guardiola didn't maintain this unusual system for long, switching to a four-man defence after 15 minutes, with Bernat dropping back to left-back – and Bayern eventually lost 3–0 after three late goals, including a memorable Messi dink over Neuer. The starting approach, however, demonstrated how Guardiola considered Neuer an eleventh outfielder, and had accordingly reduced the number of defenders he fielded.

Further forward, Guardiola continued to use unconventional centre-backs. At Barcelona he'd converted midfielder Javier Mascherano into a defender and on occasion used Yaya Touré and Sergio Busquets at the back too, explaining that because his side dominated possession and his defence played close to the halfway line, a centre-back role for his side was comparable to a midfield role elsewhere. With Bayern he did something similar with Javi Martínez, but also converted energetic all-rounder Joshua Kimmich into a defender, while full-backs Bernat, Lahm, Rafinha and David Alaba became capable of playing centrally.

These full-backs also experienced another significant revolution. Upon taking charge of Bayern, Guardiola found himself with the best full-back pairing in the world, right-sided Lahm and left-sided Alaba. Both were capable of performing the usual full-back functions, defending the wide areas of the pitch and overlapping energetically to allow Arjen Robben and Franck Ribéry to cut inside. But both were unusually talented in possession too.

Former Liverpool defender Jamie Carragher once memorably declared that no one actually wants to end up playing full-back; anyone in that position is either a failed winger or a failed centre-back. Lahm and Alaba, though, were slightly different. They were failed – if that's the right word – central midfielders. Lahm regularly played in the middle throughout his formative years in Bayern's youth system, while Alaba was converted into a left-back late in his development under Van Gaal. When he went on loan to Hoffenheim, Alaba was fielded in a central midfield role, and he also regularly played there for Austria. At possibly any other Bundesliga club Lahm and Alaba would have become central midfielders, but Bayern had such a plethora of talent in that position that they were turned into full-backs. Still, their unusual level of tactical intelligence created new possibilities for Guardiola.

Guardiola's formation structure depends on his complex rules of positional play, which involves him dividing the pitch into a grid and avoiding too many players being positioned in a line with one another, whether vertically or laterally, in the possession phase. It prevents predictable sideways passes, allows integrated movement and means his players remain distributed evenly across the pitch, ready to press if the ball is lost. One golden rule is that a full-back and winger should never be positioned in the same vertical strip. This usually means that when the full-back pushes wide, the winger will narrow his position. Guardiola, however, flipped this idea.

As with most of his tactical experiments in Germany, this idea arose because of Guardiola's determination to guard against counter-attacks. In modern football it had become commonplace to witness possession-based sides pushing both full-backs forward onto the last line of the opposition defence, stretching the play. But this proved disastrous when possession was lost; there was often 50 yards between centre-back and full-back, allowing the opposition space to break into the channels. The full-backs found themselves out of the game, too high and too wide, without any hope of retreating to stop counters. Therefore, rather than pushing the full-backs forward on the overlap, Guardiola decided to bring them inside to become central midfielders in the possession phase, sitting either side of

Bayern's holding player. Therefore, if possession were lost, Bayern's five defensive players – the four defenders and the holding midfielder – would find themselves together in a tight unit, conceding space on the outside rather than between them.

No other club possessed full-backs capable of performing in this manner. Lahm and Alaba were comfortable receiving the ball with their back to play, a very different situation to receiving the ball out wide with a clear view of the pitch. Peculiarly, Bayern had a habit of producing players who could perform competently in both central midfield and at left-back. In a 1–0 victory over Inter in February 2011, Van Gaal started Brazilian Luiz Gustavo at left-back and Danijel Pranjić in central midfield, before switching them for unspecific tactical reasons just five minutes in. Previously, between 2002 and 2009 – with a one-year break when he moved to Santos – Bayern had the wonderful Brazilian Zé Roberto, another player equally comfortable playing as a holding midfielder or a left-back. After he moved to Hamburg, Zé Roberto would sometimes play at left-back before pushing inside to become a central midfielder, a move that appeared bizarre at the time, but somewhat foreshadowed the role his ex-club would 'invent', a role for which there wasn't really a description. 'Half-back' was probably the best term – Germans used the term 'half-spaces' for the zones between the centre and the wings.

Before Guardiola started structuring his side in this revolutionary manner, he'd already fielded Lahm as a conventional midfielder during the opening period of his first season in Germany. This caused something of a stir, as Lahm had spent the last decade as a full-back; sometimes right-back, sometimes left-back, but never in the centre. In pre-season he was deployed as a number 8, tasked with getting up and down the pitch, just as he was accustomed to from a wider position, but in the Supercup game against Dortmund he switched to the deeper number 6 position, which involved more positional discipline and responsibility for switching play. It was a huge transformation, from a dynamic wide position to a more static central position, but Guardiola said his new captain was 'perhaps the most intelligent player I have ever coached'.

Lahm found himself playing a huge variety of roles. In Guardiola's first meeting with Jürgen Klopp's Dortmund, a 3–0 victory, he was fielded as a defensive midfielder, a box-to-box midfielder and then a right-back all within the same game. One commentator jokingly said Bayern's captain was a – deep breath – *'verteidigende Mittefeldgflügelstürmer'*, a defender-midfielder-winger-striker. He was a universal player, capable of aggressively overlapping or dictating play from the centre. 'Football has changed, you'll hardly find a player these days who can only play one position,' Lahm said. 'Modern footballers are very flexible. When you think back 10 or 15 years, you'd see many players who were strong and tall, but now that only holds true for goalkeepers and centre-backs, and maybe the central striker. Everyone else on the pitch is basically a midfielder.' That, of course, had been one of Guardiola's obvious aims at Barcelona.

Alaba's role was different. Although he was accustomed to playing a proper midfield role for his national side, Alaba wasn't fielded as a conventional midfielder by Guardiola during that first campaign and instead remained at left-back – on paper, at least. Gradually, however, it became clear that Alaba wasn't overlapping as readily, compared with his performances under Jupp Heynckes, and instead was drifting in-field when Bayern had possession. By dragging the opposition right-winger inside to mark him, he opened up space for Franck Ribéry to drop deeper and collect possession away from the opposition right-back.

Guardiola increasingly used this approach as the season continued. Lahm was sometimes fielded in the hybrid role, half right-back and half central midfielder – half-back. 'Jupp was terrific and he got us playing well, but our opponents got to know us and how we like to do things,' said Lahm. 'Now we play a bit differently and that's a good thing. For the full-backs it's a big deal because we have permission to insert ourselves into an attacking move wherever it seems best to do so. We can move inside, go outside, and we are allowed almost constant licence to attack.'

Starting with a 4–0 victory over Schalke in September 2013, it was obvious that Bayern's full-backs should be considered part of the midfield unit rather than defenders. On that occasion, Lahm was the holding midfielder with Alaba and Rafinha either side, and the formation was effectively 2–3–4–1. Alaba and Rafinha had licence to drift inside when necessary, and overlapped at other times.

But the most extreme version of the system came in a 3–1 Champions League quarter-final victory over Manchester United. Guardiola had been disappointed by the structure of his side in the previous round, when they were exposed to Arsenal's counterattacking, and Alaba and Lahm were therefore allowed less freedom. They always moved inside to form the outside points of a diamond, with Toni Kroos at the base, and Mario Götze at the forward point. Ribéry and Robben covered an entire flank each, with Thomas Müller and Mario Mandžukić up front. It was a remarkable system, which Guardiola announced to his squad as a 2–3–3–2 when revealing his starting XI – a day earlier than usual, such was the mental preparation required to absorb and then apply the system. But the formation made perfect sense; Bayern offered passing quality in midfield, despite the absence of both Thiago Alcántara and Bastian Schweinsteiger, and their flying wingers had more space out wide.

In truth, Bayern's performance was a little sluggish, and worked better when Rafinha replaced Götze, with Lahm playing more permanently in midfield. Patrice Evra's fearsome strike had given

David Moyes's Manchester United a shock lead, before goals from Müller, Mandžukić and Robben sealed the victory for Bayern. It was difficult to definitively declare that any of the goals arose from the unusual system, but Bayern enjoyed almost constant dominance and largely prevented any counter-attacks.

According to Martí Penarnau's account, however, Guardiola celebrated the victory extravagantly with a bottle of champagne, precisely because he'd deployed such an unusual system. The performance was no more dominant than most had expected – nor the margin of victory any greater – in a contest between the runaway Bundesliga leaders and the side that would finish seventh in the Premier League. But Guardiola was delighted because he'd evolved his strategy and helped to create an almost entirely new position, without losing any quality. 'My understanding of the role of full-backs has changed in Germany,' he subsequently reiterated. 'I no longer think of them as overlapping wing-backs, but as central midfielders, and this will let me develop central midfielders who are very different to the players I have used there in the past.'

This was a response to the quick counter-attacks that dominated the Bundesliga, although the previous season's Bundesliga-winning manager wasn't entirely convinced. 'The Germans have difficulty understanding this idea,' Jupp Heynckes mused, 'because it leaves the two centre-backs isolated and puts the full-backs right up alongside Kroos. It's a move which German football has found a little shocking.' Guardiola was always delighted to surprise other coaches.

For the national side, Löw didn't seek to copy Guardiola's halfbacks, but he did replicate his use of Lahm – the third hero – as a proper central midfielder, deploying him in the holding role for Germany's first four matches of the 2014 World Cup. In truth, Lahm didn't perform particularly impressively, and both he and Germany improved after he switched to his more familiar right-back berth.

But with fitness concerns over various central midfielders going into the tournament, Lahm's versatility got Germany through a potentially disastrous period. This wouldn't have been possible without Guardiola's tinkering at club level.

The fourth hero was Toni Kroos. Guardiola had changed his role significantly, because Kroos had spent 2012/13 pushing forward from a number 10 position to support Bayern's centre-forward. Guardiola flipped the tilt of the midfield and therefore inverted Kroos's positioning, redeploying him as a deep playmaker, the role Guardiola had himself perfected in his playing days. 'Over the years I've been moving further back bit by bit, and that's fine by me,' Kroos said.

Few players were capable of playing every midfield role so expertly, and Kroos played somewhere in between the two roles for Germany at this World Cup. In a midfield that chopped and changed regularly he was the only constant, Germany's most consistent player at the tournament, offering reliable passing from deep, combined with occasional driving runs. His performances earned a move to Real Madrid, where he played wonderfully as both a deep playmaker and then a number 8.

Up front, meanwhile, an interesting situation had developed. Ahead of every international break, Germany had started to publish their squad list in an unconventional manner, broken into three sections rather than four: goalkeepers, defenders and midfielders/strikers. The previously accepted distinction between the latter two categories had vanished. After all, Germany's squad sometimes only contained one out-and-out striker, Miroslav Klose, and he was competing for a place in the starting XI with players who were often considered midfielders, Thomas Müller and Mario Götze. It recalled Vicente del Bosque's statement that David Silva, Andrés Iniesta and Cesc Fàbregas were forwards. For Europe's two most dominant international sides, proper strikers had almost become extinct.

Müller, who was Germany's top goalscorer at the 2014 World Cup and therefore the fifth hero, was the most fascinating player. He wasn't merely versatile, he was impossible to categorise – he was somewhere between an attacking midfielder, a right-sided attacker and a centre-forward. 'I don't enjoy being classed as a striker; I don't see myself as one,' he protested. 'I like to be active in the space in behind the opposition's midfield, that's where I can hurt the opponent most. I'm a mix between a striker and a midfielder.' Guardiola found Müller almost uncoachable because his game was so instinctive, and Müller had informed him that that he was happiest when he didn't have any responsibilities, which simply wasn't viable within Guardiola's system of positional play.

Müller didn't possess the discipline to remain in midfield and didn't boast the trickery to play wide. It was difficult to work out exactly what he excelled at, other than scoring goals – and even when fielded up front he looked awkward and unnatural because he couldn't make his trademark late runs into the box. 'Thomas is a very unorthodox player, and you can't really predict his lines of running,' said Löw. No one could quite comprehend Müller, and the best description of his role was provided by the player himself.

'It's hard to compare your style with another player. Can you think of one?,' Müller was asked in an interview with *Süddeutsche Zeitung*. 'No, somehow I am unique,' he responded. 'There are wingers who are quite similar, and also strikers, but really, what am I?' The interviewer pressed on – 'Yes. What is Müller?' – and was rewarded for his persistence. 'Hmm, well, what am I? A *Raumdeuter* [space interpreter]? Yes, I am a *Raumdeuter*. That would be a good headline, right?'

It wasn't merely a good headline; it became regarded as an entirely new tactical role. Within a couple of years the hugely popular *Football Manager* computer game offered five options for users to assign to wide players: winger, wide midfielder, wide target man, advanced playmaker – and raumdeuter. Müller had defined, and named, his own position. The German language famously contains plenty of words, generally compound nouns, for concepts for which other languages need a lengthy phrase. Now it provided a term for a floating, late-running, versatile, goalscoring attacker.

Germany's raumdeuter got off to a flying start at this World Cup, scoring a hat-trick against Portugal in the eventual champions' opener, and he finished the tournament with the Silver Boot, a neat accompaniment to the golden one he'd won four years earlier. Like Neuer, now renowned as a sweeper-keeper, and Lahm, who personified Guardiola's peculiar half-back position, Müller was a subtle tactical revolutionary.

Finally, there was the sixth hero: Götze. At this stage he was widely expected to become one of the world's great players, having been Guardiola's first signing as Bayern manager because he could theoretically become his new Messi. Götze had previously played as an attacking midfielder at Dortmund, but Guardiola intended to convert him into a false 9. Götze's Bayern career wasn't successful: he suffered from injuries, subsequently returned to Dortmund after Guardiola's departure in 2016 and was omitted entirely from Löw's 2018 World Cup squad.

But Guardiola's determination to make Götze into a false 9 proved crucial in 2014. He'd occasionally provided crucial moments in that role – most significantly when opening the scoring on his return to Dortmund as a Bayern player, the first time Guardiola had deployed him as a false 9 – so Löw had the option of playing him up front. On three occasions at the 2014 World Cup he started in a front three alongside Müller and Mesut Özil, the trio rotating to keep the opposition guessing. He eventually lost his place when Löw returned to an old-school number 9, Klose.

But 36-year-old Klose couldn't last 120 minutes in the final against Argentina, and Löw therefore turned to Götze. 'I said to him: "OK, show the world you are better than Messi and can decide the World Cup," Löw remembered afterwards. 'I told him that. I always had a good feeling about Götze – he is a miracle boy. He can play any position up front.' Götze played as the central attacker and, seven minutes from the end of extra-time, received a left-wing cross from André Schürrle, controlled the ball with his chest and volleyed home with his weaker left foot.

It was a technically excellent goal, but the tactical back story was striking. Guardiola had created the false 9 role for Messi at Barcelona, had moved to Bayern, signed Götze to become his new Messi, then Löw introduced him in the World Cup Final against Messi's Argentina, told him to prove he was better than the Argentine, and he scored the winner from the position he was only playing in because of Messi's influence.

In 2012 everyone had expected Germany to overtake Spain and become Europe's dominant nation, courtesy of the Spanish influence on their play. It didn't quite happen. In 2014, however, they overtook Spain and defeated Argentina – courtesy of the Spanish–Argentine influence on their forward play.

# Transition: Germany–England

2016 witnessed the most remarkable title victory in the history of the English top flight, when Claudio Ranieri's Leicester City – 5000/1 outsiders – remarkably triumphed ahead of the expected favourites to win the Premier League.

It was an incredible story, a genuinely unthinkable success that attracted admiration from across the world. It was also evidence, however, that the Premier League desperately needed rebooting. The big clubs, with wage bills far higher than that of plucky Leicester, had faltered because their managers had underperformed – and the English clubs' poor displays in European competition also suggested they'd fallen behind.

One by one, however, Europe's most revered managers started to gather in England. The first was two-time Bundesliga winner Jürgen Klopp, who joined Liverpool early in 2015/16. The passionate, animated Klopp always felt like a good fit for Liverpool, and he underlined his suitability with a dramatic 4–3 victory over his former club Borussia Dortmund in the Europa League quarter-finals to win the tie 5–4.

By that point it had already been confirmed that three-time La Liga winner, three-time Bundesliga winner and double Champions

League-winning manager Pep Guardiola would leave Bayern Munich and join Klopp in the Premier League, having been tempted to Manchester City because of the presence of some old Barcelona friends in the club's hierarchy. The two managers who had done so much to make the Bundesliga fascinating would now be competing in England.

Guardiola would be reprising his *Clásico* rivalry with José Mourinho – who, having been sacked by Chelsea midway through 2015/16, now found himself at Manchester United. His reputation had taken a battering after his exit from Stamford Bridge, but Mourinho still boasted eight league titles from four different leagues, plus two Champions League successes.

Meanwhile, Chelsea had appointed Antonio Conte, three-time Serie A winner with Juventus and seemingly a good fit for a club who placed less emphasis on style than their title rivals, and whose fanbase were happy to win games through strategy and guile.

Elsewhere, Arsène Wenger was still at Arsenal, Mauricio Pochettino was working wonders at Tottenham and three-time Eredivisie-winning manager Ronald Koeman had joined Everton from Southampton. This was the most exciting and diverse set of managers the Premier League had ever hosted, and there would be no repeat of Leicester's incredible success.

While Ranieri's side had won the Premier League with 81 points, the subsequent two title winners managed 93 and 100. Leicester's achievement shouldn't be belittled, but the standard had risen considerably thanks to the arrival of Europe's best coaches. By 2018/19, the decline of German football and the new English dominance was clear – the Premier League contributed four of the eight Champions League quarter-finalists, and three had eliminated Bundesliga sides in the second round, by an aggregate score of 17–3.

This English period was different to the Dutch, Italian, French, Portuguese, Spanish and German periods. It wasn't about the promotion of an English style of play, but about how the English style was influenced by that of its neighbours. Therefore, for those who had followed European football closely over the past quarter of a century, the Premier League now produced a series of familiar strategies and storylines.

Part Seven

# Football, 2016–20

## 19

# The Mixer

By 2016, English football was home to the most impressive collection of managers anywhere in Europe – but none of them were English. It was therefore not only impossible to claim that the Premier League's return to prominence represented the rise of an English style of play; it was also increasingly difficult to work out whether any discernible 'English style' still existed at the highest level.

Across Europe, the English game is perceived in very clearly defined way. Italians refer to a lenient referee who fails to punish tough tackles as an 'English referee'. Former Barcelona defender Eric Abidal once explained of Andrés Iniesta, 'He was forever getting me out of trouble. You'd give him the worst possible pass, an "English pass", and you knew he would still control it.' Even in England itself, an 'English-style' coach refers to an old-school, back-to-basics manager who largely eschews in-depth tactical thinking, demands hard tackling and favours long balls into attack. By the mid-2010s, however, none of the Premier League's top coaches preached this style, and even the second tier was increasingly dominated by foreign managers who implemented a more technical style of football.

But there remained a group of Premier League coaches who, to varying extents, represented the old English game. There was Sam

Allardyce, who started this period in charge of the national side, but lasted just a single match after being secretly filmed claiming that FA rules on player transfers could be circumvented. He would subsequently take charge of Crystal Palace and Everton, but remains most well known for his earlier stints at Bolton and Blackburn: unfashionable clubs in the north-west who punched above their weight thanks to Allardyce's use of direct, route one football. He was actually one of the Premier League's more innovative coaches in terms of sports science, but Allardyce used these methods to fine-tune his side's old-fashioned football.

Another old-school coach was Tony Pulis – Welsh rather than English – who was now in charge of West Brom, but was also better known for an earlier stint, in charge of Stoke City, who effectively became 'the new Bolton' when promoted to the Premier League in 2008. Pulis cared little for possession play, and his Stoke side were infamous for their dependence on Rory Delap's long throws, to the extent that they often played long balls into the channels with the purpose of tempting the opposition to head the ball out of play, enabling Delap to hurl the ball into the box. They were prolific from set-pieces, packed their side with tall players and were also renowned as the Premier League's most physical side. 'You cannot say it is football any more – it is more rugby on the goalkeepers than football,' said Arsène Wenger of Stoke's physical approach at set-pieces. By 2016 Pulis was using the same approach at West Brom, sometimes fielding four centre-backs across defence. At the opposite end, centre-forward Salomón Rondón netted a hat-trick of headers in a 3–1 victory over Swansea City – only the second time that such a feat had been achieved in Premier League history. It spoke volumes about Pulis's favoured approach play.

There was also Burnley coach Sean Dyche, who had achieved promotion to the Premier League for the second time ahead of

2016/17, and took an unremarkable squad packed with English players to top-flight survival and then finished seventh in 2017/18. He was another who represented traditional English football; Burnley reprised the role of Allardyce's Bolton and Pulis's Stoke, playing long balls into attack, defending deep with plenty of last-ditch blocks and showing little interest in possession play. 'It was a myth that came out about five years ago that possession wins you games,' Dyche chuckled after a 2–0 victory over Liverpool early in 2016/17.

Dyche's Burnley recorded the lowest pass-completion rate in their first two seasons back in the top flight, although in 2018/19 were 'beaten' in this respect by Neil Warnock's Cardiff City. Warnock was another who liked long balls and maximising set-piece opportunities. 'What do you want as a fan? Do you want to see shots on target or do you want us to pass the ball across the pitch on the halfway line?' he offered, responding to criticism of his style. Cardiff had achieved promotion to the Premier League with a 57 per cent pass-completion rate, an alarmingly low figure even for England's second tier.

Dyche and Warnock were two of only four English managers in the Premier League in 2018/19. Roy Hodgson's Crystal Palace occasionally played attack-minded football and always fielded direct wingers, but he was still largely considered a cautious manager with no interest in dominating possession. 'A lot of possession is kept amongst the back players or between midfielders and back players,' Hodgson said during his stint as England manager. 'So I don't regard statistics, especially possession statistics, as being particularly important.'

The only English manager who played genuinely positive, technical football was Bournemouth's Eddie Howe, but he remained an exception to the rule. Allardyce, Pulis, Dyche and Warnock represented the classic idea of English football, but their primary role in the development of the English game involved protesting against the increasing popularity of possession play and complaining about any attempt to clamp down on hard tackling.

There are many reasons for the English obsession with direct football and physical challenges. The weather certainly plays a major role; of Europe's major seven footballing nations, England has both the rainiest and windiest climate, which makes the run of the ball unpredictable and means pitches are often too muddy for passing football. Even though Premier League pitches are now largely immaculate, the effect of poor surfaces at grass-roots level can't be overlooked.

The impact of rugby, a sport that developed out of football and retains basic similarities to it, partly explains the level of physicality in the English game. Rugby, in both its codes, is a full-contact sport and its supporters relentlessly emphasise its toughness compared with football, which in response has felt compelled to prove its machismo by fetishising hard tackles more other European nations. Meanwhile, rugby union became the default winter sport of private schools, with football considered a purely working-class sport, which isn't the case elsewhere in Europe. Football was often patronised, considered a pursuit unworthy of academic or scientific attention. There remains a deep-rooted anti-intellectualism within the English game, and until recently managers were evaluated purely in terms of motivation and man-management, rather than in tactical terms.

Perhaps most pertinently, tactical thinking within English football was influenced heavily by Charles Hughes, the Football Association's director of coaching in the 1970s, who selectively used statistics in an attempt to emphasise the value of long-ball football. He stressed the importance of launching the ball into the box towards the 'position of maximum opportunity', an idea that influenced managers to encourage their players to 'get it in the mixer'. Hughes's theories were arguably taken too literally – to the detriment of the English game – although many still have merit; he emphasised, for example, the importance of pressing.

Hughes's focus on hoofing the ball towards the opposition box, and regaining it there when possible, showed that English football was more about territory than possession, another feature that can be likened to rugby strategy. As late as 1990 Hughes was still dismissing the importance of possession play, claiming that 'world football has been moving in the wrong strategic direction for the better part of 30 years', a remarkable statement sadly typical of English footballing ideology. Since then, football in England has gone through periods of standing still, and periods of desperately playing catch-up, but innovation has never come, at least in the modern era, from within the English game.

Meanwhile, no English manager has won the English top flight since Howard Wilkinson triumphed with Leeds in 1991/92, the final season before the start of the Premier League – and, more significantly, the final season before the introduction of the back-pass law. Wilkinson's Leeds were a direct side who found their long-ball football compromised after the law change. 'Previously goalkeeper John Lukic would hold the ball and he'd launch it to us high up the pitch,' remembered midfielder Steve Hodge. 'Now, Lukic would have to launch it from the floor and the ball wasn't going far enough down the pitch. We were much less of a threat because the ball wasn't landing or being flicked to the edge of our opponents' area, it was bobbling around in midfield. Also, teams would now really push up and make Lukic kick it quickly.' It's remarkable that the simple fact of a goalkeeper being unable to boot the ball far enough caused the English champions such problems, but that wasn't atypical of the English game. Leeds eventually slumped to 17th the following season, and over a quarter of a century later the Premier League is still searching for its first title-winning English manager.

What is the typical English style today? Well, it's remained largely remained unchanged for decades, while the English top flight has become dominated by foreigners – first players, then managers and eventually owners. English football simply hasn't been producing enough high-quality players or coaches to dissuade top-flight clubs from looking overseas. Equally damagingly, Englishmen have traditionally been reluctant to venture abroad themselves, and instead have complained about the lack of opportunities in their homeland. Not only has this hampered their development; it has also meant there has been little chance of an English style becoming appreciated elsewhere. Of course, the national side's consistent underachievement at international level – often because of tactical failings rather than a lack of individual quality – did little to promote English football in its strictest sense overseas, while the multinational Premier League has become hugely popular across the world.

So, from 2016/17, while the classic English style was played solely by the Premier League's mid-table sides or relegation strugglers, the top teams represented the footballing styles that had defined every other major European country over the previous quarter of a century. Each era of dominance – in the Netherlands, Italy, France, Portugal, Spain and Germany – was represented by a manager of one of England's top seven.

The Dutch period, between 1992 and 1996, was represented by Ronald Koeman, the wonderful free-scoring, ball-playing defender from Johan Cruyff's Barcelona and the Dutch national side, now in charge of Everton. Koeman had retired from playing in 1997, and worked as an assistant for both Holland and Barcelona, before taking charge of Ajax, PSV and Feyenoord in his homeland, winning three Eredivisie titles, and also enjoying stints at Valencia and Benfica.

Koeman initially preached the classic Dutch model: a high defensive line, aggressive pressing and playing out from the back. He arrived in the Premier League in 2014/15, succeeding Mauricio Pochettino and taking Southampton to seventh in his first season and sixth in his second, the club's highest finish for 30 years. Koeman's coaching of the defence, as you would expect, was particularly impressive. His Southampton side had the second-best defensive record in the Premier League in 2014/15, conceding only one more goal than Chelsea. And whereas José Mourinho's champions defended deep, Koeman's Southampton maintained a Dutch-style offside trap.

Koeman worked wonders with on-loan Toby Alderweireld, a Belgian who had risen through the Ajax youth system. He struggled slightly in a defensive-minded Atlético Madrid side, but Koeman's approach at Southampton revitalised him. Alderweireld moved on to Pochettino's Tottenham, so Koeman turned to a fellow Dutchman, Virgil van Dijk, who explained the benefit of playing under Koeman. 'He was an amazing player himself,' Van Dijk said of his manager. 'I never saw him play live but obviously I've seen clips, and you know the stories. I can learn from him.' He would grow into the Premier League's most dominant centre-back.

After moving to Everton ahead of 2016/17, Koeman made a positive start with 13 points from his first five matches. In Yannick Bolasie and Kevin Mirallas, Everton played with two direct wingers. At the back they had arguably the Premier League's best attacking full-back duo in Leighton Baines and Séamus Coleman, while the defence kept a high defensive line, with goalkeeper Maarten Stekelenburg – who rose through the academy at Ajax and played for the first team under Koeman – sweeping behind. Koeman often linked his approach to what he'd learned from Cruyff. 'Still, sometimes when I need to make decisions I go back and ask myself what he would do, or what kind of decision he would make, because he was a really big inspiration,' Koeman said midway through his first season at Everton, where he guided them to sixth.

A more significant example of Cruyff's influence came at Manchester City, now coached by Pep Guardiola – Koeman's old defensive partner and roommate at Barcelona. Twenty-five years on, Koeman and Guardiola were showcasing the Dutch style together in the Premier League, with Koeman copying some of Guardiola's training sessions. 'Ronald is a man I know very well and have the greatest respect for as a player, a coach and a man,' Guardiola said. 'I have learned from him. Over the years we have talked a lot about the game and how we think it should be played. There are many things on which we agree.'

Guardiola insisted on his side playing out from defence in the classic Cruyffian style, and his first major decision at Manchester City was informing Joe Hart, England's first-choice goalkeeper, that he wasn't required because his distribution wasn't good enough. In his place Guardiola signed Barcelona's Claudio Bravo, who was accustomed to playing as a sweeper-keeper. Bravo was in the Cruyff mould: he played incredibly far off his line and was brilliantly composed in possession, but wasn't particularly adept at shot-stopping. At one stage, midway through a difficult debut campaign, the Chilean conceded 14 goals from 22 shots on target. John Stones, the centre-back signed from Everton, was a similar case; he was a fine ball-playing defender, but seemingly lacked natural defensive skills. Both Stones and Fernandinho, a Brazilian holding player, were sometimes deployed as part-defender, part-midfielder, shuttling between the two positions. It was an unusual role, but recalled the way Frank Rijkaard had played for Louis van Gaal's Ajax and how Guardiola sometimes played for Cruyff's Barca, dropping back to cover for Koeman.

Whereas keeping a high defensive line and playing out from the back were almost purely 'Dutch' concepts in the early–mid-1990s, they had now become the default approach for title-challenging clubs in England. A good example came at Tottenham Hotspur, whose manager Mauricio Pochettino was Argentine, but whose Dutch-style philosophy can be compared to Guardiola's. Pochettino's main influence was Argentine Marcelo Bielsa – who would later pop up in the English second tier with Leeds – whom Guardiola places alongside Cruyff and Juanma Lillo as one of his coaching idols. Pochettino had preceded Koeman at Southampton, and had immediately concentrated on implementing heavy pressing and an aggressive defensive line, which explained why Koeman settled so well.

Having moved to Tottenham in 2014/15, Pochettino created the division's best centre-back pairing, comprising Alderweireld and his Belgian international teammate Jan Vertonghen. Tellingly, both had risen through the Ajax academy and then played together for the first team, so they had developed a fine relationship and instinctively understood how to defend close to the halfway line. There was almost literally an Ajax defensive line in the Premier League, because when Pochettino decided that Tottenham required a third centre-back, he turned to Colombian Davinson Sánchez – signed from Ajax.

Guardiola, meanwhile, showcased another classic Dutch concept – proper width down both flanks. This was somewhat unexpected. At Barcelona Guardiola used wide forwards charging in behind the opposition defence to collect through-balls, while at Bayern he used inverted wingers cutting inside to shoot from long-range. But his Manchester City side featured right-footed Raheem Sterling on the right and left-footed Leroy Sané on the left, running down the outside and delivering a stream of low balls across the six-yard box. This tactic ensured City scored a huge number of goals from open play, finished either by the winger on the opposite side or by City's all-time record goalscorer, Sergio Agüero.

Koeman, meanwhile, only lasted one full season at Everton, and during the first couple of months of his second season it was difficult to detect much Dutch influence in the team's play. But after leaving Everton he was appointed Holland manager, tasked with turning around the fortunes of his home country, who had failed to qualify for both Euro 2016 and the 2018 World Cup. Despite the lack of attacking talent, Koeman started well, partly because he was overseeing the development of Ajax youth products Matthijs de Ligt and Frenkie de Jong, two defender-midfielders renowned for their composure on the ball in deep positions. The Dutch were still masters at producing ball-playing defenders in the Koeman mould.

Back in the Premier League, the Italian era of 1996–2000 was represented by Chelsea manager Antonio Conte, the hard-working midfielder who had captained Juventus throughout that period. Conte retired from playing in 2004 after 13 seasons at Juventus and spent the next couple of years studying for his coaching qualifications at Coverciano, where his dissertation was entitled 'Considerations on 4–3–1–2 and the analytical use of video'. After stints in charge of Arezzo, Bari, Atalanta and Siena, Conte returned to Juventus in 2011 as first-team coach. At this stage Juve were something of a fallen giant; having been relegated to Serie B in 2006 because of the *Calciopoli* scandal, they'd worked their way back to the top half of Serie A, but at the time of Conte's arrival had finished seventh in the previous two league campaigns. Under Conte, however, they immediately won three straight Serie A titles, the first of them undefeated.

Having originally played a 4–4–2 with aggressive wingers, midway through his first campaign at Juve Conte switched to 3–5–2, mirroring the Serie A norm of the late 1990s, when the three-man defence re-established its dominance over the back four. Conte could count on three outstanding centre-backs: aggressive markers Andrea

Barzagli and Giorgio Chiellini, and the more cultured, technically gifted Leonardo Bonucci. This wasn't a proper *catenaccio* system with rigid man-marking, but Italians still defended in more of a marking-orientated fashion than their European rivals, while Bonucci effectively played as a *libero*. When Conte took charge of the Italian national side in 2014 he deployed the same system, and the same three Juventus defenders. Italy were one of only two sides to use a back three at Euro 2016, including for the most tactically impressive display of the tournament, their 2–0 victory over holders Spain in the second round, before being eliminated by Germany on penalties. Conte immediately started work at Chelsea ahead of 2016/17.

Conte initially used the defensive-minded 4–3–3 system that Chelsea had largely deployed since José Mourinho's first spell at the club. Conte's Chelsea started well, with three victories – but then drew at Swansea, suffered a home defeat to Liverpool, then travelled to Arsenal and found themselves 3–0 down by half-time, prompting Conte to switch to a 3–4–3 formation. 'That decision changed our season,' Conte later recalled. Although it wasn't enough to prompt a comeback at the Emirates, Conte continued with the approach the following weekend, and Chelsea won 13 consecutive league matches, taking them from eighth to top. They eventually won the league with 93 points, at that stage the second-highest points tally recorded in the Premier League.

The three-man defence wasn't Conte's original plan, but a couple of crucial signings allowed him to play in that manner. The capture of Marcos Alonso, who had been playing as a left-wing-back in Serie A with Fiorentina, meant Conte had a proper overlapping option down that flank, so previous left-back César Azpilicueta became a right-sided centre-back, exhibiting the type of defensive versatility an Italian coach would particularly admire. The surprising return of David Luiz, after two seasons with PSG, also made sense in a three-man defence. The Brazilian was never convincing as a conventional centre-back, but in this system he played Bonucci's role expertly. While reading the play intelligently and sweeping up behind his fellow centre-backs, David Luiz also became Chelsea's deep playmaker, bringing the ball forward and spraying long diagonal passes. 'The central defender must be more tactical, reflect more, find the right position and call the defensive line up and down,' Conte explained, essentially describing a *libero*.

Opponents playing a four-man defence couldn't cope with Conte's 3–4–3. The main problem came down the flanks, where Pedro Rodríguez or Willian and the brilliant Eden Hazard started in wide positions before drifting inside, dragging the opposition's full-backs narrow. In turn, that opened up space for the wing-backs, Alonso and Victor Moses, to exploit on the overlap. Chelsea effectively attacked with five players – this quartet and striker Diego Costa – which overloaded the opposition back four. With three centre-backs and two holding midfielders, Chelsea retained a solid structure to guard against counter-attacks.

Eventually, teams realised that the best way of nullifying Chelsea's 3–4–3 was to deploy a 3–4–3 themselves, with wing-backs tracking wing-backs. Chelsea's first defeat with this system came against a Tottenham side mirroring their 3–4–3, and the more sides that played in this manner, the more others felt compelled to match them. In the previous Premier League season there had been 31 examples of a side starting with a three-man defence. In 2016/17 this figure rose to 130 – of which only eight had occurred in the opening six weeks of the season before Conte had switched to 3–4–3.

Those eight instances of a three-man defence before Conte's switch were significant. Koeman's Everton had started the season playing with this formation – he had been accustomed to playing in a three-man defence at Barcelona, of course. The other two managers were Conte's compatriots, who had previously helped repopularise the three-man defence in Serie A. Francesco Guidolin had worked wonders at Udinese with an exciting 3–5–2 system, and was now in charge of Swansea. Walter Mazzarri had turned Napoli into title contenders with a 3–4–3, and was now using that system at Watford. Their success in Serie A pre-dated Conte's use of a three-man defence, and had prompted another shift towards that system in Italy. Now, they'd brought their Italian influence to the Premier League.

It was Conte, however, whose 3–4–3 proved the real inspiration. 'We started the season with another system, but I noted in some circumstances we didn't have the right balance,' Conte explained. 'For this reason we switched to the new system of 3–4–3 ... I always knew the squad could play with this 3–4–3 system. In my mind there was always this possibility; I knew the characteristics of the players, and for this reason, when I spoke to the club and we planned the season, this system was an alternative.'

Chelsea became the first side since Everton in 1962/63 to win the English top flight with a three-man defence; an Italian manager's tactical tinkering had ended half a century of flat-back-four dominance. 'What Antonio has done here in the Premier League, maybe the people don't realise,' Guardiola marvelled. 'He introduced another way to attack, with five at the back, another system. A lot of teams, even Arsenal, had to do a lot of imitating to do that. Tactically, he is a master. I think Conte is going to leave something in English football – I'm sure of that.'

Guardiola's use of 'even Arsenal' was pointed, because Conte was only denied a Double in his first season after Chelsea were defeated by Arsenal in the FA Cup Final, after the Gunners had switched to a Conte-esque 3–4–3. Arsène Wenger had previously gone over 1,000 games without deviating from a back four, but he now felt compelled to copy Chelsea's system and eventually used it to defeat them at Wembley.

Wenger, of course, represented the French period between 2000 and 2004. By now, many of Wenger's methods, revolutionary upon his arrival in England in the mid-1990s, were either established practice or outdated, and Arsenal increasingly slipped backwards until Wenger's departure, after 22 years at the helm, in 2018. But there was still a strong French influence up front at Arsenal. Wenger had broken the club's record transfer twice in his final year, first for Lyon's Alexandre Lacazette, a talented, elusive all-round forward who could come short and run in behind, and then for Dortmund's Pierre-Emerick Aubameyang. Although Aubameyang represented Gabon, following in the footsteps of his father, he was born and raised in France, and was a classic modern French striker, based around devastating speed.

Upon his arrival at Arsenal, Lacazette was asked about the legacy of previous French forwards at Arsenal – Nicolas Anelka, Sylvain Wiltord and, of course, Thierry Henry. 'Anelka and Wiltord were a bit before my time – I was very young when they were playing their best football,' Lacazette said. 'As for Henry, I was always a fan of his, of course, so I followed his career closely. He was a huge role model for me.'

Aubameyang was the more similar of the two to Henry, especially as he started in a left-sided position and would typically drift inside and finish into the far corner, so it was perhaps appropriate that he wore Henry's old number 14 shirt. After Aubameyang scored a fine goal in a 4–2 derby win over Tottenham, teammate Aaron Ramsey underlined the similarity. 'He does that in training all the time,' the Welshman said. 'He just eases the ball into the corner, but with pace as well. It reminds me of Thierry Henry's finishes.' Wenger made the same comparison, because of 'the quality of his runs'.

Wenger generally favoured deep-lying playmakers rather than classic defensive midfielders during his last decade at Arsenal, but the French water carrier was represented elsewhere in the Premier League by N'Golo Kanté. He'd risen to prominence during Leicester's extraordinary title-winning campaign of 2015/16, when he became renowned for his tireless energy. Upon joining Chelsea in 2016/17 he performed a similar role, becoming the first player to win back-to-back Premier League titles with different clubs, and in both seasons his combined tackling and interception figures were the highest in the division. 'I need to anticipate if an attack is going wrong, and what is needed to be done to stop the counter-attack,' he explained. 'It's important to always think what could happen, offensively and defensively.'

Kanté's distribution was tidy rather than incisive, and he only sporadically pushed forward into attack. He was the classic French *domestique*, happy to get through the dirty work, just like his compatriots Didier Deschamps and Claude Makélélé, both for Chelsea and the national side. France manager Deschamps deployed Kanté as his defensive midfielder for the World Cup victory in 2018, while Makélélé regularly highlighted his successor's quality in that role. 'People talk about the Makélélé role, but I am old and it is time everybody called it the Kanté position,' he said. 'N'Golo deserves that.'

Kanté proved particularly popular in English football, being voted PFA Player of the Year in 2016/17, precisely because he was such a prolific tackler, a quality valued more in England than elsewhere. When Kanté was pushed into a more advanced role by Conte's successor, Maurizio Sarri, it prompted a remarkable backlash at the club because Kanté was no longer making so many tackles.

Kanté's former club, Leicester, replaced Kanté with another Frenchman, Nampalys Mendy, who had previously played under manager Claudio Ranieri at Monaco. 'The first time I met Ranieri he called me "the new Makélélé", Mendy remembered. Now, Ranieri wanted him to become the new Kanté. Later, Mendy was deployed alongside Wilfred Ndidi, who recorded Kanté-esque ball-winning statistics, making the most tackles of any Premier League player in 2017/18. By this stage it was relatively unusual for a Premier League side to deploy two pure defensive midfielders together, but then Leicester were now managed by Frenchman Claude Puel. He'd been a tough-tackling defensive midfielder for Wenger's Monaco back in the day, and still favoured the old French model of multiple ball-winning midfielders.

The Portuguese era of 2004–08 was chiefly represented by the familiar figure of José Mourinho. He'd returned to English football with Chelsea in 2013, winning the title in his second season before being sacked midway through a disastrous 2015/16, and then re-emerging as Manchester United manager. His teams continued to play more defensively than in his Porto days; in his first season at Old Trafford Manchester United had the second-best defensive record in the Premier League, conceding only 29 goals in 38 games. But they only scored 54 goals, whereas the five sides that finished above them all managed at least 77.

Mourinho remained excellent at navigating his way through cup competitions, however, winning first the League Cup, then the Europa League with a 2–0 victory over Ajax in which he predictably allowed the Dutch side possession and ordered his players to play on the break. United improved in Mourinho's second season. While they finished a distant second to Manchester City, they managed to postpone City's title party at the Etihad, coming back from 2–0 down at half-time to win 3–2, meaning Guardiola's side needed to wait another fortnight before clinching the title.

But that summarised what Mourinho had become – the anti-Guardiola rather than anything truly positive. He was dismissed midway through a familiar tricky period, his third season, a stage during which he'd repeatedly fallen out with key players first at Real Madrid, then Chelsea and now Manchester United. That recalled the famous pronouncement of Béla Guttmann, who exerted such an influence on Portuguese football during the 1950s and 1960s: 'The third season is fatal.'

There was further Portuguese influence elsewhere in the Premier League. Marco Silva took charge of Hull City, Watford and then Everton, and stressed that coaches like him were only given opportunities because of Mourinho's initial success. 'For all Portuguese managers, he had a fantastic impact when he appeared,' Silva explained. 'He achieved fantastic success with Chelsea, Inter Milan and Real Madrid, and it opened big, big doors for Portuguese managers to come and work abroad. Portugal had very good coaches in the past as well, but mostly working in Portugal. José changed that.'

One of Mourinho's obvious protégés was Nuno Espírito Santo, the back-up goalkeeper in his Champions League-winning Porto side – and, notably, Jorge Mendes's first-ever client. Espírito Santo took Wolverhampton Wanderers to promotion from the second tier in 2017/18, leading them to a comfortable mid-table finish in his first Premier League campaign. Espírito Santo depended heavily on his relationship with Mendes to sign a succession of Portuguese players, and on one occasion used seven compatriots in a single Premier League game.

While Espírito Santo was the first of Mourinho's former players to manage in the Premier League, many of his former coaching staff had done so already. André Villas-Boas was Mourinho's opposition scout and later coached Chelsea and Tottenham. Brendan Rodgers, who has coached Swansea, Liverpool and Leicester, credits much of his education to working at Chelsea during Mourinho's first stint, while Mourinho's former assistant Steve Clarke enjoyed a spell at

West Bromwich Albion. Meanwhile, the two symbols of Mourinho's first period at Chelsea, John Terry and Frank Lampard, had both started their coaching career in the English second tier, and were considered potential future Chelsea managers. It's also worth considering that various managers now incorporated tactical periodisation in their training process, another part of Mourinho's legacy in England.

Neatly, the primary representative of the first four eras left the Premier League in turn.

Koeman was dismissed by Everton in October 2017, Wenger and Conte departed at the end of 2017/18, while Mourinho was sacked by Manchester United in December 2018. That left two eras: Spain and Germany. Sure enough, the Premier League was now dominated by Pep Guardiola's Manchester City and Jürgen Klopp's Liverpool.

Assessing Guardiola's impact on the Premier League upon his arrival in 2016 is difficult, because the English top flight had already been heavily influenced by the dominance of Barcelona and Spain several years beforehand, many Premier League managers having decided to play a more possession-based game. Statistics concerning ball retention tell the story neatly. In the ten years from 2003/04 to 2013/14 the Premier League's pass-completion rate rose from 70 per cent to 81 per cent. Over half of that 11 per cent rise took place solely between 2009/10 and 2011/12, the period when Barcelona and Spain's dominance was most pronounced. Leading English clubs had already, in various ways, attempted to replicate Barça's style: playing out from the back, more patient build-up play, more technical players in midfield and the occasional use of a false 9. Furthermore, David Silva, Santi Cazorla, Cesc Fabregas and Juan Mata had directly introduced Spanish invention into Premier League midfields.

But Guardiola's style wasn't purely Spanish. For a start, the Spanish style he helped to define was heavily influenced by the Dutch game, as mentioned previously in relation to his use of outright wingers at City and his insistence on defenders playing out from the back. But, more importantly, Guardiola had spent the previous three years in the Bundesliga, and admitted that his beliefs had changed dramatically. Having intended to import the Barcelona approach onto Bayern, he eventually arrived at a compromise between the Spanish and German styles. He transferred that model onto Manchester City.

From the outset Guardiola used a system that would have been unthinkable under City's previous manager, Manuel Pellegrini, who had generally used a 4–2–3–1 formation that featured both Silva, a silky playmaker, and the more direct Kevin De Bruyne in the trio behind Sergio Agüero. Injury problems meant Silva and De Bruyne didn't start together regularly under Pellegrini, but City never looked comfortable with both in the side – they sacrificed width and become too predictable. But there was little criticism of the roles Silva and De Bruyne were deployed in; most managers would have done the same.

Not Guardiola. From the outset he completely changed City's midfield structure, moving to the 4–3–3 system that was his base formation at Barcelona and Bayern. This meant Fernandinho became the sole holding midfielder, a role he'd never previously played. 'I think Fernandinho can play in ten positions,' Guardiola said before the start of his first Premier League campaign. 'He has the quality to play wherever. He's a quick, fast player, so intelligent, aggressive and strong in the air.' Deploying him in front of the defence meant a familiar decision for Guardiola: dropping Yaya Touré. Just as he had preferred Sergio Busquets in 2010, now he preferred Fernandinho in 2016.

Touré wasn't used in one of the more advanced roles either. Instead Guardiola shifted Silva and De Bruyne into conventional midfield roles, where they had more responsibility for conducting play, rather than solely providing decisive contributions in the final third. This created a highly technical midfield trio, the likes of which had never been witnessed in the Premier League. It appeared doubtful they could withstand the physical demands of English football, where tackles are harder, pitches are boggier and the Christmas schedule leaves players exhausted. But Guardiola wasn't about to compromise.

This genuinely felt like something entirely new. Silva and De Bruyne, accustomed to receiving the ball between the lines on the half-turn, were now storming through midfield together while swapping passes. Both were transformed, and they represented the blend of Guardiola's Spanish and German approaches. Silva was the pure Spanish technician, and started to resemble Andrés Iniesta, slaloming past tackles and playing the pass before the assist, rather than the assist itself.

De Bruyne was Belgian rather than German, but had spent three seasons in the Bundesliga before moving to City, excelling in a counter-attacking Wolfsburg side. Indeed, after Guardiola's Bayern won the Bundesliga by ten points from Wolfsburg in 2014/15, it was De Bruyne who was voted Player of the Year. He was more direct and more powerful than Silva, and his dangerous balls into the forwards were often crosses rather than through-balls. 'It's a different role,' De Bruyne acknowledged. 'It's a little change but it's all right. The coach has his own tactics. I play not as a number 10, but as a free 8 with a lot of movement everywhere.' De Bruyne, much like Thomas Müller, had invented and named his own role – the 'free 8'.

With De Bruyne and Silva pushing forward, Guardiola ensured that City weren't overrun in midfield by sometimes reprising his Bayern Munich strategy of bringing his full-backs inside. This proved ineffective with the full-backs at Guardiola's disposal in his first campaign, when the team only just scraped into the Champions League places.

But in Guardiola's second campaign, the approach worked much better. Right-back Kyle Walker arrived from Tottenham Hotspur, but rather than overlapping, would sometimes hold a position as part of a three-man defence. Benjamin Mendy was supposed to push forward on the opposite wing, but missed the majority of the 2017/18 campaign through injury. Without a natural left-back to replace him, Guardiola converted box-to-box midfielder Fabian Delph into a full-back, and he was inevitably more comfortable pushing inside. Young attacking midfielder Oleksandr Zinchenko was also sometimes used at left-back, as was right-sided full-back Danilo, with both taking up narrow positions to cover for the 'free 8s', while winger Leroy Sané provided the left-sided width. City also offered more technical quality at both ends of the pitch: centre-forward Sergio Agüero improved his link play, while goalkeeper Ederson was a significant upgrade on Bravo.

While many doubted Guardiola could win the Premier League with such a technical approach, Manchester City reached new heights in 2017/18, becoming the first side to reach 100 points in the English top flight. They also scored a record number of goals, 106, and won 19 of their first 20 matches, the only exception coming in a 1–1 draw with Koeman's Everton when they went down to ten men before half-time. City had effectively won the Premier League before Christmas, and thereafter the question wasn't about whether they'd lift the title, but about whether they could win it undefeated and lift the European Cup as well.

City were unable to achieve either of these feats, coming unstuck both times against the same opposition: Klopp's Liverpool. The Reds recorded a 4–3 league victory over City in January to end their unbeaten run, and then ran out convincing 5–1 aggregate winners at the Champions League quarter-final stage. Both contests had a similar feel; Liverpool burst out of the traps and dominated the opening period, and played with a renewed energy after the half-time break, but City steadily grew into each half. In the 4–3 league win Liverpool scored in the ninth minute of the first half, and then in the 14th, 16th and 23rd minutes of the second. City's goals came in the 40th minute of the first half, then in the 39th and 45th minutes of the second. Then, in the first leg of the Champions League quarter-final Klopp's side blitzed City in the opening half-hour, finding themselves 3–0 up and out of sight. The game summed up the difference between the sides. City built possession play and tired the opposition out like Guardiola's Barcelona; Liverpool would offer an intense but unsustainable burst of energy like Klopp's Dortmund.

Klopp had joined Liverpool in October 2015 and immediately introduced his heavy-pressing approach for a goalless draw at Tottenham. He'd spent all his training sessions focusing on pressing, which meant that although Liverpool regained the ball quickly they didn't know what to do with it. In his technical area Klopp theatrically celebrated successful tackles in the opposition half, underlining his insistence on winning possession back quickly. 'I am happy because in the first 20 minutes we were pressing and were very aggressive,' he said after his Premier League debut. 'We were a little bit nervous when we got the ball, because our pulse was a little too high.'

Like at Dortmund, Klopp shunned pure holding midfielders, instead playing box-to-box players like Jordan Henderson who could push up and pressure opponents rather than simply protect the defence closely. 'Gegenpressing' became an accepted term in English football, and Klopp – who had made his name in Germany as a pundit – appeared on Sky Sports' *Monday Night Football* a year after his appointment to outline his interpretation of the concept. He became a pundit for the evening, moving counters around a digital screen to demonstrate how his centre-forward should position himself and direct his run to funnel the opposition's passing down one flank, before his teammates would box the full-backs in towards the touchline. Graphics displayed statistics to show Liverpool were top in terms of sprints per game and tackles per game. 'No play-maker can be as good as a good counter-pressing situation,' Klopp reiterated.

Throughout Klopp's first couple of seasons Liverpool were often outstanding in big games against technical opposition, when they could press them into submission. Klopp's first major victory was a 4–1 win over Pellegrini's Manchester City – but Liverpool had been defeated 2–1 at home to Crystal Palace the previous weekend. This set the tone. Against teams who played direct football, Klopp's team were unable to press and regain possession high up the pitch, and their possession play wasn't proficient enough to break down deep defences. They were also poor at defending in traditional situations and conceded too often from set-pieces.

Gradually, Liverpool evolved into more than a pressing side. They added counter-attacking threat with the signings of wide forwards Sadio Mané and then Mohamed Salah, who won the Premier League Golden Boot in his debut campaign. They became more measured and purposeful in possession, breaking down opponents with clever passing combinations. They also ironed out their weaknesses in defence, partly due to the signing of Virgil van Dijk, the world's most expensive centre-back. Two goalkeeping howlers from Loris Karius cost Liverpool in the 2018 Champions League Final, but Brazilian Alisson proved a significant upgrade. By 2018/19 Liverpool were ready to launch a serious title challenge, and while still capable of starting games at incredible intensity, were no longer solely about pressing.

Klopp's incorporation of more intelligent possession play hinted at Guardiola's influence on his coaching, and the best example was his use of Roberto Firmino up front. The Brazilian had arrived as an attacking midfielder, seemingly to provide the likes of Christian Benteke and Daniel Sturridge with service. But Benteke was omitted and then sold, while Sturridge found himself on the fringes. Firmino became Liverpool's false 9, their equivalent of Leo Messi. 'There is a wide spectrum of types of strikers,' Klopp explained. 'Roberto is a very offensive player, so he is a striker. Everyone asked me, "What about Firmino? We need a real target striker!" Roberto *is* a striker. A lot of strikers are 1.6 metres – Lionel Messi, what is he? Firmino can play, and score goals, and he is flexible and in brilliant shape. He gets in the box, and then something happens.' After wearing number 11 for his first couple of Liverpool campaigns, Firmino switched to number 9, reflecting his change in role, and started to score more poacher's goals, as well as starting the press and dropping deep to link play.

One Liverpool goal, scored in February 2019 in a 3–0 win over Bournemouth, displayed Klopp's philosophy perfectly. Three Liverpool players – Mané, Naby Keïta and Andy Robertson – boxed Bournemouth's Jordon Ibe in towards the touchline. Mané won possession, Keïta collected the loose ball and Robertson did the damage by chipping the ball over the defence for the onrushing midfielder Gini Wijnaldum, who finished excellently with the outside of his right foot. Wijnaldum had found space because Firmino was positioned deep, between the lines, which dragged Bournemouth centre-back Steve Cook up the pitch. The goal exemplified the two major features of Klopp's Liverpool: the energetic pressing to win possession quickly and the subtlety of a false 9 to create space.

The two managers challenging for the title, Guardiola and Klopp, had influenced one another, and both were using something between the Spanish and German models. But they found themselves forced to adapt to the English style too, and Guardiola seemed genuinely shocked by the focus on set-pieces. 'I understood English football the day I watched one game at home, Swansea versus Crystal Palace – nine goals, eight from set-pieces,' he laughed, midway through his first campaign. 'You have to control that, and we are unable [to do so] right now. Eight goals from set-pieces – corners, free-kicks, throw-ins – that is English football and I have to adapt, because never before have I experienced that. Of course, elsewhere there are corners, but not with that kind of influence on the game.'

Guardiola also dismissively spoke about tackles. 'I am not a coach for the tackles. I don't train for tackles,' he muttered after a 4–2 defeat to Leicester. 'What I want is to try to play well and score goals. What are tackles?'

But a major issue was around the concept of the 'second ball', when possession ran free after a duel. 'Many times the ball is in the air more than on the grass, and I have to adapt,' Guardiola admitted on another occasion. 'I was in Munich and spoke to Xabi Alonso about the Premier League, and he said, "You have to adapt. It's the second ball, the second ball!" – but really, you have to adapt to the second ball, and the third ball, and the fourth. I never before was focused on that, because in Barcelona or in Spain, more or less the players try to play for the culture. That's why they won World Cups, European Championships, Champions Leagues, Europa Leagues, all the time, all the years. In Germany it was physical, but not like here … the teams are taller, stronger, physical, and you have to adapt and build from that.'

After a 2–1 victory over Arsenal in December 2016 Guardiola said he'd specifically worked on second balls – even ahead of a game against a technical side like Arsenal. 'In the last three days we spent two and a half hours on second balls on the training field,' he explained. 'It works. It is part of the game here. You have to be compact for the second balls, and in the last couple of games we have been better in that sense.'

Klopp, meanwhile, although he'd professed a love for the 'English style' of football when coaching in Germany, also found himself surprised by the reality of the Premier League – particularly the weather and the physicality. 'The English game is not faster than the German game – perhaps there are a few more sprints – but there is a different style of football here, partially due to the weather,' he explained. 'The wind can be quite extreme in England. We are not familiar with that in Germany, and you have to keep things simple. Players who are not from the UK have to get used to the winds, and I have to adapt my style of football as a result, as well. Often you are forced to keep things simple. And there are a lot more duels for the second ball here. English referees are not like their German colleagues.'

This hinted at Klopp's annoyance at the ferocity of tackling in England, which became apparent when Liverpool faced Sean Dyche's Burnley in December 2018, winning 3–1 but losing Joe Gomez with a lower-leg fracture, which kept the defender out for several months. 'We won the game but the challenges from the beginning, the sliding tackling on that wet ground, I really think the referee should have said something earlier,' Klopp complained. 'The injury threat is massive. That was hard. You get the ball, nice, but it's like bowling because you get the player as well. It happened four or five times.'

Dyche, the representative of the old-fashioned English way, hit back. 'I thought some of the timing of the challenges was superb,' he said, before defending the traditional style of playing that's still respected in England. 'You've got to win the ball, you've got to challenge against these boys. I don't think there's many fans in this country that want to see tackling go out of the game.' That was a reasonable supposition, certainly in comparison to fans in Germany or Spain.

Foreigners who arrive in England with a purely technical style, whether players like Cristiano Ronaldo or managers like Guardiola, are encouraged to toughen up. English football certainly doesn't want to banish technical foreign talents from the country, but it does demand that they adapt to their new surroundings.

But while a focus on physicality, tackling, set-pieces and second balls remains the dominant approach for relegation strugglers, this approach has been left behind at the highest level. And while still failing to produce top-class coaches, English football has developed a fine generation of talented young technical players, and in 2018 England enjoyed a run to the World Cup semi-finals, their best performance in the Premier League era.

Manager Gareth Southgate, who found himself in the job almost accidentally after Sam Allardyce's ignominious departure, concentrated on picking technically gifted footballers, many of them youngsters who had played for his U21 side. Southgate was not considered a high-class coach upon his appointment – aside from the U21s, his only previous coaching post was as manager of Middlesbrough a decade earlier, which featured relegation from the Premier League and his subsequent dismissal a few months into Boro's campaign in the Championship. But Southgate's thoughtful approach turned him into an unexpected national hero and prompted a newfound wave of positivity towards the England side. It was easy to identify the influences of leading Premier League coaches on his strategy.

England used an unusual system at the 2018 World Cup, a 3–5–2 sometimes described as a 3–3–2–2. In goal, Southgate replicated Guardiola's decision to drop goalkeeper Joe Hart – a regular throughout qualification – not just from the starting XI but from the squad entirely. Instead, he used Everton's Jordan Pickford, who was renowned for his superior distribution and could send pinpoint drop-kicks to attackers.

At the back, England lined up with a three-man defence at a major tournament for the first time since Southgate's playing days. This would have been almost unthinkable a couple of seasons beforehand, but with the influence of Conte on the Premier League meaning almost every top side had experimented with the system, it made sense. Chelsea's Gary Cahill, a regular as the left-sided defender in Conte's 3–4–3, was part of the squad, but Southgate instead favoured Harry Maguire of Leicester. John Stones, who had developed under Guardiola at Manchester City, played as the spare man and brought the ball forward well, while his club teammate Kyle Walker, who sometimes tucked inside into a back three for City, was deployed on the right. Previously considered a purely attack-minded right-back, it's difficult to imagine Walker would have been fielded there if it hadn't been for Guardiola's coaching.

Kieran Trippier and Ashley Young were used at wing-back – rather than the more obvious options of Walker and Danny Rose – primarily for their set-piece ability. This was therefore the most typically English section of the side, and of England's 11 goals at the tournament, six came from free-kicks or corners, with another three from penalties.

The midfield zone also reflected Premier League developments. Jordan Henderson was fielded as the sole holding midfielder, a role he hadn't played until Klopp's arrival at Liverpool. He was joined by Spurs' Dele Alli and Manchester United's Jesse Lingard. Both were considered more adventurous players, attackers in a 4–2–3–1 rather than proper central midfielders. But Guardiola's technical approach at Manchester City had changed perceptions of a midfield trio, and Alli and Lingard therefore played as 'free 8s', to use De Bruyne's expression, constantly making off-the-ball runs in behind the opposition defence. Up front, Harry Kane won the World Cup Golden Boot, although his primary role in open play was about creating space for Raheem Sterling, now comfortable as a centre-forward, having sometimes been deployed there by Guardiola.

It was easy to get carried away with England's run to the semi-finals. Ultimately they defeated only Tunisia, Panama and Sweden, drew with a decent Colombia side before uncharacteristically progressing on penalties, and lost to serious opposition – Croatia, and Belgium twice. They hadn't actually defeated a World Cup contender. But a subsequent 3–2 victory away in Spain in the inaugural Nations League proved more promising, with Kane, Sterling and Marcus Rashford combining excellently on the break to put England 3–0 up before half-time. England demonstrated tactical intelligence and counter-attacking speed, while an early Eric Dier tackle on Sergio Ramos, which earned him a booking, also pleased the traditionalists. 'The beautiful game? No. Get in, British bulldog, let's have a bit of that,' was the succinct analysis provided by Burnley manager Dyche the following week. 'Virtually every comment was that the Dier tackle changed the game. A tackle? Is that allowed? We have been hearing for ages that 400 passes change games. Who remembers the last time someone wrote about a tackle changing a game? Who knows, it might start a revolution and we'll be allowed to tackle again.'

That was largely an isolated incident, however, and England have moved in a positive, technical direction. In recent years there has been an obvious attempt to define precisely how English sides should play, with the FA's launch of the 'England DNA', a set of guidelines that prescribes 'the playing and coaching philosophy of the England teams'.

Its mission statement emphasises that a focus on pressing, as witnessed in the German model, is 'an important part of the England DNA', while also featuring a Spanish-style statement that 'England teams aim to dominate possession'. English football now produces a large number of wide players who are skilled in one-against-one situations, like in Portuguese academies, while the national side is noticeably blessed with quick players up front, à la France. The 'England DNA' document also mentions the requirement to 'adopt varied playing styles and formations', typical of Italy's Coverciano school, and declares that 'England goalkeepers will play a key role' in the side's ball retention, a legacy of the Dutch philosophy.

The 'England DNA' is essentially a general summary of modern European footballing style, rather than anything genuinely innovative. But in the absence of progressive domestic coaches, that's all English football can ever be – a mirror to the rest of Europe, an importer of ideas. It's worth remembering Charles Hughes's declaration in 1990, that world football had been moving in the wrong direction for the last 30 years. Now, English football is no longer ignoring 30 years of overseas football, but instead using it as the inspiration for its own identity.

# Epilogue

In one sense, maybe footballing identity matters less than ever. After 25 years of European champions failing to retain the Champions League, Zinedine Zidane's Real Madrid won three in a row between 2016 and 2018.

Their footballing identity was difficult to decipher, and it had little relation to any country's style. This wasn't a particularly Spanish side, nor was it typical of its manager's nation in the way Johan Cruyff's Barcelona felt Dutch or Fabio Capello's Real felt Italian. Zidane was French, but his approach had noticeably changed when playing in Italy and then in Spain.

Real's players, too, hailed from a variety of nations. There was a Costa Rican goalkeeper, a defence drawn from Spain, France and Brazil, a midfield trio featuring a Brazilian, a Croatian and a German, and attackers from Portugal, France, and Wales or Spain, depending on Zidane's tactical preference. This was possibly the most cosmopolitan top-class side of the modern era, but given their serial Champions League success, Real's fans weren't complaining that they weren't overwhelmingly representative of the Spanish style, or any other style.

Following football, however, isn't solely about winning trophies. Supporters chant about past glories, but they also chant about their club's history and about local pride. That partly manifests itself in supporters wanting their side to play in a manner that befits the club's traditions – an identity that has clearly been influenced by the country in which they play.

Even modern football's most dogmatic philosopher, Johan Cruyff – whose vision of the game has been embraced across the continent – believed teams must reflect their geographic location. 'The way to improve is not by copying what happens in Spain or Italy, but by looking first at yourself. And looking at yourself means determining your abilities and addressing your shortcomings. You can't demand that a German must play football like a Dutchman, or an Italian,' he said. 'I can't turn up as a Dutchman in England or Italy and go and play football the way that pleases me. No. You play football the way the public wants you to.'

Crucially, UEFA have an entrenched belief in the heterogeneity of styles. 'UEFA's grassroots football mission is founded on the essential belief that football is for everyone,' European football's governing body stated in 2018. 'In addition, given that the strength of football lies in its grassroots, UEFA believes in the importance of preserving football's local, regional and national identities.' There's an active desire for teams to represent their roots and retain a diversity of styles.

This diversity isn't solely important in a footballing sense. Football is, for millions of people across Europe, the best opportunity to discover more about their neighbours. Whether the topic is Dutch liberalism, French multiculturalism or Catalan independence, football – and footballing style – often provides the introduction. That's why football remains a window into other cultures, and a valuable artefact. European football pits countries against one another, but only for 90 minutes. In a wider sense, it does much more to bring them together.

# Bibliography

Agnew, Paddy. *Forza Italia*, London, Ebury, 2006

Ancelotti, Carlo. *Il mio albero di Natale*, Milan, Rizzoli, 2013

Ancelotti, Carlo. *Quiet Leadership*, London, Penguin, 2016

Auclair, Philippe. *Thierry Henry*, London, Macmillan, 2012

Balague, Guillem. *Pep Guardiola*, London, Orion, 2012

Balague, Guillem. *Messi*, London, Orion, 2013

Balague, Guillem. *Ronaldo*, London, Orion, 2016

Ball, Phil. *Morbo*, London, WSC Books, 2001

Barend, Fritz. *Ajax, Barcelona, Cruyff*, London, Bloomsbury, 1998

Bergkamp, Dennis. *Stillness and Speed*, London, Simon & Schuster, 2013

Bliss, Dominic. *Erbstein*, London, Blizzard Books, 2014

Borst, Hugo. *O, Louis*, London, Yellow Jersey Press, 2014

Brassell, Andy. *All or Nothing*, Oxford, Trafford, 2006

Burke, Greg. *Parma*, London, Gollancz, 1998

Burns, Jimmy. *Barca*, London, Bloomsbury, 2000

Burns, Jimmy. *La Roja*, London, Simon & Schuster, 2012

Caioli, Luca. *Ronaldo*, London, Icon Books, 2016

Cameron, Colin. *Football, Fussball, Voetbal*, London, BBC, 1995

Condò, Paolo. *Duellanti*, Milan, Baldini + Castoldi, 2016

Cox, Michael. *The Mixer*, London, HarperCollins, 2017

Cruyff, Johan. *My Turn*, London, Macmillan, 2016

Dauncey, Hugh and Hare, Geoff. *France and the 1998 World Cup*, London, Frank Cass, 1999

Della Pietra, Ray and Rinaldi, Giancarlo. *Football Italia*, London, Virgin, 1993

Desailly, Marcel. *Capitaine*, Paris, Stock, 2002

Digby, Adam. *Juventus*, Huddersfield, Ockley Books, 2015

Djorkaeff, Youri. *Snake*, Paris, Éditions Grasset, 2006

Duff, Alex and Panja, Tariq. *Football's Secret Trade*, Chichester, John Wiley & Sons, 2017

Dugarry, Christophe. *Le foot*, Paris, Éditions Hugo & Cie, 2009

Eriksson, Sven-Göran. *Sven*, London, Headline, 2013

Escher, Tobias. *Vom Libero zur Doppelsechs*, Reinbek, Rowohlt Taschenbuch, 2016

Ferguson, Sir Alex. *My Autobiography*, London, Hodder & Stoughton, 2015

Fieldsend, Daniel. *The European Game*, Edinburgh, Arena, 2017

Fitzpatrick, Richard. *El Clasico*, London, Bloomsbury, 2012

Foot, John. *Calcio*, London, HarperCollins, 2006

Fort, Patrick and Philippe, Jean. *Zidane*, Paris, Éditions de l'Archipel, 2017

Franck, Dan. *Zidane*, Paris, Éditions Robert Laffont & Plon, 1999

Glanville, Brian. *The Story of the World Cup*, London, Faber & Faber, 2014

Goldblatt, David. *The Ball Is Round*, London, Penguin, 2007

Gullit, Ruud. *How to Watch Football*, London, Penguin, 2016

Hawkey, Ian. *Di Stéfano*, London, Ebury, 2016

Hesse, Uli. *Tor!*, London, WSC Books, 2002

Hesse, Uli. *Bayern*, London, Yellow Jersey Press, 2016

Honigstein, Raphael. *Das Reboot*, London, Yellow Jersey Press, 2015

# Bibliography

Honigstein, Raphael. *Bring the Noise*, London, Yellow Jersey Press, 2017

Hunter, Graham. *Barca*, Scotland, BackPagePress, 2012

Hunter, Graham. *Spain*, Scotland, BackPagePress, 2013

Ibrahimović, Zlatan. *I Am Zlatan*, London, Penguin, 2013

Iniesta, Andrés. *The Artist: Being Iniesta*, London, Headline, 2016

Jankowski, Timo. *Successful German Soccer Tactics*, Maidenhead, Meyer & Meyer, 2015

King, Jeff. *Bobby Robson's Year at Barcelona*, London, Virgin, 1997

Kormelink, Henny. *Louis van Gaal and the Ajax Coaches*, Pennsylvania, Reedswain, 1997

Kundert, Tom. *A Journey through Portuguese Football*, Lisbon, Chiado, 2013

Kundert, Tom. *The Thirteenth Chapter*, Lisbon, Chiado, 2017

Kuper, Simon. *Football Against the Enemy*, London, Orion, 1994

Kuper, Simon. *The Football Men*, London, Simon & Schuster, 2007

Lahouri, Besma. *Zidane: une vie secrète*, Paris, Flammarion, 2008

Lawrence, Amy. *Invincible*, London, Penguin, 2014

Leboeuf, Frank. *Destin, quand je te tiens*, Flammarion, 2002

Lehmann, Jens. *Der Wahnsinn liegt auf dem Platz*, Cologne, Verlag Kiepenheuer, 2010

Lizarazu, Bixente. *Lizarazu*, Paris, Grasset, 2007

Lourenço, Luís. *José Mourinho*, Stockport, Dewi Lewis, 2004

Lowe, Sid. *Fear and Loathing in La Liga*, London, Yellow Jersey Press, 2013

Lyttleton, Ben. *Twelve Yards*, London, Bantam Press, 2014

Lyttleton, Ben. *Edge*, London, HarperCollins, 2017

Makélélé, Claude. *Tout Simplement*, Paris, Éditions Prolongation, 2009

Marcotti, Gabriele. *Capello*, London, Transworld, 2010

Martin, Simon. *Sport Italia*, London, I.B. Taurus, 2011

Meijer, Martin. *Guus Hiddink*, London, Random House, 2006

Meijer, Martin. *Louis van Gaal*, London, Ebury, 2014

Michels, Rinus. *Teambuilding*, Leeuwarden, Uitgeverij Eisma, 2001

Montague, James. *The Billionaires Club*, London, Bloomsbury, 2017

Neveling, Elmar. *Jürgen Klopp*, London, Ebury, 2016

Özil, Mesut. *Die Magie des Spiels*, Cologne, Bastei Lübbe, 2017

Perarnau, Martí. *Herr Pep*, Barcelona, Roca, 2014

Perarnau, Martí. *Pep Guardiola: La metamorfosis*, Barcelona, Roca, 2016

Petit, Emmanuel. *À fleur de peau*, Paris, Éditions Prolongations, 2008

Pires, Robert. *Footballeur*, London, Yellow Jersey Press, 2004

Pirlo, Andrea. *Penso Quindi Gioco*, Milan, Mondadori, 2013

Ramsay, Arnaud. *Laurent Blanc*, Paris, Éditions Fetjaine, 2012

Reng, Ronald. *Matchdays*, London, Simon & Schuster, 2013

Rinaldi, Giancarlo. *I Classici del Calcio*, Dumfries, Rinaldi, 2015

Rivoire, Xavier. *Arsène Wenger*, London, Aurum Press, 2007

Rouch, Dominique. *Didier Deschamps*, Paris, Edition 1, 2001

Rühn, Christov. *Le Foot*, London, Abacus, 2000

Sacchi, Arrigo. *Calcio totale*, Milan, Mondadori, 2006

Saha, Louis. *Thinking Inside the Box*, Kingston upon Thames, Vision, 2012

Seban, Alexandre. *Les bleus à l'Euro*, Paris, De Boeck Supérieur, 2016

Siguero, Santiago. *Zinedine Zidane*. Madrid, Al Poste, 2015

Theiner, Egon and Schlammerl, Elisabeth. *Trapattoni*, Dublin, Liberties Press, 2008

Thuram, Lilian. *8 Juillet 1998*, Paris, Anne Carrière, 2004

Torres, Diego. *The Special One*, London, HarperCollins, 2014

Totti, Francesco. *Mo je faccio er cucchiaio*, Milan, Mondadori, 2006

Trapattoni, Giovanni. *Coaching High Performance Soccer*, Pennsylvania, Reedswain, 1999

Trezeguet, David. *Bleu ciel*, Paris, Hugo Sport, 2016

Vella, Christian. *Roger Lemerre*, Paris, Éditions du Félin, 2002

Vialli, Gianluca. *The Italian Job*, London, Transworld Press, 2006
Vieira, Patrick. *Vieira*, London, Orion, 2006
Wahl, Grant. *Football 2.0*, Scotland, BackPagePress, 2018
Williams, Tom. *Do You Speak Football?*, London, Bloomsbury, 2018
Wilson, Jonathan. *Inverting the Pyramid*, London, Orion, 2008
Wilson, Jonathan. *The Outsider*, London, Orion, 2012
Wilson, Jonathan. *Angels with Dirty Faces*, London, Orion, 2016
Winner, David. *Brilliant Orange*, London, Bloomsbury, 2000
Zauli, Alessandro. *Soccer: Modern Tactics*, Michigan, Data
    Reproductions, 2002

**Magazines**
*11 Freunde*
*Blizzard*
*Champions*
*Football Italia*
*FourFourTwo*
*France Football*
*Soccer Laduma*
*World Soccer*

**Newspapers**
*AS*
*A Bola*
*Bild*
*Corriere dello Sport*
*Daily Mail*
*Daily Telegraph*
*De Telegraaf*
*Die Zeit*
*El Gráfico*

# Bibliography

*El País*
*Guardian*
*Het Laatste Nieuws*
*Independent*
*L'Équipe*
*La Gazzetta dello Sport*
*La Nación*
*La Repubblica*
*Marca*
*Mundo Deportivo*
*O Jogo*
*Record*
*Sport*
*Süddeutsche Zeitung*
*The Times*
*Tuttosport*

**Websites**
bbc.co.uk
bdfutbol.com
espnfc.co.uk
footballia.net
football-lineups.com
kassiesa.home.xs4all.nl
portugal.net
skysports.com
spielverlagerung.com
whoscored.com
wikipedia.com
youtube.com
zonalmarking.net

# Acknowledgements

For the second time, Jack Fogg and everyone at HarperCollins have been a pleasure to work with. Thanks to Mark Bolland, Simon Gerratt, Ben Murphy, Graham Holmes and Alan Cracknell for crucial behind-the-scenes work, to Simeon Greenaway for designing another absolutely brilliant cover, and to Orlando Mowbray and Josie Turner for their marketing and publicity work. Thanks to my literary agent Chris Wellbelove for encouraging me to get cracking on a second book straightaway.

I'm indebted to various people, many of whom I have never met, for the overwhelming amount of research that this book required. Ahmed Abdel-Hamid helped immensely by watching dozens of matches and providing detailed analyses. I'm hugely grateful for his assistance.

I also required plenty of translation help. The Italian section was the trickiest; Alessandro Pugliese, Steve Mitchell and Gregory Caltabanis composed brilliant summaries of Serie A campaigns, and Jan Mazza provided interview translations. Will Beckman researched a lot, and also simply knew a lot, while Jack Unwin offered London's most comprehensive archive of *Football Italia* magazines. London Kim delivered a remarkably detailed dossier on mid-nineties Juventus.

Priya Ramesh helped with the Dutch section in return for pints at a Wolf Alice gig, and Ali Maxwell spent his summer 'off' ploughing through French football books to unlock the true meaning of the Makélelé role. Tiago Estêvão put me right about Portuguese football and Rob Hunt translated some interviews. Lewis Ambrose translated some key German texts.

Thanks to Jack Lang, Rupert Cane, Duncan Alexander, Tom Williams, Rupert Fryer, Luke Lacey, Mark Sadler and Rob Fielder for answering various questions. Jamie Cutteridge transported about 100 *World Soccer* magazines from Poole to a Kingstonian game. The video for 'Hard to Explain' by The Strokes provided the inspiration for the 'flashback' nature of the English section.

The bibliography provides a complete list of sources, but it's only right to highlight the works of David Winner, Tom Kundert, Guillem Balague, Graham Hunter, Martí Perarnau and Raphael Honigstein, who have written definitive books on key countries or teams featured. I also learned a lot from Rene Maric and Adin Osmanbasic, who have advanced the level of online tactical analysis significantly.

I'd also like to credit those who have provided European football coverage over the years: James Richardson and *Football Italia* opened up a different world for many of us, while Simon Kuper, David Goldblatt, Gabriele Marcotti, Andy Brassell and Jonathan Wilson have also been big inspirations. It was also a great pleasure to go through 30 years of *World Soccer* magazine, an incredible resource that, in the days before the internet, was essentially the only place where you could find out about foreign football.

Thanks to everyone whom I previously thanked in the previous book for roughly the same things, although my parents deserve a particular mention for plenty of moral support, and also because they own a working printer. Also thanks to those at *The Totally Football Show* for allowing me to interrupt my usual appearances with two month-long stints away to get this finished.

Finally, huge thanks to everyone who provided feedback on *The Mixer*, my first book. It has been fantastic reading reviews on Amazon and Goodreads, checking the Instagram hashtag and seeing which passages have been highlighted frequently on the eBook edition. Had it not been for compliments about that book, I wouldn't have spent two years doing little else other than writing this one.

# Index

# Index

# Index

430

# Index

# Index

# Index

# Index

# Index

# Index

**Michael Cox** is the author of *The Mixer*. A soccer writer for *ESPN* and a former contributor to the *Guardian*, he is also the founder of the Zonal Marking website. He lives in south London and is a season-ticket holder at seventh tier Kingstonian FC.